ON PARADOX

ON
PARA

THE
CLAIMS
OF
THEORY

—

ELIZABETH
S.
ANKER

DOX

DUKE UNIVERSITY PRESS
Durham and London
2022

Project editor: Bird Williams
Designed by A. Mattson Gallagher
Typeset inPortrait Text, ITC Garamond, and Helvetica Neue
by Westchester Publishing Services.

Library of Congress Cataloging-in-Publication Data
Names: Anker, Elizabeth S. (Elizabeth Susan),[1973–] author.
Title: On paradox : the claims of theory / Elizabeth S. Anker.
Description: Durham : Duke University Press, 2022. |
Includes bibliographical references and index.
Identifiers: LCCN 2022020038 (print)
LCCN 2022020039 (ebook)
ISBN 9781478016335 (hardcover)
ISBN 9781478018971 (paperback)
ISBN 9781478023609 (ebook)
Subjects: LCSH: Paradox. | Paradox—Political aspects. | Paradox—Social aspects. |
Critical theory. | BISAC: PHILOSOPHY / Political | LITERARY CRITICISM /
Semiotics & Theory
Classification: LCC PN228. P2 A554 2022 (print)
LCC PN228. P2 (ebook) |
DDC 801—dc23/eng/20220805
LC record available at https://lccn.loc.gov/2022020038
LC ebook record available at https://lccn.loc.gov/2022020039

To my parents, Roy and Ellen Anker

Contents

Acknowledgments

It is always tempting (if not fun) to play the "but for" game: this book would not have existed but for X, or Y, or Z. In this book's case, that game is fairly short and easy. When I approached Ken Wissoker with this project, its arguments were significantly abbreviated, focused on merely two of its chapters with a few ancillary reflections. As a supportive editor, Ken informed me that he'd be happy to publish it in its then-current form, if that's what I wanted. However, Ken also prodded me, urging me that he thought I was onto "something much bigger," that I was still figuring things out. Thankfully, I took that advice, allowing this book to grow in directions I never could have imagined. Since those early conversations, Ken has pushed, inspired, focused, and nurtured this project in countless ways that leave me humbled and thankful.

A number of lengthier collaborations left a particularly decisive imprint on this book's arguments. Perhaps more than anything, efforts to assess the state of critique with Rita Felski (which happily sprouted into ongoing conversations) helped to shape its assertions. Dialogue with Bernie Meyler about certain limits of humanistic scholarship on law were similarly crucial to the book's development. I am grateful to both Bernie and Rita for their friendships. At later stages of the writing process, the chance to edit projects with Justin Desautels-Stein and Grant Farred honed and clarified a number of core positions.

I remain forever grateful to the many colleagues both at Cornell and beyond who have read drafts of either particular sections or overviews of this book, offering patient and engaged criticism. Those readers include Paulo Barrozo, Lior Barshack, Ayelet Ben-Yishai, Christopher Brown, Diane Brown, Emilio Christodoulidis, Elisha Cohn, Debbie Dinner, Rita Felski, Dean Franco, Jenny Mann, Irena Rosenthal, and Caleb Smith. Anna Kornbluh has become one of my longest-standing friends in the academy, and her incisive comments on large parts of this book have been irreplaceable. Martha Nussbaum has been an invaluable reader and interlocutor, and her mentorship and friendship is inexpressibly dear to me. A few friends read drafts of the entire book over the years—and multiple versions of some chapters, no less. I am indebted to both Caroline Levine and Aziz Rana for keeping our mutual writing schedules on task, and even more for their rigorous and generative feedback on diverse iterations of this project. Caroline and I have often laughed at the prospect that we were "writing the same book," and I can only hope those synergies will continue. The chance to have people like Aziz and Odette Lienau as not only brilliant colleagues but also trusted friends is what makes Ithaca feel like a genuine home.

In this respect, one of the best parts of academic life involves the fact that many of my favored partners in crime have been ardent and engaged interlocutors. In composing these acknowledgments, I have found myself reliving so many thrilling conversations, with Tanya Agathocleous, Amanda Anderson, Ian Balfour, Nathaniel Berman, Lauren Berlant, Wendy Brown, Zahid Chaudhary, Joshua Clover, Eleni Coundouriotis, Margo Crawford, James Dawes, Maks Del Mar, Wai Chee Dimock, Dan Edelstein, Ellis Hansen, Duncan Kennedy, Mahinder Kingra, Jonathan Kramnick, Sophia McClennan, Sam Moyn, Crystal Parikh, Eduardo Penalver, Brian Richmond, Paul Saint-Amour, Alexandra Schultheis, Lily Sheehan, Judith Surkis, Chantal Thomas, Nelson Tebbe, Antoine Vauchez, Bryan Wagner, Sarah Winter, Dag Woubshet, and many others.

This book is an artifact of the rich and lively intellectual community at Cornell, and I could not have written it without immersion therein. So many colleagues in the English department and across the humanities at Cornell helped to foster and inspire this book, among others Kevin Attell, Mary Pat Brady, Bruno Bosteels, Laura Brown, Cathy Caruth, Cynthia Chase, Jonathan Culler, Jason Frank, Peter Gilgen, Paul Fleming, Phil Lorenz, Tracy McNulty, Tim Murray, Simone Pinet, Camille Robcis, Neil Saccamano,

Shirley Samuels, Dan Schwartz, Anette Schwarz, Derrick Spires, Lyrae Van Clief-Stefanon, and Helena Viramontes. While I wasn't aware at the time, a Mellon Sawyer Seminar on Political Will sowed the seeds for some of its arguments, so I am grateful to the Mellon Foundation as well as a number of people involved with that seminar (beyond those already named, Paula Epps-Cepero, Michaela Brangan, and Eric Cheyfitz). A few friendships over the years have been essential to keeping me on track on all levels. Thank you to Diane Brown, Elisha Cohn, Sital Kalantry, Renee Knake Jefferson, Chantal Thomas, and Samantha Zacher. I am also deeply grateful for my siblings and their spouses: Christina and Brian, and David and Milay.

In its final stages of completion, I was welcomed as a full-time and tenured member of the faculty at Cornell Law School. I am infinitely thankful to Eduardo Penalver and Jens Ohlin (and Nancy) for overseeing aspects of that transition and, more importantly, for their friendship. Along with those mentioned above, I am so lucky to be part of a community that includes Emad Atiq, Dan Awrey, Cynthia Bowman, Sherry Colb, Michael Dorf, Valerie Hans, Andrei Marmour, Saule Omarova, and Brad Wendel and Liz Peck.

The chance to teach and work with graduate students at Cornell University has also been vital to the evolution of this book's interventions. As one section discusses, a seminar on Theory and Method in the fall of 2018 was a turning point in my thought, so a particularly hearty thank you to that group. During the time I've been working on this project, it's been an absolute delight to work with Kelly Hoffer, Molly MacVeagh, Katie Thorsteinson, Christina Fogarosi, Kristin Angierski, Daniel Haefke, Gabriella Friedman, Meredith Shepherd, and many others. In this book's final stages, Jonathan Culler lent his irreplaceable support. Many sections would look very different without Austin Lillywhite's impeccable research, savvy editorial suggestions, and other smart comments.

Lively audiences at various lectures were also formative. It was a gift to have the chance to present versions of this book's arguments in talks, presentations, or workshops at Amherst College, Binghamton University, Boston College Law School, Católica Global School of Law, Clark University, Freie Universitat Berlin, Harvard University, Reichman University, Indiana University, NYU, Oregon State University, Penn State University, Princeton University, Queen Mary College (University of London), Stanford Law School, UC-Berkeley, Université Catholique de Louvain, the University of Connecticut, the University of Haifa, Wake Forest University, and Yale University.

I had the chance to explore early articulations of some components of its ideas in the following publications: "The Architecture of Critique," symposium issue of *Yale Journal of Law and Humanities* 31, no. 2 (2021), edited by Justin Desautels-Stein and Samuel Moyn; "Uncensorable Speech and the Snares of Illiberalism," forthcoming in *Law and Illiberalism*, edited by Austin Sarat, Lawrence Douglas, and Martha Umphrey (University of Massachusetts Press); "Beyond Ambiguity and Ambivalence: Rethinking the Tools of Critique," special issue, "The Fatigue of Critique?" *On Education* 9 (December 2020); "Human Rights," *The Oxford Handbook of Law and the Humanities*, edited by Maks Del Mar, Bernadette Meyler, and Simon Stern (New York: Oxford University Press, 2019); "Postcritical Reading, the Lyric, and Ali Smith's *How To Be Both*," *Diacritics* 45, no. 4 (2017); "Postcritique and Social Justice," *American Book Review* 38, no. 5 (July/August 2017); "Why We Love Coetzee; or *The Childhood of Jesus* and the Funhouse of Critique," in *Critique and Postcritique*, edited by Elizabeth Anker and Rita Felski (Durham, NC: Duke University Press, 2017); and "'The Scent of Ink': Toni Morrison's *Beloved* and the Semiotics of Rights," *Critical Quarterly* 56, no. 4 (December 2014).

Two other "but for"s necessarily conclude these acknowledgments. First, my infinite gratitude to Mitchel Lasser for his patience and support over the many years I've been consumed by this project. Mitchel, Sacha, and Zoe Lasser have been all too forgiving of so many hours at my computer. But this book is also the byproduct of endless joyful hours of repartee with Mitchel sitting *en terrasse* in Paris, Lisbon, L.A., Berlin, Palo Alto, and so many other favorite haunts. I hope that this is the first of many projects that will be blessed by such enthusiasm, commitment, and generosity. This book's arguments never would have come together without Mitchel's constant encouragement as well as dialogue.

Finally, this book is dedicated to my parents, Roy and Ellen Anker. Insofar as it recounts something of an intellectual biography, that story begins with my parents. From a very young age, my parents imparted to me the relish for intellectual discovery, play, and ideas to which this book is, more than anything, a testament. From the beginning, moreover, that pursuit was always closely tied to matters of social justice, value, and the dilemma of figuring out what truths are worth believing in. Of course, those links were never uncomplicated, but they represented an unfailing point of departure and return for any intellectual conversation. It is above all under my parents' influence that I have therefore worked on this book. They continue to model not only intellectual curiosity and dedication but the right reasons one might endeavor to embark on a life of ideas. Thank you to my parents.

INTRODUCTION
On Paradox

"Was that a paradox?" asked Mr. Erskine. "I don't know. Perhaps it was. Well, the way of paradoxes is the way of truth. To test reality we must see it on the tightrope. When the verities become acrobats, we can judge them." —Oscar Wilde, *The Picture of Dorian Gray* (1890)

He played with the idea and grew wilful; tossed it into the air and transformed it; let it escape and recaptured it; made it iridescent with fancy and winged it with paradox. The praise of folly, as he went on, soared into a philosophy, and philosophy herself became young ... —*The Picture of Dorian Gray*

A paradigm can, for that matter, even insulate the community from those important social problems that are not reducible to the puzzle form, because they cannot be stated in terms of the conceptual and instrumental tools the paradigm supplies. —Thomas Kuhn, *The Structure of Scientific Revolutions* (1962)

Paradox is what happens to Dorian Gray, Oscar Wilde's iconic protagonist. Wilde's 1891 novella follows Gray's corruption by the worldly-wise Lord Henry, setting in motion an aging process reflected only in Basil's painting of Dorian (rather than on Dorian's face). It is through paradox that Lord Henry—dubbed "Prince Paradox" by Dorian himself—cajoles

Dorian. When they first meet, the "wilful paradox" of Lord Henry's words possesses a "subtle magic" that "touched some secret chord that had never been touched before, that [Dorian] felt was now vibrating and throbbing to curious pulses." Throughout, Lord Henry champions the logic of paradox not only for its "acrobatic" skill but also for staving off a "creeping common sense."[1]

This book argues that we are all heirs of Wilde and compatriots of Lord Henry in our shared dedication to paradox. Its thesis is that faith in paradox has been a hallmark of left intellectual life, in particular defining what it means to do theory. Even for scholars (whether of history or law) with no special investment in literature or art, the logic of paradox governs our inquiries, discoveries, puzzles, methods, commitments, and self-images. Since the advent of theory within the Anglo-American academy, this has been true across the humanities—within scholarship, classrooms, and beyond.

Such devotion to paradox has not always been the case, and this book therefore asks: how did such a spirit install itself within critical and humanistic thought? How and when did we become, like Dorian, seduced by paradox and, like Lord Henry, its ambassadors? What are the features and effects of reasoning through paradox; how has it shaped our intellectual habits and pursuits? What circumstances have allowed paradox to operate as its own epistemology: a way of perceiving the world that more or less dictates how and what we can imagine and even think?

Wilde's epigrammatic thought suggests initial answers to these questions, illustrating a few recurring aspects of paradox and its logic. Wilde's memorably irreverent style is representative in countless ways: theorists today inherit not only a Wildean fascination with paradox but other of his doctrines as well. Wilde's appeals to paradox are frequently overdetermined, entwining a cluster of meanings. Paradox serves most immediately for Wilde to diagnose a given reality, although in a diagnosis that unmasks what he thereby derides as complacency and the status quo. In so doing, Wilde's witticisms capture why the logic of paradox has been indispensable to critique—as I'll argue, perhaps its defining technology. While reminiscent of the instinct to define theory itself as a disputing of common sense, that tactic of leveraging paradox to debunk the taken-for-granted also echoes the Oxford English Dictionary's first entry for that word: "a statement or tenet contrary to received opinion or belief."[2] There is accordingly a self-consciousness about Wilde's tributes to paradox, staged within Mrs. Erskine's question ("Was that a paradox?") in the epigraph above. As we will see, one badge of theory has been reliance on paradox as a method and analytic mode.

But that is not all: still more is at stake within Wilde's many hymns to paradox. In issuing both diagnoses and critiques, Wilde's paradoxes foretell access to elevated forms of truth—or to "the verities" "on the tightrope." Despite being playful, Wilde's paradoxes encode more complex, nuanced, deeper—and hence exclusive or exceptional—ways of knowing. These expectations for paradox have also been fundamental to theory. With such appeals, Wilde's writing further invests that logic with aestheticized (even erotic) qualities: his paradoxes are pulsing, throbbing, and "iridescent with fancy." These lyrical, metamorphic, tropological, charismatic dimensions of reasoning through paradox are similarly far from unusual: an embrace of paradox specifically as a _style_ has united theorists of all inclinations.

By no means last, it is hard to escape the autobiographical thrust of Wilde's relish for paradoxes, evident in his claim that the characters Basil, Dorian, and Lord Henry are all varying reflections of himself. This reflexivity plays out in multiple ways. Basil's painting assumes such metacritical significance, embodying Wilde's ambition to invent "a new personality for art" that would at once be a statement of "modern times."[3] Indeed, we'll see that the language of paradox has offered one of the most authoritative and enduring frameworks for describing the experience _not only_ of modernity (as a political, socioeconomic, cultural, and psychic condition) _but also_ of art. Wilde's self-referentiality thus taps into a time-honored romance of the legendary artist or thinker as a gadfly or pariah—exiled to the socially marginalized, contrarian location of the _para doxa_. Much like Wilde, humanists have long seen themselves in paradox, projecting their missions, desires, and fears of persecution onto that logic. While naming the burdens of the outcast, however, paradox has simultaneously provided a vehicle for rhapsodizing that plight, in thinking that exalts what I will explain as various "paradoxes of exclusion" not only for purveying keener, heightened understanding but also as the provenance of notions like justice, ethics, and democracy.

Since these vast expectations for paradox have not always existed, one goal of this book is to disentangle the many threads—historical, political, cultural, scholarly—that wove paradox into a comprehensive and accommodating explanatory fabric. Some possessing deep philosophical roots and others forged in the cauldron of the mid-twentieth century, a web of disparate though now tightly enmeshed influences came together to fashion paradox into what I will conceive as a type of intellectual paradigm.[4] To grasp how a generalized spirit in the postwar air evolved into an all-encompassing and tenacious cosmology, this book's examples range far and wide within (and beyond) what one might denominate as the "theory canon." Its case studies are comparatively sweeping. What follows investigates how ideas about paradox *both* orchestrated *and* were themselves implanted by proliferating debates about the character of modernity; the fortunes of legal and political rights; radical social movements post-'68; the value of a liberal arts education; crucibles of trauma and witnessing; and much, much more.

As an explanatory prism, the term *paradox* naturally consorts with a chain of mutually reinforcing and often interchangeable rhetorical-analytic cousins (contradiction, antagonism, aporia, ambivalence, irony, ambiguity, indeterminacy, Otherness, opacity, complexity, dialecticism, and so on). While I'll parse the distinctions separating these and other near synonyms for paradox, this book's main project is to raise questions about such thinking's epistemic sway: to inquire into everything that the logic of paradox has come to engulf—and in the process, to obscure and to discard. It argues that faith in paradox has been transacted at an increasingly exorbitant price, and it sets out to recover intellectual-political resources and horizons that such a mindset surrenders and forbids. But as an internal critique, this book argues less for abandoning paradox than for its containment: for offsetting such thinking's conceptual dominance with an expanded, diversified toolkit of criticism and theory. Its reservations about the intellectual equipment of paradox flow above all from the concern that critical theory has lost sight of that tradition's guiding ambitions. Conviction in paradox has diverted us from goals like just coexistence, social belonging, principled resistance and dissent, collective action, and, perhaps above all, critical, humanistic inquiry broadly. To track the many (mis)adventures of paradox, the following analyses will therefore journey through encyclopedic topics of debate as well as down certain rabbit holes, grappling with what "theory" "is" and from whence its many guises came.

The Genetics of Theory

Like most if not all books, this one tells stories—or, more accurately, a maze of interlocking ones. Each chapter revisits what is really the same story involving the many forces that aligned to consecrate paradox as a way of knowing and a left intellectual creed, although by adopting a series of divergent perspectives on those developments. With alternating protagonists—ranging from modernity to literary criticism to human rights to higher ed—each chapter unfolds microchronicles that replay a parallel narrative trajectory and recurring set of themes. Recursive, this web of intellectual genealogies all converging on paradox as a near talismanic answer offers one angle on why that spirit has functioned as a governing edict for whole generations of scholars, including schools of thought otherwise far from compatible or sympathetic. While many of this book's examples magnify points of disagreement over paradox and that logic's implications, its accumulation of varied thinkers and debates all independently endorsing the truth claims of paradox is designed to capture such thinking's supple adaptability as well as power. The sheer array of intellectual puzzles such a logic has *both* inspired *and* proficiently unraveled will illustrate why paradox came to be naturalized as a self-propagating worldview.

This book is, on the one hand, a testament to the industry of such thinking, and it aims to vivify the dynamic energy and often giddy excitement that led paradox to be enshrined as *the* conceptual prism of our times. One clear source of that authority lies with the basic accuracy of paradox as a diagnosis. It is hard to imagine a world—or frankly a life worth living—without paradox, complexity, ambivalence, and contradiction. Many aspects of contemporary existence are wildly paradoxical; as a result, many (if not most) intellectuals have flat out labeled modernity a condition of avalanching paradox, as we will at length consider. Even more, it is near impossible to conceive of critical inquiry—or for that matter thought itself—without paradox. Much of the pleasure of theory lies with the operations of paradox: with the epiphanic, cunning, delicious, unexpected discoveries that paradoxes often elicit. Yet precisely given these attractions, this book, on the other hand, scrutinizes the pitfalls and snares of such a mind-set. It examines the perils of intellectual engrossment with paradox, and it argues that too much has been sacrificed on that altar. While demonstrating why intellectual obeisance to paradox can tend to stultify, it simultaneously seeks to retrieve registers of thought throttled or interdicted by that logic, suggesting why paradox will not always be the best or the only answer to every question.

Along the way, the book recounts something of a perfect intellectual storm: a storm that overtook left intellectual life amid the same decades that witnessed the rise and institutionalization of theory. That dawn of theory, it argues, inculcated a religion of paradox that remains a calling card of the radical, academic, progressive, and theoretically informed left. Poststructuralism, Marxism and the Frankfurt School, Foucault, psychoanalysis, critiques of race and gender oppression, existential philosophy including theology, post-Saussurean theories of representation: these influences and more arrived on the doorsteps of Anglo-American universities to be ordained as "theory"—and to go on to revolutionize higher education.

Taking up initial residence in language and literature departments, that thriving body of thought annexed many of those fields' preoccupations, namely with the literary, poetic, or aesthetic. Radiating across the humanities and into pockets of the social sciences, the innovations now associated with theory spurred not only contagious anticipation but also deep conflicts and rifts. While precipitating canon wars that overhauled the syllabi and research archives of entire disciplines, that ferment also spawned now semi-independent academic programs (like Science and Technology Studies or Feminist Gender and Sexuality Studies), with the net effect of remaking the structure and orientation of major sectors of the university as we know it. This commotion within the ivory tower eventually found itself popularly disseminated, chaperoning (and capitalizing on the enthusiasm of) innumerable legal-political movements for sociopolitical change and overcoming. And while spreading the gospel of paradox far and wide, this prospering of theory simultaneously augmented the meanings and associations of paradox as an alluring language—in albeit subtle ways.

Beyond such upheaval within the academy, the transitions charted in this book are a byproduct of the peculiar sociopolitical and cultural climate of especially the 1970s and '80s. As others have suggested, the "theory era" harnessed many energies orphaned after the dissipation of 1960s-style radicalism, as the broad ethos and certain principles of the counterculture and student protest were redomiciled within then-blossoming scholarly leftisms and, eventually, the humanities classroom. Academic discourse repackaged many rallying cries of '68: anti-authoritarianism, nonconformism, anti-institutionalism, experimentalism, moral transgressiveness, a symbolics or aesthetics of politics, and belief in impromptu or "free," uncensorable expression.[5] Just as for Wilde almost a century earlier, the lens of paradox has synthesized these commitments, amalgamating them into a cohesive yet intoxicating philosophy. As a repository for the 1960s' unspent yearnings, the language of paradox has channeled not only that era's exuberantly mind-freeing (and even psychedelic) élan but also its consciousness-raising and justice-oriented mandates, which prevail to this day.

Simultaneously, intellectual life during the 1970s was indelibly imprinted by the Cold War. That context also bequeathed theory multiple warrants for paradox, along with a lingering fixation on that geopolitical era's phantoms. The anti-authoritarianism (and anxieties regarding totalitarianism in particular) understandably rampant during the Cold War readily colluded with the residual mood of '68, as those dual vectors of paradox cross-pollinated and fused. In addition, the Cold War injected the language of paradox with charged and historically precise valences still redolent within many if not most areas of theory. As intellectuals across the ideological map (including liberals and conservatives) wrestled with Cold War politics, they regularly anatomized totalitarianism in terms of a hostility to paradox and everything that quality was understood to telegraph (uncensorable speech, human rights, pluralism, Otherness, justice). And whereas the spirit of paradox was conceived as intrinsically antitotalitarian, democracy (being totalitarianism's foil) was increasingly viewed as a bastion of unmasterable paradox. Such thinking hallows paradox as an almost gnostic code binding those dual political forms together, impregnating each with an intimate if inverted inner logic. Once imbued with such a cocktail of ethical-just-democratic and protolinguistic qualities, paradox was further weaponized as a poison pill geared to sabotage power's encroachments. This premise that paradox and its armory (contradiction, ambivalence, dialecticism, indeterminacy, and so on) are vital to the unmasking and defeat of potentially authoritarian power remains a methodological staple for many.

Meanwhile, a congeries of philosophical-intellectual shifts helped to ingrain other emergent expectations for paradox—expectations that confirmed and redoubled all of the foregoing. These shifts recalibrated the tenor and resonances of that language (and its adjacent terminologies), infusing paradox with a distinctly rehabilitative if not transformative aura. One such innovation lies with what is often dubbed the linguistic turn, and especially its post-Saussurean incarnations. As Toril Moi suggests, the "doxa concerning language and meaning" within the humanities remains post-Saussurean, and this book's arguments build on Moi's assessment.[6] Whether transmitted via Lacan or deconstruction or a radicalized pedagogy operationalized by critiques of power, one thing the linguistic turn did was to install paradox within essentially *all* claims to meaning, representation, truth, identity, subjectivity, politics, justice, ethics, and more. In its wake, it has been axiomatic that basically all "representations" (political, literary, identitarian, or otherwise) must be deciphered with reference to their enabling "exclusions" and other "necessary failures"—in a relay that deems paradox both constitutive and brimming with consummate (albeit recondite) meaning.

What thus transpired with developments like the linguistic turn was a growing impulse to highlight the redemptive promise (rather than the structural oppressions) encoded by the language of paradox. Theorists for centuries (if not millennia) have relied on paradox and other dialectical maneuvers as an apparatus of critique, unsettling orthodoxy by exposing the contradictions it camouflages. But the instinct to valorize the mind-opening, emancipatory aspects of paradox was encouraged by the arrogation of two specific philosophical traditions that have historically enlisted paradox to negotiate various legitimation crises—crises mirroring those increasingly understood to plague all meaning-making practices. One such source is theology, à la a blend of diverse variants one might very differently associate with Soren Kierkegaard, W. E. B. Du Bois, and legal thinkers like Robert Cover and Carl Schmitt. Established genres of paradox (i.e., theodicy) borrowed from religious thought contained a trove of strategies for explaining why apparent limits (i.e., God's ineffability, silence, allowance of evil) could in fact be insignia of glory and greatness. A text like Kierkegaard's *Fear and Trembling* thus recounts such "struggles of faith" through a vocabulary composed of paradox and other familiar grammars that today reverberate across theory: incalculability, incommensurability, impossibility, singularity, unintelligibility.[7] Instead focused on "political" paradox, Schmitt's presence has similarly towered, among other things bestowing on the exceptional and excluded—or the marginalized positionality of a paradox—a privileged, "sovereign," constituent power. Not last, Du Bois's famed notion of "double consciousness"—which Du Bois himself labels a "paradox"—makes separate recourse to theological vestiges of paradox, although to convert the pain of oppression into a grace-like font of insight and renewal.

Just as important, aesthetic criticism has provided theorists with another storehouse of tools for contending with paradoxes. After all, a paradox is a rhetorical figure (like apostrophe, simile, metonymy, irony, and so on), so it is not surprising that lyrical-metaphorical resonances would, as for Wilde, animate that logic. But those associations also activate a long tradition of accounting for the peculiar truths procured by encounters with art and literature through a deep grammar of paradox. Over the centuries (if not millennia), paradox has been widely taken as a, if not the, signature of the aesthetic: of what makes art *art*. While here too partner to a retinue of related terminologies, in particular has the language of paradox been taken to designate art's unique province. Within aesthetic criticism, that grammar fulfills functions strikingly analogous to those at play within theology, disclosing ostensible deficiencies or limits (such as art's tenuous evidentiary status) to be replete with epistemic bounty. It is not hard to comprehend why art would suffer a legitimation crisis: one rehearsed ever since Plato's infamous charge that "fictions lie." But those "liar's paradoxes" of art and its ambiguous claims to truth have simultaneously been heralded as its sine qua non. Whether in the early modern period's many rebuttals of Plato or contemporary discourses on art's singularity, the technicities of paradox have converted art's lack of real-world or calculable bearings into a predicament worthy of veneration, just as anti-instrumentalist creeds of paradoxically "mattering without mattering" have been oft-sloganized within popular defenses of the humanities.

These multiple conduits for paradox assembled into the definition of a Kuhnian paradigm. As I'll show, certain features peculiar to reasoning through paradox (versus irony, or ambiguity, or contradiction and the dialectic) worked to synchronize those threads, merging them into a concordant and self-sustaining intellectual fabric. Precisely that eclecticism has rendered the logic of paradox versatile and elastic: a conceptual scheme readily transported to digest a host of far-flung topics and debates. Yet what also happened is that well-established metrics for reckoning with paradox inherited from theology and aesthetics were grafted onto sites of paradox not, however, so clearly aesthetic or symbolic or spiritualized in their fiber. Whether trauma, or democracy, or the radicalized liberal arts classroom, the dynamics of such phenomena have been widely modeled upon—and dissected according to—genres for navigating paradox crafted within alternate disciplines and arenas. As a result, those phenomena, first, became permeated with redemptive energies one might be inclined to confine to realms of experience like religion or literature. Second, discrepant scales, calibers, and auspices of paradox came to be collapsed: conjoined into—and capable of being delineated by way of—a single and all-enveloping explanatory matrix. Paradox has been the connective tissue cohering that matrix, just as it has acted as the axis around which those multiform inquiries (into art, politics, law, modernity, agency, history, the subject, and more) collectively rotate. Hence, this book explores the consolidation of a style of thought that has been, on the one hand, formulaic in its tendency to naturalize paradox as a mind-set and fait accompli but that, on the other, has been strikingly capacious in the plethora of issues it has adjudicated. Another perplexity of paradox and its logic involves those many homogenizing, routinizing repercussions.

By now, it should be clear that this book is, more than anything, a meditation on the state of theory and in particular on its successes and failures. Insofar as it paints an unusual picture of that landscape, that account foregrounds the diverse traffic conducted by paradox. One reason such a logic has dictated so much involves its frequently exhaustive frame of reference: as for Wilde, a single allusion to paradox can embed a discovery, a diagnosis, a critique, an objective, an ethos, a modality of thought, and almost autobiographical ruminations. This is also why the book's analyses cover such an expansive territory, ranging across broad swaths of commonly anthologized, taught, and otherwise exalted theories, thinkers, and texts. In mapping an intellectual formation fully engineered by paradox, that scope is devised to place into high relief what reasoning through paradox not only confers with the watermark of momentousness or authority but also overlooks and shuns. Although rewarding scholarship brandishing its complexity, irony, difficulty, and ambiguity on its sleeve, the edicts of paradox also abjure quite a lot. What follows therefore investigates everything that the logic of paradox forecloses and expels: what it prevents its practitioners from thinking and arguing and valuing and seeing. This is especially crucial because the truth claims of paradox are secured by various negative theologies: by stipulating (in keeping with the structure of the *para doxa*) what a given domain (whether the humanities or justice or modernity) is *not*, or with reference to what something appears to supersede and to banish. In such ways has theory similarly been constituted by its exceptions, exclusions, bans, and refusals: by all that it purports *not* to be. And insofar as belief in paradox can be self-reinforcing, that prophetic status centrally derives from what its logic occludes from view—even while being wholly dependent on those omissions for its very existence.

Only Paradoxes to Offer: The Story of Rights

This book ended up in a very different place from where it began. It started with a narrow objective: to weigh in on the explosion of interest in human rights across the humanities, including my own field of literary studies, during the first and second decades of the twenty-first century. In taking stock of that efflorescence, I was struck by the regularity and even predictability of certain default assumptions regarding rights. Over and over again, attempts to theorize rights arrived at one or another stock conclusion regarding their paradoxes, even while holding out that insight as surprising if not revelatory. Whether to deem paradox fatal or fertile, essay upon essay after book upon book presented paradox as the chromosomal makeup of rights. Whereas for some a preliminary diagnosis, and for others the culmination of lengthy analyses, paradox seemed to emerge as its own governing principle. At once, I was astonished by the manifold roles paradox played within many such studies, representing *both* problem *and* solution—if not an uncanny providence. Far from last, a given citation to paradox frequently pertained to multiple facets of rights simultaneously, fast becoming overdetermined. I asked: how could one property carry out such intricate theoretical labor, and for so many otherwise inharmonious thinkers?

While wrestling with what felt like an odd (and unremarked) consensus, I gradually observed such patterns of thought to extend far and wide beyond the narrow purview of debates about rights—and even beyond the precincts of theory. Worship of paradox started to show up every place I looked. Any random book from my shelves, whether acquired the week prior or in college, already contained diligently underlined sections that zeroed in on disclosures of paradox and contradiction. As I proceeded, my research for this project often felt eerily straightforward, given that I had already marked the exemplary passages providing fodder for my arguments years ago: passages all verifying paradox as a way of knowing and belief structure. Some best-selling theory texts made my research even easier by staging paradox in their titles: *Cruel Optimism, The Right to Maim, Ugly Feelings, The Queer Art of Failure, Vibrant Matter, Revolution of the Ordinary, The Emancipated Spectator, Black and Blur, Transnational America, The Cunning of Recognition, Enlightenment Orientalism*.[8] Seemingly everywhere did paradox operate simultaneously as riddle and clue, enigma and cipher, the key to virtually anything that mattered—or at least to any question meriting theorization. Hence, I slowly began to accept that I was writing a book about questions much bigger than those besetting rights: that I was trying to apprehend something vaster than any discrete line of inquiry. Rather, I was investigating deep structures of thought, sacred ideals, foundational methodologies, and vocational callings—plainly put, the nostrums of theory.

Notwithstanding this project's ever-amplifying scope, rights have continued to offer an ideal platform for entertaining its main arguments. This is partly due to the fact that rights—arguably more than any other legal-political-philosophical construct, and since their modern inception—have been outright defined with reference to their incurable paradoxes. The premise that rights have "only paradoxes to offer" (per a book by Joan Scott) and that we must "suffer the paradoxes of rights" (per Wendy Brown) has been doctrinal.[9] On the one hand, this view of rights is undoubtedly correct. Paradox has haunted rights' fortunes on nearly every level, causing the world's hopes for rights to be impaled on paradox after endless paradox. If anything, the globalization of rights has only multiplied those hazards, aggravating the sorts of worries ventured long ago by a thinker like Jeremy Bentham when he wittily called the idea of *natural* rights "nonsense upon stilts."[10]

But on the other, theorists have responded to that diagnosis of paradox in markedly different, even opposing ways. In sorting theories of rights, I was therefore confused by what appeared a balkanized intellectual landscape. On one side was a healthy tradition of rights skepticism, wedded to a vision of paradox as structural, chronic, and lethal. For many, the determination that rights are riddled with paradox levels a damning verdict: a basis for jettisoning or otherwise disparaging rights. On the other side were cadres of thinkers who instead celebrated rights as vessels of justice, ethics, and democracy—and not *despite* but rather *because of* their plentiful paradoxes. These thinkers tended to seize on the *exact same* paradoxes of rights that elsewhere prompted condemnation—however, to celebrate that property rather than to lament its existence. Within both camps, moreover, a lot more than rights was implicated within the discovery of paradox: paradox acted as a linchpin demanding parallel conclusions about related phenomena comparatively afflicted by tenuous legitimacy or an exclusionary architecture. Marveling at this ostensible divide, I wondered: what occurred that allowed some theorists otherwise committed to a staunch "anti-legalism" to exalt rights as uniquely redemptive? And on the very grounds (paradox) that had conventionally toed the line of rights skepticism and refusal (paradox)?

Just as telling, certain theorists' forays into rights seemed to have triggered watershed advances carrying broad significance. Jacques Derrida, Karl Marx, Jacques Lacan, Giorgio Agamben, Claude Lefort: these thinkers' efforts to anatomize rights stimulated broad, thoroughgoing transitions in their respective oeuvres. Moreover, it was precisely due to overlapping paradoxes that rights came to be enmeshed within—and to glean larger lessons into—*both* the institutions embedding them (e.g., democracy) *and* abiding dilemmas understood to face law, politics, justice, ethics. This privileging of paradox also appeared to generate a type of conveyor belt inviting transference back and forth across contrasting and even unrelated problematics and domains, permitting the paradoxes of rights to be patterned on the foreclosures of the subject or deferrals of a text or an antinomian grace. Some of these relays struck me as unsurprising, for instance given trauma theory's role in fostering academic interest in rights. But all of this traffic undeniably endowed the logic of paradox with chameleon, ambidextrous qualities—enabling sleights of hand, slippages, and conversions. This book looks to rights as one laboratory in the incredible virtuosity of reasoning through paradox.

Joan Scott's 1996 *Only Paradoxes to Offer: French Feminists and the Rights of Man*, an intellectual history of the centuries-long struggle for women's rights in France that later chapters revisit, can afford an initial demonstration of this colossal labor frequently conducted by paradox. Followed by a colon in Scott's title, paradox issues a double diagnosis, indexing *both* the exclusions constitutive of rights *and* the plight of feminists fated to embody such failed universality. Yet to be expected by now, Scott's appeal to paradox signals a lot more simultaneously. For one, Scott plots feminist activism over history as a litany of successive encounters with paradox that, moreover, are held out as the recipe for *all* radicalized agency. In Scott's thinking, radical agency comes to be near synonymous with paradox, and for reasons that mirror other influential accounts of the resistant insurgency of society's marginalized and downtrodden. This is because feminist agency is above all actuated for Scott by the symbolic enactment of "inconsistency and ambiguity—of self-contradictoriness—within an orthodoxy that strenuously denies [its] existence."[11] However, we can pause to note a certain tension (which I'll extensively probe): paradox *both* denotes the machinery of women's oppression *and* harbors eye-opening, prolific, and even justice-oriented faculties. Not last, paradox is a bedrock of Scott's own method as a revisionist historian who sets out to excavate sites of heterogeneity, ambiguity, and fragmentation in the record—or what Michel Foucault would call "mak[ing] visible all of those discontinuities that cross us."[12] A symmetrical justificatory framework thus connects Scott's genealogical project as a revisionist historian seeking to uncover paradox with the radicalized agency mobilized by her French feminists—offering one early glimpse of why the logic of paradox tends to become autobiographical for theory.

Scott's kaleidoscope of paradox, like Wilde's, is far from anomalous. Over its course, this book examines a panoply of thought comparatively riveted by the transformative and consciousness-raising powers of paradox. To be sure, paradoxes are not foreign to the intellectual-political traditions often juxtaposed with theory: humanism, analytic philosophy, law, normative inquiry, (neo)liberalism. As Bertrand Russell once observed, "The point of philosophy is to start with something so simple as not to seem worth stating, and to end with something so paradoxical that no one will believe it."[13] I'll therefore question the common gambit of accusing nonhumanistic, social scientific, quantitative disciplines of indifference to paradox: that move creates cartoonish straw men—albeit straw men that many regnant defenses of the humanities have fully required. Even more worrisome, we'll see, is the fact that crying paradox by no means represents an exclusively left or progressive or radical strategy, but rather is just as prone to smuggle in right-wing or reactionary agendas. Indeed, the jury is out over whether the machinations of paradox have increasingly embezzled not only the politics of theory but also contemporary public life and civic debate. Nevertheless, it is also true that theory has been exceptionally spellbound by paradox and its charisma; other disciplines and variants of thought typically confine that logic to a much narrower intellectual berth. Only within theory has paradox overseen such multitudinous, vertiginous functions, dominating all stages and components of the reasoning process to emerge as a kind of oracle-like cipher.

This book, then, reckons with the intellectual-historical collisions that catalyzed these exorbitant aspirations for paradox. Those high hopes, we'll see, are both old and new. Although it is descended from fabled philosophical origins, something unusual transpired when growing ranks of left intellectuals began to regard paradox in a newly rejuvenating and metamorphic light, extolling the logic of paradox as something to be reveled in, promoted, and pursued. Flowering into its own self-sufficient explanatory principle, that logic has swallowed more and more and more. What follows consequently asks: when and why did paradox begin to legislate and presort our theoretical puzzles? How did paradox become *the* impetus for intellectual inquiry—occasioning, shepherding, and guaranteeing what, in the context of this study, will start to appear foregone conclusions? What environmental factors allowed paradox to acquire this unrivaled conceptual and critical acumen? Even more, what syndromes take hold when a single metric becomes so massively overburdened?

Autobiographies of Paradox

One such syndrome involves that logic's propensity to become intimately personal as well as self-referential. And in fact, this book in part recounts my own intellectual biography. Its beginnings stem from some of my earliest memories, traceable to a vision of my eight-year-old self poring over my father's study shelves. Like many academics during the late 1970s and early 1980s, my father (a professor of nineteenth-century American literature) had amassed a collection of books all differently haunted by the "age of atrocity" and that era's many crimes against humanity.[14] Already at a young age, I internalized such an onus to tackle political evil head on. Later, my undergraduate education was constellated by philosophy and English majors that provided endless avenues for my continued probing of such matters, although primarily routed through existential and "postmodern" philosophy. Whereas college found me transfixed by thinkers like Mikhail

Bakhtin and Derrida and Fred Jameson, even in law school I convinced my professors to let me write seminar papers on Max Weber, Foucault, Virginia Woolf, Milan Kundera.

When I returned to the academy to write a dissertation on postcolonial literature and theory's relevance to human rights, Yale school approaches to that interdisciplinary juncture provided my main compass. In many respects, I was drawn to theories of human rights precisely because of their dizzying, irresolvable paradoxes. My first book wrestled with what I characterized as one distinct paradox of human rights: that "liberal" discourses of rights presume a strangely abstract and decorporealized subject, eviscerated by rationalist individualism. (My hiring talk at Cornell was titled "The Human Rights Paradox.") Even more telling, my book's rejoinder to that anemic subject of rights hinged on a methodology (adapted from phenomenology) for revealing apparent limits of rights to be, lo and behold, reservoirs of ethical, just, fecund paradox. My analyses thus relied on that logic to effectuate the very sorts of alchemy this book calls into question. Since then, my scholarship has frequently proceeded from the assumption that awakening submerged paradox can liberate law from its errors, just as my investment in literature will always rest on a hope that the vicissitudes of paradox attune us ethical and other complexity.

My classrooms have similarly paid frequent homage to paradox. Even today, nearly every novel or film or theoretical text I teach procures lessons in the virtues of qualities like indeterminacy and ambivalence, which I contrast with the moral hazards of stability, intelligibility, closure, transparency, resolution, and more. The twenty-first century academy certainly bears some responsibility for making available a literary canon stocked with texts verifying that wisdom, as chapters 4 and 5 discuss. But the point is that my classrooms and research alike have found me a regular evangelist for paradox; and on some levels, I am still a believer. The language of paradox will always conjure my sense of vocation, including the passion and exhilaration of a life of ideas. That love is something this book does strive to capture: to recreate the thrill of an intellectual mode that has captivated and defined entire disciplines and academic generations and sociopolitical movements and schools of thought. Despite its reservations, this book attempts to do justice to the radiance of a philosophical tradition that has proven world-altering and electrifying for so many.

However, what follows is foremost a chronicle of mounting frustration. When I began this project, my curiosity was piqued by what struck me as a startling predictability and homogeneity of thought. Reliance on paradox had become rote and programmatic. But as I slowly recognized those bearings to be compulsory, claustrophobia set in. Allegiance to paradox had, with great irony, congealed into its own orthodoxy, into a regimen that suffocated free thinking and stymied creativity. Rather than provoking nuance or sophistication, insistence on paradox seemed to annihilate thought: to administer a kind of intellectual anesthesia. Every book in my theory library performed the exact same moves on what felt like autopilot, walking lockstep through a worn-out methodological repertoire. Texts that had previously invigorated me started to feel dead, robotic, and unoriginal. In too many talks at too many academic conferences, paradox might have ghostwritten the gag lines in advance. Perhaps counterintuitively, I was overwhelmed (rather than pleased) by the sea of evidence supporting my arguments, as literally every thinker or text I perused served to confirm what I was seeing.

These frustrations only deepened the longer I lived with this project. Beyond how the logic of paradox ossified thought, I grieved over its disciplinary effects. Careers were threatened for those who broke from its ranks. It also seemed one matter to dictate practices of reading literature, and yet another to submit life-threatening issues of politics or justice or law to such a threadbare machinery. Don't get me wrong, I have and will remain a proponent of many founding commitments of critical theory: to social justice, to defeating structures of oppression, to freedom from ideological conformity, to the critique of power, and even (à la Wilde) to the unmasking of philistine common sense. However, the clutches of paradox have too often sabotaged those principles, leading theory to forsake everything it has advocated. Of late, it has become a cottage industry to blame certain imperatives (like critique or paranoia or symptomatic reading) for selling theory out, and this book may well be numbered among those indictments. Nevertheless, blind adherence to paradox has appeared a tragedy of the worst, lowest common denominator winning out, despoiling other elements of an otherwise rich, lively, engaged intellectual formation.

Ongoing immersion in this project thus intensified my wariness regarding the intellectual habits that the arithmetic of paradox both entrenches and gratifies. In diagramming those priorities, I became dismayed by more than default positions or foreordained outcomes. Belying a frequent mystique of singularity and difference, that logic more accurately encourages facile homologies and sweeping parallels, often gaining momentum precisely by toggling seamlessly from one domain (say, semiotics or aesthetics) to another (say, politics) only to collapse them into a single economy of meaning and valuation. The same algebra recruited to decipher the meaning-making practices of a text can thus be applied to account for political agency or rights. All the while, the humanities classroom gets touted as a microcosm of the political, teeming with consciousness-raising opportunities paralleling activism in the streets. Relatedly has democracy's lack of secure foundations been ransomed by the same apologetics enlisted to redress the justificatory crisis facing the ailing humanities, and precisely by modeling both those spheres' paradoxes of representation (of democracy's people and of the humanities' marginality) on the arbitrary slippages and deferrals that harbor a text's elusive "meaning." While such analogical transfers can be stirring, their emulsifying effects have felt disabling if not downright destructive. To me, a tradition staked on fantasies of radicalism seemed to have fallen victim to the very syndromes it sought most vigilantly to combat. As an edict, paradox appeared to have set theory up to succumb to its worst fears—to install itself as a universalism, a pure form and formalism ripe for cooptation.

Beyond my own peculiar intellectual pilgrimages, this book tells a wide network of stories, many of which I hope will feel recognizable (if not biographical) to my readers. Some of those tales concern developments that are resoundingly positive, whereas others are more mixed. For some readers, this book will recount the shifts that refurbished their home disciplines and departments, as many humanities fields became caught up in canon wars and other efforts to give voice to the paradoxical exclusions underwriting their historical foundations and ambit. For others, this book will describe the terms that presided over their primary fields' birthplace, as those mandates simultaneously inseminated new programs and majors across the liberal arts. For others still, it will explain the critical movements that swept through disciplines with partial footings in the social sciences, like sociology or psychology or law. There is no question that these innovations that rebuilt higher education, and thereafter rippled throughout popular culture, number among the most beneficial gifts of theory. However, the complex stakes of those gifts will appear less clearly salutary when tied to enchantment with paradox.

Readers with Marxist sympathies will likely approach this book as an odyssey of the dialectic and, perhaps, of its betrayal. In certain ways, this book does track the dialectic's fate in the aftermath of 1960s-style radicalisms, the institutionalization of theory, and the apex of poststructuralism. It examines dissipating hopes for the utopian transcendence promised by revolution—hopes superseded by a spirit of vagrant and irresolvable dialecticism. But this is not a book about the dialectic, and, more important, its main fights are not internal to vying factions of Marxist theory. At best, debates about the dialectic surface intermittently, although it also submits that reasoning through contradiction (the usual métier of the dialectic) is ultimately cut from the same cloth as that of paradox. On the one hand, there is much truth to the notion that a spirit of paradox did colonize and overtake the dialectic, supplanting its status as the primary engine of history, change, power, domination, agency, and so on. Hence, the ensuing chapters ratify one standard rendition of the dialectic's trajectory post-'68: its replacement with an exuberant "modernism in the streets" of the sort chronicled by Marshall Berman.[15] At the same time, one might counter Berman and wager that what more accurately triumphed was a negative dialectics akin to Theodor Adorno's, or a dialectic that foremost serves as a mediating device allowing conflictual, incommensurable ideals to coexist together. Nevertheless, what undoubtedly did ensue is that an uncabined dialecticism became something virtually every student of theory could get behind, papering over these and other schisms.

So on the other hand, I would put pressure on a retort this project has often met with: "well, what about the dialectic?" That impulse to distance Marxism from deconstruction and its ilk by appealing to the dialectic is all too easy. For one, the annals of Marxist theory are filled with many ardent crusaders for paradox—and not only figures like Slavoj Žižek, whose bravura performances tantalize precisely because they culminate with omnipresent paradox. Indeed, paradox is a punch line that Žižek's 2001 *Did Somebody Say Totalitarianism?*—an ostensible takedown of deconstruction—converges on a total of sixty-one times.[16] Seminal thinkers like Georg Lukacs, Louis Althusser, and Fred Jameson are all celebrants of paradox, often substituting paradox for "properly Marxist" terms like contradiction or antagonism perforce.[17] Hence, there is no question that Marxist brands of the dialectic deserve due credit for aiding and abetting the consolidation of paradox as an epistemology.

I expect some readers will therefore experience this book as a saga of competing radicalisms, or a battle for methodological-institutional dominance amid the academic peak of theory. Yet while parsing such quarrels, its main goal is to understand how otherwise acrimonious schools of thought settled their differences—all assenting to a common catechism of paradox. Despite how different sites of paradox can in fact incur competing responses (as we'll examine throughout), those contentions risk obscuring the significantly more profound and thoroughgoing consensus that set in across theory for its practitioners. That consensus was both choreographed and secured by a shared devotional of paradox. So notwithstanding eruptions of internecine warfare like those roiling a field like literary studies amid this book's completion, rarely if ever has that infighting questioned paradox and its paramount authority.

Given that literary studies represents one of this book's backdrops, some readers may try to pigeonhole it accordingly, such as to take it as a statement of postcritique. However, those attempts would similarly miss the mark. While invested in rethinking the methodological precepts administering theory, this book does so in effort to better integrate our theory into our critical praxis. It therefore examines the reasons those projects have been sundered—with praxis, as Bernard Harcourt suggests, getting short shrift.[18] The problem, in turn, is not with critique per se but rather that critique has been bowdlerized, truncated, and diverted along lines that increasingly prevent it from living up to task. This book's explanation for that depletion lies with the spell of paradox. Far from tangential or occasional, paradox has been *the* architecture of critique, as we will see again and again and again. It is this beholdenness to paradox that leaves critique in disrepair, although the final chapter proposes one itinerary for its renovation.

Other of this book's subplots will, I hope, indulge readers' specialized or idiosyncratic interests in varying ways. The status of critical work on law, inside and outside of the legal academy, is a theme within many chapters. As I argue, "anti-legalism" (often paired with "antinomian" visions of an antirationalist justice dispensed by versions of grace) is one artifact of conviction in paradox rife within much of the humanities. Debates about power and its guises also recur, along with theorizations of modernity; of the contours of radical agency; of aesthetics; and of selfhood and the subject. Lacanian psychoanalysis helped to naturalize a logic of paradox: an entire section of Lacan's *Seminar VII: The Ethics of Psychoanalysis: 1959–60* is focused on (and titled accordingly) "The Paradox of *Jouissance*."[19] Later thinkers incorporated such an itinerary of the subject into accounts of disciplinary power analogously scaffolded by paradox, as Judith Butler's 1997 *The Psychic Life of Power: Theories in Subjection* declares: "As a form of power, subjection is paradoxical."[20] This book contains many such underdeveloped leads begging for elaboration.

Still others will discern a narrative of theory's attempts to metabolize various allegations. As Thomas Keenan notes, "paradox" (like the epithet "postmodernism") was a standard ground for disparaging a thinker like Foucault (as in the antiquated term "paradox-monger").[21] Yet that tactic of leveraging paradox as an accusation has not been alien to theorists' own civil wars. As John Searle recalls, Foucault himself claims to have charged

Derrida with something similar: with practicing a method of *obscurantisme terroriste*.[22] Yet even more instructive is the reasoning that emerged to neutralize complaints like those differently directed at Derrida and Foucault. Indeed, what thinkers like Keenan self-consciously did was to accept the basic diagnosis of paradox but to dispute its essence and implications. Actively recalibrating the meanings and significance of paradox, what others mistook as a philosophical deficit or lapse (paradox) was instead embraced as the vector of an insurgent agency and ethics (paradox). Reliance on the logic of paradox to effectuate a type of transubstantiation links many of this book's examples.

With thinkers like Butler and Keenan in mind, this book further considers the dynamics that rendered theory a hodgepodge or melting pot of approaches and schools. Theory in the twenty-first century begs to be characterized by its eclecticism, of which Butler's blending of Foucault with Althusser with Hegel with psychoanalysis with deconstruction is prototypical. Here, too, the trappings of paradox are *both* what enabled *and* essential to that pluralism. Especially when harnessing the figural or tropological dimensions of paradox does such reasoning not only concatenate synergies and analogies (as metaphors and other rhetorical figures are wont to do) but also broker the merger and acquisition of disparate and arguably incongruous problematics into a single explanatory prism. To be sure, such catholicism is contagious in how it transgresses intellectual pieties, but it can simultaneously produce a kind of methodological grab bag from which one can pick and choose.

But the point is that *all* these different stories are present, just as an array of topics ranging beyond this book's remit would comply with its individual chapters' mirroring narrative arcs. Notwithstanding small points of departure, those tales are all, at their core, one and the same. One way to understand that consistency is as a textbook case of a "paradigm," as Thomas Kuhn famously theorized scientific orders of knowledge. Kuhn emphasizes the fact that a research community can adhere to a paradigm "without agreeing on, or even attempting to produce, a full interpretation or rationalization of it" or the existence of "any full set of rules."[23] Rather, the sheer number of "puzzles" and problematics that a paradigm works to assimilate, digest, and inspire will ensure its combined purchase and resilience. That the conceptual architecture of paradox has incorporated so many far-flung inquiries, issues, and debates—spinning off subsidiary frameworks and even theoretical microcommunities—thus tells us everything we need to know. As Kuhn explains, the crux of a paradigm is to be sufficiently "open-ended" as to motivate a wealth of seemingly endless sites of application each of which conspires to reinforce the naturalness of that basic schema.[24]

One of Kuhn's agendas in reflecting on the nature of a paradigm is to make sense out of a research community's seeming imperviousness to "incommensurabilities"—and hence striking immunity to change and challenge. In fact a successfully functioning paradigm will "often suppress fundamental novelties because they are necessarily subversive of its basic commitments."[25] In drawing on Kuhn to contend with the grips of paradox, this book therefore foregrounds such thinking's intolerances: its congenital allergies, resistances, and denials. Yet Kuhn's formulation of a paradigm also registers the irony that precisely the throng of narratives a paradigm reconciles and absorbs can foretell its exhaustion. The very attributes enabling a paradigm's survival can lead to its fatigue (if not looming extinction). Having incorporated so much, faith in paradox indeed writes off what Kuhn would call "anomalies"—or a gathering host of disturbances that call its foundational premises into dramatic question. Hence, still another cardinal feature of a paradigm lies with that community's inability to recognize itself as thus beholden—even while that denial leads to a silencing of outliers with all the more militancy and vigilance.

The Logic of Paradox

The peculiar technicities of reasoning through paradox have themselves worked to enforce such fidelities and decrees. While ordaining certain substantive commitments, in particular has the veneration of paradox as a *style* sealed such reasoning against anomalies and other challenges. What is it about paradox as a stylistics, genre, and mode that exerts such control? As we will see, that logic often serves to harmonize clashing frequencies, as for Butler pacifying what might be sites of friction. On the one hand, this is because paradoxes are hoarders: they tend to stockpile heterogenous meanings, often playing them off one another like Wilde in his clearly literary fashion. Hence within allegory, "paradox" has sometimes been personified as a flesh-and-blood character, allowing such a medley of meanings to loom larger than life. Like other rhetorical figures, paradoxes summon parallels, homologies, repetitions, and metamorphoses. Rather than to magnify dissimilarities, they tend to activate synchronicities that only contribute to their gravitational pull. But on the other hand, such thinking's critical, contrarian orientation renders it simultaneously prone to scramble and unsettle its referents, thwarting stabilization and predictability. Paradoxes frequently self-complicate (if not self-detonate)—which is exactly why they have been prized within theory. It is this endless volley of provisionalities, subversions, and remainders that can magnetize, pulling more and more into such reasoning's conceptual orbit.

Over the following pages, we'll probe this agility and acuity. Although one might distinguish contemporary theory by its penchant for paradox, that investment is by no means a niche or a recent invention. In fact, early modern thinkers were attracted to paradoxes for reasons akin to those that mesmerize us to this day. For instance, Rosalie L. Colie's 1976 *Paradoxica Epidemica* studies the burst of such reasoning during the Renaissance, which Colie analogously attributes to its dexterity and versatility. Colie singles out many of the same properties as does this book, among others the propensity of paradoxes to amuse, to equivocate and even be duplicitous, to be self-critical, to "do two things at once," to be dialectical, to defy their own categories, and to reduce truth and meaning to a "hall of mirrors."[26]

As Colie further suggests, many facets of that logic have inspired cathexis or self-identification. Paradoxes can be cunning vehicles of critique, which is why talk of paradox flourished in the late eighteenth century alongside other portals of modern doubt and suspicion. Indeed, paradoxes have offered particularly adept tools for demolishing hierarchies and outing hypocrisies, in an often reflexive manner. Reasoning through paradox can appear to place the terms of inclusion-exclusion under perpetual renegotiation—an itinerary theorists have extolled as not only theory's own but also the kernel of democracy, justice, and ethics. Paradoxes are often protean, mobile, shape-shifting, energetic, and restless—and, given that fugitivity, hard to pin down. Not surprisingly, many thinkers have sought to rhetorically and formally emulate those qualities, routing their analyses through the torsions, meanderings, and other frequencies of paradox. Bringing to mind the recursive style of Lacan or Derrida as well as contemporary thinkers like Fred Moten or Hortense Spillers, reasoning through paradox often hovers about, undercutting its own inchoate recognitions, forever blurring boundaries and on the move.

While dramatizing these sorts of features, this book mainly strives to illustrate why such thinking becomes problematic. Like any analytic tool or argumentative maneuver, paradoxes are extremely good at certain things and less so at others. Staging a paradox is a highly effective way to liquidate substance and content—an enterprise chartering whole schools of theory. However, that logic is less good at telling us what should come along to fill that ensuing vacuum (other than still more paradox), or what might prevent invidious causes from profiteering from the normative-evaluative abyss that reasoning through paradox often creates. These tendencies are exacerbated by a related proclivity to interrupt efforts to equilibrate or rein such thinking in: paradoxes tend to short circuit the drawing of lines, the proposing of values, and the application of evaluative or prescriptive criteria. One reason their logic thwarts such differential analysis (which chapter 5 instead defends) stems from the ways paradoxes almost organically spawn synergies, correspondences, and analogical transfers—which, however, can end up homogenizing (if not totalizing) wildly discrepant circumstances and phenomena. Just as that logic can muddle the drawing of granular and other distinctions, it is at constant risk of running roughshod over ideals, norms, facts, truths, principles, standards, and commitments—even those that urgently require salvaging and preservation. This book puts forward various such theories of how and why the formal logic of paradox became erected into a global or omnibus theory, in the process critiquing its (crypto-) formalist bracketing of content, autonomization of discourse and style, and antifoundationalist foundationalism.

Still other common aspects of reasoning through paradox tend to self-armor it against efforts to moderate or curtail its workings. As we saw with Wilde, paradoxes deign to be smarter: to startle, unmask, and outwit. Yet despite acting as trump cards in a stacked deck, the predicament of a paradox is simultaneously to be derivative and parasitic: contingent on the original or dominant upon which its logic preys. Tellingly, theorists (ranging well beyond Wilde) have often glorified that very contingency as both libera-tory and a defense mechanism impeding ideological capture. A paradox (much like theory itself) brooks no desire for assimilation into the rule or dominant or center; those outcomes are more accurately what that logic religiously guards against, installing intellectual trip wires prone to get tripped whenever a goal like inclusion or resolution is on the table. Compounding all of this is that such reasoning typically knows no stop-ping point: its migrations can become almost hypnotic in their endless self-complications. Although acclaimed as consciousness-raising and gal-vanizing alike, reasoning through paradox, our case studies will recurrently show, is just as likely to do the opposite: to produce a haze of indecision; to apologize for handwringing and inertia; to mystify (if not stupefy) thought; and to offer succor in the face of real moral, political, and other difficulty.

It is also true that the world looks very different today than when de-votion to paradox came of age. Once upon a time, that logic was surely eye-opening, provocative, and even revolutionary—with regard to *both* the surrounding sociopolitical environment *and* the academic hierarchies it shook up. Today, however, we face a radically altered geopolitical landscape that can seem to expose faith in paradox as a relic of a distant era. At the time of this book's completion, the circumstances conspiring to betray that paradigm's obsolescence (a global pandemic, rising authoritarianism, mass protest, raging wildfires) seem only to mount. But beyond those atmospheric factors, the larger reality is that such reasoning is no longer the sole possession of intellectuals or of the left; critical theorists are no longer the only ones skilled at the weaponization of paradox. Of late, it has been au courant to worry, à la Bruno Latour, that "critique" and other historically left agendas have "run out of steam," whether due to their own subsidence or susceptibility to right-wing takeover.[27] The fate of reasoning through paradox can appear to vindicate those fears, causing concerns about critique to pale in comparison. Not only has crying paradox become a favored missile in the right-wing arsenal, used to derail more than particular arguments or ideological standpoints but the basic conventions of fair, open-minded, civic debate. In addition, that logic's therapeutic aura has been popularized: rebranded and watered down as today's face of common sense. One subtext of this book is accordingly to ask whether the tides of history have rendered faith in paradox not only outmoded but fully dangerous. Insofar as devotion to paradox was gestated within a bygone sociohistorical milieu, can it still equip a left, progressive politics for the future? As one example among many, does the authoritarian personality still behave in the same manner as during the Cold War, seeking to devour paradox and everything it stands for? Or does tyranny instead thrive within the very throes of indeterminacy and indecision long espoused by theory? And what about rising generations of students; if paradox manufactures ideology in the twenty-first century, will throwing still more paradox into the mix really rupture that façade?

Notwithstanding these liabilities, the problem is *not* that reasoning through paradox is inherently limiting or pernicious. Its logic has been and will continue to be irreplaceable, and especially to the forms of critical inquiry cultivated by an education in the humanities. Over the decades, the habits of thought dissected herein have radically transformed, along with intellectual life, our available imaginaries regarding politics, law, justice, and more, dramatically expanding the range of what we can realistically hope for and endeavor. However, this very world-altering power raises the question of why the more damaging, deadening tendencies of such thinking have increasingly won out—eclipsing if not stifling its many contributions.

It is hard to deny that paradox has simply engulfed too much, subsuming more and more to become all-determining (if not deterministic) within a lot of theory. That syndrome is in dire want of moderation, and this book argues more than anything that investment in paradox requires supplementation with other intellectual resources and goals. Such an integration with alternate analytic modes promises to better tailor theory to a praxis, including to reattune that tradition to pursuits it has erroneously jettisoned. A diversification of the repertoire and horizons of theory is therefore what this book above all endorses.

Plainly put, the logic of paradox cannot solve all of our puzzles, and it is even less suited to help us figure out how to act. Having "only paradoxes to offer" is not something to be celebrated: it is a dereliction. Yet in a state of denial, we continue ramping our dosage up and up, believing that the discovery of more durable, more foundational paradoxes will deliver us. But in actuality it is this bottomless insatiability that needs to be curbed.

Each chapter of this book offers a different angle on the dynamics that hardwired paradox into the genetics of theory. Those forays begin with the axiomatic link between modernity and paradox, although by interrogating the warrants subsidizing that modernity-as-paradox thesis. Intellectuals of all stripes have been in basic agreement that modernity represents a condition of escalating paradox. Discourses of modernity are therefore a playbook in the precepts and moves that have allowed paradox to supervise nearly all dimensions of theory, functioning as diagnosis, critique, method, philosophy of agency, ethics, metacritical self-commentary, and—when all is said and done—a type of panacea. Causing even contrasting accounts of modernity to appear strange carbon copies of one another, this consensus can also index larger debilities afflicting the logic of paradox. Among others, the equation between modernity and paradox has hinged on the positing of various pre- or anti-modern antitheses and foils; those exclusions from modernity, not surprisingly, map onto predictable sites of sociopolitical exclusion operative still today. Nevertheless, even theory committed to interrogating modernity's "othering" undercurrents has requisitioned paradox as a key apparatus of anticolonial and other critique. This chapter ventures tentative explanations for blind spots such as these, contending with perplexities that the rest of the book goes on to probe more fully.

Thereafter turning to debates about rights, chapter 2 investigates why a robust tradition of rights critique has often responded to the paradoxes of rights by ontologizing them—or by substantializing paradoxes that might otherwise be viewed as purely abstract or conjectural. For many that assessment has further meant that those limits are fatal and incurable—in extreme cases, motivating the view that rights logic is a blueprint for state-sanctioned and other organized injustice, violence, and oppression. According to versions of such reasoning have Marxist critics handcuffed rights to capitalism, whereas others (Arendt and Agamben) blame "legalization" for bankrupting rights. This impulse to ontologize paradox is part and parcel of the "anti-legalism" that remains a methodological a priori within many humanistic fields.

The middle section of the book addresses how, with the debut of theory, the predominant valences of paradox mutated to increasingly harness that grammar's uses within aesthetic theory, theology, and linguistics—although to decipher a spectrum of legal and political constructs and debates including rights. To illustrate what exactly was thus appropriated, the first Interlude takes a detour through the aesthetic criticism canon. In many ways, the nexus between aesthetics and paradox is even *more* doctrinal than that linking modernity to paradox. But what permitted a notion like rights to be infused with genres of paradox devised to make sense out of art and literature? And what happened when those literary-aesthetic vectors of paradox were enlisted to navigate deep quandaries that are preeminently legal and political, not only aestheticizing but also redeeming them along the way?

Given this book's attempt to vivify the protean workings of reasoning through paradox, that logic's aesthetic texture and figural-rhetorical bearings animate certain of its own arguments. While problematizing many facets of those dynamics, what follows also seeks to undergo and inhabit the vitality of paradox as an intellectual mode. Paradoxes, as suggested, often propagate metaphorical and allusive connections, and parts of this book draw freely from such strategies—and precisely to elucidate how and why that logic took on a life of its own. My own intermittent recourse to paradox as a stylistic mode should further clarify that this book is not "against paradox": it is an internal critique inspired and outfitted by the very intellectual tradition it scrutinizes.

In key ways, aesthetic criticism laid the groundwork for theorists to embrace rights, although that embrace was simultaneously facilitated by other intellectual and historical influences canvassed in chapter 3. While the peculiar geopolitical climate of the 1970s found many left intellectuals newly championing rights, that acclimation was not an isolated phenomenon but instead was stimulated by a budding wave of enthusiasm for paradox. The turn to rights was also enabled by their redefinition as linguistic claims or utterances; a Cold War preoccupation with censorship; psychoanalytic theories of "inhuman" justice and ethics; various poststructuralist rebuttals of Marxism; and more. While clearly incited by the dual specters of atrocity and totalitarianism, persisting long beyond that historical milieu have been decidedly redemptive hopes for paradox—and for everything projected onto that quality.

Chapters 4 and 5 explore the many channels through which these intellectual developments traveled far and wide beyond the chambers of high theory and even the academy. Even while nascent hopes for paradox midwifed key transformations within the university, theory capitalized on certain residues of '68, especially the ethos of the counterculture and radicalized youth protest. Chapter 4 inventories the countless social justice movements that, beginning in the 1970s, were enrolled under the banner of a "politics of exclusion." Giving voice to exclusion and its paradoxes was a central mandate that not only rebuilt the liberal arts but also piloted many popular consciousness-raising agendas. Not coincidentally, a near-identical justificatory framework and conviction in exclusion have underpinned many prevailing defenses of the humanities, which chapter 4 further examines. However, that genre of the humanities defense exemplifies the double binds created by reasoning through paradox.

These consciousness-raising initiatives have been accompanied by both therapeutic and pedagogical ambitions for paradox, considered in chapter 5. During the 1980s and '90s, a spirit of paradox was widely imagined to radicalize the humanities classroom, a mood that coined new vocabularies (hybridity, alterity, in-betweenness) and inspired teaching philosophies dedicated to an (often autobiographical) bearing witness. While ushering in many beneficial advances, those yearnings for a hyperpoliticized classroom have been among the more mixed bequests of theory. These innovative pedagogies were also subsidized by trauma theory, which left its own lasting imprint on many humanities fields. Especially in its early formulations, trauma, too, was conceived as a project of "giving voice to exclusion": here, the paradoxical repressions and foreclosures of traumatic remembrance.

This book concludes by venturing a series of proposals for mitigating the dominance of paradox. It connects those proposals by appealing to an "integrative criticism" receptive to the analytic yield of noncontradiction. Among other things, that notion of the integrative embeds a plea to supplement paradox with a wider arsenal of critical strategies better catered to tackling whatever diverse challenges arise. Given the antinormativity of paradox, that logic has discounted if not obstructed forms of differential evaluation and analysis, whether the drawing of distinctions regarding varying objects of critique, alternate manifestations of a given syndrome, or the comparative merits of one truth claim versus another. Relatedly, insistence on friction, fractures, divisions, and dualities has blinded us to realities "when things hold together," a phrase taken from Virginia Woolf. To consider how such a criticism oriented toward encounters with integrity and integration might instead proceed, the book's final chapter returns to the isolated scene of reading often allegorically envisioned as a laboratory in critique, attempting to practice a different kind of criticism and theory. In so doing, it strives to reclaim a disavowed intellectual space—a space where paradox does not have all the answers, where paradox is instead one resource among many, a resource that is sometimes fruitful but at others a dire threat to our very being.

1

—

ALL THAT IS SOLID MELTS INTO PARADOX

The Idea of Modernity

Baudelaire is intensely personal, yet close to universal. He wrestles with paradoxes that engage and enrage all modern men, and envelop their politics, their economic activities, their most intimate desires, and whatever art they create. [Baudelaire's writing] has a kinetic tension and excitement that re-enact the modern condition it describes. —Marshall Berman, *All That Is Solid Melts into Air: The Experience of Modernity* (1982)

Anyone who abides in a paradox on the very spot once occupied by philosophy with its ultimate groundings is not just taking up an uncomfortable position; one can only hold that place if one makes it at least minimally plausible that there is *no way out*. —Jürgen Habermas (1990)

"To be modern is to live a life of paradox and contradiction."[1] So opens Marshall Berman's 1982 *All That Is Solid Melts into Air: The Experience of Modernity*. In that classic text, Berman tells a familiar story: a story of modernity today near universally affirmed. That standard tale, more than anything, is one of mounting, pervasive, and incurable paradox. Whereas Berman's title highlights modernity's "experiential" dimensions, insistence on paradox has governed debates about modernity through and through, whether it is conceived as a historical process, a way of knowing, a predicament of the self, a "crisis concept," or by way of its central institutions (democracy, capitalism, rights, the nation-state). In a site of rare intellectual unanimity, thinkers of all leanings cite paradox as *the* watermark of what it means to be modern.

Books upon books have naturally been written about modernity and its DNA. Arguably few notions have been pored over with greater scrutiny and persistence. Indeed, the very notion *modernity* has acted as a placeholder for seemingly infinite things. That term has been taken as a referendum not only on modernity's endemic violence but also on its more mixed endowments (secularism, democracy, the industrial and scientific revolutions, globalization, and even literary innovations like the novel). At once, allusions to modernity often conduct philosophical ruminations over more nebulous principles like universalism, humanism, reason, freedom, individualism, critique, historicity, and more. Given these myriad associations, it is not surprising that the sheer idea of modernity would incite seemingly inexhaustible commentary and analysis.

At the core of these debates about modernity lie the epistemic claims of paradox. Indeed, almost every received account of modernity echoes what I will refer to as the modernity-as-paradox thesis, even as disputes over that notion have been waged on paradox and its terrain. As a result, it can be hard to find influential discussions of modernity that do not delimit that category according to a grammar composed of paradox and adjacent properties like contradiction, ambiguity, irony, antagonism, ambivalence, and more. Whether seen as a curse or a blessing, fatal or redemptive, modernity's main effects have been both identified and distilled according to such a logic. While on the one hand indexing modernity's overwhelmingly dark sides, on the other paradox has provided a lens for simultaneously grasping what are deemed modernity's complex fruits: the peculiar species of agency, resistance, heightened consciousness, ethics, and politics that the cauldron of modernity makes newly available. Appeals to specifically modern *paradox* thus tend to telegraph multiple facets of modern social, cultural, political, economic, and historical existence at once, including their fraught imbrications. Meanwhile, there is no doubt that the very plethora of meanings summoned by discourses on modernity is one reason the grammar of paradox has been overriding.

No real question exists whether modernity and virtually everything about it are rife with paradox and contradiction. That assessment has been a necessary and important one, which is why it can feel near impossible even to begin to think or talk about modernity without invoking one variant of paradox or another. Just as the basic idea of modernity is overdetermined, the equation between modernity and paradox is prone to conjure a welter of hopes, fears, desires, and antipathies that are difficult to disentangle. Here, too, that very hypersaturation of meanings suggests why that equation has been an intellectual default position, as well as why attempts to adjudicate those warring links are fated to become mired in paradox. Notwithstanding these and other snares, broad consensus over the modernity-as-paradox thesis itself helped to erect paradox into an epistemology: into a comprehensive framework of knowing and of making sense out of the world.

Still other phenomena can explain why that thesis has been fully doctrinal. In fact, most efforts to theorize modernity deploy the logic of paradox to carry out manifold, multidirectional intellectual labor. Almost without fail, paradox oversees all stages and components of the reasoning process. That property embeds a diagnosis; critiques modernity for its wrongs and derelictions; offsets the modern from its antecedents; scripts a philosophy of radicalized agency; delineates the guiding spirit of modern intellectual-*ism*; and ultimately serves as an all-enveloping method. These divergent analytic roles orchestrated by paradox often coexist, operating in tandem within any given study. What follows consequently asks: how did the logic of paradox come to possess this versatility? What has permitted a single metric to fulfill so many diverse functions? How did what arose as a diagnosis ("modernity is paradoxical") become assembled into a full-blown method as well as a captivating intellectual style? What allowed a verdict on modernity's unspeakable crimes to become infused with rehabilitative, emancipatory, and even ethical valences? In short, how has the modernity-as-paradox thesis evolved over time? These questions occupy more than this opening chapter but rather the entire book.

On one level, looking to paradox as a telltale sign of modernity is an old move—one that arose hundreds of years ago alongside early discourses on modernity as a historical process. Similarly, reliance on paradox as a vehicle of critique descends from a long lineage traceable to ancient Greek philosophy. But on another, the instinct to venerate paradox as the kernel of a self-rejuvenating agency and ethics claims a more recent intellectual vintage; these expectations for paradox prospered along with the rise of theory in the Anglo-American academy. As a diagnostic and critical lens, moreover, paradox makes good sense: countless factors led left intellectuals to converge upon paradox as an optics for wrestling with the twentieth century's unprecedented technologies of mass death (whether the trenches or the camp) and other horrors. Among other things, that language registers the dizzying proximity between human reason and radical evil, including the enigma of how ostensible pinnacles of human progress could sow lethal seeds of devastation. Hence, it is perhaps inevitable that paradox would be consecrated as modernity's regnant (if infernal) logic.

But in the decades following World War II, something happened to that received framework for contending with the utter irrationalism of modern life and its illusions of civilizational advancement. The explanatory prism of paradox began to assume a whole new cast, and due to a complex of dynamics this book's opening chapter merely begins to delineate. While long crystallizing modernity's dualities and deceptions, that prism increasingly probed the ways abundant gifts could seem to spring directly from modernity's grimmest tragedies. The aesthetic resonances of literary modern*ism* simultaneously rose to the surface, as the creative, transformative species of paradox at play in literature and art ransomed modernity from its many failings. "Critique" has of course represented one affirmative bestowal frequently espoused as theory's special province, and, in turn, the blossoming of theory also saw the spirit of paradox become increasingly autobiographical for its proponents. So while a web of complicated intellectual developments unfolding during the postwar decades precipitated shifts in the meanings not only of modernity but also of those properties heralded as its main indicia, paradox emerged as a philosophy unto its own.

Clearly, all of the above is not confined to debates about modernity, although they offer an ideal perch for observing the incredible virtuosity of paradox in motion. This chapter's study of philosophical accounts of modernity and its maelstrom of paradox therefore serves as a type of second introduction: a panoptic overview of the driving force and multitude of roles performed by that logic within theory. It seeks to illustrate, by way of formative accounts of modernity, why and how paradox became the intellectual air we all breathe—so much so as to inure us to those atmospheric conditions. What follows therefore moves quickly through a representative sampling of foundational texts and thinkers. Right away, we will see how a recurring diagnosis of modernity (paradox) acts inextricably as the backbone of method (paradox), only to see that quality transmute into an intoxicating and often poeticized rhetorical style. And whereas debates about modernity are relatively self-contained, it was also a peculiarly postwar engrossment with modernity as a problem that engrained paradox as a broad mind-set and ethos. Efforts to reckon with modernity thus inculcated a generalized conviction in paradox, disseminating a faith that would spread to infect virtually everything.

Paradox as Diagnosis

As a diagnosis of modernity, paradox is so routine that its alternate formulations hardly bear rehearsing. Whether to understand modernity as a stage of history, a way of knowing, or a condition of the subject, that basic language gained currency during the same era that engendered modernity as a predicament. To some degree, paradox therefore offered a common approach to explaining modernization amid its very genesis, including the vertiginous transitions ushered in by modernity's intertwined revolutions in science, government, economics, trade, knowledge, demographics, religion, culture, literacy, power, and more. For instance, a Google Ngram shows surging uses of the word *paradox* from 1750–1800, measuring the sudden escalation of such a sensibility. However, this familiar linkage between modernity and paradox donned a panoply of new meanings as the events of the twentieth century unfolded—meanings that, with the dawn of the "theory era," became progressively redemptive.

Certain of those emancipatory frontiers are implicit to the dialectic. Indeed, Hegel's *aufheben* (typically translated as "to sublate") is itself a term harboring contradictory meanings, implying both "to cancel or suspend" and "to lift up" or "to preserve." This chapter's title clearly puns not only on Berman's study of the 1960s and its aftermath but also on Karl Marx and Friedrich Engels's renowned 1848 pamphlet, which Berman similarly quotes. A key passage beginning *The Communist Manifesto* reflects on the conditions of production under capitalism: *realism*

> All fixed, fast-frozen relations, with their train of ancient and venerable prejudices and opinions, are swept away, all new-formed ones become antiquated before they can ossify. All that is solid melts into air, all that is holy is profaned, and man is at last compelled to face with sober senses his real conditions of life, and his relations with his kind.[2]

That oft-quoted passage gives voice to a now stock rendition of modernity conceived as a break with the stability of the past: a rupture of tradition, collapse of foundations, and ensuing disillusionment.

Marx's modernity naturally enshrines capitalism as its dominant logic, attributing such psychospiritual privation to alienated or estranged labor, which "tears from [man] his *species life*" (violating the human) and "degrad[es] spontaneous, free activity to a means."[3] Yet Marxist thought is also a natural starting point for observing the centrality of paradox and contradiction, beyond ideas about modernity, to the intellectual formation of theory.[4] For Marx, modernity's many layers of contradiction and antagonism are crucial to grasping more than either capitalism's essence or how capitalism installs contradiction at the heart of "the human" and of modern social relations (or, for that matter, to the workings of the dialectic). Rather, Marx's account inscribes contradiction at the core of Marxist analysis. Whereas ideology masks the many contradictions resulting among other things from capitalism's exploitative nature, the primary objective of Marxist critique is to unearth that property: to uncover its submerged existence. Along with the "contradiction of estranged labor" identified by Marx as the subject of political economy,[5] his thought is preoccupied with elaborating the many antagonisms both stemming from and lending fuel to capitalism—many of which Marx deems all-governing.[6] Phrases such as "the antagonistic character of capitalistic production and accumulation" thus recur throughout a text like *Capital*. And although Marx favors certain such terms over others, paradox is not foreign to his vocabulary, much as little doubt exists whether phenomena like commodity fetishism and the money-form are not steeped in paradox. *Capital* Vol. 1 accordingly contends with a sequence of realities such as that "the economic paradox, that the most powerful instrument for shortening labor time, becomes the most unfailing means for placing [that time] at the disposal of the capitalist."[7]

So while endemic to if not wholly constitutive of capitalism and its brutality contradiction simultaneously operates for Marx as an essential apparatus of anticapitalist critique. Given this, that property can seem to take on a life of its own. From one angle (and partly due to its role within the dialectic), Marxist thought imbues contradiction with near agentive force, of a magnitude certain of Marx's heirs have only amplified. Hence, Mao Tse-tung's 1937 "On Contradiction" meditates at length on the ways contradiction is absolute and all-encompassing. For Mao, internal contradictoriness is "the fundamental cause of the development" of all things, including their "motion" and "movement." Citing Engels for the universality of this principle that "motion itself is a contradiction," that property for Mao governs not only the class struggle but also physics, chemistry, and mechanics.[8] Today, one need not look far for examples of this reflex to treat contradiction as quasi-volitional: a lead entry on the "Communist Party US" website thus declares that it is "the contradictions of capitalism [that] are holding us back."[9]

The rhetorical strategies through which Marx vivifies that agency are especially illuminating. The often incantatory, rhapsodic style of a text like *The Communist Manifesto* is readily apparent, and that lyricism injects Marx's prose with a frequently figural, tropological quality—a quality that no doubt leads a critic like Berman to insist that the "paradoxes at [the *Manifesto's*] heart" become "manifest almost from its very start."[10] For Anna Kornbluh, such a style animates Marx's corpus broadly, and it is in particular when elucidating the "mysterious" aspects of capitalism, such as the relationship between commodities, that Marx enlists literary-poetic devices like personification and metonymy. Kornbluh suggests that *Capital* thereby "impute[s] a quasi-subjective status to capital in order to underscore the strangeness of the capitalist metaphysic."[11] Indeed, such devices not only conjure capitalism's seductive allure but also dramatize its predatory energies, as in Marx's memorable depiction of "capital [as] dead labor, which, vampire-like, lives only by sucking living labor, and lives the more, the more labor it sucks."

Importantly, Marx relies on similarly colorful imagery and tropes to monumentalize the driving force of properties like contradiction and antagonism. Speaking of the absolute contradictions of industry, Marx relates "how this antagonism vents its rage in the creation of [the] monstrosity [of] an industrial reserve army,"[12] endowing "antagonism" with emotions and an almost despotic will. Elsewhere in *Capital* contradictions and antitheses "impress themselves" and "assert themselves," just as antagonism "makes itself forcibly felt."[13] At certain points, that demonstrative power becomes near mythic in its proportions, leading Marx to describe how "this antagonism between the quantitative limits of money and its qualitative boundlessness, continually acts as a spur to the hoarder in his Sisyphuslike labour of accumulating."[14] Such rhetorical strategies vest contradiction with an influence just as decisive yet baffling as that of capitalism—and especially in light of that property's dialectical destiny to outlive any given stage of world history. Given how buried contradiction determines the underlying architecture of capitalism as a structure and a system, Marx (and his contemporary exponents) can seem bent on rhetorically enacting the divinatory power of that authority. Insofar as certain aspects of capitalism are ineffable, contradiction and its unearthing are what ultimately disclose that strangeness.

This chapter's introductory tenor invites another brief yet final detour through a recurring issue (although one that is ultimately a cul-de-sac): to what extent are "contradiction" and "paradox" (along with other protoliterary terminologies that today permeate criticism and theory) overlapping versus distinct intellectual modes? Although conceptual cousins, are those properties not separate? Have they not been incarnated in measurably different intellectual styles? Shouldn't Marxist critique motored by contradiction (and the dialectic) be meticulously distinguished from the mystique of paradox that has enthralled many since theory's heyday?

As I will continue to argue, yes and no. On the one hand, yes, the intellectual diet that thrived with theory's domestication was conditioned by a distinct intellectual-historical milieu that this book overall investigates. In a different sense, yes, within rhetoric, paradoxes are prone to "evoke" and to "conjure"—and therefore laden with incipient meaning-making potential that arguably participates within an alternate figural economy than reasoning through contradiction. Chameleon and prolific, paradoxes are often synthetic, orchestrating and merging discontinuous meanings and analytic functions. Their logic also encourages analogical thinking, in ways that can tend toward the assimilative and pluralistic. So yes, something novel and unusual transpired when paradox was elevated into an article of left intellectual faith and doctrine.

But on the other hand, no, Marxist thought cannot feign innocence regarding the gravitational pull of paradox. As we have already seen, Marx's own vocabulary—with his penchant for lively tropes and figures—reveals the territory dividing contradiction from paradox to be murky if nonexistent. This is even more so for Marxism's present-day inheritors, including for thinkers who outwardly pledge doctrinal purity. A certain rhetorical prodigality has characterized the work of many prominent Marxist critics, who move fast and loose between allusions to contradiction or antagonism versus a brigade of corresponding terms of art. Thus does Jameson's *The Antinomies of Realism* recount the novel's evolution: "it is to be grasped as a paradox and an anomaly, and the thinking of it as a contradiction or an aporia."[15] Slavoj Žižek, as the introduction suggested, is an ardent evangelist for paradox. Yet it is within modes of analysis perhaps best associated with Louis Althusser that a logic of paradox fully engulfs and supplants that of contradiction. Again and again throughout *Reading Capital*, Althusser diligently rereads and thereby reframes Marx's statements of contradiction as lessons in "paradox," going so far as to deem Marx's own relationship to method and especially his borrowing from Hegel thoroughly "paradoxical."[16]

This book's arguments, however, lie not with minor squabbles but instead with the common ground linking what might appear to be inhospitable philosophical approaches, including the ground connecting these contrasting

Marxisms to other criticism and theory. Critical thinkers (whether more or less indebted to Marx) have near unanimously ratified his basic thesis regarding the contradictory character of modernity and its existential fabric, echoing that account with a regularity rendering it a kind of philosophical second nature. In so doing, they have also endorsed Marx's expectations for the intellectual yield of paradox and contradiction—the exposure of which is invariably imagined to reveal apparent forms of progress and advancement to cloak hidden liabilities and perils. As for Marx himself, a bedrock of theory has therefore been reliance on a conceptual matrix composed of paradox, contradiction, and other cognate terms—which intellectual preoccupation with modernity has only reinforced. Even when capitalism per se is demoted to a minor character, modernity is without fail plotted as a story of material, epistemic, and psychospiritual disembedding, dissolution, and fracture.

Merely a few (re)statements of these themes can establish the pervasiveness of versions of both Marx's underlying insights and his basic methodological approach. A narrative wherein burgeoning paradox becomes an unavoidable fact of modern existence is, for instance, implicit in Max Weber's rationalization thesis. For Weber, modernity entraps the individual within an "iron cage" or "steel-hard casing," metaphors registering the intensified modes of bureaucratization, efficiency, calculation, and control counterintuitively accompanying its lure of freedom.[17] A similar vein of analysis structures Weber's *The Protestant Ethic*, which instead wrestles with the paradoxes sprouting from the unexpected liaisons between Protestantism and capitalism's "spirit." That the "irrational elements" of a religious calling fueled a process of instrumentalization is for Weber deeply ironic, prompting him to mine perplexities such as that capitalism could be driven by an "ascetic compulsion to save" and that moral duty could sanction unequal wealth distribution.[18] As for Marx, the paradoxes Weber isolates demonstrate what might seem benign phenomena to be highly ambivalent.

As Weber's thought (like Marx's) suggests, one reason paradox and contradiction have been methodological staples derives from this premise that their detection will not only indict modernity's violence but also divulge the deceptive character of its enabling myths—political, institutional, philosophical, and otherwise. Such an objective underlies Sigmund Freud's 1930 *Civilization and Its Discontents*, in which lurking paradox is what betrays the promise of "civilization" as a mirage. Rather than progressively freeing, modernity for Freud imposes deepening constraints upon both individual and society. As he recounts, the demand made by "civilization" for a "renunciation of instinct" induces "'cultural frustration' [that] dominates the large field of social relationships between human beings,"[19] prompting Freud to conclude that civilization

> is largely responsible for our misery, and that we should be much happier if we gave it up and returned to primitive conditions. I call this contention astonishing because, in whatever way we may define the concept of civilization, it is a certain fact that all the things with which we seek to protect ourselves against the threats that emanate from the source of suffering are part of that very civilization.[20]

Like so many, Freud thereby understands modernity to exacerbate the very afflictions it aims to alleviate, compounding individual neurosis to an extent that, for psychoanalysis, becomes resistant to cure. Further far from accidental is how Freud's diagnosis takes shape with reference to background assumptions about the "primitive," "happier" circumstances that modernity overtakes—in another gambit that, as we will see below, the logic of paradox engineers.

One cannot observe these methodological affinities between Marx and Freud without gesturing at the same time toward Friedrich Nietzsche's formidable presence.[21] It has been de rigueur to conjoin the three, although critics vary regarding the best or appropriate basis for so doing. That triumvirate was dubbed the "three masters" of the "hermeneutics" or "school of suspicion" by Paul Ricoeur in his 1965 *Freud and Philosophy*.[22] Althusser's contemporaneous *Reading Capital* analogously links Marx to Nietzsche and Freud, although on account of their common investment in "symptomatic reading."[23] A now peripheral text like Richard Rorty's *Contingency, Irony, and Solidarity* also connects them, however by emphasizing the concurrently metaphorical and antireformist elements of their thought.[24] But still another basis for aligning that triad lies with their shared conviction in the eye-opening power of paradox and contradiction, properties around which the thought of Marx, Nietzsche, and Freud collectively rotates. For all three of Ricoeur's "masters," suspicion flows directly from the encounter with those properties. For Althusser, paradox is more than a defining feature of the symptom: it is what symptomatic reading breeds. And notwithstanding recent calls to shed such symptomatic and suspicious modes, paradox and contradiction remain methodological bulwarks of theory.

Ricoeur and Althusser are also telling reference points given that both their seminal coinages are at base commentaries on the predicament of modernity and its peculiar cognitive burdens. Ricoeur's suspicious hermeneutic, for instance, emanates from a larger reckoning with a "crisis in language" that Ricoeur attributes to a conflict between "two poles" of interpretation: a restoration of meanings versus "demystification" and the "reduction of illusions."[25] While tying suspicion to the latter, Ricoeur nevertheless generalizes that *mentalité*, surmising: "From the beginning we must consider this double possibility: this tension, this extreme polarity, is the truest expression of our 'modernity'"—a prospect notably problematized via scare quotes.[26] Differently for Althusser, Marx is pivotal in launching a distinctly modern "transition" in critical analysis. As Althusser avers, Marx institutes "a new practice of reading, and [...] a theory of history capable of providing us with a new theory of *reading*."[27] With those assessments, Ricoeur and Althusser foreground the dualities and divisions intrinsic to modern knowing, offering another window on the logic yoking modernity and paradox together as flip sides of the same coin. It is for Ricoeur a "logic of double meanings" that renders hermeneutics "full," but not without riddling modern truth with "double motivations" and "double possibilities."[28] Althusser, too, ventures something similar regarding Marx, describing Marx's "new theory" as "a double reading" and "in principle a *dual* reading, [...] which introduced into a question an answer given to its absent question."[29]

It is important again to acknowledge the basic correctness of these diagnoses that would cement the equation between modernity and paradox, whether put forward by Marx, Nietzsche, and Freud or the legion of others who theorize modernity as a state of omnipresent paradox. Also understandably did the unparalleled and anonymous violence of the twentieth century incline later thinkers to behold those assessments as a kind of premonitory writing on the wall, much as the traumas of the Great War had already left their imprint on a body of thought like psychoanalysis. To be sure, such reasoning claims other decisive roots beyond these lodestars of theory—whether one cites interwar modernism (with its attunement to fragmentation and indeterminacy) or the fin de siècle avant-garde (with its own mantras of rupture and experimentation). However, what subsequently ensued with theory's maturation not only guaranteed that the finding of paradox and reasoning through paradox would become inextricable, binding diagnosis and its mode of discovery in a self-mirroring, self-reinforcing symbiosis. In addition, the modernity-as-paradox thesis evolved to become explicitly self-referential. Embedding an (often not-so-subtle) auto-commentary on the agency (and conundrum) of theory, that increasingly routine account of modernity inscribes within theory's genetics, along with a specific vision of modernity, a self-regenerating (and often self-congratulatory) spirit of paradox. While highly versatile, that metatheoretical anatomy of modern paradox has thus (and arguably from its beginnings) conducted a long sequence of referenda on the self-image, ambitions, and promise of theory.

This autobiographical thrust of modern paradox is palpable in a study like *Reading Capital*, a self-avowed symptomatic reading of Marx (who Althusser simultaneously credits with inaugurating symptomatic reading). Althusser's 1965 discussion memorably begins with the proviso "there is no such thing as an innocent reading."[30] Luxuriating in Marx's invitation to "play on words" (a phrase Althusser takes from Marx directly),[31] cognizance of "knowledge as a production" compels Althusser to foreground the "guilt" and "culpability" of any and all possible readings of Marx—in an insistence surely required by Althusser's historical moment. Yet whereas that spin on modern paradox adduces the implicatedness of postwar Marxism within the cataclysms of history (whether atrocity, global war, or that era's many purges), Althusser presents such a sensibility as the overarching and necessary fabric of left intellectual life. Marx's rendition of modernity is thereby reframed and expanded both to interpellate the critic and to limn the double bind of theory. It is in a seeming attempt to charismatically rejuvenate a sullied, depleted Marxism that *Reading Capital* assiduously redacts and replaces Marx's many assertions of antagonism and contradiction with the exuberant reflexivity of paradox.

Self-implicating discourses on modernity like Althusser's have also had the effect of codifying paradox as the emblem of sophisticated thinking—or the badge of the "critical" and of theory. While we will encounter such assumptions again and again, a brief return to Weber's reception can further elucidate those (auto)biographical bearings. In the introduction to one recent edition of *The Protestant Ethic*, the sociologist Peter Baehr not surprisingly praises Weber's study for "prompting successive generations of readers to wrestle with the paradox at its core."[32] Baehr elaborates:

> If Weber's "thesis" were self-evidently true, simple, or translucent, it would never have engaged a critical audience or survived to become a classic. "Mere" solutions to a problem impede a text's ascent to greatness for the simple reason that they offer no challenges for contemporaries to embrace and successors to ponder. [...] Weber's achievement was not to definitively answer a riddle but to stake out a territory fertile of new puzzles. [...] That Weber's argument raises—or begs—a hundred questions is inseparable from its eminence and renown.[33]

Baehr's commentary certainly recalls the familiar instinct to define theory as a disputing of self-evidence and common sense—or via the logic of the *para doxa*. Yet for Baehr, Weber's achievement derives not strictly from his insights' perspicacity but rather from the inexhaustible perplexities they spawn: from how Weber's account of modernity self-complicates into "a hundred" "puzzles." That Weber's thought opens up a Pandora's box of paradox is what establishes its lasting relevance. However, accolades like Baehr's also leave us with twinned ironies: first, that Weber would be celebrated according to the same logic he identifies as modernity's peculiar autograph; and, second, that this very signature of the modern would be consecrated as the measure of seminal philosophy.

Critique and the Paradoxes of Modern Knowing

It should be clear why methodological reliance on paradox fast becomes overburdened. Among other things, the exact properties heralded as modernity's signposts have represented the main levers enlisted to critique that category and everything it has been taken to signal. Moreover, those same properties (paradox, antagonism, contradiction, and so on) thus implicated within modernity's untold crimes have simultaneously been deployed to register its more ambivalent, even salutary handiwork. In one sense, this multidirectionality has helped to naturalize the modernity-as-paradox thesis, seeding it with a medley of conflictual meanings. In offering a type of Rorschach test, however, that thesis also works to indulge and verify a given critic's preconceived desires and preoccupations, reflecting back whatever one wants or expects to see. Along with this tautological character, the governing status of that thesis has just as much been confirmed by the near impossibility of disaggregating its interwoven layers, whether paradox is chiefly seen to reside within modern knowing, selfhood, politics, economics, power, "interpretation," art, or elsewhere. Inescapably, then, to be modern is to inhabit an epistemology of paradox.

Few intellectual faculties (at least within the annals of theory) have been more fully synonymous with modernity than "critique." Not surprisingly, statements regarding the centrality of paradox and contradiction to critique abound. As Bernard Harcourt explains of Etienne Balibar's thought, *contradiction* is "a form of praxis and critique" that "keeps the political space alive," being "essential to maintaining political life."[34] That said, critique is also one modern bequest claiming a strikingly mixed inheritance—and hence for thinkers like Reinhart Koselleck fated to itself become ambivalent.[35] From one angle, perhaps no legacy of the enlightenment has occasioned greater reluctance for theorists than reason, held to task among other things for the organized bloodshed and persecution that has dominated global modernity. Thus do Frankfurt School theorists Max Horkheimer and Theodor Adorno in their 1947 *Dialectic of Enlightenment* blame specifically "instrumental" reason for even relatively quotidian phenomena like the social homogenization accompanying a consumer culture industry, the commodification of interpersonal relations, and other abstractions. In so doing, Horkheimer and Adorno characterize their study as a now-standard lesson in modern paradox: in how "the gifts of fortune themselves become elements of misfortune," with the consequence of rendering "enlightenment as totalitarian as any system."[36]

But from another angle, it is also true that the brand of critique practiced by critics like Horkheimer and Adorno, as they acknowledge, is a devise of the enlightenment and of enlightenment reason—or exactly such a "gift" fated to sow "misfortune." Foucault's thought offers another helpful point of entry into these tensions, seeing how much of his corpus undertakes what is at bottom a protracted reckoning with modernity's main guises. Much like Horkheimer and Adorno, Foucault reflects on the enlightenment in terms that understand critique to straddle an ambivalence and, in his bicentennial tribute to Immanuel Kant's 1784 "What Is Enlightenment?," engages in self-commentary regarding those murky debts:

> I have been seeking, on the one hand, to emphasize the extent to which a type of philosophical interrogation—one that simultaneously problematizes man's relation to the present, man's historical mode of being, and the constitution of the self as an autonomous subject—is rooted in the Enlightenment. On the other hand, I have been seeking to stress that the thread that may connect us with the Enlightenment is not faithfulness to doctrinal elements, but rather the permanent reactivation of an attitude—that is, of a philosophical ethics that could be described as a permanent critique of our historical era.[37]

While claiming to disarticulate critique's two "threads," Foucault's rhetorical "on the one hand" and "on the other" simultaneously underscores their enmeshment. Like others, Foucault sets out to wrest critique as an intellectual posture and "philosophical ethic" from the more invidious strands of enlightenment rationalism, and that effort, first of all, leads him to insist on the "permanence" of such a stance of "philosophical interrogation": on critique that knows no limits or boundaries, holding nothing sacred including the category of "man." Of second importance is what Foucault substitutes for Kant's self-authoring, autonomous subject in his purport to salvage critique from its liberal humanist origins. In many respects, he leaves us with a vision of a modern experience, selfhood, governance, politics, and more thoroughly steeped in paradox—even while he conceives critique to actively incubate such conditions.

It is hard to dispute that Foucault conceives paradox to pervade modern existence, even though he only occasionally uses that precise terminology. *Discipline and Punish* instead inventories the "ambiguities," "tensions," and "innumerable points of confrontation, focuses of instability, each of which has its own risks of conflict, of struggles" that comprise the "micro-physics" of modern disciplinary power.[38] The account of normalization that emerges across a text like *History of Sexuality* analogously describes how the "relative uniformity" of discourse surrounding sexuality was "broken apart, scattered, and multiplied in an explosion of distinct discursivities" to become all the more insidious.[39] Rather than negative or repressive, power for Foucault is paradoxically productive; instead of uniform or centralized, it is dispersed and diffuse. Yet at the same time as variants of paradox diagnose these decisive features of biopolitics, discourse, power, subjecthood, and more throughout Foucault's oeuvre, it is also the case that the excavation of buried frictions and discontinuities escorts Foucault's own distinctive manner of analysis; those properties both pilot and are the upshot of Foucault's critical method. Genealogy, for instance, relies on a conceptual matrix composed of such properties in order both to challenge mainstream historicism and to craft a revisionist historiography, as is considered below. As Foucault cautions, the field of history risks collaborating with power and its "subjugations" when it deceptively casts history as organic, cohesive, unbroken, and inevitable—and, as such, suppresses the fractures, accidents, and disparities that perforate the historical record. In contrast, genealogy sets out to "fragment what was thought unified," "introduce discontinuity into our very being," and lay bare the "unstable assemblage of faults, fissures, and heterogeneous layers," "systems of subjection," and "hazardous play of dominations" that haunt the writing of history.[40] The same conceptual matrix that Foucault cites as the albeit shrouded insignia of power is thus the backbone of his own intellectual-political project.

Part of this ambivalence confronting modern critique naturally concerns its role, as Foucault suggests, in assassinating the subject, whether that "death" is ultimately eulogized or lamented. Another centerpiece of nearly all accounts of modernity, as we have already seen, is this premise that modern selfhood entails splitting, duality, self-estrangement, and chronic uncertainty. Mirroring views about other of modernity's fraught gifts, so, too, is it axiomatic that registers of paradox will dictate modern subjectivity and experience. While implicit to coinages like Emile Durkheim's *homo duplex* or to the psychoanalytic unconscious, this proposition is one also adhered to within philosophical traditions ranging well beyond the usual compass of theory. Indeed, even canonical texts of moral philosophy subscribe to such a vision of the paradox-besieged subject. Alisdair MacIntyre in his classic *After Virtue* thus understands modernity to "partition each life into a variety of segments," entailing "the liquidation of the self into a set of demarcated areas of role-playing."[41] Similarly for Charles Taylor, the "moral world" of the moderns is "full of gaps, erasures, and blurrings."[42]

Nonetheless, how different philosophical traditions have responded to that basic assessment offers another perspective on the postwar decades and how the flourishing of theory updated the modernity-as-paradox thesis. In a clear disciplinary divide, for moral philosophers like MacIntyre modernity's paradox-afflicted subject is exiled to a moral universe tragically "after virtue" (the title of his 1981 study): a world painfully divested of coherence, "social structure," and the potential "to think of a human life as a narrative unity." Whereas MacIntyre decries that shattering of moral thought and participation in a classically Aristotlean sense,[43] it is within many variants of theory, however, that near identical conditions of self-rupture and loss are instead welcomed—if not fully valorized. Hence, for a theorist like Judith Butler (whose thought absorbs later chapters), the very "foreclosures" and "threats" of "dissolution" troubling MacIntryre are recast as a "paradox of subjection" indispensable to the opportunity for ethics.[44] An ethics like Butler's, of course, descends from Jacques Lacan's thought including his collected *Seminar VII: The Ethics of Psychoanalysis*—one section of which entitled "The Paradox of *Jouissance*" probes what Lacan deems the "forbidden" status of *jouissance* and its resultantly "enigmatic" relation to law.[45] In chapter 3, the ethical valences newly implicit in the language of paradox during the late Cold War are examined across a breadth of theory. But for now, fault lines such as these surely invite multiple approaches to taxonomization, whether vis-à-vis a rift between philosophy and theory, humanism and posthumanism, rationalism and its critique, or (as the above suggests) conventional morality and ethics. But while indicative of an oft remarked standoff between theory and philosophy, exclusive focus on such schisms also risks submerging what is ultimately a striking intellectual consensus: a consensus regarding the fact that to be a modern subject is to be torn between competing and irreconcilable imperatives.

As one result, it is today a near truism to say that modern *truth* is similarly destined to be riven with clefts and fissures, whether those fractures are exalted or instead cause for despair. Berman thus describes the modern condition: it "leave[s] [modernity's] questions echoing in the air long after the questioners themselves, and their answers, have left the scene."[46] As Berman's allusion to "questioners" suggests, those paradoxes riddling modern truth and knowing are also the progeny of critique, offering another perspective on its fundamental ambivalence as well as the "permanent reactivation of an attitude" advocated by Foucault. The predicament of theory, as we know already is that critique itself bears a certain responsibility for proliferating epistemic and other paradox. And insofar as critique has been compulsory, so, too, will a spirit of paradox become a veritable obligation.

Efforts to delineate critique have often looked in allegorical fashion to the isolated scene of reading or exegesis—including, as for Althusser, its propensity to spawn paradox. Correlatively, critique is frequently expostulated in terms of—and seen to be actuated via—a specific set of interpretive habits. Invariably *self*-critical, critique is in particular seen to induct as well as to require self-detachment, self-objectification, and self-scrutiny (sowing division within the critical subject). But while imagined to vest critique with neutrality, such a posture—to be expected by now—is significantly more complicated—due for many to a relay wherein critique and modernity are together understood to proceed from a decoupling and opposition of two (or more) ostensibly inhospitable ways of knowing. It is therefore in opposition to supposedly immediate, self-present modes of intellectual-perceptual engagement that critique (and its superior faculties) is seen instead to lie with the distanced, abstracted, and mediated. However, that mind-set casts doubt not only on established orders of truth and authority but also on the building blocks of unfiltered perception—in an economy of valuation that can seem to inject paradox into the most rudimentary levels of consciousness and experience. As Michael Warner observes in characterizing critique as a "duty," "critical reading" since Kant has been predicated on "a clear opposition between the text object and the reading subject—indeed, critical reading could be thought of as an ideal for maximizing that polarity, defining the reader's freedom and agency as an expression of distance from a text that must be objectified as a benchmark of distanciation."[47] Whether requiring what Warner distinguishes as "disengagement or repudiation," it has nonetheless been a baseline supposition that critique legislates a disconnect and resulting conflict (reminiscent of Ricoeur) between alternate planes or spheres of knowing and understanding.

For many, these sorts of tensions have only been exacerbated by the overarching institutional structures that administer modern regimes of truth. Here, too, a narrative of dissonance and fracture has mapped the logic according to which modernity, in deracinating truth, simultaneously sequesters alternate domains of expertise, placing them into friction if not competition. Whether quarantining morality from politics (for Reinhart Koselleck) or "knowing" from belief (for Jürgen Habermas) or science from politics (for Bruno Latour), modern knowledge, it is widely maintained, is fated to be not simply bifurcated in a Cartesian or dualistic sense but comprehensively disintegrated, compartmentalized, and embattled.[48] For Latour, this siloing of disciplinary authority is furthermore what causes the perception of paradox to burgeon. As *We Have Never Been Modern* recounts, modernity's emergent orders of knowledge were confronted with new burdens of self-justification, given their combined lack of support by and unrelenting attacks on traditional bastions of power. One way they acquired authority, responding to the very legitimation crises they (like critique) worked to instigate, is through what Latour calls the work of "purification" and "dividing up the tasks,"[49] wherein increased specialization served to credentialize otherwise insecure claims to validity. Yet with this concentration of expertise came both disciplinary enclosure and perceptions of incommensurability—or alleged schisms that have themselves redoubled the presumption that all versions of truth will prove chronically relative, foundationless, and divided. So beyond inseminating institutional rivalries rampant still today, the rise and standardization of the disciplines separately christened modern knowledge with incurable and thoroughgoing paradox.

This chapter's quick tour through merely a few permutations of the modernity-as-paradox thesis could clearly continue to contemplate yet additional sites of paradox that similarly engrained such a sensibility as the fabric of modern existence, including to detail their points of mutual overlap and reinforcement. But one crucial reason that thesis became controlling involves how it mutated along with the geopolitical landscape of the midcentury. Just as an optics of paradox helped many to grapple with the twentieth century's merciless decimation of all illusions of progress, that grammar has articulated a sense of complicity with those calamities. Yet it was also during the same historical juncture that saw "theory" assume its contemporary contours that left intellectuals became newly preoccupied with modernity as a problematic. Amid that engrossment did the language of paradox catch fire—and precisely as a framework for replenishing the darkened vistas of a radical tradition shipwrecked on modernity's debris. Hence, a habitual lens for reckoning with modernity and its many catastrophes began to accrue additional meanings, donning a fresh light and web of associations that by the late 1970s and certainly 1980s dominated. An explanatory scheme long deployed to come to grips with various historical crises and debacles thus increasingly summoned (and often inextricably so) those very tragedies' peculiar "gifts of fortune," in reasoning that came not only to be transposed onto specific challenges like democracy, ethics, and rights but also to telegraph the revived promise of theory.

We can therefore pause to ask: why was this the case? Why did critical thinkers embrace paradox as an antidote to the scourge of modernity? What allowed a language that for many prophesied modernity's blackest midnight to become rehabilitative? And what permitted a stock diagnosis of modernity's ailments to be converted into a resplendent cure—although a cure almost too perfectly mirrored in regnant philosophical accounts of radical evil? The recipe for that cure also became widely generalizable: just as applicable to politics as to ethics as to law as to the most integral claims of criticism and theory.

Although a full answer to this line of questioning will come together over this book's course, a few initial explanations should be apparent. The first concerns critique and its wager of more sophisticated, self-aware knowing. Especially when purified of its instrumental, colonizing, liberal humanist geneses, critique has epitomized modernity's remarkable duality, including why sources of seeming blight might ward off a repetition of the left's gravest errors. (In fact, we'll see that the spirit of paradox has been oft touted as precisely such a defense mechanism.) So in essaying modernity's vast wreckage, critique could arise from the ashes relatively unscathed—although not without its own constitutional ambivalence. Itself a key germinator of modern paradox, the critical spirit has been implicated in nearly all of modernity's hazards, and one consequence is that critique on its own has not provided an exit from the fatalism overshadowing the twentieth and twenty-first centuries. As Habermas remarks of Horkheimer and Adorno (in a quote providing one of this chapter's epigraphs), "Anyone who abides in a paradox on the very spot once occupied by philosophy with its ultimate groundings is not just taking up an uncomfortable position; one can only hold that place if one makes it at least minimally plausible that there is *no way out*."[50]

A second reason why the modernity-as-paradox thesis came to harbor restorative promise is also implicit in Habermas's observation, and it involves the legitimation crises that modernity (and modern critique) inaugurated—and that, by most accounts, continue to plague modernity's core institutions still today. With its traditional foundations swept away, modern life was plunged into a justificatory abyss. This is one dynamic that has caused not only modernity but also critique to be saddled with responsibility for authoring a climate of ever-escalating uncertainty. Summed up in a title like *Critique and Crisis: Enlightenment and the Pathogenesis of Modern Society*, Koselleck attributes such epidemic anxiety to "the series of concepts and counterconcepts that mark the literature of the Enlightenment and its countervailing forces."[51] Something analogous obtains for Latour, although he describes a spiraling legitimation crisis that has beleaguered modern disciplinary orders, propagating forms of paradox. For Habermas, such a justificatory vacuum more accurately afflicts the whole of philosophy, turning philosophy's central problem into that of "modernity's *self-reassurance*" (regarding Hegel) or "the paradoxical task of obtaining standards of its own for the contingency of a modernity that had simply become transitory"(regarding Walter Benjamin).[52] Due to precisely such recognitions has the basic term *modernity* been deemed a "crisis concept," as Matei Calinescu argues.[53]

Yet while distilling a mood of crisis, the logic of paradox has simultaneously redeemed the very justificatory deficits and resulting sense of emergency partly engendered by that logic's own operations. Modernity's assault on the strongholds of convention and authority has naturally been vertiginously freeing for many, opening up untold possibilities and vectors of meaning. However, the logic of paradox also generates a scheme for romanticizing the underlying tenuousness of modernity's surrogate (if not foundationless) foundations, even to warrant revelry in those conditions of tentative (if not absent, groundless) legitimacy. Hence, the self-same logic recruited to diagnose why modernity's gifts could contain hidden terrors has served to name the unexpected fruits flowering from those catastrophes—in obviously circular (if not tautological) thinking. Yet in encapsulating the perplexity that circumstances of loss and privation could, lo and behold, be awash with plenty, that optics performs a certain alchemy, transforming sites of strife and error into something meriting worship and adulation. The postwar decades thus saw the logic of paradox become progressively recuperative, as paradox was embraced as a vehicle for metamorphosizing sources of crisis, failure, insecurity, and indeterminacy into (albeit irrationalist) reservoirs of potency, resilience, and creative renewal. In short, theory refashioned the logic of paradox into a remarkably versatile and compelling apologetics.

The dialectic—although less in its classically Marxist or Hegelian forms than the generalized spirit of dialecticism that prevails today—offers a third window on why the modernity-as-paradox thesis could spell something other than unmitigated disaster. Just as for Koselleck the nexus between "critique and crisis" emanates from opposing "counter-concepts," many have understood modernity to be composed of clashing or warring threads: of co-existent yet rival modernities. Thus does Berman recount how a pluralized "dialectics of modernization and modernism" rescued the dialectic's stalled trajectory following '68, in the process replenishing the left's deflated hopes by divorcing them from the expectation of either transcendence or reconciliation.[54] Although tinged with disappointment, Berman's description of that lapsed faith is by no means negative, as he reflects on the tenor of 1960s protest:

> This meant that our project was shot through with paradox from the start. [...] So long as we grasped our self-divisions, they infused the New Left with a deep sense of irony, a tragic irony that haunted all our spectacular productions of political comedy and melodrama and surreal farce. Our political theater aimed to force the audience to see that they, too, were participants in a developing American tragedy: all of us, all Americans, all moderns, were plunging forward on a thrilling but disastrous course.[55]

As elsewhere, such thinking recasts "division" (here internal to social movements) as rejuvenating—and exactly by ascribing to it the mood of "irony" that has similarly predominated. So while evoking "tragedy" and "disaster," Berman can nevertheless characterize modernity as "thrilling"—and precisely by pitting "bad modernization" against "good modernism" glory in the latter. In the hands of many—and not only convalesced Marxists—a spirit of "paradox" has thus augured a revitalized dialectic—and one often notably unmoored from Marx's own structuralist materialism.

Appeals to tragedy and melodrama like the above point to another influence that imbued the modernity-as-paradox thesis with new resonances and contours: as Berman suggests, an aestheticized conception of modernity (and of paradox) was also ascendant. While an instinct present within interwar modernism, it became broadly imperative to comprehend modernity as a distinctly aesthetic phenomenon, and for many overridingly so. In labeling modernity a "crisis concept," Calinescu thus construes "aesthetic modernity" as "a threefold dialectical opposition to tradition, to the modernity of bourgeois civilization (with its ideals of rationality, utility, progress), and, finally, to itself, insofar as it perceives itself as a new tradition or form of authority."[56] Differently for Habermas, the need to "[ground] modernity out of itself first comes to consciousness in the realm of aesthetic criticism," which explains the "core aesthetic meaning" that attaches to discourses of modernity still today.[57] Whereas for Rorty, it is an outwardly poeticized dialecticism ("the attempt to play off vocabularies against one another") that culminates with a defense of ironism as a political mode.[58] Indeed, even MacIntryre treats modern selfhood as a primarily literary and narrative agenda.

For a host of thinkers such as these, the notion of modernity has therefore been refracted through (and enmeshed within) a set of specifically aesthetic(izing) currents, and it is quite possibly this aestheticizing impulse that most fully ransoms modernity from its deadly liabilities. Much as Berman envisions the literary-poetic-cultural-artistic *style* of moder*nism* to issue a rejoinder to (and stave against) moderni*zation*'s many instrumentalizing forces, the reconfiguration of modernity as a fundamentally aesthetic category has purveyed a kind of absolution for its crimes. As will become clearer, this literary-poetic derivation of modernity is, to a degree, understandable—and due to more than the boundary-breaking experiments of modernism and the avant-garde. Spanning the history of aesthetic criticism, it has been standard to demarcate "the literary" or aesthetic vis-à-vis the same grammar of paradox (and irony, ambiguity, indeterminacy, ambivalence, and so forth) that we are seeing to betoken modernity and its habitat. These conspicuous echoes have inclined many to discern within *both* modernity *and* paradox decidedly creative, transformative, self-replenishing energies.

That aestheticizing impulse has been partner to a near-Romanticist lionization of the great artist-thinker-inventor as a paragon of such a spirit (as we already observed of Weber). Yet few figures have been more consistently sanctified as high priests of modern paradox than Charles Baudelaire, whose life and oeuvre are taken to epitomize everything augured by aesthetic modernity in particular. A prominent section of Calinescu's *Five Faces of Modernity* entitled "Baudelaire and the Paradoxes of Aesthetic Modernity" exalts Baudelaire's investment in paradox as "a qualitative turning point in the history of modernity as an idea" and especially its "time awareness so strikingly new." [59] Calinescu's tribute notably builds on Paul de Man's 1970 essay "Literary History and Literary Modernity," which similarly lauds Baudelaire as the embodiment of a "modernity" that de Man elaborates via a long sequence of paradoxes.[60] Berman devotes an entire chapter to Baudelaire and how he "wrestl[es] with paradoxes that engage and enrage all modern men, and envelop their politics, their economic activities, their most intimate desires, and whatever art they create."[61] Indeed, even Foucault venerates Baudelaire on almost identical grounds, in "What Is Enlightenment?" extolling Baudelaire's *dandysme* and "ironic heroization of the present" manifest in art.[62] These tributes illustrate more than the allure of drawing upon the literary-poetic as a vehicle for salvaging (if displacing) the modern condition. Exemplifying the personification of paradox (here via Baudelaire) in their own right, they capture why worship of paradox is, perhaps inevitably, destined to become autobiographical: why the paradoxes of modernity have offered a screen projecting back to theorists all the ambivalences plaguing their own self-images.

Gatekeeping the Modern

Curse and blessing, sickness and remedy, poison and tonic: the modernity-as-paradox thesis can appear so saturated with discordant meanings as to cease to tell us much of anything, even while becoming predictable. Yet as a badge of modernity, paradox has also policed that category's borders, hypostasizing everything modernity is imagined to exorcise and to surpass. Along with the precise term paradox, a matrix of corresponding values, here again, has charted the horizons of modernity, although in terms that simultaneously marshal assumptions about those lives that deserve and are even capable of achieving modernity as a threshold. Thus has the inverse of such properties—nonparadox or noncontradiction—denoted what it means to fall short of or to betray the modern—and along the same lines as those that continue to license history's many oppressions.

It might not be surprising that theories of modernity would depend on an image of the pre- or not-yet-modern. Given modernity's plotting as a course of rupture and dissolution, it may be unavoidable that its rendition will hinge on ideas about what modernity comes along to marginalize, vanquish, and supersede. Yet those myths regarding the transparence, coherence, and unity of the world views that modernity overtakes have performed essential work in not only engineering that category and its presumed trajectory but also, by extension, scripting the parameters and bearings of theory. So while fictions of the not-yet-modern serve to equate "ancient" cultures with a dearth of paradox and everything that property has telescoped, they just as much expel certain truths, arguments, and imaginative possibilities from the purview of theory.

In particular have fables regarding the "integrated" nature of Greek and other ancient cultures fortified modernity as a conceptual framework. Georg Lukács's 1914–15 *Theory of the Novel* sets forth a routine formulation of those links. While foremost a literary-intellectual history of the novel's rise, Lukács's account of that genre's evolution rests on an opposition between a modern versus an ancient world view. Conceiving the Greek world as harmonious, homogenous, rounded, and totalizable, allowing for a "passively visionary accept[ance] of ready-made, ever-present meaning," that experiential coherence of "integrated civilizations" (the title of Lukács's first chapter) is mirrored in the epic form, within which "life and essence are [...] identical concepts."[63] In contrast, the novel for Lukács internalizes the many "fissures and rents," "fragmentary" or "antagonistic" realities, and larger "transcendental homelessness" of the modern condition.[64] As Lukács explains of the novel's formal logic, it enacts a "paradoxical fusion of heterogeneous and discrete components," into "a semblance of organic quality which is revealed again and again as illusory."[65]

With such remarks, Lukács enshrines "paradox" as the frontier separating a modern sensibility from its antecedents. As he clarifies of that "line of thought,"

> [It can] take us some way towards understanding the secret of the Greek world: its perfection, which is unthinkable for us, and the unbridgeable gap that separates us from it. The Greek knew only answers but no questions, only solutions (even if enigmatic ones) but no riddles, only forms but no chaos. He drew the creative circle of forms this side of paradox, and everything which, in our time of paradox, is bound to lead to triviality, led him to perfection.[66]

Everything distinctive about modernity is thus distilled into paradox, which Lukács heralds as not only the signature of "our time" but also a clearly demarcated perimeter. Cast as irreversible, modernity is further aligned with multiple indicia already well-known within this chapter: riddles, questions, chaos, antagonism, fragmentation. Given Lukács's focus on the novel, those properties assume a palpably literary-aesthetic texture.

It is hard to overstate the pervasiveness of such thinking, which we will discover in unexpected places time after time. Within theorizations of modernity, versions of Lukács's oppositions are so doctrinal as to be evoked with passing casualness, just as his assumptions have not been confined to the universe of critical theory. MacIntyre's *After Virtue* imagines "heroic" societies to experience "morality and social structure [as] in fact one and the same," entailing that premodern art forms (again, the epic) "embody" that givenness.[67] Taylor's *Sources of the Self* hinges on a parallel contrast, claiming that "earlier civilizations" espoused "frameworks" of belief and judgment that remained fundamentally "unquestioned."[68] Freud's *Civilization and Its Discontents*, we saw, differentiates the many ills bred by modernity from the "happier" ways of "primitive conditions."[69] Ricoeur's influential "hermeneutics of suspicion" is prominently juxtaposed with the "univocity of meaning" inherent to Greek culture and especially to Aristotle's law of identity.[70] Not last, Althusser's exposition of symptomatic reading attributes that "new conception of *discourse*" to a break with "the religious complicity between Logic and Being; between the Great Book that was, in its very being, the World, and the discourse of the knowledge of the world; between the essence of things and its reading"—all of which are disclaimed as "those tacit pacts in which the men of a still fragile age secure themselves with magical alliances."[71] Such a catalog could obviously continue.

There are, it should go without saying, many reasons to be wary of these "magical" divides that have secured modernity as a category, and, in some respects, the "Othering" dimensions of that logic have been vigorously debunked. Indeed, entire fields like postcolonial studies arose from the mandate to expose modernity's dependence on the construction of a premodern, precivilizational, colonial foil and antithesis. A field-creating text like Edward Said's *Orientalism* thus begins with the recognition that "Europe gained in strength and identity by setting itself off against the Orient as a sort of surrogate and even underground self."[72] The preface to Gayatri Chakravorty Spivak's *A Critique of Postcolonial Reason* analogously describes its "aim, to begin with, [as] to track the figure of the Native Informant through various practices: philosophy, literature, history, culture," in a circular effort to "make visible the foreclosure of the subject whose lack of access to the position of narrator is the condition of possibility of the consolidation of Kant's position." Spivak cautions that such a figure (defined as "a name for that mark of expulsion") "is crucially needed by the great texts; and it is foreclosed."[73] One guiding impetus for anticolonial critique has accordingly been to reveal the tales of European enlightenment shoring up the conceit of modernity to fully necessitate such a fantasy structure of the excluded Other deemed incapable of modern self-representation or rationality.

Yet while stagist discourses of modern development have been well chastised for their colonialist ancestry, the logic of paradox has been indispensable to—often fully piloting—such critique. So even while a rote equation between modernity and paradox has authored history's many expulsions from that category, complaints about its colonialist derivation have nevertheless enlisted an architecture of critique wholly scaffolded by paradox—or by what is simultaneously deemed modernity's enabling logic. In their charges, critics have singled out a range of faculties (reason, critique, self-abstraction, self-determination) seen to underwrite modernity's role as an exclusionary benchmark. But we can observe by now that paradox has both laid the groundwork for and connects many of those bases for stigmatizing the not-yet. For example, "historicity" (like critique) is one such yardstick reinforcing the usual linkage between paradox and modern ways of knowing. As Koselleck's *Futures Past* describes, "historicity" involves "a temporalization of history, at the end of which there is the peculiar form of acceleration which characterizes modernity."[74] Talal Asad rightly cautions that such views have functioned to congratulate European dominance, so that "the West defines itself, in opposition to all non-Western cultures, by its modern historicity."[75] This is partly because, like ideas about modernity, historicity requires a picture of what such a consciousness allegedly surpasses, meaning that "actions seeking to maintain the 'local' status quo, or to follow local models of social life, do not qualify as history-making."[76]

From one angle, concerns like Asad's generatively dispute the problematic warrants subsidizing one particular permutation of the modernity-as-paradox thesis (historicity): few things disobey the logic of paradox more completely than blind captivity to stasis, normalcy, or a "status quo." Asad is also right that the ruse of historicity, with its romance of a "time awareness so strikingly new" (as Calinescu comments of Baudelaire) works to exile certain world views from modernity's ambit. But from another standpoint, Asad actively draws from the armory of paradox to launch his critiques; for Asad, the logic of paradox maintains all its critical edge. Indeed, Asad laments the worrisome "paradoxes" that modernity's enabling myths have introduced into anthropology, a discipline that conventionally constructed its objects of analysis as "culturally marginal" to Europe and is therefore itself "dependent on [a] contrastive sense of the modern."[77] While one might expect Asad to challenge (along with historicity) a range of properties for smuggling in complementary biases, he freely enlists what is arguably *the* distinguishing guise of modernity (paradox) to spearhead his critical project.

In parallel ways have secularism and specifically *secular* modernity been condemned for enforcing a plethora of neocolonial interdictions—and on grounds that, for many, also implicate critique. As Wendy Brown and Judith Butler preface the volume *Is Critique Secular?: Blasphemy, Injury, and Free Speech*, "a particular conception of secularism is crucial to the identity of the West (liberal, democratic, tolerant, critical), juxtaposed against its imagined other."[78] In so doing, Brown and Butler's title underscores the fact that secularity has been braided with the fortunes of critique and its prototypically modern habits of knowing. Hence, the volume's contributors contend with the ways secularism is achieved vis-à-vis the sort of critical reading Warner attributes to Kant, and therefore rests on norms regarding what Saba Mahmood terms "improper reading practices."[79] With that notion, Mahmood does more than censure ideas about secularism for privileging certain rationalist, self-distancing modes of interfacing with textual objects. In addition, she characterizes secularism as a normative framework that, like modernity, is naturalized with reference to the practices (and world views) it purports to adjure, quarantine, and transcend. Such reasoning thereby understands secular modernity to be erected upon a polarity that divorces both critique and secularism from immersive, absorptive, and proximate registers of engagement—penalizing the latter for a presumed lapse of detached self-bracketing. Although itself a religious ideology, secularism thus sanctions certain (non-Judeo-Christian) cultures and manifestations of belief for being insufficiently neutral, aloof, divided, and self-critical—or, we might say, insufficiently paradoxical—impugning them for an implicit miscarriage of modernity and its requirements. Discourses of secularism can consequently function just as much to chasten integrated and integrationist ways of knowing for noncompliance with modern critique as to instill paradox at the heart of modern knowing.

For both Mahmood and Webb Keane, these protocols administering critical-secular-modern regimes of truth both stem from and are corroborated by a highly specific account of language and of how language works, including the nature of symbols and signs. As Mahmood relates, secularism "presuppose[s] a semiotic ideology in which signifiers are arbitrarily linked to concepts," and it is that ungrounded account of representation that works to disparage the structures of attachment and belonging that oversee meaning and interpretation within many non-Judeo-Christian belief cultures.[80] Relatedly for Keane, the crux of the secular hostility to many world views of the global South lies with such deracinated theories of language. As Keane explains of modernity's logic, "the materiality of signifying practices comes to be identified with external constraints on the autonomy of human agents" and a dereliction of modernity's "link[age of] moral progress to the practice of detachment from and reevaluation of meaning."[81] Keane traces such reasoning comprehensively, locating it (like Warner) within seminal theories of modernity, including social scientific literature (Weber and Durkheim) and Continental thought (Marx and Heidegger, who both equate modernity with objectification).[82] For Keane, post-Saussurean linguistics represents the apex of such an antimaterialist conception of language that is intrinsically hostile to non-European cultures.

This chapter could continue to hold other tokens of modernity to the fire—whether individualism, autonomy, enterprise, humanism, contract, or law broadly—to demonstrate how they are consolidated by not-yet-modern inversions. Such a genre of analysis, I've suggested, has been vital to many indictments of modernity's organized violence. Thus does Saidiya Hartman embroil Enlightenment humanism within the institution of slavery, arguing that "the slave is the object or the ground that makes possible the existence of the bourgeois subject and, by negation or contradistinction, defines liberty, citizenship, and the enclosures of the social body."[83] Not so different are Said's charges against the imperial imaginary, which he accuses of manufacturing a misleading "internal consistency" that cloaks the "battery of desires, repressions, investments, and projections" actually shaping imperialism's discursive field.[84] There is no question that studies like Hartman's and Said's shed invaluable light on modernity's deeply compromised foundations: its total dependence on institutionalized structures of abuse and dispossession. However, such studies also place inordinate faith in the unmasking and critical power of paradox and contradiction. While the inordinacy of that faith will become ever clearer, it has nevertheless been the common ground of theory.

The Agency and Aesthetics of Paradox

Given how the logic of paradox both avouches and guarantees modernity as a horizon, it could seem puzzling that anticolonial thought would rely on an itinerary of critique itself coordinated by paradox. Nevertheless, the very logic that has rationalized modernity's exclusions has been widely recruited to expose and condemn global modernity's Othering projections. Being engraved within method across theory, reasoning that leverages paradox and contradiction as the first step in a larger odyssey of critique has also been the bread and butter of anticolonial thought, much as Asad evokes "paradox" to crystallize his reservations about anthropology's colonialist liaisons and "ambivalent phenomenology."[85] Earlier sections of this chapter already began to delve into the derivation and impetus for such thinking: into certain sources of left intellectual conviction in paradox. A few other ingredients will become visible within three different examples of revisionist historiography.

A textbook exhibition of anticolonial genealogy, Dipesh Chakrabarty's *Provincializing Europe* explains imperial modernity in terms that simultaneously conduct the sort of disciplinary self-reckoning that consumed many humanities fields with the incursions of theory (explored in chapter 5). In that book, one of Chakrabarty's goals is to charge historicism with promulgating a "'waiting room' version of history" that provides "justification for denial of 'self-government' to the colonized" and consequently "enabl[ed] European domination of the world in the nineteenth century."[86] Among other offenses, historicism's tendency (like, for Asad, anthropology's) to conceive its analytic objects as "internally unified" and "developing over time" divulges that conspiracy not only with empire but also with "a particular formation of the modern subject."[87] India for Chakrabarty has therefore provided a necessary foil to colonialist history-writing, as he explains: "European thought has a contradictory relationship to such an instance of political modernity (as India). It is both indispensable and inadequate."[88] Importantly, Chakrabarty's reliance on genealogy further compels what we'll recognize as default assumptions about the operations of power: precisely the crime of "repressing" and mastering sites of paradox is what inculpates history within global modernity's violence.

Yet Chakrabarty proceeds from that standard diagnosis-cum-critical apparatus of paradox to develop an account of how the same matrix of qualities that historicism disingenuously submerges can become rehabilitative. Hence, an optics of paradox, while arraigning modernity for its offenses, simultaneously rescues history writing from its liaisons with power, sowing anticolonial revisionism with near-redemptive promise. That promise, however, straddles its own double binds that ensue from the unavoidable failure and impossibility of that task. Like Althusser insisting on the complicity of all possible readings (here, of history), Chakrabarty asserts that "the project of provincializing Europe must realize within itself its own impossibility."[89] Relatedly does Chakrabarty promote another now-recognizable recipe for thus guarding genealogy against historicism's errors: "The idea is to write into the history of modernity the ambivalences, contradictions, the use of force, and the tragedies and ironies that attend it."[90]

We have already encountered this instinct to evoke modes like "tragedy" and "irony" as the flip side of modern*ization*'s lethal operations—and will do so repeatedly. In Chakrabarty's hands, those qualities serve as more than instruments of the usual critique and dismantling, such as to blame mainstream historicism for blindness to the "double bind" of Indian history writing.[91] Although tools for self-critically evading conventional historicism's mistakes, those paradox-laden qualities serve just as much to script a philosophy of agency that Chakrabarty champions for ushering in unprecedented opportunities for just coexistence. Chakrabarty elaborates on his distinct brand of dialectical thinking by juxtaposing two "contradictory" historical modes that exist "in a state of permanent tension." Contra "History 1"'s "indispensable and universal narrative of capital" without which "there is no political modernity," Chakrabarty advocates:

> thought about diverse ways of being human, the infinite incommensurabilities through which we struggle—perennially, precariously, but unavoidably—to "world the earth" in order to live within our different senses of ontic belonging. These are the struggles that become—when in contact with capital—the History 2s that in practice always modify and interrupt the totalizing thrusts of History 1.[92]

Jettisoning stagist versions of historical progress to instead envision change motored by "infinite incommensurabilities" and unending "struggle," such a passage embraces dialecticism for more than its capacity to immunize history-writing against the risk of inadvertently "totalizing" more complex phenomena. Even more, Chakrabarty's dialecticized terms ("being," "belonging," "diversity," "worlding") are suggested to carry profound implications for matters of justice and ethics.

In alluding to these variants of paradox, however, Chakrabarty's reasoning effectuates a certain sleight of hand, seeing how qualities like ambivalence and incommensurability function simultaneously as levers of critique and as emancipatory vistas ("incommensurabilities" are what allow one to "world the earth"). The logic of paradox thus allows Chakrabarty to extract an affirmative itinerary for "living" and "worlding" from a standard diagnosis of historicism's misdoings (its disrespect of ambivalence), transmuting paradox that is toxic when submerged into something grace-like in its untapped potentiality. As a consequence, a term like ambivalence gestures multidirectionally, merging diverse analytic functions (diagnosis, critique, method, solution) into a single—and itself unifying—cosmology. The same properties that betray historicism to be in league with empire thus come to be infused with ethical-just-political renewal.

Beyond this warehousing effect that we will also observe to be incredibly common to reasoning through paradox, further slippages haunt theories of modernity like Chakrabarty's—although those misprisions become particularly poignant within anticolonial critique. Chakrabarty's main complaints against historicism, we have seen, concern its justification of empire and resulting exile of the colonial subject to modernity's margins. But in leveling that charge, Chakrabarty requisitions the very conceptual framework long deputized to gatekeep the modern, to barricade the global South from full access to that category. The same indicia denied the "developing world" as confirmation of its failed modernity are thus enlisted by Chakrabarty to critique modernity's logic. In effect, Chakrabarty marshals a powerful ideology in the hopes of subverting that self-same ideology, mobilizing the exact economy of valuation that has *both* consolidated modernity as an ideal *and* expelled certain lives from its ambit. Hence, there is a way in which methodological investments like Chakrabarty's can appear self-undermining, fated to solidify the very edifice of oppression that *Provincializing Europe* purports to unsettle.

Two other revisionist histories that similarly recruit an algebra of paradox to transact parallel conversions can shed further light on the roots of such reasoning. Joan Scott's *Only Paradoxes to Offer: French Feminists and the Rights of Man*, as the introduction suggested, was one catalyst for this book's arguments. In that text's journey through key episodes in French feminism's centuries-long march, paradox fulfills all the protean functions we have just considered—and more. Indeed, Scott's opening chapter, "Rereading the History of Feminism," pays extended homage to paradox, which Scott directly exalts as the "constitutive condition of feminism as a political movement throughout its long history."[93] Scott's playful title commemorates these grand ambitions through the words of Olympe de Gouges, the only woman executed for her political writings during the French Revolution. For Scott, de Gouges was an expert tactician in the logic of paradox— encapsulated in de Gouges's aphoristic self-description as "a woman who has only paradoxes to offer and not problems easy to resolve." De Gouges's riposte deftly stages a paradox precisely in order to expose the exclusionary design of, in this instance, rights.

But the "paradoxes" alluded to in Scott's title are many, piled one upon the next. That term indexes multiple dimensions of rights, feminism, modernity, liberal individualism, and more, even while it pledges Scott's own allegiance to historical revision. As before, paradox issues a sweeping diagnosis that critiques the historical denial of rights' universal protections to women. At once, Scott's (and de Gouges's) "only" is tongue-in-cheek, given how it also modifies the "feminists" following her title's colon. As Scott explains, "it is precisely because feminism embodies paradox that it has been trivialized or consigned to marginality by those seeking to protect the foundations of whatever status quo they represent."[94] While evoking dictionary entries for *paradox*, in the same breath Scott makes recourse to another frequent gambit: she lauds the elevated awareness of that "marginal," excluded, outsider vantage point personified in paradox. No doubt, this is in fact the tenor of de Gouges's consciousness-raising quips, which leverage paradox in order to awaken cannier, more sophisticated insight and understanding. As within other theorizations of modernity, that grammar thereby allows Scott to toggle between—and, arguably, to muddy—the negative versus affirmative species of paradox that have, for better and for worse, shaped feminism over history.

A similar metric adumbrates the liminal agency made available by that predicament of paradox. Clarifying that her study contends with paradoxes that are not simply "strategies of opposition, but the constitutive elements of feminism itself,"[95] that logic, as for Chakrabarty, brokers more than sheer critique:

> Indeed feminists' agency consisted exactly in this: they were women who had "only paradoxes to offer." The courage and inventiveness of individual feminists, the subversive power and historical significance of their collective voice, lay (still lie) in the disturbing spectacle presented by paradox. For the identification and display of inconsistency and ambiguity—of self-contradictoriness—within an orthodoxy that strenuously denies their existence is surely destabilizing and sometimes even transformative. Ideological/political systems such as French republicanism work by endorsing the notion that coherence is a requirement for social organization and then by presenting themselves as fulfilling the requirements for coherence. In order to do this they deny or repress internal contradiction, partiality, or incoherence.[96]

Scott here endorses a conception of power (seen as disavowing paradox in service of "coherence" and common sense) that we are quickly observing to be a theoretical mainstay. And she continues thereafter to inventory more precise rationales for women's subordination over history, such as "that feminists were unreasonable and themselves dangerously incoherent" and that "feminist paradoxes have [...] usually been interpreted as the products of their own confusions, and this interpretation has then become the justification for their continued exclusion."[97] "Paradox," as Scott notes, has represented a pejorative label rationalizing women's subjugation; yet in the same passage, Scott recuperates that epithet to redescribe such an ostensible curse as the main artery of feminism's "transformative" agency. In one sense, precisely because power (in Scott's thinking) cannot tolerate paradox does that property become supercharged in its disruptive potential. But in another, the transfigural (if not aestheticizing) dynamics of paradox simultaneously alchemize apparent liabilities (i.e., incoherence) into a font of distinctly *creative* resistance and renewal.

Revealing in turn are Scott's debts to aesthetic theory. Already in the fourth page of her introductory chapter, Scott unpacks her reasoning to acknowledge that it is inherited from a cluster of roles played by paradoxes within aesthetic theory, conspicuously instilling her philosophy of agency with those literary-artistic properties. Along with its "poetic creativity," she extols that logic for enabling "the ability to balance complexly contrary thoughts and feelings."[98] At the same time, Scott's readings of discrete historical events repeatedly seize upon "the disturbing spectacle presented by paradox," or what we might describe as the theatrical texture of such agency. While visually redolent (as in eyeglasses), the Oxford English Dictionary's first entry for *spectacle* reads, "a specially prepared or arranged display of a more or less public nature (esp. one on a large scale), forming an impressive or interesting show or entertainment for those viewing it," and another suggests kinship with drama ("a piece of stage-display or pageantry").

Yet in the same breath as she appeals to the epiphanies stimulated by art, Scott alludes to still another variant of paradox germane to aesthetic criticism: the paradox of art's tenuous, "fictional" evidentiary status and truths. Crucially, Scott herself points out that paradoxes involve something analogous within formal logic, wherein they denote "an unresolvable proposition that is true and false at the same time."[99] With this explication of her title (and of de Gouges's sayings), Scott locates the spirit of feminism—and, for that matter, of modernity broadly speaking—within that movement's fraught burdens of justification. Analogizing the legitimacy deficit faced by feminism over history to art's abundant fictions, Scott can thereby champion that very dearth or absence of received authority as the source of feminism's emancipatory frontiers. It is the logic of paradox that generates this arithmetic capable of transforming what on the surface is a lack of empirical or established legitimacy into an opportunity to redraw the boundaries governing what can and cannot be asserted and imagined. These dense links are elaborated across this book. For the time being, Scott's study is instructive in spelling out the interdisciplinary borrowings that allow her to model feminist agency on, among other things, the protean, metamorphic, world-building faculties of art and literature.

As should be clear, Scott's account of feminist agency is intensely meta-critical. Like that of other revisionist histories, her own methodology stages paradox in a fashion parallel to that performed by feminism.[100] Scott, too, excavates and parades the "inconsistencies and ambiguities" perforating not only the historical record but also philosophical constructs like the "abstract individual" and "rights"—which is to say that Scott's labors as a historian are magnetized by the same compass of disruptive, transfigurative, consciousness-raising paradox as feminist activism sets out to harness. This project of "reading" and "Rereading the History of Feminism" (to recall her first chapter) for paradox—a tactic Scott characterizes as "technically deconstructive"[101]—thus offers another perspective on why a stigmatizing epithet (paradox) can turn out to be redemptive (paradox). In a characteristically deconstructive (if not Althusserian) manner, Scott's insistence on "rereading" feminism's annals further permits her to revel in the ways "symptoms" like "repetition" and "difficulty," rather than hindrances, become endlessly productive—for Scott within a text, just as much as for feminist activism in the streets.[102] And in summoning these many interwoven tributaries of paradox, Scott can aver that feminism plainly and simply is paradox; what might appear negative "difficulties" are more accurately feminism's fertile enabling conditions. To be sure, one could here interrogate Scott's reasoning on similar grounds as Chakrabarty's, since she, too, recuperates the exact logic that has condoned modernity's exclusions to espouse it as the vessel of an agency inspiriting both leftist historicism and feminism together. Despite censuring "abstract individualism" for its masculinist pedigree, Scott promotes and performs the very itinerary of self-distanced, divided, mediated "reading for paradox" that has long sanctioned injurious assumptions about women's lack.

Further questionable is Scott's conviction in what she calls the "formal similarity of paradox," which she cites as the connective tissue linking feminism to other emancipatory crusades. Notwithstanding the historical distance separating her book's different examples, Scott maintains that they are all governed by a self-replicating and formally equivalent logic—a logic therefore transposable onto other scenarios far and wide. Scott is explicit about her thinking's generalizability, wagering that such opportunities to stage the "disturbing spectacle" of paradox "still lie" with feminism today. And indeed, Scott is correct that the machinery of paradox is what facilitates such transit, allowing not only feminism but also revisionist history-writing to be deciphered according to a unifying metric across context and time. In the process, however, that overreach sweeps a host of far-flung phenomena into an all-enveloping conceptual orbit—an orbit fully synchronized by paradox and its gravitational pull. One recurring concern of this book involves how such a homogenizing prism can work to neutralize and obscure meaningful *dis*-similarities between disparate occurrences, just as in Scott's study vexing paradoxes stemming from invidious patterns of structural oppression (women's lack of rights) flower into—and risk getting mistaken for—the exhilarating symbolics of the eye-opening "spectacle."

Synthesis of such themes into a cohesive theory orchestrated by paradox informs a lot of contemporary criticism and theory, as later chapters show. But before moving on, one additional example, again of anticolonial history, can illuminate other common expectations that have permitted faith in paradox to rescue modernity from its many crimes. In *Conscripts of Modernity: The Tragedy of Colonial Enlightenment*, David Scott (no relation to Joan) instead rereads C. L. R. James's classic 1938 *The Black Jacobins*, and to spur similarly broad ruminations on modernity, struggle, and what Scott deems the birth of the "modern intellectual:" Toussaint Louverture. Exalting the Haitian Revolution as "one of the founding events of the modern age," Scott enlists recognizable reasoning to establish that event's emblematic status.[103] First, Scott affirms various default assumptions about modernity's fraught "cognitive-political terrain" and perennial "social crisis, the collision of embattled and irreconcilable social forces."[104] Second, Scott presents his protagonist Toussaint's plight as quintessentially modern: as being "obliged to act in a world in which values are unstable and ambiguous" and to confront "a broken series of paradoxes and reversals in which human action is ever open to unaccountable contingencies—and luck."[105]

These dualities further prompt Scott to describe Toussaint's predicament as one of "conscripted agency" within modernity's vicissitudinous throes. For Scott, that coinage also highlights Toussaint's complicity; Scott emphasizes that the "cognitive-political terrain of modernity [...] was not [Toussaint's] to choose" and that Toussaint "could not choose *not* to be modern."[106] But what exactly does such circumscribed agency entail? By now to be expected, what at first blush appears a liability is reimagined by Scott to be fertile and productive, engendering in Toussaint amplified awareness regarding "the *paradox* of enlightenment" (Scott's italics).[107] Scott relatedly trumpets "the doubleness of knowledge: how it can obscure even as it reveals, how it can disable as much as it enables, how it can imprison at the very moment that it emancipates." Toussaint is thus anointed with the very qualities that over history have been cited to deprive lives like his of the capacity for modernity, here lending ideological support to slavery.

In another routine move, those same terms that redeem Toussaint and his ordeal issue an auto-referential commentary on the goals not only of Scott's book but also of theory broadly, causing the unique crucibles undergone by Toussaint to assume almost allegorical, metatheoretical significance. Scott presents James's original study as a meditation on modernity at large:[108]

> If *The Black Jacobins* is a book about enlightenment, still, as these sentences suggest, it is a book about the paradox of enlightenment, not its pathos. It is a book about the enigma of enlightenment, not its transparence. *The Black Jacobins* is a book about enlightenment's recalcitrant ambiguity, the collocation of vision and blindness, knowledge and ignorance, illusion and reality. And Toussaint Louverture, C.L.R. James's doomed hero, is the embodiment of this irrepressible illusiveness of enlightenment.[109]

Much should be familiar in these reflections. Indeed, one might mistake them for Joan Scott's statements about feminism or, alternatively, for other reflexive ruminations on the seductive elusiveness of everything conjured by modernity as a philosophical predicament. Relatedly does Scott evoke rival modernities, which lets him cast Toussaint as a harbinger of an exuberantly modern*ist* "political desire" capable of metabolizing modernity's destructive undercurrents.[110] Further evident is the dialectic*ism* of Scott's thinking; in fact, he dismisses the prospect of resolution as crude and "reductive" to instead cite Horkheimer and Adorno as a basis for "holding the contradictions of modernity in a more productive nonreductive tension."[111] As before, paradox might seem to supplant contradiction to rehabilitate a rigidified, tired structural materialism. Yet regardless of distinctions such as these, it should be clear by now how such a logic works a kind of magic. Hence, Scott can surmise that "Toussaint's weaknesses sprang from the very qualities that gave him his strength, his insight from the same qualities that blinded him."[112]

A lot more than the dialectic and its operations is accordingly at stake within such assertions, bringing me to the lyrical qualities of Scott's own writing. The above excerpt's repetition of declarative sentences—"it is" and the phrase "book about enlightenment"—is incantatory and rhythmic, building momentum. Those cadences are also beseeching, almost mimicking a sermon or political oratory. The "if-then" structure of Scott's opening sentence (a stylistic tic he resorts to regularly) problematizes enlightenment as a category while rhapsodizing its chimerical aura. Speculative, Scott's revisioning of Toussaint thus hovers in its own liminal space bridging "illusion and reality" (here again resembling the plight of art and literature).

In fact, Scott deliberately encases both Toussaint's biography and his rereading of it within precise literary-aesthetic genres. One of *Conscripts of Modernity*'s stated projects is to position Toussaint's life within scholarly debates about "tragedy," a lens for Scott capturing "tragic dilemmas" such as that Toussaint's "intellectuality is at once the source of his magnificent successes and of his doom."[113] To such ends, Scott also enlists what he terms a "poetics," and in particular a "poetics of tragedy" that requires him, rather than treating *The Black Jacobins* as a strictly social scientific text to examine "the poetics that constitute [James's] dramatic narrative about slavery and freedom, and the figuration that establishes the presence of its historical subject [Toussaint]."[114] Elaborating on the significance of that approach, Scott clarifies that a poetics trains attention on "the literariness of the historical text" and "style of representation" informing a given history rather than solely on a work's ideological content or historical accuracy.[115]

In part, these are overtures to Hayden White and his influential *Metahistory*, which White himself characterizes as a "formalist approach to the study of historical thinking."[116] An exemplary instance of literary criticism's migration into historical study, White explains that he draws (like Joan Scott) on a "linguistic paradigm" to distinguish between varying historical modes.[117] Tellingly, White defends that method by negatively cataloging the many considerations a poetics must sideline: in other words, formalism requires him to specify what a prioritization of the literary, figural, and stylistic elements of history-writing intentionally leaves off the table. White notes in a proviso: "I will not try to decide whether a given historian's work is a better, or more correct, account of a specific set of events or segment of the historical process [...]; rather, I will seek to identify the structural components of those accounts."[118] As White submits, a poetics eschews judgments regarding the truth status, content, and normative fiber of a given work, skirting those evaluative determinations. That onus to bracket if not proscribe such inquiries, importantly, has not been confined to theories wearing those methodological commitments on their sleeve; to the contrary, reliance on variants of formalist analysis has been part and parcel of reasoning through paradox, as this book argues. It should go without saying that such a pretense of deferring matters of "betterness" and "correctness" can be a ruse—especially insofar as highly specific stylistic and formal features (i.e., paradox, irony, contradiction, tragedy) denominate those objects meriting serious scholarly inquiry to begin with. And no doubt, returning to David Scott, it is indeed a formalist poetics that encourages his vast generalizations, permitting him to extrapolate from Toussaint's particularized struggles to venture global conclusions about theory as an enterprise. In the process, the paradoxes of tragedy, modernity, theory, history, and Toussaint's life become interchangeable—one and the same "irrepressibly illusive" phenomenon digestible according to a single conceptual schema.

The Modern Intellectual

For Scott, Toussaint also epitomizes "the emergence of a new type of human being," "the modern colonial intellectual."[119] This chapter has already touched on this impulse to enthrone the iconic, pathbreaking artist-intellectual-creator-theorist as an exemplar of modernity and its inexhaustible paradoxes, and, in thus lauding Toussaint, Scott joins a tradition that has similarly immortalized Baudelaire. It is above all Toussaint's "intellectualism" that for Scott propels him on a "paradigmatically" "paradoxical journey" that can be universalized as one "we have never ceased—and perhaps it is our fate to never cease—rehearsing."[120] This link between intellectualism and paradox has also been pervasive, rampant far beyond the corridors of theory. Yet beyond being the badge of momentous thought or ideas, paradox has also been taken to encode the personal attributes of the revered thinker, including amorphous things like character, behavior, ethos, and demeanor.

So far, we have considered multiple factors that have rendered an ethos of paradox autobiographical for theory, in a consanguinity implicit even in that term's etymology. Inherently (self-)critical, the logic of paradox has been near synonymous with deeper understanding. On the one hand, it has therefore summed up the intellectual play, innovation, and discovery much admired as theory's domain—hence, Berman's appeal to "comedy and melodrama and surreal farce" and Foucault's nod to the *dandysme* of Baudelaire. Yet on the other, that grammar inextricably registers the experiential fabric of loss, victimization, suffering, and oppression, as later chapters probe. To inhabit the place of a paradox, we know, is to be excluded from the dominant and the status quo, infusing that language with the suggestions of exile and marginalization accompanying such outsider vision. But precisely in so doing does that grammar index another duality: that those trials of the pariah are disposed to awaken elevated, more complex ways of knowing.

These expectations for the exceptional vision aroused by encounters with paradox clearly underwrite the equation between paradox and modern intellectualism evoked by Scott. However, that mode of personifying paradox can smuggle in its own apologetics—and especially when paradox is transposed onto the persona of the prodigious thinker. Such a slippage, for instance, structures Stephen Greenblatt's *Renaissance Self-Fashioning: From More to Shakespeare*. Traveling for us well-trod territory, Greenblatt's study extends from the recognition that "in the sixteenth century there appears to be an increased self-consciousness about the fashioning of human identity as a manipulable, artful process."[121] That quintessentially modern exercise is both catalyzed by and works to incur heightened cognizance of paradox, along with that property's usual counterparts. Greenblatt strikes predictable chords by associating modernity with "irony," mobility, "protean adaptability," "histrionic improvisation," "perpetual self-reflexiveness," "self-estrangement," "playfulness," and a "complex interplay [...] of self-fashioning and self-cancellation." But those bywords of the modern serve to modify not only intellectual-artistic talent or schools of philosophy but also the identities and lives of Greenblatt's subjects. To be sure, one might expect Greenblatt to lend preeminence to art given his expertise in literary criticism, and, indeed, he describes as his study's "proper goal, however difficult to realize, a *poetics of culture*."[122] Relatedly, it might seem far from accidental that Greenblatt's study was published on the cusp of the much-debated rebranding of the "Renaissance" as "Early Modern" within literary studies over the 1980s and '90s, a shift in part incited by Greenblatt's own method, which came to be termed the new historicism. Nevertheless, modernity plain and simply *is* an aesthetic phenomenon for Greenblatt, "function[ing] without regard for a sharp distinction between literature and social life."[123]

Early modern *self*-production, moreover, is simultaneously conceived as a laboratory in the fashioning of *theory* and its anatomy: those twinned enterprises are together actualized vis-à-vis highly specific reading practices that Greenblatt models and performs. In Greenblatt's opening chapter on Thomas More, Hans Holbein's *The Ambassadors* (Greenblatt's cover art) memorably inspires such metatheoretical commentary. Just as Greenblatt welcomes Holbein's spur to "radical questioning" and "restless shifting of perspective,"[124] his analysis converges on a cascade of "paradoxes" (Greenblatt's term). Along the way, Greenblatt serves up a menu of the usual indicia we have seen to unleash modern paradox. Whereas the painting's provocation derives from how Holbein subverts "the very concept of locatable reality" to adopt the "marginal position" of the "periphery," Greenblatt recounts how it enacts:

> a subtle but powerful countercurrent to the forces of harmony, reconciliation, and confident intellectual achievement embodied elsewhere in the picture's objects and figures. None of these antitypes is immediately visible. [...] To see the large death's-head requires a still more radical abandonment of what we take to be 'normal' vision; we must throw the entire painting out of perspective in order to bring into perspective what our usual mode of perception cannot comprehend.[125]

In professing the slant, outsider vision of paradox, Greenblatt opposes his own (and More's and Holbein's) interpretive habits to certain telltale markers of modernity's supposed antecedents. "Harmony," "reconciliation," and intellectual certitude thus act as foils to the revolution in perspective imagined to be inaugurated by modernity. Rather than esteemed as idealized relics of experiential wholeness, those precursors for Greenblatt occasion critique, evident in his assertion that More's greatest achievement is to "return[] again and again to the unsettling of man's sense of reality, the questioning of his instruments of measurement and representation, the demonstration of blind spots in his field of vision."[126] One might read such a call to arms as a paean to theory (rather than to "More").

Greenblatt's panegyric leads him still farther, including to graft More's literary-intellectual feats onto his character, life, and personality. Hallowing More's life as a vindication of modern paradox, Greenblatt relishes the idea that More was possessed of multiple "shadowy selves" and experienced a "life lived at a perpetual remove from reality" and "as histrionic improvisation." Greenblatt identifies the pinnacle of More's achievements thus: "To make a part of one's own, to live one's life as a character thrust into a play, constantly renewing oneself extemporaneously and forever aware of one's own unreality—such was More's condition, such, one might say, his project."[127] Reminiscent of feminism's "spectacle," More's alleged pageantry of performances and disguises is cause for adulation—just as Greenblatt applauds modern critique's parallel destabilization of all registers of empirically verifiable truth and knowing. Thus are modernity's very crises of legitimacy, once again, glorified, contributing for Greenblatt to a corresponding romance of derivativeness and imitation. So whereas the politics of feminism are for Joan Scott steeped in protoliterary qualities, Greenblatt's historical subjects are fully costumed by an atelier more appropriate to art or to literature. It is the spell of paradox that, first, encourages this copious aestheticization: of life, ideas, theory, history, political activism, personality, and more. But second, that logic of paradox simultaneously renders such cross-disciplinary borrowing and exchange semi-automatic, ultimately causing the diverse "unrealities" of modern truth, knowing, experience, art, and individual identity to be conflated. As a result, Greenblatt can exalt how the enigmas of More's character are inseverable from his genius—with myths of intellectual greatness providing their own kind of pretext and cover.

This willingness to confuse intellectual paradox (i.e., genius) with the biography and character of the sage theorist has been ubiquitous. Baehr's introduction to *The Protestant Ethic*, for instance, moves seamlessly between reverence for Weber's corpus to idolization of Weber the individual, remarking "and behind the essay stands a man of remarkable qualities and paradoxes."[128] In such a tribute, the language of paradox migrates from the socioeconomic realities Weber detected, to Weber's distinctive intellectual style, to being a personality trait—with that very synchronicity elevating Weber into something larger than life. But that mythologization of Weber and his oeuvre further buys into a worrisome cult of the tragically marginalized, tormented, and misjudged artist-writer-philosopher. As Greenblatt analogously suggests, to be paradoxical is indeed to inhabit the periphery—and, by extension, to court chronic misunderstanding. So in the same breath as Baehr extols Weber's "encyclopedic genius" and "prodigious versatility," he can chide his own contemporaries for such a failure: for being "ill equipped to understand a man who was in most respects [the present's] antithesis."[129]

This manner of praise has become so commonplace as to resemble its own genre of eulogization. Turning to one other example among countless, elisions like Baehr's similarly inform a 2016 encomium for Friedrich Kittler by Hans Ulrich Gumbrecht. Describing Kittler as a "man of paradoxes," Gumbrecht elaborates: "These paradoxes have the potential to explain how scholars and intellectuals coming from very different premises have often converged in their fascination for Kittler's work—a work that is linked to his personality in a particularly intense fashion." For Gumbrecht, moreover, Kittler's are "appealing paradoxes," with "charismatic effects,"[130] in a combined aestheticization and personification of that quality. Even worse, that accolade injects paradox with near erotic, seductive undercurrents, breeding another type of confusion between "appealing" behavior versus "appealing" ideas. Mesmerizing scholarship, it is implied, will make the great thinker equally hard to resist, while the word *charisma*'s suggestion of a divinely bestowed brilliance adds a separate layer of extenuation to that description.

Just as instructive is the ecumenical flavor of Gumbrecht's homage to Kittler. Kittler's "appealing paradoxes" are imagined to collectivize, to explain why scholars "coming from very different premises" gravitate toward his corpus. Gumbrecht in essence answers the quandary of why so many have congregated around Kittler by citing paradox, at the same time as paradox finesses Gumbrecht's attempt to establish Kittler as a scion of theory. Gumbrecht is right: paradox has been a beacon within that intellectual formation, gathering even otherwise inhospitable thinkers into a mutual intellectual fold. However, another spin on that pluralism involves how the logic of paradox can deceptively harmonize, minimizing if not obscuring meaningful frictions and discordances. While the ability to merge everything and everyone into a single confederacy of paradox has been such reasoning's power, it nevertheless mystifies crucial distinctions far more significant than those separating momentous ideas from individual identity.

Statements like Gumbrecht's can consequently furnish an apologetics for bad behavior. Although faith in the heightened, savvier truths procured by the excluded viewpoint of paradox has served to empower many, that linkage can just as readily salvage or excuse phenomena better left unredeemed. Should the justficatory logic of paradox condone paradoxes of personality, pardoning the quirks and foibles of the contrarian thinker? What happens when the indulgences of paradox sugarcoat contradictory or ambiguous behaviors and personality traits? The very magnetism of such thinking can confer a kind of atonement, sanctioning (if not glamorizing) the vagaries, whims, and idiosyncrasies of the "difficult," "complex" individual. No doubt, this sort of ruse becomes particularly alarming when that "charisma" is not only poeticized or figural but also shorthand for an erotics.

To be sure, the lore of the socially persecuted, maligned genius claims a long history, and one that gained new currency post-'68. Relatedly, it is a truism that all fields venerate their pioneers, memorializing their lives and accomplishments. However, what has distinguished theory and its economy of valuation is the instinct to reward and even fetishize the esoteric, recondite, and ambiguous—privileging insights deemed inaccessible to those trapped within "normal" vision. As we have seen, those priorities descend from a conception of modernity that equates such consciousness with epistemic paradox, all the while stigmatizing world views allegedly stagnated by a dearth of that quality. Yet what ultimately emerges is a mind-set that sanctifies nonconformity, elusiveness, and transgression as proxies not only for landmark ideas but also for the legendarily quixotic thinker. And when that aura of paradox portends intellectual eminence, it can offer an alibi for attitudes that would be quickly dismissed as morally or socially reprehensible in other arenas.

It should go without saying that such an alibi is not universally available across subject positions. To the contrary, the accoutrements of paradox dress up idiosyncrasy in ways only selectively permissible—along predictable lines.[131] Those privileges are also intrinsic to the modernity-as-paradox thesis, given how it disallows the label not only of modernity but also of "theory" to certain (noncontradictory) expressions of truth, subjectivity, meaning, value, identity, and experience. Just as the category of modernity is shorn up by projecting its antitheses onto gendered, raced, classed, and other subordinate lives, so, too, has theory required the negative relief of everything it purports to interdict and expel.

Deep questions therefore surround the ways worship of paradox can collaborate with disparities of power and rank in the academy (and beyond) today. Clearly, not everyone gets to enact or embody paradox with the same license or liberty. As a badge of intellectualism, paradox guards and distributes merit along vectors that both reinforce existing entitlements and turn a blind eye on the injustice of those allocations. We can consequently ask: whose claims will be burnished and authenticated when cloaked in the language of paradox? Conversely, for whom will qualities like "complexity," "indeterminacy," and "inconsistency" backfire (whether as scholarly or personality traits), serving not as insignia of worth but rather as bases for reprimand or even disbarment? Who gets to hide behind the mystique of paradox, versus who will be shamed or penalized for daring to don that mantle?

In sum, there are countless reasons to be leery of this nexus linking paradox and intellectualism. I've tried to show why the instinct to espouse paradox as (auto)biographical for theory is far from surprising, given how that logic telegraphs many of left intellectual life's most abiding commitments. But it is one thing to be dazzled by paradoxical ideas, and another to transfer those intoxicating puzzles onto the demeanor or life of the fabled thinker. That move risks mortgaging the central goals that have long inspired the project of theory, while also ratifying enduring bastions of elite enclosure and privilege. Later chapters examine additional reasons why obeisance to paradox can jeopardize everything valuable conventionally associated with theory. Yet within some humanities fields, that onus has also been compulsory, causing failure to comply with paradox as an edict—or with dialecticism or with critique or with modernity—to exact an exorbitantly steep price.

Conclusion

As we have seen, the equation between paradox and modernity has been so automatic that it can be hard to find theories of modernity that do not confirm such a thesis. But representative accounts of that link also pose many perplexities: a thicket of lingering questions with which the rest of this book wrestles. Among others, should we be worried about the synergistic, chameleon nature of the logic of paradox? Are the plethora of roles it plays a warning sign of intellectual exhaustion and inertia, or merely of the inevitable homogeneity that sets in within any intellectual tradition? It is hard to deny that, for many, paradox has acted as a receptacle for a miscellaneous blend of preoccupations; yet what enabled that openendedness? In many respects, the preliminary diagnosis of paradox is indisputable in its acumen, especially with regard to modernity. Likewise, there is little question that paradoxes provide cunning, revelatory vehicles of critique. But what happens when that logic becomes autobiographical or self-aggrandizing? Or when philosophies of agency, change, justice, history, and democracy are refracted through such an optics, in extreme cases rendering paradox the very cynosure of an ethics?

These are a few inquiries later chapters pursue, although via a web of interlocking paths. There are still complicated stories to be told about how those paths came together—about the means and turns that fashioned paradox into not only a way of knowing but also a philosophy of being and belonging. While some paths are already becoming foreseeable, a congeries of factors (intellectual, historical, and more) amassed paradox into a comprehensive scheme for making sense out of the world—and especially out of left intellectuals' relationship to it. As a starting point, this chapter has sought to apprehend that framework's incredible scope, longevity, and purchase—or to suggest why the grammar of paradox can conjure our most cherished intellectual and political yearnings. To aspire to be modern, or critical, or creative, or aesthetically attuned, or savvy, or ironic, or dissident is to be an evangelist for paradox—and to be a penitent at its altar. Yet the question remains what is thereby sacrificed: what worship of paradox forfeits, and why it can become so very blinding.

2

—

ONTOLOGIZING THE PARADOXES
OF RIGHTS, OR THE
ANTI-LEGALISM OF THEORY

No paradox of contemporary politics is filled with a more poignant irony than the discrepancy between the efforts of well-meaning idealists who stubbornly insist on regarding as "inalienable" those human rights, which are enjoyed only by citizens of the most prosperous and civilized countries, and the situation of the rightless themselves. —Hannah Arendt (1951)

The exception can be more important [...] than the rule, not because of a romantic irony for the paradox, but because the seriousness of an insight goes deeper than the clear generalizations inferred from what ordinarily repeats itself. The exception is more interesting than the rule. The rule proves nothing; the exception proves everything: it confirms not only the rule but also its existence, which derives only from the exception. —Carl Schmitt (1922)

Perhaps no legal-political-philosophical construct has been more consistently spoken of in terms of *paradox* than rights. By most accounts, the history of rights has been one of disappointment if not failure, as rights have run aground on their many paradoxes—again and again and again. Since the eighteenth-century recognition of rights principles in law, much energy has been devoted to grasping those paradoxes and other limits, often prompting the conclusion that rights have "only paradoxes to offer" (to recall the plight of the French Revolutionary feminist Olympe de Gouges). As a result, many if not most theoretical accounts of rights outright conceptualize rights with regard to paradox. While sparring over the extent to which those paradoxes jeopardize rights' success, scholars have overwhelmingly assumed that paradox will prove fixed and immutable: that it is something we must "suffer" (as Wendy Brown puts it) and endure.[1] This emphasis on chronic paradox has oftentimes justified forms of rights skepticism—skepticism occasionally so intense that recent book titles describe a "human right to dominate" and a "right to maim."[2] That mind-set, I'll argue, has been accompanied by an "anti-legalism," or a suspicion of law and legalization that is compulsory across many fields, including humanistic work on legal matters. This chapter explains these interrelated phenomena of anti-legalism and rights skepticism as natural outgrowths of the instinct to *ontologize* paradox: to treat paradox as foundational, structural, and permanent. To call something a "paradox" is, of course, an abstract, philosophical assessment. Yet one signature of contemporary theory is to endow that quality (and its counterparts like contradiction, antagonism, and ambivalence) with concrete, constitutive actuality and force—or to see paradox as a determining feature of contemporary political, social, economic, cultural, and other existence and reality.

Since the modern emergence of democratic rights and their subsequent codification in law, paradox has so thoroughly troubled rights' fortunes that little doubt remains about their paradoxical nature. While a crowning achievement of modern law, rights have nevertheless been plagued by violence and tragedy on basically every level, and the grammar of paradox has indexed those liabilities—much as chapter 1 observed of the modernity-as-paradox thesis. Of course, this nexus between rights and paradox derives in part from the fact that rights are artifacts of modernity—and incarnate all of modernity's prodigious, vertiginous tensions. And as such a bequest, rights have naturally been inculpated for the untold destruction, exploitation, and other terrors broadly tied to modernity and its relentlessly unfolding logic. Thus has the philosophical construct of rights, for instance, been saddled with all of the damning contradictions imagined to afflict instrumental reason, including other enlightenment ideals like universalism, humanism, and liberal freedom. Relatedly has the practical protection and enforcement of rights been not only beset with false starts and double binds but also condemned as a tool of global dominance and oppression—crimes often seen to be directly (and paradoxically) engineered by rights' legalization, as suggested by Hannah Arendt in the epigraph above. Far from last, discourses of rights have proven particularly slippery and precarious, liable to constant abuse and manipulation.[3] Yet whereas the language of paradox has served to critique those hazards, the inevitability of that diagnosis has led many to conclude that the failures of rights are destined to remain insurmountable if not fatal.

Importantly when it comes to rights, neither the diagnosis of paradox nor analysis thus animated has been confined to leftist or critical thought. To the contrary, thinkers of all orientations have tended to foreground paradox when evaluating rights—as well as to deploy it as a weapon of rights critique. Especially when discussing *human* rights, it has been pro forma (whether for mainstream liberal and conservative critics or for humanitarian activists) to begin a conversation about rights by canvassing their many pitfalls and dilemmas. Even when succeeded by normative proposals for how those paradoxes might be mitigated or overcome, paradox has represented a routine starting point. Although sometimes married to anti-legalistic rights skepticism, this linkage between paradox and rights also illustrates the susceptibility of reasoning through paradox to co-optation. Offering a demonstration of why insistence on chronic paradox can actively sabotage considerations of justice, equality, fairness, and everything we might associate with a principle like rights, theories of rights offer a key case study in the troubling costs of unbridled intellectual faith in paradox.

Within the humanities, scholarship exploring the paradoxes of rights has proliferated to such an extent as to become its own genre, and instantiations of that genre only continue to grow. As elsewhere, this conviction in paradox has united theoretical schools (i.e., Marxism and Foucauldian genealogy) and thinkers. To recall discussions of modernity, the discovery of paradox haunting rights issues more than a mere diagnosis; almost invariably, that appraisal marshals a critique, a methodological agenda, and a pre-set roster of outcomes and conclusions. With striking regularity, attempts to theorize rights therefore follow an established itinerary: a given right or rights debate and its paradoxes is isolated, then enlarged, then inspected, then globalized—all leading to the inexorable view that paradox is systemic and inescapable. With paradox simultaneously held out as a recondite truth and total social fact, that conclusion is rarely restricted to discrete difficulties or scenarios confronting rights but instead generalized to contaminate virtually everything it touches—in a sequence that grants the logic of paradox vast explanatory reach. Insofar as those paradoxes are lethal—as they understandably were for Arendt writing in the shadow of the Holocaust and for countless others contending with global modernity's unspeakable violence—they are furthermore presented as lessons in the casualties of law and of legalization in general.

A veritable genre unto itself, this approach to rights both descends from and has memorialized certain iconic thinkers, texts, and watershed events: the French (and occasionally American) Revolution, Karl Marx, World War II, midcentury fascism and totalitarianism, and Arendt, among others. As milestones, those thinkers and events are heralded as not only inaugural but also authoritative in laying bare paradoxes intrinsic both to rights and to the larger institutions embedding them: law, politics, capitalism, constitutional democracy, and even modernity overall.[4] This stock cast of characters and plots driving many if not most accounts of rights has (as with modernity) subsidized what this book describes as an epistemology of paradox—or a way of knowing and perceiving that finds paradox in nearly anything worthy of theorization. Just as it has become practically impossible to talk about rights without pointing to paradox, theorizations of rights will, as before, enable us to examine what happens when paradox is formalized into a comprehensive method. By studying a perhaps unexpected blend of both oft recounted and understudied episodes in the joint adventures of rights and "theory" beginning in the late eighteenth century, we'll see that disputes over rights have played a far more driving part in theory's evolution than is usually acknowledged, as a range of seminal theorists' encounters with rights precipitated crucial intellectual turning points and advances. Yet while engaging intellectual history, this chapter complicates certain prevailing narratives. Instead of questioning the formidable impact of figures like Marx and Arendt, I'll mainly challenge the default assumptions and styles of analysis naturalized by scholarly engrossment with their oeuvres.

While a standard diagnosis of rights, paradox notably has not inspired a single, uniform response, even among thinkers invested in nearly identical issues, texts, and references. Even when citing the *exact same* paradoxes of rights, different theorists have drawn polar opposite conclusions about *both* rights *and* the nature of paradox. Although one take on such a split would map the diverging horizons of structuralism versus poststructuralism, I'll argue that a lot more is going on. Whereas the next chapter considers reasoning that inseminates rights with an antinomian justice-ethics, this one investigates the widespread—and frequently generative—instinct to reckon with paradox by ontologizing it. Why has that tack been both useful and provocative? As chapter 1 showed, one reason an optics of paradox acquired purchase was as a framework for wrestling with the tragic character of modernity, with the recognition that staggering loss and devastation could flower from ostensible pinnacles of progress. In such a manner have properties like paradox and contradiction similarly offered indispensable tools for laying bare the architecture of structural oppression; among other things, those properties have elucidated the logic according to which seemingly distant sites of violence are inexorably linked. The many thinkers addressed below conceive of paradox as ontological precisely to fathom such ravages of modern history, including the perplexity of rights' participation within them.

But in what follows, the term ontologization captures still other features of methods of rights critique that deem their paradoxes to be fatal. First, such reasoning often treats isolated, abnormal, exceptional incidents and truths as elemental and controlling, in the process privileging the heightened, exemplary modes of awareness awakened by apparent anomalies or aberrations. For theorists like Robert Cover and Carl Schmitt, the "extreme case" and "exception" have thus been understood to ground, constitute, and enable the rule and the norm, sowing purportedly reason-based orders like law with a fundamental irrationalism. Second, another common feature of the reasoning explored below is that it endows an abstract quality (paradox) with concrete, determinant actuality and consequence, guaranteeing that paradox will be revealed as innate and insurmountable—in some cases, "totalizing" paradoxes of exclusion like those plaguing rights into a full-blown "paradigm" of modernity (as in biopolitical theory). Far from last, theory that ontologizes paradox frequently blames that effect on *legalization*: specifically law and legal codification are accused of ensuring that purely speculative eventualities (e.g., rights abuses) will prove foregone and unavoidable. The move to ontologize the paradoxes of rights has therefore gone hand-in-hand with the premise that law, legality, and the juridical will unfailingly corrupt otherwise salutary ideals.

This chapter works through a series of different "modes" of ontologization. Contemporary theory indebted to Marx typically relies on a variant of this logic that affixes rights to the economic-material and other structural conditions of capitalism. The second section turns to Arendt's famed reflections on the "perplexities" and "ironies" of rights in *The Origins of Totalitarianism*, where Arendt bewails how midcentury attempts to legalize rights unwittingly set the stage for their violation by totalitarian regimes. Much as for Arendt the "exclusions" of rights and citizenship loom dangerously large, political theology has furnished separate rationales for privileging exceptions and outliers. Thereafter, this chapter explores what I'll characterize as the apotheosis of anti-legalist suspicion of rights: biopolitical theory like Giorgio Agamben's popular work. Finally, it concludes by questioning the implications of this ubiquitous tendency to ontologize contradiction and paradox within a few representative texts of contemporary critical race theory, which demonstrate why that methodological instinct can ultimately detract from and obscure urgent matters of social justice.

The Roots of Rights Skepticism and Critique

It is well established that modern articulations of rights find their origins in the sweeping changes that overtook the late eighteenth century, even as those germinal rights statements ushered in those very transitions. By the end of the eighteenth century, rights occupied a central place in the postrevolutionary French, American, and soon thereafter Haitian constitutions, and this clearly marks a dramatic intellectual, legal, and political innovation. The fact that theorists still today wrestle with those early statements of rights and everything they signify testifies to that era's ongoing relevance. Since the late eighteenth century, rights, of course, have served as beacons for democracy and its core values (freedom, resistance to tyranny, equality, justice). But those newly minted legal rights simultaneously posed political-legal challenges that were also evident from the start. In the very midst of their incorporation into law, eighteenth-century political philosophers therefore questioned rights' purpose and design—and frequently in terms that remain operative. Even more important than specific critiques, the late eighteenth century launched a distinct vein or genre of rights analysis that anatomizes rights with respect to their paradoxes and contradictions.

From those beginnings, rights were naturally ensconced within and dependent on larger constitutional orders, a genesis seen to encumber rights with the same hurdles facing democratic founding and legitimacy. As Etienne Balibar explains, rights enact "a constitution of the constitution,"[5] which is to say that they harbor almost identical paradoxes as those that hamper yet enable democracy. At times, celebratory narratives have accounted for these mutual paradoxes. Much political theory today, for instance, incorporates rights into a genealogy of radically democratic paradox traced to Jean-Jacques Rousseau and his 1762 *The Social Contract*. Rousseau's insight that the incorporation of a democratic People requires "recourse to an authority of a different order" has been taken to crystallize perennial dilemmas of democratic legitimacy that implicate not only constitutional founding but also the authority of a construct like rights.[6] Yet for many, that democracy rests upon legitimacy "of a different order" is viewed not as a deficiency but instead as that institution's vital abundance, in reasoning the next chapter considers.[7]

The late eighteenth century's fledgling attempts at rights and constitutionalism have simultaneously been looked to as cautionary tales foreboding inevitable catastrophes fated to sully those twinned legal-political inventions. Certain of those inaugural trials for rights, faced by the nations that first authored revolutionary constitutions, have therefore been widely extrapolated from to yield broad, comprehensive lessons about rights' philosophical and legal makeup. In particular, those early crucibles in rights have been read as lessons in rights' *exclusionary* architecture—or in the exceptions and limits intrinsic to rights' very complexion. In the American and French contexts, the institution of slavery and disenfranchisement of women have naturally been thus understood to disclose foundational limits destined to compromise any and all expressions of rights, whether real-world or abstract and regardless of their authors' or founders' intent. Indeed, this is the spirit of de Gouges's epigrammatic sayings, such as that "women have the right to mount the scaffold; they should likewise have the right to mount the rostrum." That quip stages a paradox stemming from women's exclusion from rights protections purported to be universal.[8] Yet pithy insights like de Gouges's have consistently been globalized: written into the philosophical-legal blueprint of rights and taken to prophesy an infinite succession of future such lapses and omissions.

While a window on the exclusions imperiling rights, early endeavors to constitutionalize rights can exemplify other of their unavoidable limits. Gazed upon retrospectively, the late eighteenth century has thus been imagined to foreshadow hazards that would come to terrible fruition during later epochs like the mid-twentieth century. And whereas the grammar of paradox has often registered the irony that rights have provided nation-states with a pretext for abusing their own (and other) populations, other more complicated impasses confronting a genuine human rights universalism have also been encapsulated by that language. Far from either an exclusively European or singularly nefarious phenomenon, Haiti's successive efforts at constitution-writing have offered their own case study in the inescapability of paradox. In *Modernity Disavowed: Haiti and the Cultures of Slavery in the Age of Revolution*, Sybille Fischer reads the six successive Haitian constitutions adopted between 1801 and 1816 as visionary instances of expressive lawmaking that nevertheless dramatize such barriers. Although anticolonial in principle, those constitutions for Fischer were doomed by rights' inseverable tethering to the institution of citizenship. Whereas Haiti's second 1805 Constitution decreed all Haitians to be Blacks, its 1843 Constitution sought instead to transcend the confines of nation-state sovereignty and bestow Haitian citizenship on all Blacks transnationally.[9] Needless to say, realities of territory and geography frustrated those ambitions—and in ways shown by Fischer to expose legal and practical obstacles that extinguish hopes for a true human rights internationalism to this day.

The late eighteenth century also germinated the seeds of distinct genres or modes of rights critique that would, over the intervening years, become dominant. Among Jeremy Bentham's many contributions to contemporary philosophy, his reflections on rights undertake a method of analysis that seizes upon paradox and contradiction as the chief basis for rights skepticism. Bentham gave us perhaps the most memorable witticism regarding rights—calling rights "nonsense upon stilts," a phrase memorialized by Jeremy Waldron in the title of his 1987 compilation of Bentham, Marx, and Edmund Burke's writings on rights.[10] However, Bentham's foremost objection to eighteenth-century discourses surrounding rights was their grounding in "natural" law. In contrast, Bentham's *Anarchical Fallacies* (composed in 1791–95 and published in 1816 in French) sought to preserve rights as strictly legal artifacts, or inventions of positive law and the social compact—in a position that simultaneously disputes certain premises of social contract theory. Hence, Bentham calls ideas about the "origination of governments from a contract" a "pure fiction, or in other words, a falsehood."[11] As Bentham cautions in a retort just as applicable to rights, "Contracts come from government, not government from contracts." Yet one further problem with natural law justifications for Bentham is that they cast rights as "imprescriptible" and, especially when rights lack legally stipulated boundaries, render them "open-ended," limitless, and "indeterminate." Although Bentham thereby decries qualities today valorized by many theorists, he sees these risks as particularly acute given the slippery nature of rights rhetoric. Hence, Bentham worries about the "figurative," "unbounded," "loose," and "ambiguous" character of rights talk, which not only invites "dangerous" and "mischievous" manipulation but also enflames the unchecked "passions," fomenting a "propensity to perpetual insurrection."

Beyond the substance of Bentham's objections, crucial for us is that he unfolds these and other concerns via the exposure of lurking paradox. Bentham dissects one right after another—beginning with "liberty," and thereafter "property," "security," "resistance to oppression," and so on—by divulging and, in the process, magnifying their many "inconsistencies" and incoherences. As he inveighs,

> *Liberty*, then is imprescriptible—incapable of being taken away—out of the power of any government ever to take away liberty—that is, every branch of liberty—every individual exercise of liberty; for no line is drawn—no distinction—no exception made. What these instructors as well as governments of mankind appear not to know, is, that all rights are made at the expense of liberty—all laws by which rights are created or confirmed. [...] Laws creative of rights of property are also struck by the same anathema. How is property given? By restraining liberty; that is, by taking it away so far as is necessary for the purpose. How is your house made yours? By debarring every one else from the liberty of entering it without your leave.

In such fashion, Bentham inventories one conundrum after the next, through a maze of dependent clauses and interrogatories rhetorically staging the "anathema" bedeviling rights. In a line of attack culminating with the charges that rights are "fictional" and a ruse of "power," Bentham finally dismisses them as fully "a system of contradictions and impossibilities."

While today familiar, Bentham's methodological style is nevertheless striking: his analysis pursues, mines, enlarges, and inhabits the many quandaries posed by rights, undergoing the intellectual vicissitudes, turns, and convolutions of those paradoxes. Whereas each complaint is independently probing, Bentham's argument also gains power by accumulating a cascade of such perplexities. And although Bentham does not himself specifically cite paradox (versus a network of adjacent, near-interchangeable terms), his discussion is steered by the presumption that the excavation of submerged "anathema" and "contradiction" will provoke rights skepticism. Beyond the substance of his doubts, that intellectual mode enshrines those paradoxical qualities as a cardinal feature of rights. Moreover, it is precisely by layering one source of "nonsense" upon the next that Bentham captures why such a morass of paradox will, in the end, prove "systemic." Today, Bentham's view that rights are not only awash with contradiction but precipitously so typically functions as a baseline and preliminary supposition within rights critique.

Even more monumental an influence on theory than Bentham, of course, has been Marx, whose early yet formative "On the Jewish Question" (1843) engages in a modality of rights critique not so far afield from *Anarchical*

Fallacies. Whereas for Bentham paradox suffuses rights as a discourse and philosophical-legal construct, the early Marx of "On the Jewish Question" yokes rights to the conditions of privation and exploitation that his later work would theorize in terms of capitalism: a world-historical process that, as the last chapter saw, both thrives upon and multiples paradox and contradiction. "On The Jewish Question" focuses specifically on the rights to liberty, property, equality, and security as contained within the 1789 French Declaration of the Rights of Man and of the Citizen. Famously, Marx excoriates those "so-called rights of man" as the possessions of "egoistic man, of man separated from other men and from the community" and of "the *circumscribed* individual, withdrawn into himself."[12] As Marx also comes to argue of capitalism, a construct like rights therefore injects contradiction into the human, humanism, and social relations. Marx explains the institution of property:

> The right of property is, therefore, the right to enjoy one's fortune and to dispose of it as one will; without regard for other men and independently of society. It is the right of self-interest. This individual liberty, and its application, form the basis of civil society. It leads every man to see in other men, not the *realization* but rather the *limitation* of his own liberty.[13]

In Marx's thinking, rights exacerbate (rather than temper or counteract) all of the predatory, socially atomizing behaviors that he understands capitalism to reward. Rather than to foster political community or "species-being," rights actively jeopardize it. Disseminating seductive yet illusory notions about freedom and "private interest," they do more than rationalize egoism but furthermore protect it within law. As one result, Marx finds it "incomprehensible" that a revolutionary project oriented toward the fragile aim of establishing a genuine political community would install rights at the heart of its national ethos, betraying the French Revolution to be "in flagrant contradiction with its theory."[14]

Just as Marx's wariness about rights remains authoritative, so too has his basic modality of rights critique exerted enormous sway. Mirroring his theory of capitalism, the central technology of Marx's brand of rights analysis is the unearthing of contradiction, and precisely those contradictions riddling rights explain why their logic both tears man from himself and divides community, inducing forms of social loss and isolation. Given his towering influence, it is simultaneously essential to distinguish Marx's own conclusions regarding rights from the typical assumptions held by many of his intellectual heirs. Whereas Marx's reflections merely anticipate his emerging account of capitalism, almost every theorization of rights remotely indebted to Marx (or concerning an economic order like neoliberalism) ever since has characterized rights logic as, to varying degrees, capitalism's handiwork. So whereas Marx's insights into rights are largely gestural, subsequent iterations of his theory quite seamlessly incorporate rights into the edifice of capitalism, all the while redoubling his view that rights are fundamentally antisocial. Whether viewed as bedfellows to capitalism, class hierarchy, the division of labor, neoliberalism, globalization, or other economizing regimes, rights are therefore imagined to breed near identical contradictions and antagonisms as are endemic to capitalism. It has consequently been axiomatic that rights will both aggravate and excuse the many hyperindividualistic, predatory, and privatizing behaviors ingrained by capitalism as an economic order.

As chapter 1 addressed, properties like contradiction, antagonism, and paradox play a complicated role within Marxist thought as well as other variants of the dialectic. While those qualities possess an incredible dynamism, they are often absolutized in ways that elevate them into governing principles of sorts: they are substantialized as decisive aspects of modern reality. That instinct to objectivize paradox has also organized Marxist theories of rights. So even as Marx pioneered a method of critique piloted by contradiction and antagonism, his adherents attribute a structuralizing force to those properties that, in many ways, renders them not merely systemic but fully ontological, as we will continue to see. Contemporary iterations of Marxist thought have only accentuated this dimension of his reasoning, vesting paradoxes like those vexing rights with a determinant authority, fixity, and exhaustiveness. Marxist theory has thereby generated one distinctive logic of, and justification for, the ontologization of paradox.

Current Marxist thought has assembled diverse kinds of support verifying the premise that rights are capitalism's progeny. To canvass a few brief examples, Ian Baucom's *Specters of the Atlantic: Finance Capital, Slavery, and the Philosophy of History* regards the late eighteenth century as the birthplace of the modern subject—and exactly because it saw rights, democracy, and finance capital collectively originate as mechanisms for securing the economic risks posed by the slave trade. Rather than separate or discontinuous from other contemporaneous developments, justice-oriented principles like rights were for Baucom from their inception handmaidens to trade and other economic practices of dispossession. In one haunting example, Baucom reads the 1781 *Zong* massacre of more than 130 enslaved Africans to substantiate his assertion that the coterminous escalation of economic speculation and of slavery together wrought "the financialization of a system of justice, the transformation of the legal system into a scene of exchange, its reinvention as a mechanism designed not to dispense justice but money."[15]

Many studies of humanitarianism deploy such a frame of reference to draw parallel conclusions, magnifying the deep irony that a philosophy like humanitarianism would become hostage to regimes of economic exploitation. Here, too, that paradox has been viewed as wholly determinant of rights' real-world fortunes. Especially when cast in the mold of neoliberalism, global economic barriers and flows are usually understood only to deepen rights' collusion with capital, internationally and domestically. If anything, the efflorescence of work on neoliberalism has led theorists to double down on Marx's somewhat more ruminative observations. Pheng Cheah thus argues that the globalization of human rights norms ironically facilitates rights' conscription, or "contamination," by supranational market-based factors, causing rights to operate not merely as private and court-enforced weapons (versus shields) but also as active tools of international policing and coercion.[16] Among other examples, Cheah points to rights' frequent conspiracy with the usurious and predatory lending practices of financial institutions like the World Bank and International Monetary Fund, particularly when targeted at the global South. Needless to say, a further contradiction besetting humanitarian activism involves its common gratification of consumerist desire; hence, Alain Badiou dismisses rights as "the self-satisfied egoism of the affluent West, with advertising, and with service rendered to the powers that be."[17]

Parallel cautions have been raised about neoliberalism's impact on rights within domestic contexts, exemplified for Wendy Brown in the economization of speech rights in American legal reason. Brown's *Undoing the Demos* demonstrates how "neoliberal jurisprudence" "replaces the distinctly political valences of rights, equality, liberty, access, autonomy, fairness, the state, and the public with economic valences of these terms."[18] Indeed, Jasbir Puar argues something analogous about the deleterious consequences of rights logic on disability activism, including legal gains like the Americans with Disabilities Act. While the final chapter revisits Puar's study, Puar dismisses rights as mechanisms of value extraction that ultimately reduce disability to a "commodity."[19] As she submits, "rights based frames sustain the relation of perpetual, normalized crisis" that feed into a "biopolitics of debilitation."[20]

Notwithstanding certain of those assessments clear accuracy, one by-product of this focus on the damning paradoxes of rights is that rights skepticism can seem compulsory, acting as a litmus test for properly critical theory. Take Foucauldian analysis, which can illustrate the categorical nature of the positions often extending from such an outlook. Ben Golder's *Foucault and the Politics of Rights*, for example, is inspired by what Golder holds out as an inconsistency: Foucault made increasing appeals to rights at late stages in his career, even though the critique of rights is central to his oeuvre. Yet in treating rights as a privileged shorthand for Foucault's overall politics, Golder must first concede that Foucault's turn to rights was motivated by something more than either pragmatism or unwitting selling out. Golder instead maintains that Foucault's self-aware mission was to de-familiarize rights logic in order to facilitate its repurposing.[21] Beyond this assessment, however, Golder's underlying assumptions are immensely telling. First, Golder presumes that his audience shares in deep suspicion of rights and of law in general, effectively blessing rights critique as the only admissible progressive, critical, or theoretical stance. Only within such an intellectual landscape does it make sense to devote an entire scholarly monograph to uncracking the riddle of Foucault's apparent endorsement of rights. Second, Golder's approach to navigating this disjunction is just as representative. Golder pinpoints an alleged incoherence—here, internal to Foucault's own views—and plumbs its depths with the expectation that it will disclose intractable dilemmas constitutive of rights and politics overall. Golder thereby undertakes a sequence of recurring moves that usually spell rights skepticism, although deploying them to dissect the corpus of a thinker (Foucault) responsible for ingraining such a methodology.

It may be tempting to discount rights skepticism as peculiar to pro-gressive or leftist thought, but that mind-set prevails well beyond strictly theoretical circles. More mainstream legal and other scholars have also cited paradox and contradiction as the signature of rights and their many pitfalls. Rights skepticism, along with what the philosopher Joshua Cohen refers to as "rights minimalism," has therefore functioned as a default posi-tion for many.[22] This normalization of rights critique beyond the outposts of critical theory is evidence of more than an unusually broad consensus regarding rights; it also exemplifies the mainstreaming of paradox as an analytic mode. In one sense, a text like David Kennedy's 2004 *The Dark Sides of Virtue: Reassessing International Humanitarianism* is a prime case of how certain complaints about rights have become so summary as to invite cataloging. Kennedy's first chapter asks "The International Human Rights Movement: Part of the Problem?," with section headings that walk through a list of now rote objections: "Human Rights Occupies the Field of Emancipatory Possibility," "Human Rights is Limited by Its Relation-ship to Western Liberalism," "Human Rights Promises More Than It Can

Deliver," "The Human Rights Movement Strengthens Bad International Governance," and so on.[23] Kennedy effectively presents these and other paradoxes of rights as established if not objective fact.

Even more alarming, rights critique that emanates from the mining of paradox and contradiction can serve notably different goals in different hands. Even Michael Ignatieff—hardly a left radical—engages in such a performance of rights skepticism and corresponding mood of resignation, a mood apparently sanctioned by Ignatieff's rehearsal of a long sequence of predictable limitations afflicting rights.[24] However, *Human Rights as Politics and Idolatry* traverses that standard portfolio of limits—the imperialism of rights, what Ignatieff memorably terms "rights inflation," and more— only to stage a defense of rights grounded in deliberation and reasoned decision-making.[25] In what is ultimately an apologia for distinctly *liberal* rights,[26] the steps of Ignatieff's argument are particularly instructive. Ignatieff seemingly credentializes his pro-rights stance by first acceding to the sorts of charges normally wielded by the progressive left as rationales for either rejecting or curtailing the scope of rights. Yet Ignatieff does little more than pay lip service to those concerns, in a prototypical demonstration of why rights skepticism need not end up in a particular politics. Crying structural and disabling paradox, in other words, does not prevent Ignatieff either from espousing a decidedly liberal world view or from incorporating rights therein.

Indeed, when debates about rights are on the table, conservative, libertarian, and liberal thinkers alike regularly latch onto paradox as a baseline proposition, even when the goal is to scoff at certain reservations as overly squeamish. Like Ignatieff, Eric Posner's 2014 foray into human rights law relies on numerous of the moves we've already studied. In particular, it is Posner's self-styled "realism" that entails his decidedly bleak view of human rights: for Posner, the inability of rights treaties to exact compliance betrays our era to be "the twilight of human rights law," having "made a mockery of" the human rights movement.[27] That feint of a reality check is supported by other maneuvers that should start to appear predictable. Posner opens his introduction with an epigraph that, as he explains, "encapsulates a paradox about human rights," and his first chapter thereafter travels through a list of real-world examples designed to show human rights to be "puzzling."[28] Those examples itemize multiple paradoxes we have already encountered. Posner, too, notes that already in the eighteenth century a dilemma arose: "the very idea that rights are universal conflicted with the imperative of building a nation."[29] Even more, he throws a bone to humanists, acknowledging that "the expansion of literacy and reading" of imaginative literature like novels was necessary to cultivate the moral awareness tied to human rights.[30]

Posner thereby adopts what might appear an ecumenical approach, although only to smuggle in a domineering, neo-imperial foreign policy. In fact, Posner's stated goal is to defend the use of "foreign aid" as an inevitable and excusable "tool of coercion" by "wealthy countries," which should be wielded regardless of whether a given nation "complies within human rights treaties" or not.[31] The ease with which Posner leverages paradox and rights critique as a pretext for licensing overtly paternalistic and aggressive practices is nothing short of remarkable. One could certainly shrug off Posner's proclivity for the "puzzling" as a diversionary tactic meant to placate and disarm his audience by courting their fancies, tilling the ground to make it more receptive to his rightwing views. Likewise, we could question whether Posner, like many, has learned to purloin and redeploy an arsenal of what were perfected as left, critical strategies—plundering to which the logic of paradox, we will see, is particularly susceptible. Or maybe Poser is genuinely convinced about the literary-cultural origins of legal constructs like human rights.[32]

But these matters of intellectual theft and sincerity are a distraction from deeper questions about the yield and politics of reasoning like that scaffolding many critiques of rights. Posner coyly recruits such reasoning to defend a muscular, neoliberal foreign policy, and he apparently does so with full awareness of what paradoxes do: they defamiliarize (to recall Golder) and thereby evacuate normative-moral principles of their established content and bearings. As Posner shows, the logic of paradox is extremely successful at creating a moral-ethical vacuum—and one that leaves Posner just as free as anyone to fill it with whatever suits him. Posner's favored solution, of course, contravenes everything one might hope for human rights. Yet the truth is that Posner both extrapolates from and weaponizes paradox in ways we will come to recognize as far from anomalous, offering a tutorial in why reasoning through paradox can be, in Bentham's words, a "mischievous" affair. As theorists have long submitted, and as Posner confirms, paradox-fueled critique most certainly *does* confiscate rights' preconceived, normative meanings, and that resulting emptiness *does* create new argumentative openings. This accomplished, however, the logic of paradox does nothing to delimit or prescribe what should come along to replace whatever principles it has abolished or cleared away.

World War II, Rights, and the "Legalization" of Paradox

World War II profoundly changed both the urgency and terrain surrounding debates over rights—and especially *human* rights. The war of course led to the high-profile 1948 adoption of the Universal Declaration of Human Rights (the UDHR) by the United Nations, although critics have rightly protested the lionization of not only that document but also its most eminent champion, Eleanor Roosevelt. For a time, triumphalist and moralizing narratives regarding the UDHR held sway, often involving its whitewashing as a testament to global harmony and cross-cultural dialogue.[33] Much energy has therefore been devoted to downsizing the UDHR (and Roosevelt), frequently by challenging the mythologization of human rights as an unbroken tale of progress.[34] Many revisionist historians have instead developed genealogies of rights catered, as Samuel Moyn puts in it *The Last Utopia: Human Rights in History*, to tell a story "of construction rather than discovery and contingency rather than necessity."[35] Indeed, as Philip Alston comments of Moyn's work, "there is a struggle for the soul of the human rights movement, and it is being waged in large part through the proxy of genealogy."[36] We can briefly recall from the last chapter the centrality to genealogy of qualities like friction, contradiction, and paradox—here, qualities fruitfully enlisted to unmask and destabilize overly congratulatory, sanguine human rights narratives.

Needless to say, not only World War II itself but also celebrated efforts to theorize rights in its aftermath have consumed thinkers over the ensuing years. Midcentury inquiries into rights gave us a number of methodological edicts and preoccupations that remain hardwired, among others a profound (and, at times, understandable) wariness of law and the legal system—of the juridical sui generis and the specific consequences of "legalization." The interwar political landscape in particular has been widely understood to have materialized the dangers, first, of legally codifying otherwise salutary or just principles and, second, of submitting left or progressive political projects to law and its domain. This fear of legalism—which we'll see was partly engineered by efforts to confront distinct paradoxes of rights made newly visible in the decades leading up to the war and to the UDHR—goes largely unquestioned within theory today. Yet already for many postwar thinkers, the UDHR and global ascendency of human rights were imagined not to vindicate rights principles but only to proliferate and compound their most damaging paradoxes. Resulting attempts to account for that disconnect between rights as ideals versus rights in practice generated a separate (although often interrelated) mode of ontologization than the one inherited from Marx: a mode of ontologization that blames legalization for actualizing—and, in fact, nothing short of guaranteeing—certain fatal byproducts of constitutive paradox, and especially those flowing from the snares of citizenship and nation-state jurisdiction. Given the insidious work of denationalization programs before and during World War II along with plight of scores of refugees thereafter, these endemic paradoxes have often been deemed deadly. As such that midcentury climate has also been deemed a turning point for confirming the centrality of "exclusion" (i.e., from citizenship) to those debacles of rights, consecrating exclusion as a master or governing paradox—of rights, law, and more.

How did this all play out? Midcentury attempts to legislate human rights understandably prompted a whole new wave of doubts about their shortcomings and dilemmas, practical and philosophical. Without question the most theoretically renowned of those appraisals occurs in Hannah Arendt's 1951 *The Origins of Totalitarianism*; few commentaries on rights have inspired greater analysis, just as certain of Arendt's phrases have been pored over like a kind of scripture.[37] *The Origins of Totalitarianism* attributes its stirring reflections on human rights to the massive refugee crises that overwhelmed first interwar and then postwar Europe, as the redrawing of national borders and other repercussions of those conflicts displaced staggering numbers of people, leaving many stateless.[38] Arendt therefore laments the functional hollowness of human rights for the very populations in most dire need of their assurances.[39] For Arendt, the exact situation (of statelessness) that one might expect to activate the protections of human rights instead exposed their façade of universality to be a sham. Given their contingency on citizenship in a rights-respecting nation, Arendt describes human rights as a "barbed labyrinth" for those desperately seeking to rely on their safeguards—a fiasco unleashing inestimable "Perplexities of the Rights of Man," the title of one of her book's sections. Arendt's discussion therein spins a tangled web of paradox, which she presents as stemming from intractable features of citizenship, the nation-state, "civilization," humanism, and more. The paradoxes of rights—or as Arendt at one point terms them, "calamities"—are thus conceived as wholly foundational to the modern geopolitical order.

Addressing "irony" after "irony" of rights, Arendt ponders tragic dilemmas such as that "only with a completely organized humanity could the loss of home and political status become identical with expulsion from humanity altogether."[40] Rather than a pinnacle of humanism, the very category of "man" broke down when confronted with people reduced to "the abstract nakedness of being human and nothing but human;" this became the "greatest danger" for stateless populations, as it provided cover for their persecution.[41] At one point, Arendt bitterly concludes: "The paradox involved in the loss of human rights is that such loss coincides with the instant when a person becomes a human being in general [...] *and* different in general, representing nothing but his own absolutely unique individuality which, deprived of all expression within and action upon a common world, loses all significance."[42] As Arendt consequently argues, what matters are not rights per se but rather "the right to have rights" and "a right to belong to some kind of organized community."[43]

While volumes have been written about Arendt, in particular four elements of her thought helped to endow paradox with near-proverbial truth, within rights theory and beyond. The first involves Arendt's notably lyrical, impressionistic writing. Gestural, Arendt's remarks are rife with ambivalences almost primed to elicit outpourings of commentary, which has often been similarly ruminative. The almost cult following (spawning entire schools of theory) provoked by Arendt's poetic phraseology is without question tied to this indeterminacy and open-endedness of her coinages: "the abstract nakedness of being nothing but human" (a phrase versions of which Arendt incants), "the right to have rights," or the claim, "Their plight is not that they are not equal before the law, but that no law exists for them; not that they are oppressed but that nobody wants even to oppress them."[44] Beyond the aphoristic flavor of Arendt's language, each successive observation stages yet another paradox, and that orchestration of paradox into a rhetorical-intellectual *style* has been emulated far and wide. Although Arendt purports to unravel a thicket of paradox, her writing more accurately elongates and dwells within that discovery's implications almost infinitely, as paradox starts to devour all of modern political existence. Aestheticized via the repetitive, incantatory, rhythmic, almost musical quality of her writing, the paradoxes of rights are melded by Arendt into something like their own rhapsodic poetry.

Second, paradox for Arendt is clearly not a diagnosis that can be disambiguated or alleviated or resolved or overcome. To the contrary, she dwells within it. On one level, something circular or tautological sets in: a preliminary finding of paradox stockpiles an accumulation of mounting paradoxes to imbue that initial discovery with near-prophetic freightedness.[45] In a type of feedback loop, the avalanching paradoxes of rights can thus seem to verify the sense that rights are fated to be paradoxical. On another level, a certain relish for paradox and its infinitely self-complicating, peripatetic meanderings animates Arendt's reasoning, sowing her prose with enigmas resembling those she claims to uncover. True, enacting the fabric of paradox serves to register the terrible magnitude and irrevocability of the unthinkable horrors that capsized the world during her lifetime. But Arendt's web of paradox becomes more than all-enveloping or threatening; paradox becomes almost mystical in its resplendence.

Arendt's tautologies bring us to another frequent feature of reasoning that ontologizes paradox. Just as paradox engulfs virtually everything related to rights, it compels Arendt to conclude that their failed universality is an inherent, insurmountable property of rights themselves. In the process, however, Arendt inscribes paradox within the genetics not only of rights but also of law and legalization. In some ways reminiscent of Marx, her argument takes what might remain a purely abstract, philosophical quality (paradox or contradiction) and objectivizes it, vesting it with concrete, real-world actuality. What might look like strictly academic or hypothetical "perplexities" of rights thus become chronic, innate, inescapable failures—and mortal failures, at that. Colored by despair if not fatalism, Arendt's meditations on the fully ontological nature of paradox consequently leave her unable to imagine an alternative to her own assessment—as she ultimately universalizes the very poisonous limits that she blames for annihilating rights. It is no wonder, then, that chapter 9 of *The Origins of Totalitarianism* paints a picture of Europe wracked by "disintegration," "deterioration," and disaster. While certainly justified by her historical milieu, Arendt's relationship to paradox is simultaneously what demands an outlook that is both dark and all-governing.

Arendt is quite lucid about the implications of her own reasoning. In fact, her conclusions about rights both provoke and extend from her account of legalization: of what happens when otherwise abstract paradox is codified in law, giving it teeth and consequence. It is when formalized in law that implicit, unstated paradoxes of rights become tangible and liable to exploitation. In effect, Arendt suggests that the juridification of a paradoxical construct like rights objectivizes otherwise theoretical or speculative categories of sociopolitical exclusion by making them a decisive matter of legal status. As Arendt explains of the peace treaties and minorities treaties following the Great War, beyond doing little to ameliorate the plight of the stateless, they actively backfired by acknowledging "in plain language" the grave consequences of nationality and citizenship for human rights. Only when legalized were rights emptied out by their own loopholes, consigning certain lives to a state of "illegality" that drastically increased the likelihood of their oppression. In a way, Arendt here contends with what is perhaps the deepest tragedy of human rights: that midcentury attempts to deal with the mounting refugee crisis made the vulnerability of those very lives patently obvious, ripe for abuse. Many passages of *The Origins of Totalitarianism* grapple with the repercussions of this fundamental double bind (e.g., that human rights become accidents of birth), which in the end reduces human rights to "the evidence of hopelessness or idealism or fumbling feeble-minded hypocrisy."[46]

It is through this indictment that Arendt develops what is best explained as another basis for ontologizing the paradoxes of rights. Whereas Marx's heirs tether rights to all of the material and structuralizing contradictions of capitalism, Arendt's account of what legalization does produces parallel effects. For Arendt, it is precisely when rights are given legal backing and positivity that their paradoxes become substantialized and concrete. However, that conclusion also ties Arendt's hands: it bars the possibility of antidotes or alternatives, whether to the evisceration of rights or to the broadly sinister outcomes that transpire whenever law colonizes otherwise noble undertakings. Such an impasse arises in part because Arendt's reasoning undertakes the exact moves she complains of—which is to say that her own argumentative logic, wherein purely hypothetical paradox becomes ontological, prevents her from envisioning another course that might depart from the atrocities of midcentury European history. Such thinking thus falls victim to a determinism; the grievous letdowns of rights essentially become impossible to mitigate or transcend. And whether narrowly confined to rights or globalized, Arendt's devastating prognosis has reinforced a larger reflex to regard law and legality as integral to the production of structural violence—if not the primary technology authoring institutional oppression. We will see again and again over later chapters theory that, like Arendt's, perfunctorily identifies law and the juridical as the main culprits in the manufacture and perpetuation of political-economic injustice—in a view that, as for Arendt, can circularly confirm the pervasive, systemic scope and design of oppression. Notwithstanding Arendt's understandable despair over the realities she chronicles, this premise regarding law has survived to long outlive that era—and to be endowed with even greater weight and inexorability in some contemporary theory.

Later chapters will continue to understand "exclusion"—a term today summoning a lot more than what Arendt blames for the midcentury catastrophes of rights—as a master paradox that has since operationalized nearly *all* contemporary social justice movements, inside and outside of the academy. Indeed, Arendt's diagnosis of the deadly consequences of exclusion enshrines that category as a kind of secret or riddle that is essential to deciphering the fortunes of human rights yet fundamentally unsolvable. Whether in "the right to have rights," "the abstract nakedness of being human," or other of her epigrammatic sayings, Arendt returns again and again to that enigma of exclusion, which she clothes in almost religious language. This privileging of exclusion as near talismanic also extends from political theology, which the next section considers.

Political Theology and Law's Enabling Exceptions

Arendt's premise that their exclusionary architecture is the crux of rights' vulnerability to abuse dovetails with legal theory that draws cognate (if inverted) conclusions about the ontology of law: theories of legal interpretation and judgment rooted in "political theology" and descended from scriptural exegesis. Whereas for Arendt legalization ironically fortifies the lethal exceptions from rights, the work of Carl Schmitt and to a somewhat lesser degree Robert Cover offers a separate if related basis for prioritizing law's exclusions: for looking to what law on the surface exempts or omits from its ambit for indispensable insight into its anatomical makeup. It has become well-established that law is constituted by, and in turn dependent on, the very phenomena it appears to "exclude" or "except," in thinking that, like Arendt's, grants methodological and conceptual primacy to exclusionary paradox. While geographically and historically distant, both Schmitt and Cover differently regard the "exception" or anomalous case as crucial to grasping underacknowledged dynamics regarding law, jurisprudence, and what Schmitt terms "the political." For Schmitt, those exceptions are furthermore what vest law with "sovereign" authority, even while they are uncodifiable (Schmitt's theory here diverges from Arendt) and therefore exiled from law's formal purview. Despite (or rather because of) the theological bent of their work, Cover and Schmitt have proven so consequential that their ideas are regularly cited by not only the left but also the right—above all, for insight into the "irrationalism" of the only nominally reasoned and neutral operations of law and politics.

As a Weimar jurist and member of the Nazi Party, Schmitt and his legacy have naturally been caught up in debates about the vexed role of law in both forging and rationalizing fascism. Notwithstanding this, Schmitt is widely credited with ascertaining essential, if elusive, truths about law—truths that midcentury totalitarianism came to apotheosize. While promulgating an alluring terminology (sovereignty, political theology, the exception), Schmitt also locates antagonism at the heart of political and legal existence. For instance, he views the "friend-enemy" distinction as "decisive" and "primary," superseding all other vectors of socio-economic conflict.[47] Even more widely echoed has been Schmitt's plea for thinkers to come to grips with the unavoidable irrationalism of politics, as he cautions that a neglect of that imperative can set the stage for fascism and other political evil. Even more important today, Schmitt's insistence on the unreasoned elements of politics flows from a critique of liberalism—here, too, an agenda attractive to both the left and far right.[48] As Schmitt forewarns, liberal commitments like proceduralism, reasoned deliberation, and humanism problematically conceal (casting what Leo Strauss calls a "smokescreen" over) "the political," occluding its most vital elements.[49]

For our purposes, it is critical to appreciate that the friend-enemy distinction is "primary" precisely because it emerges through the exceptional or extreme case. For Schmitt, it only gains meaning amid the real threat of killing—or through the most inordinate manifestations of political struggle. Schmitt explains:

> That the extreme case appears to be an exception does not negate its decisive character but confirms it all the more. [...] One can say that the exceptional case has an especially decisive meaning which exposes the core of the matter. War as the most extreme political means discloses the possibility which underlies every political idea, namely, the distinction of friend and enemy.[50]

Rather than locating politics within its ordinary, self-evident, commonsense workings, the political for Schmitt resides within instances so extreme as to appear anomalies or deviations, and one result is that politics and law paradoxically necessitate for their "possibility" tensions that liberal rationalism pretends to resolve but in fact dangerously overlooks and submerges.

A cognate structural logic organizes Schmitt's theory of the norm, which he explains as similarly parasitic on its own enabling violation and antithesis.[51] For Schmitt, the norm or juridical rule requires, and is determined by, the "sovereign" declaration of "the exception," even while such a decree will both elude received structures of legal-political justification and remain alien to law on the books. For Schmitt, the exception "defies general codification" and cannot be encompassed by or "made to conform to a preformed law," arguably staving off the sorts of legal objectivization feared by Arendt.[52]

That said, the norm is simultaneously consolidated by its own abrogation in ways that "are not peripheral but essential"—meaning that key aspects of law will be unintelligible to reason and thereby installing paradox at the core of the legal order.[53] Both Schmitt's conviction in paradox and his doubts about liberal rationalism are thus vividly infused by what he himself terms a political theology (or *Politische Theologie*, in the title of his 1922 essay). Ultimately fueled by a wish to restore vitalism and transcendence to politics (evident in his comparison of the legal exception to a religious miracle),[54] this theological lineage is further instructive for other reasons: namely, Schmitt adopts a relationship to paradox routine within theodicy and philosophical defenses of the existence of God. Paradox, as later chapters address, is integral to various genres of legitimation long relied on within religious discourse: genres the primary function of which is to transform apparent liabilities (i.e., the impossibility of objectively proving the existence of God) into repositories of near divine bounty and revelation. So just as Schmitt's antiliberalism protests the sanitization of charisma and wonder from modern political experience, he espouses an antinomianism that extols certain realities (like spiritual faith) precisely because they outwardly defy rational verification and legitimacy.

Bob Cover's influential 1986 *Yale Law Journal* essay "Violence and the Word" reproduces such a characteristically Schmittian scheme, albeit within the left liberal context of Yale Law School. In this iconic text, Cover grapples with the ways law's monopoly on violence haunts even the most mundane of legal acts, as his opening sentence dramatically intones: "Legal interpretation takes place in a field of pain and death."[55] For Cover it is a mix of theology, literary and cultural criticism, then emergent work on hermeneutics, and psychology (including the Milgram experiment) that warrants this observation. Key, moreover, is that Cover's work was a conduit for the incursion of those modes of thought into more mainstream legal study.[56] Without citing Schmitt, Cover nevertheless echoes his thesis that one must examine the exceptional or rare instance (for Cover, death penalty cases or martyrdom) to grasp law's most essential workings. In perfectly Schmittian terms, Cover observes:

> Martyrdom, for all its strangeness to the secular world of contemporary American Law, is a proper starting place for understanding the nature of legal interpretation. Precisely because it is so extreme a phenomenon, martyrdom helps us see what is present in lesser degree whenever interpretation is joined with the practice of violent domination. [...] And the

miracle of the suffering of the martyrs is their insistence on the law to which they are committed, even in the face of world-destroying pain. [...] A legal world is built only to the extent that there are commitments that place bodies on the line."[57]

Cover further finds "such an act of rebellion" with the miraculous genesis of "our own [US] constitutional history."[58] Thus invested in a specifically American vitalist tradition, one of Cover's goals is (like Schmitt's) to reveal law as neither stable, nor unitary, nor rational. Rather, the arbitrariness of legal interpretation and judicial decision-making only compounds law's intimate connection to pain and violence, here again exemplified in apparent outliers and exorbitant cases.

Schmitt and Cover hold much in common that should, at this point, also be familiar. Both thinkers are deeply suspicious of the presumed transparency, order, and naturalness of legal norms, and they set out to divulge law's randomness precisely to interrogate orthodox assumptions about legal authority, challenging the legitimacy taken for granted by liberal reason. Even more, their main apparatus for disabusing law and politics of rationalism is to excavate foundational paradox—paradox that the legal order depends on yet painstakingly masks. Within Schmitt's exception, as elsewhere, paradox therefore serves to effectuate critique, shattering multiple of liberalism's fantasies. Although by interrogating law, those paradoxes of the "extreme" and "exceptional" simultaneously do a lot more, procuring a heightened if esoteric understanding that both Schmitt and Cover liken to an antinomian "miracle."

What Schmitt and Cover thereby generate is another independent framework for hallowing paradox as the cradle of elevated epistemic truth as well as legitimacy—legitimacy that is superior (and often divinatory) precisely in having been gestated in a cauldron of paradox. In certain ways, their thinking attributes even greater constitutive and explanatory force to paradox than Arendt. Whereas for Arendt juridification and legal rule-making reify paradox, for Schmitt and Cover repressed paradox ordains and enables the political as well as law. Plainly put, paradox *is* what catalyzes the sovereignty that bestows legitimacy on politics (again, in a thoroughly irrational relay). Analogous reasoning pervades Schmitt's 1928 *Constitutional Theory*, just as Cover identifies "the risk of pain and death" as the lifeblood of the American Constitutional tradition.[59] From one angle, it might seem far from surprising that especially Schmitt would be seamlessly assimilated into a political theory canon preoccupied with redemptive paradox radiating from Rousseau. But the point is that political theology disseminates its own distinct logic of ontologization that, while intersecting in certain ways with Arendt's propositions, exhibits an even stronger conviction in the world-making power of paradox. Cover and especially Schmitt essentially glory in the irrationalism of the paradoxes that pervade fully political existence. Although all three thinkers differently privilege what law excludes or disavows, for Schmitt and Cover those omissions lay the groundwork for the juridico-political in ways that border on the sacred. Hence, ontological paradox is not really a problem or worry within political theology; to the contrary, it becomes immensely fertile, injecting both law and politics with dynamic energy. Or to recall Schmitt's terms, the decision that founds the sovereign exception "parts here from the legal norm, and (to formulate it paradoxically) its authority proves that to produce law it need not be based on law."[60]

Within political theology, then, ontological paradox for all intents and purposes *is* the ultimate source of legal and political legitimacy. But while Schmitt and Cover's thinking is second nature within much theory, it is one thing to say that politics or law is fated to negotiate chronic paradox, and another to embrace that irrationalism as its own ephemeral yet governing explanatory principle and authority. This is the sort of etherealizing transfiguration that the next chapter explores in depth. Such reasoning mystifies if not mythologizes the origins of law and politics (which is often exactly the point).[61] But in Schmitt's hands, that hypothesis regarding the vertiginously foundationless foundations of politics can come perilously close to rationalizing not only such magical thinking but also troubling eschewals of law and its guarantees. Despite Schmitt's insistence on the situationalism of political decision-making, moreover, his metrics have proven attractive precisely because they can seem to include virtually anything.

Biopolitics and the Totalization of Paradox

Biopolitical theory is another case in point. In many ways, the main project of biopolitics is to propound its own unique diagnosis of modernity—a diagnosis that erects legal-political paradox into a full-blown "paradigm," in Giorgio Agamben's lexicon. With that diagnosis, biopolitics also offers a textbook exhibition of how the logic of paradox can broker facile homologies and convergences, metastasizing into a type of crypto-universalism. As an explanatory framework, theory like Agamben's combines many of the suppositions considered above into a particularly malignant cocktail that, given biopolitics' preoccupation with law, has been enormously influential within recent humanities-based and other critical work on legal and political matters, exacerbating a predisposed anti-legalism. With its fixation on World War II, fascism, and the Holocaust, biopolitical thought also amplifies whatever fatalism might be attributed to work like Schmitt's. Clearly extremist, this defeatism further derives from the reflex to substantialize not merely negative but fully genocidal conditions of paradox, vesting that quality with a deadly actuality. Such a mode of ontologization thus compounds the stakes of paradox as a diagnosis, beyond multiplying its lethal ramifications imbuing it with a gravitational pull capable of engulfing (at least within Agamben's thought) essentially all of contemporary reality.

One explanation for biopolitical theory's allure extends from the ready exportability of Agamben's main analytics. "Bare life," "the camp," sovereignty, the "state of exception" (notions drawn from not only Arendt, Schmitt, and Foucault but also Walter Benjamin): those heuristics have served to digest an impressive array of topics and scenarios. This is a syndrome Agamben's thought actively encourages, for instance as *Homo Sacer: Sovereign Power and Bare Life* explicitly analogizes the persecution of Jews leading up to the Holocaust to "the *zones d'attentes* [waiting rooms] in French international airports."[62] Likely not surprising by now, what allows Agamben to collapse those measurably distinct realities into a single, undifferentiated phenomenon is precisely his position that paradox is, in his terms, the "hidden matrix" underwriting all modern institutions of citizenship and rights. Agamben does not deny that his agenda is to generalize damning paradox onto all of modern political existence; his main thesis is that biopolitics represents modernity's defining logic and unavoidable destination.

Much of Agamben's work orbits around one of Schmitt's key concepts that Agamben similarly treats as an insignia of sovereignty: the exception. The first chapter of *Homo Sacer* opens with a section, "The Paradox of Sovereignty," wherein Agamben conceives biopolitical modernity as inaugurated by an act of exclusion that simultaneously produces the circumstances of "bare life." Like Arendt, Agamben is foremost interested in exceptions to citizenship and national belonging, even while he both broadens and refines Arendt's midcentury recognitions. Above all for Agamben, that axis of *ex*clusion inseverably *in*cludes, producing an indeterminacy (or "zone of irreducible indistinction") that renders the borders of the political community perennially mobile, porous, and uncertain.[63] His terms "bare life" and "state of exception" are devised to index those liminal "zones" of constant slippage, while marshaling his idiosyncratic take on the structural-ontological violence of modernity. For Agamben, those evanescent "thresholds" in particular render totalitarianism an ongoing threat: he thus declares an "inner solidarity between democracy and totalitarianism" that causes "Nazism and fascism [to] remain stubbornly with us."[64] As the next chapter explores, for Cold War thinkers it was standard to foreground the intimate proximity of those seemingly opposing political forms. Agamben therefore leverages an established schema for conceptualizing totalitarianism: one that understands its logic both to suppress and to capitalize on conditions of paradox. Yet within biopolitics, primary of those paradoxes ripe for fascist manipulation is the fundamental confusion between inclusion and exclusion that, while reaching its apogee within the programs of denationalization leading up to the Holocaust, continues to endanger the legal categories of citizenship and rights in the present. If we want to comprehend either totalitarianism or political atrocity, for Agamben we must therefore begin with the exclusionary paradox at stake in the state of exception—a paradox Agamben's reasoning quite consciously globalizes.

While echoing a number of theoretical commonplaces, Agamben also totalizes many aspects of whatever affinities might connect his reasoning with that of his interlocutors, including to enlarge their anti-legalism. For instance, an absolutization of mortal paradox structures Agamben's account of "the camp," which for him represents "the paradigm of modernity." For Agamben, we must "regard the camp not as a historical fact and an anomaly belonging to the past (even if still verifiable) but in some way as the hidden matrix and *nomos* of the political space in which we are still living."[65] Far from an aberration, the Holocaust becomes a natural and inevitable outgrowth of modern (bio)politics: an archetypal event laying bare the decisive features, or ontology, of all our legal and political systems.[66] To be sure, this instinct to endow the limit case with paramount importance—or to regard an apparent exception as foundational—is inherited from Schmitt. But when deemed *the* face of modernity, that case is universalized—in a move with enormously troubling implications. First, genocide and mass atrocity (rather than for Cover martyrdom or capital sentences) become ever-lurking possibilities, lying in wait within every political and legal institution. Second, extreme cases like the Holocaust become pregnant with consummate meaning, containing the secret to ontological puzzles riddling biopolitical modernity as a whole. Hence, biopolitical thought can seem to gaze upon the Holocaust and other barbarity with more than fascination but rather an expectation of supreme discernment. Third, when deemed the infrastructure of modernity, events like Holocaust also come to be normalized, almost belying a

Schmittian emphasis on the norm's exception. Thus routinized, fourth, the abyss made manifest in the concentration camp becomes determinant in ways that govern all of politics, stalking even democratic, rights-respecting institutions and practices.[67]

It is crucial to recognize that Agamben's hyperbolic views are directly dictated by his principle that lethal paradox is ontological. Hence, despite arriving at rather extravagant positions, Agamben largely relies on what are widely ascribed to, if not theoretically ubiquitous, analytic assumptions and moves—which is to say that Agamben merely embroiders upon a range of seemingly innocuous staples of theory. Precisely his reasoning's representative status should therefore alert us to pitfalls broadly haunting theory comparatively overinvested in a structuralism and/or foundationalism of paradox. For instance, recall that sovereignty (the locus of law and politics) not only emerges from but itself *is a* paradox. *Homo Sacer* begins by clarifying that its driving inquiry concerns the "paradox" that "Western politics first constitutes itself through an exclusion (which is simultaneously an inclusion) of bare life."[68] On one level, this sort of insight is so pro forma as to border on a truism. Yet on another, Agamben's paradoxes of exclusion are, first, entirely toxic and, second, exhaustive, causing that category of bare life to deterministically subsume nearly everything into its vortex. Given those dual ingredients, it should not be shocking that mortal paradox would infiltrate all of modernity's bequests, including democracy and rights. But at the same time, Agamben's positions are plainly tautological: the existence of political evil proves that political evil will be constitutive, in a circle of self-reinforcing paradox. So although Agamben's conclusions are especially panoramic, his thought's affinities with less catastrophizing schools of thought nevertheless divulges the categorical, totalizing premises that are latent if unacknowledged in a lot of contemporary theory.

In a different sense, Agamben's work also epitomizes what occurs when a diagnosis of paradox plays too many roles at once, overseeing all stages and facets of the reasoning process—much as within renditions of modernity. Like many, Agamben starts with a less-than-remarkable account of why the tragic failures of rights proved particularly bloody during World War II: that diagnosis, we've seen, singles out and incriminates the foundational paradox of exclusion. At first, paradox thereby furnishes Agamben with a trenchant angle on the mystery of how and why the same era that first incorporated human rights into law also witnessed their mind-boggling decimation. Beyond that preliminary finding, however, Agamben vests paradox with a suite of interwoven functions. As elsewhere, paradox encodes a critique, a methodological framework, repressed truths about modernity, and, when all is said and done, a foregone and relentless conclusion. The unearthing of hidden paradox not only lubricates Agamben's riveting theory; it represents its denouement. Yet while Agamben's viewpoint is bleak if not cynical, it is only when already methodologically omnipresent and all-controlling within a surrounding intellectual formation that paradox can thus be amassed into an omnibus theory: into an ontology that sees the guises of, here *deadly*, paradox absolutely everywhere. Hence, the lineaments of Agamben's thinking, we will see again and again, are incredibly common.

As suggested, Agamben further aggrandizes both the anti-legalism and rights skepticism that have been broadly espoused. Like Arendt, Agamben argues that the legalization of rights, or their formalization in law, actively invited the Holocaust to happen. As Agamben puts it, "Fascism and Nazism are, above all, redefinitions of the relations between man and citizen, and become fully intelligible only when situated—no matter how paradoxical it may seem—in the biopolitical context inaugurated by national sovereignty and declarations of rights."[69] Put bluntly, what ushers in biopolitics as an epoch? Without the codification of rights in law, Agamben effectively submits, the Holocaust never would have happened. Rather than a stave against genocide, the legalization of rights proved a particularly hospitable enabling condition. The coterminous flourishing of rights and of genocide consequently poses not merely a "perplexity" (as for Arendt) but instead a total social fact. A blueprint for the Holocaust, rights engineered genocide precisely by making legal—and therefore substantial and concrete—the ephemeral "zones of indistinction" that perforate the juridical categories of citizen and man. It is surely hard to imagine a more ruinous condemnation of rights or of their paradoxes.

As if this were not enough, Agamben distributes these fatalities onto the entire edifice of juridicality and law. As Alexander Weheliye explains, Agamben is "possessed by law" and villainizes it to an astonishing degree.[70] In part, this is because Agamben renders encyclopedic a structure of analysis that Schmitt confined to the sovereign exception and Cover to the extreme case, blanketing *all* of legality with such terms. At once, it is a structuralization of symmetrical sites of paradox that facilitates Agamben's movement from the isolated case to the entire legal system, including to philosophical notions like rights. Precisely this mirroring of cognate paradoxes allows biopolitical theory to traffic freely between the local and the global. As a result, Agamben can extract lessons from the Holocaust deemed pertinent to *all* law and to *all* citizenship practices, although only by simultaneously (and paradoxically) infinitizing and normalizing that event along the way.[71] So despite evincing an antipathy to law congenital to theory, Agamben's circular reasoning (like Arendt's) entirely foreordains the law's authorship of evil. Perhaps most distressing, then, is Agamben's argument that legalization will booby-trap even democratic systems, rigging even the best efforts at democracy to succumb to a preprogrammed biopolitical destiny. Any superficially rights-respecting legal culture or society ultimately carries a susceptibility to the Holocaust within its chromosomal makeup.

To be sure, these sorts of homologies make a certain sense in theory aiming to capture the full and unspeakable horror of organized violence, whether the Holocaust's factories of mass death or the technological warfare that the midcentury also perfected. But the simultaneously categorical and overly accommodating nature of Agamben's heuristics allows for sweeping, facile, and sometimes alarming generalities, all with the effect of prophesying genocide as modernity's only foreseeable horizon. It is by linking merely concurrent incidents (the coterminous rise of human rights and of fascism) that Agamben discerns universal truths within what are more accurately accidents of proximity. And while those synergies are transfixing, they also let Agamben off the hook, sanctioning a striking lapse of imagination. Because if cosmic paradox dictates any and all legal-political questions, Agamben need not undertake the sorts of normative, evaluative considerations ordinarily used to distinguish one site of injustice from another. In effect, his foundationalism of deadly paradox dissolves the possibility that divergent vectors or instances of oppression might *not* be fungible. While arguably typifying the antireformist mentality of a lot theory, Agamben's morass of totalizing paradox ultimately obviates any need to contemplate improvements or alterations to our existing legal and political institutions, since any viable surrogate would be just as quickly devoured by deadly paradox. As such, the albeit inflated propositions of biopolitics are nevertheless worrisomely indicative of a household resistance to the drawing of normative lines and to differential analysis.

Despite being overblown, Agamben's suspicion of law and related impulse to universalize the exclusionary paradoxes of rights have therefore been the bread and butter of theory well beyond the environs of biopolitics. In fact, Agamben's basic premises underlie most, if not nearly all, critiques of law that zero in on its constitutive exclusions and double binds, predisposing those critiques to arrive at comparatively exaggerated conclusions. As one example, Werner Hamacher's essay "The Rights to Have Rights (Four-and-a-Half Remarks)" offers a characteristic snapshot of reasoning that samples from the human rights theory canon to support its eventual assertions. Genu-flecting toward Arendt in his title, Hamacher also enlists Marx to corroborate the (by now tired) view that rights are "paradoxical, self-contradictory, and possibly self-defeating in their definition."[72] Further predictably, Hamacher construes those paradoxes in global terms, deeming them "fundamental and unresolvable,"[73] and he describes legalization as a particularly "horrendous paradox," echoing (without citing) Agamben. Hamacher explains:

> According to their internal structure, the "rights of man"—as private rights and rights of property and protection—are thus elements of a law of international civil war, in which the enemy can be declared to be a criminal, a nonhuman, a "rogue," or "scum of the earth." In the concentration and extermination camps, the essential content of human rights—its antisocial and antihuman and thus suicidal content—made itself manifest. These camps are, in every meaning of the word, the end, not only of human rights and thereby of rights in general, but also the end of the possibility of conceiving of what is called "man" within legal concepts.

Dystopian, Hamacher's assessment of rights prompts him to speculate whether "far more terrifying epochs" than World War II are yet on the horizon. However, such a sinister worldview only becomes semi-automatic when paradox is ontologized into a "structural and historical fact," which, thus accomplished, allows Hamacher to decisively condemn rights as "un-redeemable" artifacts of the "antihuman" and of Marx's "antisocial" man.[74]

Not coincidentally, Hamacher follows this denunciation of specifically juridified rights by appealing to a messianically "open" and antinomian "right to have rights" that resists codification—anticipating the countervailing instincts taken up by the next chapter. For now, it is enough to observe, here too, the ways thoroughgoing anti-legalism can stunt one's vision. When paradox infects everything, of course it will foreclose alternatives—although not without inducing imaginative enfeeblement, if not full-blown paraly-sis. When a finding of paradox acts as *both* the invitation *and* the upshot of theory, of course its ontological certainty will occlude other angles of seeing, contributing to forms of intellectual inertia. Scapegoating law thus becomes too easy, distracting attention from the vastly more complicated, subtle, multivariable dynamics surrounding many real-world injustices.

At the same time, analytics like Agamben's (whether bare life or the camp) are so open-ended and capacious as to allow one to discover biopo-litical "truths" in virtually any phenomena, which surely helps to explain his wide following. While sensationalizing ordinary aspects of modern life, rendering them terrifying (if thrilling) portents of the biopolitical, Agamben's metrics are simultaneously so commodious that they cease to tell us much of anything. Whether airport security or police brutality, the facts of modern existence slot all too easily into biopolitical categories—expediting the work of totalization that Agamben's own analysis sets in motion—however not without creating slippages that can, indeed, make evil look banal. When all is said and done, a simplistic determinism thus takes hold, as Agamben's biopolitical categories can start to seem pre-fabricated, guaranteed to be replenished by an endless parade of horribles. And given law's structural disposition to forsake even noble aspirations like those accompanying rights, a similarly disastrous outcome would presumably befall any good faith attempt to do better.

The Anti-legalism of Theory

Biopolitical thought probably represents the acme (or, more accurately, the nadir) of the impetus to ontologize—and, in the process, routinize—fatal paradox. Yet the basic topography of reasoning like Agamben's is deeply engraved in the theoretical landscape. Within many fields, it is settled if tacit doctrine that law and legal institutions deserve vigilant and unflagging critique, breeding a skepticism further understood to implicate a gamut of associated terminologies (liberalism and neoliberalism, rationalism and reason, institutionalism, instrumentalism, conformity, morality, hierarchy, discipline, normativity and normalization, reform and progress, and many others). While ensuing chapters explore additional bases for this posture, thinking like Agamben's has fostered an at times paralyzing fear that recourse to law will trigger automatic self-betrayal or selling out. As Wendy Brown and Janet Halley preface the volume *Left Legalism / Left Critique*, "submitting left projects to the terms of liberal legalism translates the former into the terms of the latter, a translation which will necessarily introduce tensions with, and sometimes outright cancellations of, the originating aims that animate left legalism in the first place."[75] In such a vein are the channels of law presumed invariably to sully, if not to ruin, otherwise valuable or ethically minded ideals and endeavors.

This skepticism has been particularly acute within critical race theory—and in many ways for good reasons. In the American context, the institution of property has (given Marx's legacy) naturally offered a recurring target and placeholder for everything seen as broken in the legal system. Hence,

Stephen Best's *The Fugitive's Properties: Law and the Poetics of Possession* asserts, "Slavery is not simply an antebellum institution that the United States has surpassed but a particular historical *form* of an ongoing crisis involving the subjection of personhood to property."[76] Saidiya Hartman's *Scenes of Subjection: Terror, Slavery, and Self-Making in Nineteenth-Century America* similarly charges: "The question persists as to whether it is possible to unleash freedom from the history of property that secured it, for the security of property that undergirded the abstract equality of rights bearers was achieved, in large measure, through black bondage."[77]

While little doubt exists whether property law or frankly the entire American legal system protected if not invented slavery as an institution, such reasoning extends those crimes far and wide, much as Hartman amplifies her indictment of property to cover everything from US constitutionalism, "the liberty of contract," rights (submitting that rights directly "facilitate[ed] relations of domination"), legal personhood, and more.[78] Here, too, it is true that historians have all too thoroughly documented the use of deceptive contracts to dupe illiterate blacks into signing away their rights and thereby consenting to debt peonage and other forms of bondage during Reconstruction, producing what Douglas A. Blackmon terms "slavery by another name."[79] Relatedly, the carceral state and Michelle Alexander's account of "the New Jim Crow" offer a trove of evidence demonstrating the legal system to be horribly biased.[80]

However, the logic of ontologization blankets essentially *all* legal practices with these and other residues of indeed widespread yet nevertheless historically specific injustices, among other things creating the illusion that an unbroken narrative connects slavery to the prison industrial complex. While not to dispute the explanatory power of such accounts, the analytic sway of paradox can fully demand certain elisions—fast at risk of becoming reductive. Formulaic, such critiques furthermore proceed through what are, for us, a sequence of boilerplate steps and assumptions. For example, the entry for "Property" in the 2007 *Keywords for American Cultural Studies* walks through what we can recognize as a sequence of stock moves that often spell forms of determinism. The entry's author, Grace Kyungwon Hong, explains:

> The keyword "property" thus indexes a contradiction between the ostensible universal endowment of the rights to property for all US citizens and the uneven actualization of that right through forms of racial and gender dispossession. US culture is a crucial site where this contradiction is managed, troubled, and destabilized. Diverse cultural artifacts and

practices disavow this contradiction, even as they serve as sites where the histories of the propertyless can be articulated.[81]

Less a definition than a critique, Hong's entry begins by pinpointing a "contradiction" intrinsic to property, which both law and culture are charged with "managing" and "disavowing." Those deceptions expose property to be "uneven" and predicated on "forms of dispossession" that "belie the ostensible universality of propertied citizenship" (in other words, that derive from citizenship's exclusions). Over its course, Hong's entry walks through a series of other such contradictions infecting property, support for which she finds in not only Marx but also texts like Cheryl Harris's "Whiteness as Property."[82] Once uncovered, moreover, contradiction is expected almost instantaneously to "trouble" and "destabilize" an institution so vast as property. Spearheading her method, Hong thus identifies contradiction as *both* a constitutive feature of property *and* the answer to that institution's historical and contemporary wrongdoing. It should not be unexpected that, just as this assessment overtakes Hong's thinking, it would be absolutized to govern property through and through. Although Hong's commitment to documenting technologies of structural oppression like property is clearly worthwhile, her reasoning exhibits the telltale signs—and limits—of the logic of ontologization.

Another pillar of anti-legalistic critique has been to inculpate legal *reason*, including specific procedural and/or argumentative tools, within the production of structural injustice. This approach of course descends from its own multistranded genealogy, whether Frankfurt School concerns about instrumental reason or Max Weber's "iron cage" of rationalization or defenses of the humanities that accentuate their anti-instrumental tenor (see chapter 4). [83] In a garden variety statement of such thinking, Lisa Marie Cacho's *Social Death: Racialized Rightlessness and the Criminalization of the Unprotected* builds on Orlando Patterson's seminal 1982 *Slavery and Social Death* to show how contemporary American practices of criminalization consign populations stigmatized by race and class to a permanently illegal status.[84] Naturally for Cacho, these conditions are neither random nor intermittent; rather, they "*form the foundation* of the US legal system, imagined to be the reason why a punitive (in)justice system exists."[85] Here again seizing on the exclusions animating law, Cacho understands law to actively depend on such exceptions that it strategically exploits in labeling certain groups "unable to comply with the 'rule of law'" and therefore "ineligible for personhood"—with the net effect of granting objective, substantialized force to biases that might, under other circumstances, have remained purely hypothetical but for being legally set in stone.[86] Personified, law possesses something akin to volition within Cacho's study, as she explains: "Law ensures that there will always be a population of color rendered permanently rightless in the United States."[87]

Cacho extends this familiar line of attack to specific mechanisms of legal reasoning, which are similarly accused of active authorship of oppression. "Valuation" is for Cacho particularly pernicious, since value is "made intelligible relationally" and requires negative othering.[88] In zero-sum fashion, the prospects of any given social group are thus imagined only to be augmented by the inverse disfavoring of others, a concern that Cacho proceeds to broaden to argue that any and all analysis reliant on "valuation" will therefore unwittingly work to condone inequality. Cacho analogously impugns "legibility" for its inherently othering ramifications, although she warns, "there is no way out of these dilemmas." Even more noteworthy is Cacho's account of how law reconciles these and other exceptions to its purported ideals: its criminalization of black lives is wholly necessary to "[make] sense of the contradictions that ensue when according unequal access to legal universality."[89] In other words, law's omissions are a direct corollary of its need to quell the contradictions that jeopardize its stated principles, at the same time as those oppressions are what circularly introduce contradiction into the legal system to begin with. Taken for granted, then, is the notion that legal reasoning is ultimately a grand masquerade aimed at camouflaging the contradictions that are the handiwork of power. Yet notwithstanding Cacho's biting critiques, her suspicion of the tools of reason corners her into a strident antinormativity. In fact, she actively advocates a politics of "unthinkability" wherein "the critical task is *not* to resolve the contradictions."[90]

So ingrained is such anti-legalism that even scholarship disputing core tenets of biopolitics clings to the stance. For instance, many of Weheliye's reservations about biopolitics voiced in *Habeas Viscus: Racializing Assemblages, Biopolitics, and Black Feminist Theories of the Human* are highly incisive. Weheliye powerfully denounces Agamben's sidelining of race, accusing him of "largely occlude[ing] race as a critical category of analysis," and laments how a Schmittian emphasis on the exceptional erases the mundane, low-grade, pervasive nature of much Black suffering.[91] Notwithstanding these objections, Weheliye ups the ante on other aspects of the very logic he claims to reject. In particular, law and legality are viewed with a suspicion just as intense as Agamben's, despite Weheliye's complaint that Agamben suffers from a dearth of imaginable alternatives to the existing legal-political order. Perhaps not surprisingly given Weheliye's focus on race, the primary root of law's toxicity lies with the institution of property, which for Weheliye colonizes law so comprehensively as to reduce all legal membership to forms of (self-) ownership. As Weheliye charges, "the benefit accrued through the juridical acknowledgment of racialized subjects as fully human often exacts a steep entry price, because inclusion hinges on accepting the codification of personhood as property."[92] Recalling Agamben, Weheliye, too, regards law's dynamics of inclusion-exclusion as primary.

Like Cacho, Weheliye assigns special blame to distinct faculties of legal reasoning, although he foremost charges "comparison" (which Cacho favors) and "calculability" with meting out unjust effects. Whereas calculability ranks "some forms of humanity [as] more exceptional than others," comparison "merely reaffirm[s] Man's existing hierarchies."[93] Effectively condemning the rudiments of legal reason for *both* instating new paradoxes of exclusion *and* excusing pre-existing ones, Weheliye ends up issuing another sweeping indictment of law. With utter indifference to either history or context, the entire legal system is envisioned as a single, heavy-handed monolith devoid of either internal diversity or mechanisms of checks and balances. Thus totalized, law becomes Law, and Weheliye can subsume *Dred Scott* and contemporary intellectual property decisions into one and the same explanatory matrix. If the historical wrongs accompanying the institution of property sully all law, and if virtually any legal decision remotely concerning property is the offspring of *Dred Scott*, then naturally law will be synonymous with injustice. Woefully divorced from its real-world practice, law for Weheliye becomes little more than a crudely drawn straw man.

Both Cacho and Weheliye succumb to other logical missteps, with their certainty that all legal reasoning will engineer oppression. As we have seen, both mistake merely incidental analytic tools (i.e., calculability) as causally determinative, and they aggrandize others (i.e., hierarchization) to deem them *both* primary *and* independently sufficient for the perpetration of injustice. However, such reasoning cherry-picks one or two components of the complex architecture of racism through history and assigns them with disproportionate blame. While acts of differentiation (or calculation, or valuation) may indeed condone racism in some cases, those logics are neither integral nor controlling nor the primary impetus underlying racist behavior. Likewise, the fact that a given intellectual faculty has been conscripted to pardon injustice in certain (or even many) scenarios neither completely bankrupts it nor diminishes its yield in other contexts. Needless to say, one could readily imagine countless cases of discrimination in which those devices play either a negligible or nonexistent role. What results, then, is that Cacho and Weheliye criminalize the very intellectual resources urgently needed to combat structural oppression: to isolate, document, substantiate, measure, and penalize racism and its harms. Their conviction in paradox jettisons key resources in the critical armory: intellectual resources arguably best equipped to evaluate and condemn racism, including to disentangle its many diverse incarnations.

Another side effect of such categorical thinking is that rights, citizenship, political membership, and other legal entitlements are understood to exist in a zero-sum game: imagined to be distributed according to a finitely subdividable pool or pie. As Cacho wagers, any group's increase in power will immediately and proportionately detract from the net social gains, assets, and opportunities of others. However, that logic also rests on a set of faulty statistical warrants ancillary to outmoded theories of socioeconomics. No doubt, equally questionable assumptions inform Weheliye's alternative to the pessimism of biopolitical theory: an antinomian vision of messianically deferred justice. Thereby embracing a different kind of fantastical thinking, Weheliye champions the exact inverse or antithesis of the logics that he censures. Weheliye neatly substitutes "calculation" with an extrajuridical mode of "incalculability," lauding the latter as the horizon of ethics. Such patently either/or, binaristic thought itself provides an alibi for Weheliye's avoidance of the fine-tuned normative distinctions that are the fabric of real-world legal-political decision-making and justice-oriented practice.

As suggested, ontologizing paradox can in fact be an important and effective strategy for making visible the enormity and intractability of structural oppression, as for Cacho and Weheliye. Indeed, capturing the scale and resilience of racial injustice, including the legal system's entanglements with it, is the chief goal of their work. Similarly do their critiques of legal reason endeavor to outflank thinking that might dismiss or minimize structural violence as isolated, happenstance, or occasional—and conversely to dramatize why individualized cases must be grasped as inevitable, predetermined outgrowths of an unjust system so vast and consuming it can be hard to imagine its defeat or undoing. Relatedly does the ontologization of paradox stymie any temptation to write off certain injuries as purely abstract or symbolic; Cacho and Weheliye catalogue the ways subjective bias is constantly objectivized to inflict concrete wounds carrying material effects.

Yet for all the consciousness-raising virtues of such work, it should give us pause, and on numerous grounds. As I've detailed, such reasoning has instilled a striking intellectual-methodological uniformity, as study after study reproduces a set roster of conclusions that, taken together, mutually reinforce one another's collective wisdom. Its tautological character can entail formulaic views, causing (for some, lethal) paradox to become a fait accompli. Theories that ontologize contradiction and paradox usually do so to protest the failures of purportedly just-universal principles (like legal personhood or rights)—although only to end up inadvertently universalizing those very betrayals and disappointments, treating paradox as constitutive in ways that globalize its tragic effects. Such a dire outlook can surely breed fatigue if not cynicism: if damning paradox pre-programs the whole legal system, how can one possibly change a thing? If even nominally egalitarian and aspirational principles like rights are certain to backfire, why bother trying?

As the book's final chapter submits, insistence on chronic paradox ultimately shuts down normative analysis—which, we've seen, is often the whole point. Doctrinal in many fields, the optics of paradox (again, often intentionally) work to blur if not elide the sorts of fine-tuned, meaningfully qualitative distinctions that are ordinarily necessary to separate one manifestation of a given phenomenon from another. Those sorts of granular differences come to be dwarfed by the totalizing structure—and, frankly, by the omnipresence of paradox itself. Precisely when aggrandized does the logic of paradox thus short-circuit the types of reason-based, evaluative, comparative labor on which, it should go without saying, intellectual life depends. Again, for many, this mutiny of the normative is overt and knowing, but it can take a disastrous toll on any kind of praxis, leaving theory strangely unmoored from the very legal-political crises it purports to navigate.

Finally, we should observe the extent to which such thinking tends to rest on caricatured, falsifying accounts of law—accounts similarly cut off from the real world. Those clichéd, unidimensional ideas about law and its workings certainly render law a ready target.[94] But when law becomes a paper tiger, the activity of critique also becomes far too easy, delivering outcomes that are facile in their predictability. The modes of anti-legalism this book continues to confront have indeed become tacit and unthinking: a rote stance that—while reconfirmed by study after study after study—doesn't really tell us much of anything about either law or the complex circuitry that perpetuates real-world oppression. Yet what *is* guaranteed is that the critical theorist "always wins," playing "good cop" relative not only to a broken legal system but also to mainstream legal scholarship, which gets charged with an almost identical slate of offenses as legalism proper. The same basis for scapegoating law—namely, its perceived indifference to the all-enveloping status of paradox—is simultaneously finessed as the main crime of the untheoretical scholar.

Conclusion

This chapter has sought to account for certain origins—as well as liabilities—of the dual orthodoxies of rights skepticism and anti-legalistic critique. In many ways, the sheer number of arteries that feed, and thereby nourish, those entwined positions has caused suspicion of law to function as a left intellectual nostrum. Rather than a mere symptom of antinormativity, the veins of anti-legalism run deep, in part because that stance is underwritten (and, indeed, required) by methodological investment in contradiction and paradox. The conceit that rights were fledged in paradox has been partner to a corresponding instinct to ontologize that determination—in extreme cases, leading to a universalization of the most troubling flaws of rights and of the legal system together.

This view that structural contradiction and paradox offer a framework for deciphering rights' many limits can therefore be blinding. This chapter has studied the provenance of such thinking precisely to begin to reckon with its shortcomings, occlusions, and other conceptual errors. Chapter 3 instead examines an alternate yet just as influential approach to the proliferating paradoxes of rights, an approach that burgeoned during the "theory era" in the Anglo-American academy. Importantly, this divergent mode of analysis disputes *neither* the fundamentally paradoxical character of rights *nor* the decisive importance of rights' exclusionary anatomy. Rather, it responds to the same midcentury debacles of rights that preoccupied the thinkers here by recruiting paradox to conduct a very different kind of intellectual labor. Instead of viewing constitutive paradox as deadening or frozen, the body of thought we'll turn to next finds within that logic transfigural, metamorphic, and kinetic virtuosities. Many of those dynamic properties are borrowed from literary criticism, as the intervening interlude first shows.

Interlude

ANATOMY OF PARADOX, OR A BRIEF
HISTORY OF AESTHETIC THEORY

It is clear that criticism cannot be a systematic study unless there is a quality in literature which enables it to be so. —Northrop Frye, *Anatomy of Criticism* (1957)

As the tumult of ideas that came to be known as "theory" traveled through the Anglo-American academy, among those ideas' first way stations were language and literature departments. Encamping there, that body of thought naturally annexed certain preoccupations of those fields—in particular, with the literary or aesthetic. To be sure, many giants of Continental theory, whether Nietzsche or Heidegger or Sartre, had either composed or looked to literature and art as a type of philosophical muse. But with the linguistic turn and other intellectual developments of the 1970s, distinctive habits of reasoning adapted from literary and aesthetic criticism were absorbed and thereafter disseminated as methodological staples of theory. Those habits of analysis swiftly permeated discussions not only of art but also of less obviously literary phenomena like democracy and rights and modernity and the fate of the humanities.

A shared economy of paradox lubricated that traffic. Paradoxes of rights (for instance) were explained as cognate to, and thus suffused with the same energies as, paradoxes long understood by literary critics to animate art and literature. Later chapters further explore the complex historical juncture that saw theory explode onto the scene and that invested the logic of paradox with unprecedented and enduring currency. But why were theorists from other disciplines drawn to schemes for reckoning with paradox that literary critics had crafted? What exactly did theory assimilate when it harnessed a logic of paradox tailored to explain the exceptional qualities of art and literature? What crises and conundrums has that grammar served to manage? And, of course, what have been the virtues as well as liabilities of such cross-pollination?

A fleeting moment in Jacques Derrida's pivotal 1976 "Declarations of Independence" (published in 1986) can help us begin to answer these questions. This short text that chartered Derrida's turn to politics and law reproduces, in a type of aside, lines from the French poet Francis Ponge's brief poem "Fable." The impetus for this citation is Derrida's meditation on the "fabulous" nature of the signature appended to declarations of rights. For Derrida, that signature serves a paradoxical function, *both* constituting rights *and* through that constitutional act founding the subject capable of performatively undertaking such a gesture. Beyond this context, Derrida's recitation of the opening of Ponge's poem is left unexplicated: "By the word *by* begins thus this text / Of which the first line says the truth ... [*Par le mot par commence donc ce text / Dont la premiere ligne dit la vérité ...*]."[1]

With this reference, Derrida does more than appeal to artistic creativity or to literary language per se in order to reflect upon the peculiar status of rights. He also evokes long-standing debates about the truth claims of fictions. As Ponge's poem notes, literature tells lies; yet much of its power simultaneously derives from those charlatan, questionable bearings upon the objectively real or true. This conceit that poetry poses a "liar's paradox" possesses an illustrious lineage—one as old as aesthetic criticism itself. Reaching back as far as Plato's "ancient quarrel" between poetry and philosophy, literary critics ever since have sparred over the meaning and consequences of Plato's charge that poetry represents "mere imitation," asking how art should respond to its perennial crisis of legitimacy. What to do with the fact that the evidentiary claims of literature will be, at best, fraught and uncertain?

In applying Ponge's riff on Plato to rights, Derrida certainly underscores their constructed, artificial nature. In addition, he activates a storied tradition of exalting "paradox" as art's sine qua non. Indeed, it can feel virtually impossible to find canonical accounts of aesthetic experience that do not point to paradox as the essence of what makes the literary *literary*. Even thinkers like the New Critics were celebrants of paradox, manifest in the opening chapter of Cleanth Brooks's 1947 masterpiece *The Well Wrought Urn*, titled "The Language of Paradox." Today, paradox is so fundamental to ideas about the literary-aesthetic that it can be hard to describe the decisive qualities of literature or art without drawing from some such grammar, even while, given aesthetic theory's variety and breadth, the many things paradox denotes can sometimes appear a heterogeneous jumble. Over the centuries (if not millennia), paradox has provided a vocabulary for talking about art's epiphanies, dialecticism, play, singularity, critical edge, dissidence, double meanings, elusiveness, bounty, exuberance, structure, form, style, distinctive language, and on and on the list goes. Yet amid that hodgepodge, belief in paradox has provided a unifying creed: a source of agreement that congregates literary and aesthetic criticism as a field even while telegraphing different features of art for different thinkers (and sometimes a panoply of things all together).

On one level, Derrida's nod to Ponge (and to Plato) launders rights with art's plentiful paradoxes precisely to imbue them with those world-making capacities. As others have noted, especially in the French Ponge's lines are "metapoetic."[2] Aurally, "by the word *by*" [*Par le mot* par] could be mistaken for "Go word *go*!," reflexively likening the creativity of literary language to the exhortatory rhetoric found in revolutionary rights declarations. Both art and rights, Derrida reminds us, give birth to new realities. The qualifier "*ce*" is equally ambiguous, translatable as either "this" or "that." "That text" accordingly might be an allusion to the biblical acts of creation opening the Book of Genesis or, alternatively, to theodicy, a genre that wrestles with the quandary of why an infinitely good God would allow worldly suffering. On another level, however, it is by inflecting rights with the aesthetic that Derrida effectuates a metamorphosis. Like countless others pitching fights with Plato over the centuries, Derrida ultimately embraces his liar's paradox of art, in reasoning that converts what might, at first blush, appear a failing ("fiction's lie") into a reservoir of bottomless potential. Another recurring theme within literary history's *longue durée* is this impulse to champion what Plato leveled as a curse: to rhapsodize Plato's complaint as the locus of art's preeminent value. Perhaps *the* primary language and logic for doing so has been paradox.

Derrida's moves are by now doctrinal definitive of theory as a genre and mode. By enlisting aesthetics to decipher rights, Derrida thus joins a lengthy line of thinkers who have similarly leveraged expectations for paradox ingrained within aesthetic theory to contend with dilemmas of law and politics. In theoretical circles today, there are well-established frameworks for grappling with paradoxes of legal-political authority that transpose the conventions of aesthetic criticism onto those arenas. These homologies, as later chapters show, are methodologically hardwired: today taken for granted. And while influences like the Cold War and the residues of 1960s-style radicalism have enhanced such thinking's purchase, its conventions are at bottom borrowed from theology and aesthetics. Paradoxes distinct to politics, law, the modern university, pedagogy, activism, and more have consequently been routed through a conceptual machinery that was first refined within literary criticism.

What exactly transpired with this borrowing is the subject of later chapters. For now, this interlude investigates the factors that made literary criticism ripe for transport. What rendered that tradition's conventions, especially its approaches to paradox, attractive to theorists working in other fields? Why were metrics for denominating the distinguishing features of art so readily grafted onto other only nominally "aesthetic" or "creative" matters—albeit matters comparatively confounded by paradox? Most important, what diverse properties of art has the language of paradox so poignantly channeled? How has it not only lasted, surviving for centuries and through dramatic upheavals of thought to remain a potent discourse for distilling the experience of art, but also gained heightened popularity in the late twentieth century? At the same time, allegiance to paradox can appear to dictate membership within the aesthetic theory canon; what thinkers, theories, texts, and facets of the literary has it stifled—written off as unworthy of serious, scholarly attention?

THE TRUTH CLAIMS OF ART. In their love for paradox, one might conclude that critics of art and literature are more Plato's progeny than Aristotle's. If there is one thing literary studies near uniformly rejects, it is Aristotle's principle of noncontradiction, or the law that contradictory propositions cannot simultaneously be true. Arguably nothing is more alien to the epistemology of paradox than such a tenet. In contrast, critics today inherit numerous instincts from Plato, even while persistently calling his conclusions into question. Indeed, one could easily narrate the span of literary history as a succession of efforts to rescue poetry from Plato's condemnations, reversing his hierarchical subordination of poetry to philosophy. Yet even in dispute, critics have by and large acceded to key components of Plato's basic conceptual architecture. What are those Platonic foundations that literary critics espouse, even erecting their theories upon them?

Plato's views across "Ion" and *The Republic* are not entirely consistent, but certain of his insights have been authoritative. Plato's infamous call to banish the poets from his republic was, of course, motivated by distrust of "sophistry," or of rhetoric's ability to manipulate and mislead. However, that caution regarding poetry's beguiling deceptions simultaneously acknowledges its enormous power, both as "a form of drug" and regarding matters of justice.[3] It goes without saying that this unpredictable power of art has been near universally recognized. At once, Plato's suspicion of poetry was prompted by its characterization as "a third remove from that which is." Plato notoriously dismissed the poet as a mere "imitator" with "no worthwhile knowledge of the things he imitates"—thereby exiling or excluding poetry from first-order, undiluted, immanent registers of knowing.[4]

Underlying that charge of "imitation" are a series of premises that have been mainstays of aesthetic criticism, and those premises exemplify the sorts of conversions brokered by the logic of paradox. The first involves the "derivative" position of art. Whereas a problem for Plato, art's nonnatural, inorganic, contrived status has been widely extolled, for a spectrum of reasons considered below. In turn, what is ultimately a structure of negative valorization has saturated virtually all areas of literary and aesthetic criticism. Second, this view admits the prospect that art, if fundamentally nonmimetic, is fated to exist in a discordant, contrarian, and potentially subordinate relationship to other evidentiary discursive and representational orders—orders that by definition expel art from their radius. Here, too, critics have responded to that seeming predicament by instead exalting it. Along with its dissidence, art has therefore been prized precisely due to its exclusion from ordinary ways of knowing—as part of what we are observing to be a larger methodological privileging of truths deemed marginal or exceptional. Third, further stemming from Plato's philosophy is an awareness that art's truths are fated to be ambivalent, doubled, or divided, whether internally at odds or in conflict with those alternate representational orders. Plato thus imparts to literary criticism multiple warrants for why the truth claims of art will be riddled with paradox.

Anchors of aesthetic theory, these bequests have at times worked to decree that the only phenomena deserving of theorization are liar's paradoxes. This vein of Plato's reception demands to be traced at least to the Early Moderns. As the introduction addressed, "paradoxy" played a prominent and extensive role in Renaissance letters.[5] Yet while that burgeoning of paradoxy was clearly itself symptomatic of the intellectual commotion of modernity, the Early Moderns were transfixed not only with paradoxes in general but specifically with the onus to craft rejoinders to Plato's allegations, or with the paradoxes flowing from art's tenuous bearings on truth and veracity. Often, those meditations on art were merged into scriptural and Judeo-Christian genres of allegory wrestling with enigmas of theology and of religion, like the infinity, omnipresence, and unknowability of God. Ponge is surely an heir to that tradition, seeing how his couplet's riposte likens his own poetic creation to that of Genesis.

Among the Early Modern period's many restatements of Plato, Sir Philip Sidney's 1595 "The Defence of Poesy" remains most renowned in the English literary tradition. Adopting the tenor of a legal oration, many of Sidney's retorts (like his provocation that the poet "nothing affirms, and therefore never lieth") mine the liar's paradoxes posed by art.

> I will answer paradoxically, but truly, I think truly, that of all writers under the sun the poet is the least liar, and though he would, as a poet can scarcely be a liar. For, as I take it, to lie is to affirm that to be true which is false.... The poet never maketh any circles about your imagination, to conjure you to believe for true what he writes. He citeth not authorities of other histories, but even for his entry calleth the sweet Muses to inspire into him a good invention; in truth, not laboring to tell you what is or is not, but what should or should not be. And therefore, though he recount things not true, yet because he telleth them not for true, he lieth not.[6]

While divulging certain fallacies underlying Plato's reasoning, Sidney's "Defence" exhibits multiple preoccupations that have endured. Rather than mired in past or present, the poetic imagination for Sidney outstrips Plato's reductive emphasis on "what is." Such a future-oriented telos, along with a tendency to infinitize, have been hallmarks of reasoning through paradox.

In so doing, Sidney plays on varying senses of the "truly" and "true." While he purports to counter Plato by confessing to poetry's compromised bearings on objective truth, that same gesture assigns superior authority to poetry, including over "what should or should not be." Not surprisingly, the chameleon workings of paradox—the "paradoxically, but truly"—are what lay claim to that elevated jurisdiction. Welcoming what Plato denounces, Sidney deploys that logic of paradox to transpose an ostensible limit into a merit, trumpeting Plato's recrimination as the essence of what makes poetry *poetry*. As for many since, Sidney's reasoning further illustrates the self-immunizing effects of such a transfiguration. It is by willingly inhabiting the space of paradox that Sidney inoculates poetry (and himself) against Plato's insinuations.

Investment in these liar's paradoxes has been far from confined to the British literary tradition or to the Early Modern period or to studies of poetry. Rather, versions of Sidney's rebuttal have shaped accounts of the exceptional status of art across genres and over the centuries. Among many available examples is the French philosopher Denis Diderot's *The Paradox of the Actor* (*Paradoxe sur le comédien*, written in 1773-78, published in English in 1820). Structured as a dialogue, the basic form of Diderot's text pays tribute to Plato, even while his main project is to extend Plato's original targets to include the modes of subterfuge and dissimulation practiced on the stage. On one level, and as Diderot's title suggests, the professional actor must engage in "deception" and "mimicry," since their performance awakens "sentiment" in the audience that the actor does not necessarily undergo.[7] Theater's "lies" are therefore continually metabolized by the actor (and arguably less so by the audience).

Beyond this artifice perpetrated by the actor, Diderot also understands an economy of paradox to control the "meanings" and "interpretations" at issue within drama—or to oversee the labors of the critic and of criticism. At one key point, Diderot's Second Speaker inveighs meta-theoretically: "You think that in every work, and especially in this, there are two distinct meanings, both expressed in the same terms...." To which the First Speaker answers, "Yes." As Diderot suggests, that art's truth status is paradoxical means that its content will analogously be replete with "doubled meanings"; not coincidentally, Diderot inscribes that ambivalence on his own treatise ("and especially in this"). Whereas insistence on the divided, doubled, poly-valent meanings latent to art is today second nature, nevertheless striking is that, within Diderot's commentary, that insight directly proceeds from Plato's accusation regarding literature's chronic deceptions.

It should not surprise us that a figure like Oscar Wilde—an unabashed evangelist for paradox—would write in Plato's shadow. Wilde's perhaps most ardent homage to Plato, his 1891 "The Decay of Lying," elaborates extensively on the paradoxes arising from art's fictionality, while similarly being constructed as a dialogue. Therein, Wilde revels in the adulterated as well as secondary or derivative character of art. Part of Wilde's agenda is to disparage his "Realist" contemporaries, whom he accuses of fundamentally misunderstanding art. In contrast, Wilde finds vindication for his defense of "lying in art" in the Greeks and especially Plato. As Wilde remarks, "Lying and poetry are arts—arts, as Plato saw, not unconnected with each other—and they require the most careful study, the most disinterested devotion."[8] With his characteristically sardonic wit, Wilde subverts additional of Plato's priorities, for instance proclaiming that "life" is parasitic upon art rather than vice versa. He explains, "Paradox though it may seem—and paradoxes are always dangerous things—it is none the less true that Life imitates art far more than Art imitates life."[9]

"The Decay of Lying" extrapolates from Plato in such a spirit to arrive at other contrarian views that have represented veritable doctrine across much theory. Along with an antinaturalism, Wilde gives voice to an antipositivism, chiding "our monstrous worship of facts." He describes art as anti-instrumental ("Art never expresses anything but itself"). With his disparagement of "the prison-house of realism," he marshals a constructivist notion of "truth," while displaying his trademark disdain for "common sense." These and other of Wilde's positions are simultaneously brandished as autobiographical, allowing Wilde to don the mantle of the marginalized "genius." One thesis of this book is that those positions are all permutations of intellectual devotion to paradox—and, by extension, of a creed of art's (and theory's) outsider, excluded, peripheral truth value.

Notwithstanding the pretense to iconoclasm and originality informing Wilde's own oeuvre, his philosophy is routed through a romance of the derivative. Hence, Wilde's persona certainly begs to be included in the chronicles of modern(ist) "self-fashioning," "histrionic improvisation," and "perpetual self-reflexiveness" inventoried in the last chapter.[10] But while conceiving individual identity as its own work of art, Wilde's relish for the imitative is indicative of still additional reasons that theorists have oft cathected onto that logic. In Wilde's hands, a parodic mode clearly functions to aestheticize, as for many it has imbued non-aesthetic domains of experience with protoliterary or poeticized energies. But we can also observe how Wilde conscripts a recurring (and far from original) justificatory framework perfected over literary history through successive disagreements with Plato. Wilde, too, draws upon the logic of paradox to transubstantiate an ostensible debility (being derivative or "lying") into something worthy of veneration. Rather than badges of inferiority, these and other spins on Plato's allegations (the imitative, the unverifiable, the doubled) are thereby metamorphosed by Wilde into virtues transcending the limitations of the (non-existent) "originals" on which they prey—in a maneuver fully orchestrated by the "acrobatics" (to recall Wilde's epigraphs) of paradox.

It is tempting to downplay the influence of this line of thought, including—and this is key—within theory only tangentially dealing with art or literature. Although later chapters return to Judith Butler's formidable body of work, many aspects of her theory enlist exactly such a logic of justification. Particularly unmistakable is the Wildean imprint on Butler's account of drag as parody. As that thrilling discussion concluding Butler's 1990 *Gender Trouble* explains: "*In imitating gender, drag implicitly reveals the imitative structure of gender itself—as well as its contingency*. Indeed, part of the pleasure, the giddiness of the performance is in that recognition...."[11] For Butler, cognizance of gender's "imitativeness" is both freeing and resistant, among other reasons because it explodes ideas about the biological grounding of sex in nature (and the corresponding prospect that gender could be thereby policed). But read through the lens of Wilde, that constructivism breeds its own paradoxes, at risk of legislating what I'll repeatedly describe as an "autonomization of style." Butler's reasoning overtly celebrates the parasitism of a subversive practice like drag—in other words, basking in its counterfeit, derivative status. Yet while on the one hand contingent on the (albeit factitious) norm for its parodic reenactment, on the other gender simultaneously operates independently of any material backing or objective substance to which it might become hostage. As one result, a theory of gender must bracket inquiry into those nonexistent foundations, seeking to comprehend gender solely with reference to its unmoored and self-reflexive play—or, we might say, vis-à-vis the signature of its elusive yet alluring style. Returning to Wilde, he is insistent that emphasis on the imitative will feed into an (admittedly coy) philosophy of aesthetic autonomy: "It is style that makes us believe in a thing—nothing but style." In Wilde's mirthful thinking, art therefore "invents a type," which life opportunistically "tries to copy."[12]

For both Butler and Wilde (in the latter's rebuttal of Plato), an optics of paradox thereby ransoms phenomena (art, gender) otherwise imperiled by an absence of foundations, converting that position of putative lack into something exuberantly transgressive as well as creative in its meaning-making potential. An almost identical arithmetic, as we will see time after time, has dictated theorizations of a whole spate of disparate and unrelated phenomena, making it important to spell out other warrants for such common reasoning here. What Plato's charge ultimately does is to call out a legitimation deficit: to embarrass art for its constitutive dearth of empirical or rationalist or provable or uncompromised foundations. It is in response to such crisis that the logic of paradox emerges as an incredibly powerful apologetics, one capable of commuting sources of exigency into a limitless windfall. This is precisely why Butler's theory of gender makes recourse to such a structure of justification. Besides being nonnatural, nondominant genders are excluded from the (nonexistent) norm, causing them to radically defy objective verification, standardization, or measurement. That want confronts an authenticatory shortfall and ensuing crisis akin to the one afflict-ing art—and analogously religion, democracy, rights, trauma, the humanities, and more, as later chapters consider. However, the ploy of the "paradoxically, but truly" comes along not only to rescue gender but also to transform its absent grounding and exclusionary paradoxes into a source of "giddiness" and obviously aestheticized "pleasure." It is gender's very lack of founda-tions and corresponding legitimacy vacuum that thus infuses it (and art, and justice, and for Derrida rights) with a self-regenerating, transfigural, and infinitely fertile dynamism.

First and foremost among our answers to the question of why theo-rists of non-literary realities would draw so heavily (and often unwittingly) from aesthetic criticism thus lies with its techniques for negotiating such legitimation deficits and other conceptual lacuna. How to dramatize the power of something (like god, like art) that cannot be readily substantiated? How to delineate the truth effects of representational orders that lack cor-respondence with, or at best possess a fragile relation to, the objectively "real"? How to establish the paramountcy of experiences eluding rational structures of validity and corroboration? How to explain why recognitions outcast from an orthodoxy are ripe with an uncanny insurgency? Aesthetic criticism contains a storehouse of tools for alchemizing these and other apparent shortfalls into reserves of inexhaustible renewal and discovery. Hence, theorists from other disciplines have appropriated schemes for de-fending art and repurposed them to reckon with an array of nonaesthetic phenomena subject to parallel crises of representation and veracity. No doubt, this is Derrida's gambit when he conscripts Plato (routed through Ponge) to access the emancipatory promise latent in a fictional proposition so ephemeral as rights.

Of course, these conversions have not always been synthesized by the precise term *paradox*. Aesthetic criticism has relied on a web of grammars differently geared to elucidate the paradoxical texture of the strange truths afforded by art, and those diverse vocabularies have similarly been exported to manage other dilemmas of political-legal-social-disciplinary validation and legitimacy. Singularity, unverifiability, incalculability, untranslatabil-ity, indeterminacy, inarticulacy, among uncountable others: these terms, like the logic of paradox, often perform sleights of hand, transmuting ostensible failures into cradles of elevated awareness like that stimulated by art. We can quickly get a handle on these terms through a short table.

Soren Kierkegaard's presence therein naturally exemplifies the consan-guinity between literary-aesthetic species of paradox and those of theology.

TABLE INTER1.1 — LANGUAGES FOR THE TRUTH STATUS OF ART

	Representative Thinkers
Speechlessness	Schiller
	Kierkegaard
Unrepresentability	Shelley
Unverifiability	Plato
	Sidney
	Diderot
	Wilde
	Attridge
	Empson
	Spivak
Singularity	Kierkegaard
	Spivak
The Sublime	Kant
	Jameson
	Burke
Autonomy	Wilde
	Kant
	de Man
Indeterminacy	Bakhtin
	de Man
	Muñoz
Incalculability	Kierkegaard
	Spivak
	Derrida

Quotes

"However disciplined by taste and skill, the experience of literature is, like literature itself, unable to speak."—Northrop Frye

"Lying and poetry are arts—arts, as Plato saw, not unconnected with each other—and they require the most careful study, the most disinterested devotion."—Wilde

"Faith is this paradox, and the single individual is quite unable to make himself intelligible to anyone."—Kierkegaard

"Whenever this autonomous potential of language can be revealed by analysis, we are dealing with literariness."—de Man

"The novel inserts into these other genres an indeterminacy, a certain semantic openendedness, a living contact with unfinished, still-evolving contemporary reality (the openended present)."—Bakhtin

Whereas a philosopher like Kierkegaard's thought was an important conduit for the broad ethos and mood of paradox, his reception also captures the frequent imbrication of that language's literary and religious registers. In fact, scriptural exegesis and hermeneutics provided an early stomping ground for many influential theorists, including Butler. But in addition, *Fear and Trembling* (1843), published under the pseudonym Johannes de silentio, demonstrates the tendency of various conceptual cousins of paradox to function interchangeably, becoming endlessly substitutable.

Regarding Abraham as a paragon of faith and its many enigmas, *Fear and Trembling* ruminates over the perplexity of his willingness to sacrifice Isaac through a lexicon composed of qualities now engraved as autographs of the literary-aesthetic. For Kierkegaard, faith like Abraham's is beyond "calculation," resistant to "mediation," "incommensurable with the whole of reality," impossible, "absurd," and consequently "cannot speak."[13] At once, Kierkegaard casts Abraham and his predicament as singular—another bellwether of the literary. Even more telling is how these features of Abraham's belief ultimately unravel what Kierkegaard holds out as another crisis of legitimacy—a crisis to which paradox arises as a kind of solution. As *Fear and Trembling* importunes: "Is he justified? His justification is, once again, the paradox: for if he is the paradox it is not by virtue of being anything universal, but of being the particular."[14] It is Abraham's teleological suspension of the universal that, in plunging him (and Kierkegaard) into what Kierkegaard characterizes as a justificatory echo chamber—or a position defiant of reasoned, communicable, conceptualist content—can thus be touted by Kierkegaard as exemplary.

THE AGENCY OF ART. In so doing, Kierkegaard requisitions another aesthetic category—the sublime—to index the "monstrous paradox" embodied in Abraham's predicament.[15] Whereas discourses on the sublime have crystallized diverse representational paradoxes confronting among other things art, that category has also served to expound the unusual agency at stake therein. As before, what might appear a flaw or lapse of agency is instead refracted via the lens of paradox into a locus of power so incredible it verges on inexplicability. In many seminal accounts of the sublime like Edmund Burke's, art has therefore served to instantiate multiple subsets of that category, with poetry for Burke serving as a quintessential manifestation of modes like "obscurity."[16] Again striking is how Burke's treatise continually oscillates between appealing to God versus to poetry as illustrations.

In the interests of time and space, this Interlude is both synoptic and schematic, walking perhaps too methodically through the collected logics that have conspired to render paradox one of (if not *the*) overriding grammars for stipulating the unique and distinguishing features of art and aesthetic experience—logics that will resurface in what follows. But to proceed: another angle on the sublime's enduring explanatory currency lies with how it encapsulates the uncanny agency through which apparent limits can become counterintuitively productive. Accounts of the sublime like Burke's, on the one hand, grapple with the limits of human knowing, limits albeit conservative for Burke. However, such an insistence on the sublime's ability to lay bare the periphery, or outer reaches, of human cognition and understanding continues to shape contemporary theorizations of that category. This is one facet of Jameson's postmodern or technological sublime, which for Jameson gauges "the incapacity of our minds [...] to map the great global multinational and decentered communicational network in which we find ourselves caught as individual subjects."[17] But on the other, others have formulated that category in terms designed to show how and why those very impediments to human knowing become peculiarly (and hence paradoxically) empowering—and along lines that inextricably meditate over the curiously noncausal, unpredictable agency possessed by art. While in a philosopher like Kant's account of the sublime reason effectively triumphs, even for him that category contends with certain paradoxes of freedom and will.

Over the centuries, multiple vocabularies have been enlisted to denominate as well as to channel this antirationalist, nonlinear, noninstrumental, yet dramatic agency of art—of which the sublime is merely one such expression. For efficiency's sake, a few of those coinages can become quickly visible in another brief table below.

While contrasting, each term therein acknowledges the sheer difficulty of either demarcating or delineating art's nonagentive agency. In effort to do so, each, first, highlights its distinctiveness from causal ideas about the agentive, instead averring the impractical, inefficacious, and nonteleological character of art's inchoate force. Second, those terms embrace the fact that art's agency is fundamentally unpredictable and uncontrollable, even causing it to exceed the intent or design of its author. Indeed, such a paradoxical attempt to establish agency that will by definition prove both noninstrumental and ungovernable can be seen already to animate the sublime's classical articulations, displaying such debates' very long lineage. Even Longinus's first century AD treatise anticipates this anti-rationalism at stake in art's elusive power with his clarification that the sublime involves "not persuasion but transport" (*ekstasis*).[18]

TABLE INTER1.2 — LANGUAGES FOR THE AGENCY OF ART

	Thinkers
Anti-Instrumentality	Kant
	Rancière
	Wilde
	Spivak
Unpredictability	Spivak
Efficacy	Rancière
Impossibility	Kierkegaard
	Derrida
	Agamben
Rupture and Disruption	Berlant
	Bhabha
	Calinescu
Staging and/or Disclosure of Contradiction	Wilde
	Butler
	Schiller
	Rancière
	Ngai
	Jameson
	Empson
	Berman
Improvisation	Greenblatt
	Butler

"Poetry makes nothing happen."—W. H. Auden

Pedagogy is "teleo-poeisis, striving for a response from the distant other, without guarantees."—Spivak

"If there exists a connection between art and politics, it should be cast in terms of dissensus, the very kernel of the aesthetic regime: artworks can produce effects of dissensus precisely because they neither give lessons nor have any destination."—Rancière

"There is no justice without this experience, however impossible it may be, of aporia."- Derrida

"To live in the unhomely world, to find its ambivalences and ambiguities enacted in the house of fiction, or its sundering and splitting performed in the work of art . . ."—Bhabha

Regarding Baudelaire, "this makes the boulevard a perfect symbol of capitalism's inner contradictions."—Berman

This conviction in the inescapably paradoxical agency of art marshals an economy of negative valorization. In refusing to conceive art's agency in serviceably concrete or "instrumental" terms, many of the above grammars instead extol negative faculties like destruction, undoing, and the rupturing or disintegration of the stable, uncomplicated, or whole. Just as such thinking thereby assigns art with value in regard to what it disaffirms, sunders, excepts, and/or fails to do, art's liminal agency has almost invariably gained definition and meaning with active and direct reference to what it is not. Far from confined to ideas about art, we will see, that basic regime of valuation has instilled corresponding dictates within nonliterary arenas that work to place a parallel moratorium on affirmative, constructive goals and assertions, akin to how literary critics tend to shy religiously away from statements regarding art's measurable, determinant, predictable aims or outcomes. One symptom of the interdisciplinary traffic traced herein is that the logic of paradox has also governed (and curtailed) ideas about the caliber of agency analogously understood to inform politics, law, democracy, justice, a liberal arts education, witnessing, and more. A conceptual matrix inherited from literary criticism has, besides aestheticizing agency within these not-terribly-literary domains, thus coordinated views about the permissible agency of *theory*.

FORM, GENRE, LANGUAGE, AND STYLE. Typically, literature is both distinguished and internally classified in terms of things like form, genre, style, rhetoric, and the supposed distinctiveness of literary language. Here, too, the semantics of paradox have fulfilled an indexical function, inventorying those properties that render the aesthetic *aesthetic*, all the while offsetting literature from other discourses and technologies of knowing. Again, a few such shorthands can be enumerated in a table located below.

To begin, the language of literature and its uniqueness—or what literature does with words—has been thus distilled. It has been largely unquestioned, first, that the literary or poetic harnesses a distinctive—or "singular," recalling Kierkegaard—"voice" alien to other discourses. And second, part of that exemplarity has been seen to lie with the multiple—and hence paradoxical—meanings both unleashed and harbored by literary language. Like Diderot, many therefore emphasize the doubled (Ricoeur), dialogic, polyglossic (Bakhtin), and/or polysemous (Dante) species of those meanings. Others instead focus on the potential of literary language to sustain and even to breed "ambiguities" (William Empson), "ironies" (Rorty), and "paradoxes" (Cleanth Brooks) that are either "purged" or "stabilized" within other disciplines (for Brooks, science).[19] Noteworthy here is that even nominally "conservative" outliers, such as the New Critics, placed great stock in such an amalgam of qualities, including in literature's propensity to provoke and to unsettle. Brooks, too, affirms how the "language of paradox" "disrupt[s]" and "awakens the mind's attention from the lethargy of custom."[20] Yet Brooks's investment in paradox importantly did *not* prevent him from finding oneness, integrity, and wholeness within the literary object at the same time. And although Brooks's ultimate stance regarding these matters is deserving of skepticism, subsequent efforts to purge the "idealism" and elitism presumed to color values like those Brooks promotes have suffered from their own failings, namely to be unsparingly aseptic in what they sanitize.

There is much that could be said about each of the following columns, whether to chart the steps according to which each terminology naturalizes paradox as an episteme or to unpack their diverging genealogies. For instance, what Friedrich Schiller in 1795 termed "the play impulse" has inspired a rich and ecumenical lineage.[21] For Schiller, this "perhaps [...] paradoxical" orientation toward "play" aroused by the literary derives from antagonism and "contradictory demands," which, when combined, "support the whole fabric of aesthetic art."[22]

Nevertheless, delving in slightly greater depth into popular accounts of the novel's evolution can enable further insight into the intellectual factors that allowed a spirit of paradox to mushroom into a type of organizing principle. Studies of the novel have dominated certain fields of literary criticism, whether of Victorian culture or postcolonial theory. And while much controversy has surrounded matters like the novel's regnant structural logic and precise conditions of historical emergence, those debates have with great regularity been staged on a terrain that cedes conceptual authority to contradiction and paradox—ordaining those properties as the novelistic form's developmental engines as well as preeminent indicia.

It might seem inevitable that efforts to historicize and otherwise chart the novel's rise would hold out paradox as a foregone conclusion. The novel, of course, is an artifact of modernity—and thus a repository of the vertiginous, comprehensive upheaval that spawned the modern condition. Also perhaps inevitably, that genre has been understood to incarnate those tensions: to metabolize the contradictions of capitalism, liberal individualism, the public sphere, a sense of time out of joint, empire, and so on. As Jameson explains of realism, "its theorization will ultimately involve the most paradoxical of philosophical problems, namely the conceptualization of time and temporality."[23] Similarly does Ian Watt's influential *The Rise of the Novel* argue that nineteenth-century novelists "created irony" by "incorporat[ing] [...]

TABLE INTER1.3 — LITERARY FORM, STYLE, AND LANGUAGE

	Qualities	Figures
Literary Language	Doubled	Diderot
		Ricoeur
	Irony	Rorty
		Berman
		Hayden White
	Polyglossia	Bakhtin
	Paradox	Brooks
	Ambiguity	Empson
		Bhabha
	Pluralism	Andzaldúa
		Mouffe
		Rorty
Style	Play	Schiller
		Spillers
		Gates
		Derrida
		Rancière
	Parody	Bakhtin
		Butler
		Wilde
		Bhabha
The Novel	Hybridity	Bakhtin
	Irony	Watt
	Fragmentation	Lukacs
	Contradiction	Jameson

Quotes

"We need a redescription of liberalism as the hope that culture as a whole can be 'poeticized.'"—Rorty

"Is all good poetry supposed to be ambiguous? I think it is."—Empson

"In this play of paradox, only the female stands *in the flesh*."—Spillers

"The novel form is, like no other, an expression of this transcendental homelessness."—Lukács

conflicts and incongruities into the very structure of their works."[24] As one recent example, Joseph Slaughter's study of the postcolonial bildungsroman reiterates these basic theses, maintaining that the form's "capacity to sustain ambiguity and complexity" renders it "a powerful ally in naturalizing the law's paradoxes and exclusions" and making contradiction feel "common-sensical."[25] As a consequence, one can feel hard pressed to find accounts of the novel that do not lend near constitutive force to contradiction and paradox, outright categorizing that genre vis-à-vis the determinant presence of those qualities.

Since most of the thinkers and theories gathered here reckon with specifically aesthetic *modernity*, it might seem unavoidable that they would converge on various conceptual cousins to paradox. But it is also the case that recurring elements of the modernity-as-paradox thesis have governed accounts of the literary far beyond a genre fully fledged in modern turbulence like the novel. One result has been the tendency to posit a premodern foil or Other as a background against which these distinguishing features of art and literature can begin to become apparent. Much as Paul Ricoeur's influential "hermeneutics of suspicion" is juxtaposed with the "univocity of meaning" of ancient culture and philosophy,[26] and much as Georg Lukács's description of the "transcendental homelessness" pervading modern literary experience hinges on the "integrated cultures" it supersedes,[27] critics have essayed the aesthetic by envisioning exactly such a divide—a divide the last chapter also attributed to the sway of paradox.[28] Yet notwithstanding a form like the novel's clear status as an archive of modernity and its many transitions, the repudiated prospect of the nonparadoxical and noncontradictory has conducted momentous classificatory labor in shoring up what counts as art and literature. Meanwhile, a set of recurring properties are selected as antitheses to the literary (and projected onto premodernity in the same gesture): unity, integration, totality, identity, harmony, presence or immanence, organicism, wholeness, homogeneity, "roundedness" (Lukács), centralization (Bakhtin). As placeholders for all that modernity is imagined to shatter and surpass, those properties are thereby castigated as markers of tradition, conservatism, social convention, stasis, regression, and so on. In a glimpse of the deep imbrication of prominent theories of modernity and of art, that cluster of terms can furthermore summon highly specific political referents, contributing to an explanatory economy wherein discourses of art (and of modernity) are expected near automatically to embed not so subtle political commentaries.

Following his work's translation into English beginning in the 1970s (written largely in the 1930s and '40s), the Russian formalist Mikhail Bakhtin exerted a decisive influence especially on literary studies, disseminating a complex of once fashionable concepts like polyglossia, dialogism, hybridity, the carnivalesque, parody, spontaneity, plasticity, the polyglot, indeterminacy, the encyclopedic, and more. As elsewhere, a presumed gulf separating ancient Greek from modern culture is foundational to Bakhtin's theory of the novel. Elaborated in *The Dialogic Imagination*, Bakhtin's account of that genre maps such a split by explaining how the "epic world knows only a single and unified world view, obligatory and indubitably true" and characterizing the Greek "creative consciousness [as] realized in closed, pure languages."[29] In contrast, the novel enacts a struggle against those centripetal impulses, while also corrupting genetically unalloyed literary forms. Bakhtin recounts that form's impact on other genres: "They become more free and flexible, their language renews itself by incorporating extraliterary heteroglossia and the 'novelistic' layers of literary language, they become dialogized, permeated with laughter, irony, humor, elements of self-parody and finally—this is the most important thing—the novel inserts into these other genres an indeterminacy, a certain semantic open-endedness, a living contact with unfinished, still-evolving contemporary reality (the open-ended present)."[30]

This romance of the insurrectionary forces awakened by the novel leads Bakhtin to more than idealized musings about the unrivaled status of art. He ultimately leverages that polarity between modern and Greek to advance a not-so-coded critique of his immediate historical circumstances in Stalinist Russia. Opposing the novel's polyglot discourse to the "absolutism of a single and unitary language" and "centralizing" tendencies of traditional literary forms,[31] Bakhtin's insistence on the aesthetic myopia and enclosure of premodernity thus marshals a scathing indictment of political authoritarianism's backward, repressive nature. Only against that backdrop can the novel's "spirit of process and inconclusiveness" and capacity to be "both critical and self-critical" deliver an extended meditation on political freedom,[32] even while such reasoning conceives literary forms to exist in a neatly homologous relation to actual, flesh-and-blood political institutions. So while mythologized notions about the ancient Greek world view and its cultural analogues are imagined to contain the key to deciphering the domineering, absolutist leanings of *contemporary* political institutions, the same matrix of qualities that Bakhtin celebrates in the novel become artillery, geared to sabotage forms of political repression.

Versions of Bakhtin's moves and oppositions have been at the helm of critical method since the height of his vogue in the 1980s and '90s—an era that also saw thinkers like Bakhtin, Lukács, and Althusser become influential far beyond strictly Marxist circles. This popularization and eventual routinization of equations such as those Bakhtin wields were naturally invited by the late Cold War geopolitical dynamics of that episode in history, but their basic explanatory dominance has persisted. Thus today, traffic between the aesthetic and the sociopolitical is often semiautomatic, including for critics otherwise wary of the notion that literature might furnish remotely clear-cut or "translatable" political lessons. Akin to how Bakhtin takes for granted that those spheres are cognate or analogues, the operations of which can be swapped and overlaid, it has been de rigueur to draw conclusions about political forms and institutions based on insights into literary structures—and vice versa. But of particular interest here is how the mercurial workings of paradox both subsidize and expedite those smooth transfers. Perceptions of symmetrical paradox—whether of legitimacy, truth, representation, absent foundations, exclusion, or more—operationalize that movement from aesthetics to politics and back again, with the frequent effect of collapsing those contrasting domains so fully as to render them indistinguishable.

PARADOX AS METHOD. One agenda of this book is to demonstrate how and why a diagnosis of paradox evolved to become the scaffolding of an all-enveloping method, capable of adjudicating virtually any topic submitted to its machinery. In so doing, the book also probes the reasons faith in paradox has elicited such an ecumenical following: why has paradox represented an ethos seemingly everybody is eager and willing to acclaim? To be sure, there are noteworthy exceptions, although neither very many nor threatening. Even the New Critics, I've suggested, were proponents of literary paradox. That said, at least one chapter of aesthetic history would depart from this interlude's sweep: a chapter located in the eighteenth century and involving neoclassical theorists of rhetoric. Figures like Swift, Pope, Addison, and Dryden, along with a popular education shepherded by the teachings of Cicero, would require us to contemplate why an alternate set of ideals, for a time, was instead associated with the literary.[33] But that chapter's significance to contemporary theory has been minor, and it would require a lengthy detour away from another of this book's central goals: to grasp what exactly other disciplines saw when they pawned the justificatory conventions of aesthetic criticism to reckon with a spate of other, less so obviously aesthetic issues— albeit issues themselves comparatively ransacked by paradox.

Another answer to this question of why methods of reading escorted by paradox have been oversubscribed involves, as we have seen, that reasoning's tendency to become meta-theoretical: to reflexively comment on the comparatively fraught labors of criticism and theory. The very property (paradox) representing a core objective of analysis often meditates in the same gesture on corresponding paradoxes fated to bedevil the project of critical analysis. In some sense, this synchronicity has been oft-remarked. As Ricoeur observes of psychoanalysis in his 1970 *Freud and Philosophy*, one cannot reach a diagnosis without undergoing an interpretation, causing the former (the goal) to be "subordinated" to the latter (the process).[34] Hence, reading for symptoms will invariably become symptomatic.[35] Allegorical reading—a prevalent interpretive mode that extrapolates from the fictional-imaginative to the real—has relatedly encouraged such a reflex; Jameson's brand of cognitive mapping thus aims to uncover a "political unconscious" via the "subtext" of "contradictions" he deems "central to any Marxist cultural analysis."[36] Given the elusiveness of phenomena like the unconscious and symptoms, some have fixated on the structural impossibilities that will analogously dog the act of criticism. As Slavoj Žižek construes what he introduces as theory's core problematic, "the subject can 'enjoy his symptom' only in so far as its logic escapes him—the measure of the success of its interpretation is precisely its dissolution."[37]

Such mirroring of the mutual impediments fated to plague analytic method and textual-critical object has not been restricted to Marxist or psychoanalytic (i.e., symptomatic) criticism. Rather, emphasis on the constitutive yet irresolvable layers of paradox infesting a literary text has similarly beset deconstructive reading with failures, uncertainties, and deferrals—and, of course, a fascination with those stumbling blocks and ensuing relays. Paul de Man's 1982 "The Resistance to Theory," self-identified as its own referendum on the distinctiveness of literary experience, reflects on the theorist's task in exactly such terms. De Man surmises: "Whenever this autonomous potential of language can be revealed by analysis, we are dealing with literariness and, in fact, with literature as the place where this negative knowledge about the reliability of linguistic utterance is made available."[38] Perhaps not surprisingly, de Man's account of the literary actively depends on the silhouette of what literariness supposedly is *not*, or on its negation— for de Man, its "irreducib[ility] to grammar or to historically determined meaning."[39] Yet this predicament of literariness—for de Man, as for many others—also names that of theory, infusing theory's own enterprise with the same undecidabilities, displacements, "resistances," and "residues of indetermination" as those that comprise art and literature. "Theory," too, must therefore embark on a persistent "methodological undoing": a diligent bracketing of the will to understand.[40]

Whether actualized via the pursuit of autonomized and free-floating signs or the excavation of buried symptoms, these circuitries of reading for paradox can set in motion a process of universalization. As Tim Dean argues of Žižek's corpus, "having grasped the structural logic of the symptom, one may submit practically anything of interest to its explanatory grid."[41] Yet there is also something peculiar to the *paradoxes* both intrinsic to and unearthed by the symptom that concatenates such synergies: something distinctive about the logic of paradox that causes *both* its central locus or container (i.e. the symptom) *and* its traces to become near endlessly generalizable. Whether chiefly regarded as a figure, a structural element, or a critical mode, paradox names an abstract property (or properties) that are expected to recur across a limitless number of instantiations of that figure or system or practice, independent of context or content or other such variations. Clearly, one attraction of such reading habits lies with this very recyclability: as Dean suggests, with a given formal logic's ability to be grafted onto and discerned within a host of far-flung yet structurally cognate realities.

However, another angle on this iterability concerns a privileging of style—again, á la Wilde. In identifying the literary (or the symptom, or democracy, or power) through its formal features or structural logic alone, these analyses evacuate objective and measurable substance from a text, while also abstracting the activity of reading from the changing real-world circumstance that embed it, unmooring critical practice from its concrete, lived referents. For many, we have seen, this is the whole point. However, emphasis on the formal techniques distinguishing literature qua literature is fine and well when evaluating art and its province. But the heuristics this chapter has studied have been embroidered to administer myriad nonaesthetic debates, issues, domains, and problematics. Later chapters delve further into why and how a logic of paradox is what enabled such free and uninhibited cross-pollination. For now, this cursory journey through the byways of aesthetic history has begun to explain why an economy of valuation fashioned to negotiate the peculiar truth status of art would have invited rampant piracy and cooptation. As a result, innumerable phenomena comparatively hamstrung by tenuous representational authority or legitimacy (whether trauma, democracy, or the humanities) have been anatomized vis-à-vis what is at base an aesthetic regime of valuation. Hence, just as poetry was excluded by Plato from his republic, so too has political exclusion been hallowed as a badge of elevated knowing. Just as unverifiability is a virtue within some art, so too have the truth claims of theory been valorized along such lines. But while perhaps symmetrical, are the paradoxes of art—whether of representation, agency, truth, or form—really mirroring and interchangeable with those governing human rights or justice or politics? If not, what happens when aesthetic species of paradox are embellished to resolve legal-political-social matters? Does this not conflate nonfungible phenomena? To reiterate, what allowed a spirit of paradox to authorize this legerdemain?

Other ironies surely exist. One involves what I've described as a negative economy of valuation: an epistemology that locates preeminent worth and meaning within the ineffable and inscrutable. Only through the status quo's suspension will the nonevidentiary truths of paradox surface; hence, those truths have been venerated precisely for eluding proof, calculation, certainty, and clarity. But while these priorities make a certain sense for art, can they really help us navigate dilemmas of politics or law or the future of the university? One might relatedly observe how a realm (art) conceived over history as singular and irreducible would, albeit when its trove is plundered, be systematized into a recursive and all-controlling conceptual framework. Given the critiques of foundationalism and es-sentialism that launched so many variants of theory, that those schools of thought would ossify into either a crypto-foundationalism of paradox or a formalism regulated by almost mechanistic, law-like doctrines can seem nothing short of tragic.

Far from last, further quandaries concern how the marginal, contrarian play of paradox has acted as watchman, patrolling the aesthetic theory canon's borders. Whether bootstrapped by theories of modernity or other-wise, the logic of paradox has itself operated to exclusionary ends—as we have seen, as a threshold dividing liberatory and transgressive aesthetic styles (i.e., modernity) from those deemed absolutizing and regressive (i.e., modernity's others). When all is said and done, it is hard to overlook the tautological patterns thus engraved. Within much literary theory, a single optics of paradox denotes a definitional feature of art, a theme, an objective, a mode, a structural feature, a method, and a cabalistic religion of (non-)meaning—all together. Whereas those many vectors of paradox become self-reinforcing, paradox can start to have a quick-fix or feel-good aura about it. Both riddle and key, that logic is guaranteed to confirm an observer's id-iosyncratic predilections. Criticism goes questing for paradox, but through a method that foreordains its emergence. This feedback loop is another reason the explanatory economy of paradox would prove so universally beguiling.

3

REDEEMING RIGHTS, OR THE ETHICS
AND POLITICS OF PARADOX

May not totalitarianism be conceived as a response to the questions raised by democracy, as an attempt to resolve its paradoxes? —Claude Lefort (1981)

Let us practice the peculiar bias, the slant, of paradox and approach these questions
obliquely. Politically. —Thomas Keenan (1997)

E ach chapter in this book, as suggested, tells what is really the same
story albeit in different ways. Recursive, those stories each converge
on a common set of developments: developments that unfolded within
left intellectual life largely with the onset of the "theory era." With parallel narrative arcs and agendas, each chapter examines alternate roots and
the evolving contours of a distinct modality of thought—what one might
broadly identify as the intellectual formation of theory—to chart how an
ever-expanding range of topics came to be subsumed within its conceptual logic. That explanatory web was both spun by paradox and itself wove
paradox into an incredibly powerful way of knowing—or an epistemology. The book's successive chapters therefore study the many background
conditions and ideological assumptions that have allowed that logic not
only to navigate a truly encyclopedic range of debates (modernity, rights,

aesthetics, democracy, the humanities, law) but also to take hold across multiple academic disciplines during the twentieth century's last decades, ramifying beyond the departments of language and literature that initially fostered such devotion to erect paradox into a near uniformly accepted set of intellectual doctrines and overarching *mentalité*.

Like chapter 2, this one pursues the adventures of rights, although by exploring the rapidly shifting and unprecedented meanings that rights donned especially beginning in the 1970s. As it shows, those newfangled hopes for rights that sprouted during the late Cold War can shed comprehensive light on a period of intense intellectual activity coinciding with predominantly French theory's institutionalization. Why look to rights for insight into these seismic shifts? What follows ventures numerous interlocking explanations for why rights were a driving force in the odyssey of theory. More than providing a mere bird's eye view on those developments, rights were an active stimulus for multiple sea changes in left intellectual life, as efforts to contend with rights instigated landmark philosophical innovations, many recognized as among the theory era's crowning achievements. Indeed, there are real questions whether theory would look the way it does but for these attempts by now-foundational thinkers to grapple with rights. In the process, rights simultaneously acted as a bridge enabling forms of traffic that would not otherwise be so automatic. That traffic, not surprisingly, was both conducted and inspired by the logic of paradox.

The fact that rights had all along been defined with reference to their paradoxes is one reason they acted as such a catalyst. Chapter 2 considered the enduring tradition of submitting rights to seemingly endless critique—critique aimed at divulging, magnifying, and ultimately generalizing paradox to deem it structural and, with frequency, fatal. During the Cold War, other like-minded thinkers (Jacques Derrida, Jacques Lacan, Claude Lefort, among others) instead began to celebrate rights and their untapped promise—and often by citing the *exact same* paradoxes as those elsewhere invoked as the basis for rights' repudiation. The theorists this chapter engages seize on paradoxes understood by many to bankrupt or to contaminate rights and instead exalt those very limits—although in the process recalibrating the nature of paradox as a diagnosis and a mode. Rather than strictly to encode the machinery of oppression, paradox was increasingly extolled as the fountainhead of a democratic politics and theory of justice. Unfolding debates about rights can therefore dramatize the swiftly mutating stakes of paradox as a basic discovery, shedding light on the collision of factors that injected that logic with newly rehabilitative expectations. Precisely because the thinkers covered here wrestle with near identical paradoxes to those long troubling rights skeptics can their analyses lay bare the changing conditions that brought about what is in fact a major intellectual transition: one that overhauled both the significance of paradox and the emancipatory horizons of rights. In the end, paradox emerged as something to be glorified: the kernel of rights, justice, ethics, and a radicalized democracy.

In one sense, this is a Cold War phenomenon. It was against the backdrop of Cold War anxieties not only about totalitarianism but specifically about censorship that *both* paradox *and* rights became laden with what have been since touted as antitotalitarian and fundamentally untotalizable energies. With direct reference to midcentury geopolitics was paradox thus heralded as the secret or clue to grasping the (albeit proximate) distinction between authoritarian political forms and democracy. At once, these Cold War hopes for paradox colluded with other unrelated intellectual, political, and socio-historical influences that also surfaced in the aftermath of the 1960s. Along with its Cold War referents, that language has channeled the spirit of the counterculture and student protest, post-Saussurean views about language, psychoanalytic conceptions of the subject, theological genres of justification, aesthetic theory, and more. Each of those traditions furnished a separate conduit for left intellectual faith in paradox, together reinforcing paradox as an elevated way of knowing. With paradox acting as a sort of spindle weaving those diverse threads, its resulting explanatory fabric has proven notably consistent, resilient, and all-encompassing—which is to say, near endlessly recyclable across both context and history.

This chapter submits that something distinctive about the precise complexion and flavor of reasoning through paradox permitted so many diverse intellectual-historical tributaries to constellate into what has proven a relatively capacious, elastic, and unifying analytic framework. It is therefore worth, once again, enumerating how and why reasoning through paradox often departs from that focused on contradiction or antagonism, among other things being more mercurial and therefore harder to delineate or arrest. Another difference lies with the tendency of paradoxes to warehouse: such reasoning often stockpiles, redistributes, and spawns unexpected linkages and sites of rapport. This tendency is exacerbated when the grammar of paradox operates as a master trope or figure. As we know, within rhetoric a paradox *is* a figure, and like metaphors and other associative language, paradoxes often self-complicate—boundlessly proliferating unforeseen synergies and connotations. In some cases, that propagative spirit has encouraged methodological eclecticism, even going so far as to harmonize meaningful disagreements. In what follows, prospering hopes for rights will elucidate why these and other features helped to encourage a mounting veneration of paradox in the postwar years. Although centered on renowned thinkers, this chapter tracks instincts that are today hardwired: transformative expectations for paradox that remain compulsory for many.

This chapter begins with a general picture of the 1970s climate that made the left intellectual scene ripe for an embrace of rights. One ingredient circulating within that air, both in the wake of 1960s-style radicalism and given the Cold War, was belief in the unrivaled importance of insurrectionary speech. The logic of paradox, I will argue, separately subsidized that belief, at the same time as radically "free" speech was championed as a vital safeguard against the encroachments of authoritarianism. Thereafter, the chapter plots a course of swelling dedication to paradox. Whereas one angle on these transitions might cite structuralism's uneven mutation into poststructuralism, a lot more is at issue for the theorists considered below. Claude Lefort's defense of rights lays the groundwork for a critique of Soviet-era Marxism: a critique that also enshrines paradox as key to grasping the frontiers of democracy. Derrida's early reflections on rights will illustrate how the linguistic turn helped to implant paradox as the skeleton of deconstructive theories of justice and ethics. Psychoanalytic accounts of "inhuman" rights (for Lacan, Jean-François Lyotard, and Judith Butler) instead locate paradox at the heart of the subject and of ethics. Finally, Jacques Rancière's thought exemplifies the impulse to aestheticize rights and their paradoxes. While thus spinning an intensifying web of paradox, this chapter also charts a progressive aestheticization of that quality and its retinue (rights, democracy, ethics, and so forth); a deepening formalism (or cryptostructuralism) of paradox; and an expanding scope and generalizability (or crypto-universalism) of those redemptive vistas.

Rights and Insurrectionary Speech Post-'78

While '68 is often hailed as the pinnacle of popular radicalism, the late 1970s bequeathed left intellectuals the peculiar spirit of dissent that prevails to this day. That decade was a watershed for left intellectual life, retrofitting its contemporary compass and design. This is, no doubt, in part because the 1970s oversaw not only the domestication of 1960s-style protest but also theory's institutionalization, as Continental thought initially took up residence within language and literature departments and thereafter traveled throughout the Anglo-American university and abroad. As an inflection point, that decade further led to an internalization of preoccupations somewhat unique to that historical juncture: with speech and censorship, with authoritarianism, with consciousness-raising, with fears of co-optation, with rights, and more.

Rights (human and civil) certainly experienced changing fortunes during the late 1970s. However, what exactly that era meant for rights has also inspired significant debate—debate partially incited by Samuel Moyn's 2010 *The Last Utopia: Human Rights in History*. As Moyn recounts, especially the *international* human rights agenda acquired much of its (albeit Euro-American) validity and visibility beginning at the 1970s' tail end, when human rights both became an official global campaign and entered popular parlance. Citing events like Amnesty International's 1977 Nobel Peace Prize and Jimmy Carter's promotion of human rights in his inaugural address,[1] Moyn disputes the premise that 1948, the year the United Nations adopted the Universal Declaration of Human Rights (the UDHR), should be viewed as the primary birthplace of the contemporary human rights movement. To some degree, this is a Cold War story for Moyn; as he explains, "only once formal empire and direct Cold War intervention fell into disrepute did an internationalism based on rights come to the fore."[2] But the main targets of Moyn's revisionism are the assumptions, first, that rights were either a spur for decolonization or the guiding philosophy driving anticolonial activism and, second, that the Holocaust and Holocaust memory were the primary catalysts for either the UDHR or the explosion of human rights discourse by the end of the 1970s.[3]

Instead, Moyn's hypothesis is that human rights gained currency only after the miscarriage of other left idealisms, or following the collapse of "other, more grandiose dreams that [human rights] both drew on and displaced."[4] In particular, the human rights movement capitalized on the implosion of '68-style radicalism, deflecting those heady if exhausted aims into the surrogate yet noncontroversial project of human rights. Kristin Ross's *May '68 and Its Afterlives* draws parallel conclusions about France, attributing growing French support for human rights to the mutual debris of student protest and the counterculture. Key for both Moyn and Ross is that the success of human rights fully required certain disappointments among the left—and that enthusiasm for human rights therefore entailed a form of left selling out. For Ross, the left diverted its spent dreams into human rights only to abdicate responsibility for and identification with the local working class as well as the global South.[5] Or as Moyn puts it, "human rights were to crystallize as an organizing idealism only on condition of anticolonialism's decline and the general omission of its concerns."[6] For Moyn, this betrayal of left principles has at times sanctioned human rights minimalism, even if representing a "hardy utopia that could survive in a harsh climate."[7]

Moyn and Ross are correct that rights (human and civil) did undergo reinvention during the 1970s and that, in certain ways, that activity culminated with newfound zeal for rights across the liberal left. However, the motives and terms presiding over those shifts are a lot more complex, in part because the Cold War and atrophy of Soviet Marxism imbued rights with highly specific valences that made rights independently attractive to many intellectuals, including among the far left and within radicalism. More apt, then, is a distinction between the sudden allure of rights within left academic circles versus within liberal public discourse and the popular imaginary. Naturally, the factors prompting left intellectuals to look favorably on rights varied from those that fueled the popular international rights crusade. At the same time as *human* rights became an American agenda (no doubt compensating for the neglect of civil rights on the home front), rights (and the many issues they summoned) actively if unexpectedly helped to articulate and give an identity to the new brands of critical theory also resurrected from '68 and its ashes.

As a result, the 1970s saw rights become—and remain ever since—a battleground *within* the far, radical, intellectual left, and one that, for many, has made rights an unusually revealing litmus test gauging broader sympathies. That said, these feuds over rights do not always map onto clear or predictable fault lines, either within or across disciplines. Even while rights skepticism can appear near-militaristic within some corners of theory, that posture has not always transcended disciplinary boundaries. For instance, divisions within critical race theory are telling. Within the legal academy, one complaint of early work on race like that of Mari Matsuda and Kimberlé Crenshaw, as the next chapter considers, was that critical legal studies had been too hard on rights: too quick to jettison their emancipatory promise. In contrast, that rights are a primary technology of racial disenfranchisement under empire and the carceral state is axiomatic within the vast majority of work on racial oppression in fields like anthropology, literary criticism, American studies, and so on. While clearly dialing around larger disputes about normativity, liberalism, and law, these differences can just as much be boiled down to competing views about the structuralizing effects of paradox—rather than about whether paradox is or isn't constitutive of such a construct. Is paradox ontological and likely toxic? Do the paradoxes of rights, including their exclusionary architecture, buttress legalism, neoliberalism, and other machinery of oppression? Chapter 2 examined a collection of theorists who answer "yes." Or is paradox protean, subversive, rehabilitative, and metamorphic? Are the paradoxes of rights the very font of their open-endedness, fecundity, and visionary potential? In order to thus embrace the paradoxes of rights as dynamic and self-regenerating, left intellectual life required not only the linguistic turn and deconstruction but an assembly of other influences examined herein.

Many of those factors are relatively peculiar to the era that witnessed theory's American debut. To linger with the 1970s, a congeries of such influences united to replenish the enmeshed (and often interchangeable) fortunes of paradox and of rights. Much as Moyn and Ross observe regarding the popular and liberal left, academic theories of rights certainly harnessed energies orphaned following '68, redirecting them into then incipient hopes for rights. If anything, rights offered a perfect outlet for those foreclosed aspirations. In a set of moves choreographed by paradox, rights were re-imagined along lines that injected them with all the contrarianism of the counterculture. That reconfiguration of rights also rendered them anti-authoritarian (rather than helpmates to power)—although in a slippage between Cold War politics and the counterculture's anti-establishment sensibility. This gambit salvages rights from risks such as liberal legalism and complicity with power, rescuing them from the sorts of critiques canvassed in chapter 2. Yet whether seen as harbingers of a utopian "to-come" (á la Derrida) or embodying more modest goals, rights essentially became vehicles for keeping the nonconformist, rebellious, and experimental mindset of the 1960s alive.

Counterpart to such anti-authoritarianism, rights were simultaneously redefined as capacious and consciousness-raising outlets for liberatory self-expression—further suffusing them with the ethos of '60s-style radicalism. This mystique of the "free" clearly conjures *both* the shadow of the Cold War *and* the nonconformism of radicalized youth movements, including the impetus to "free one's mind." Akin to what Sean McCann and Michael Szalay maintain about theory overall, rights came to be imbued with the 1970s "new political vision built in large part on the appeal of the spontaneous, the symbolic, and ultimately, the magical."[8] For McCann and Szalay, that vision can be characterized by diverse elements: a Marcusean view that society has lost access to "spontaneity"; the prioritization of struggle waged through the "cultural apparatus"; and a psychedelic relish for magic, mysticism, risk, and the unforeseen. That mood has also conceived politics via an aesthetics of "performance, [...as] a kind of therapeutic rite aimed at the self-realization of its participants."[9] McCann and Szalay's goal is obviously to question this romance of the impulsive and transgressive, including its "fascination with the authority of 'political inarticulateness'"—or with "speech for speech's sake" divested of substance and content.[10] But the point is that these countercultural aspirations for "freedom of (self)expression" were channeled into rights to become implicit in their novel theoretical reformulations. Moreover, that impulse to extol rights as beacons of improvisatory speech (and its mind-altering fruits) was just as much encouraged by (and itself invited) the construal of rights as fundamentally *linguistic* and *performative* claims. A reflex corroborated (if not mandated) by the uptake of post-Saussurean semiotics, emphasis on the rhetorical dimensions of rights also increasingly dictated their theorization.

A religion of spontaneous self-expression thus conspired with a Cold War preoccupation with freedom of speech to deputize rights as a first and necessary line of defense against totalitarianism, further capturing why rights could become a rallying point across the countercultural *and* liberal left. Clearly, that atmosphere of the Cold War made talk of rights exceptionally freighted, and even more so when rights were viewed as eminently speech-based. Indeed, appeals to rights during the 1970s would have brought the specific threat of censorship almost immediately to mind. For thinkers of all stripes, the Cold War was a harrowing lesson in the utmost importance of protecting speech—a value circularly condensed and confirmed by fears about censorship. Those fears were only fanned by attacks on intellectuals both behind the Iron Curtain and in nations like South Africa. The tendency to link the Soviet Union and South Africa was rampant during the 1970s and '80s, evident for many in salient parallels connecting those two nations' show trials. For Cold War intellectuals, censorship therefore denoted not only the suppression of dissent and unique vulnerability of writers and public figures but also a precipitously slippery slope leading to other human rights abuses, which were explained as near automatically parasitic on the erosion of free speech. Just as censorship is widely thematized in art and literature of that era, anticensorship missions traveling behind the Iron Curtain included prominent philosophers and writers among their ranks.[11] Notably, this premise that rights are crucial staves against authoritarianism's many encroachments was also the narrative accompanying Amnesty International's Nobel Peace Prize. The Nobel organization's 1977 award ceremony speech praises Amnesty International for its fight for "prisoners of conscience," mistreated due to their "opinions" alone. While invoking the UDHR's Article 18 and 19 covering "freedom of thought, conscience, religion, opinion, and speech," the organization's presentation rigorously distinguishes between content-based versus "neutral" speech protections, clarifying that Amnesty's efforts do "not necessarily imply that the organisation shares the views of the prisoner, but that it maintains his right, under any regime, to give expression to his opinions."[12] What matters to peace and democracy, in other words, is the sheer existence of unregulated, uncoerced speech—regardless of its substance or subject matter.

This Cold War fixation on speech and censorship was verified by highly specific ideas about the anatomy of totalitarianism then circulating within academic as well as public discourse: ideas *both* about how totalitarianism consolidates itself *and* about its predatory appetites. Totalitarianism was seen above all to prey on speech: to be actively nourished by assaults on freedom of expression. Regnant accounts of totalitarianism have consequently looked to speech as a kind of gateway drug, the cusp of a snowballing barrage of other rights infringements.[13] According to such reasoning, its devouring of speech is corollary to authoritarianism's monopolization of truth and (especially political) meaning. As Lefort, who we turn to next, describes the image of the "People-as-One" manufactured by totalitarianism, "This logic of identification [...] accounts in turn for the condensation that takes places between the principle of power, the principle of law and the principle of knowledge."[14] What thus arose during the Cold War was a widespread instinct to equate the political form of totalitarianism with a totalization of truth, speech, and other expressions of meaning, in a nexus that hallows free speech as a crucial stopgap against those ever-lurking perils. A threshold right, speech either opens the door to other rights abuses or ensures that door's vigilant barricade. However, not just any old speech has been thus touted as autoimmunizing. Precisely the aleatory, undisciplined, and "inarticulate" modes of self-expression proselytized by the counterculture were—albeit underpinned by a different set of rationales—deemed intrinsically antitotalitarian. Liberal principles operative during the Cold War consequently fused with a lingering countercultural mind-set to become mutually reinforcing. Within that accord, democracy-producing political speech would similarly be treated as identifiable *not* with reference to its substance or content but instead vis-à-vis its very freedom from such strictures: its pluri- or multivocality, indeterminacy, open-endedness, uncensorability, and, plainly put, ladenness with paradox.

Along with this Cold War setting and its countercultural residues, a burgeoning focus on witnessing and testimony—a focus indulging a separate if related fascination with unspeakability, namely of the two world wars—encouraged such conflation of rights with defiantly antiauthoritarian (and antilegalistic) self-expression. So while Holocaust memory may not, as Moyn argues, have fueled popular support for the human rights movement during the 1970s, it without question midwifed left *intellectual* investment in rights over the decades to come. A novel like Don DeLillo's 1985 *White Noise* succinctly registers the extent of intellectual engrossment with the Holocaust during that era. In this satire of academia, the novel's main character, Jack Gladney, a professor at an institution referred to simply as "The-College-On-The-Hill," is renowned for pioneering the then infant field of Hitler studies, which the novel presents as a sufficiently consuming research area to warrant entire scholarly careers and even departments.[15]

Thus did the late 1980s and '90s see realities like pain, trauma, and large-scale atrocity increasingly theorized according to a framework that generated still additional rationales, *both* for privileging speech as a uniquely sacrosanct right *and* for granting conceptual authority to paradox. Then germinal work on suffering and trauma also attributes massive explanatory significance—political, symbolic, and psychological—to violated, threatened, or otherwise silenced speech. For some, that significance extends from the fact that speech represents a core insignia of the "human," as Elaine Scarry's pathbreaking 1985 *The Body in Pain* submits.[16] While trauma theory occupies this book's penultimate chapter, crucial for now is that a distinct blend of late Cold War politics and a mounting imperative to reckon with the Holocaust also helped to solidify an equation among rights, paradox, and specifically aleatory, contentless speech—an equation that, perhaps ironically, simultaneously helped popularize trauma as an infectious discourse. Work like Scarry's regards pain as instructive due to more than how it compromises if not shatters the human voice; that crisis of representation induced by pain facilitates far-reaching insights into power's anatomy. For Scarry and other trauma theorists (mirroring adjacent accounts of totalitarianism), power is aggrandized through attacks on speech and the voice; just as pain lays siege to the voice, power, too, exhibits a fundamentally totalitarian relationship to language. As Scarry explains, torture "monopolizes language, becom[ing] its only subject" and thereby enacts "the conversion of absolute pain into the fiction of absolute power."[17] Indeed, Scarry cautions that precisely when speech fails to communicate does pain become a stepping stone for "debased" forms of power.[18] Scarry's seminal insights into the phenomenology of pain—that it is "unsharable" and "world-destroying"—thus carry decidedly political stakes, much as her study's opening chapters on torture and war probe the communicational hurdles faced by activist organizations like Amnesty International along lines vividly echoing that organization's Nobel acceptance speech.[19] Paradoxical, most immediately, is the fact that a representational failure (here, of speech) would work to illuminate inescapable realities concerning the operations of power. Although in many respects a conventional humanist, Scarry nevertheless defines pain via the assumption that power is actualized by censoring or colonizing certain voices, just as she views anticensorship protections as a firewall against totalitarianism's incursions. So whereas the specter of totalitarianism per se (or at least its Cold War variants) has clearly dissipated over time, many of these conceptual lineaments remain all-governing.

Another core paradox structuring much work on trauma is that extreme pain, despite being overwhelmingly real for the sufferer, causes language to break down, refusing pain representation. This basic insight is foundational to Yale school trauma theory, with its insistence that traumatic remembrance is, on a certain level, impossible. The conceit that trauma and pain will resist rational, objectivizable communication works, in a parallel fashion as the liberal premium on freedom of expression, to define traumatic speech by way of its evacuation of determinant subject matter. Hence, trauma studies offers its own basis for valorizing "speech for speech's sake"—or speech that gains merit precisely in its inarticulacy. By explaining the act of bearing witness as a quintessentially antiauthoritarian gesture, trauma studies also theorizes that act in term that meditate inextricably on the anatomy of power *and* on the human psyche. The very psychic foreclosures, deferrals, and other absences surrounding the traumatic kernel are what render its truths productively defiant of totalization and, as such, antitotalitarian, even while that elusiveness is imagined to divulge essential truths about law, power, and oppression. Yet despite brimming with consummate meaning, trauma's capacity for unconcealment paradoxically lies with the incoherence, untranslatability, and other communicational failures of the traumatized voice—not so far afield from the "political inarticulacy" probed by McCann and Szalay.

For now, key is that all of this led humanistic work on rights to flourish. The above preoccupations primed numerous humanities disciplines for what have been dubbed various "human rights turns," fueling an outpouring of scholarship on rights. Indeed, the year 2000 is arguably the high-water mark of Continental theory's absorption with rights, whether instantiated in Judith Butler's work from the early 2000s (the books *Giving An Account of Oneself*, *Precarious Life*, and *Undoing Gender*), or the dual volumes of Oxford

Amnesty Lectures both of which were published in 1993 (*Freedom and Interpretation*, edited by Barbara Johnson and including essays by Julia Kristeva, Paul Ricoeur, Wayne Booth, Hélène Cixous, and Terry Eagleton, which was followed by *On Human Rights*, edited by Stephen Shute and Susan Hurley and including Jean-François Lyotard, Richard Rorty, and Catharine MacKinnon), or the prominent 2004 *South Atlantic Quarterly* issue "And Justice for All?: The Claims of Human Rights" (edited by Ian Balfour and Eduardo Cadava, with contributors Gayatri Spivak, Rancière, Etienne Balibar, Derrida, Thomas Keenan, Slavoj Žižek, and Avital Ronell, among others).[20] Many examples in this chapter and the foregoing come from that material.

A few added things require emphasis before moving on. First is the indispensability of paradox to this prospering attention to rights, as an object of scholarly inquiry and an emancipatory horizon. That logic is crucial to mapping the intellectual landscape to which such enthusiasm for rights responds. We have at length observed why a logic of paradox has widely administered debates about rights; little question exists over whether rights are or are not paradoxical. Second, however, something distinctive happens when speech and specifically speech rights are refracted through that optics of paradox—and, in turn, when rights are foremost taken to denote anticensorship protections. Whereas unrestricted speech gets exalted as a poison pill that totalitarianism cannot stomach, it is the logic of paradox that above all buffers such speech to inoculate it against ideological capture. Unverifiability, incalculability, plurivocality, indeterminacy, inchoacy, open-endedness, unspeakability, fugitivity, liminality, unforeseeability: those properties are thus imagined as innately fortifying. Meanwhile, the coterminous move to theorize rights as chiefly linguistic claims and shorthands for freedom of expression transfers those qualities of uncensorable speech onto rights—and onto the democracy that rights-as-utterances are imagined both to ordain and to betoken.

Third, those uncensorable (and paradox-riddled) indicia acquired potency under the shadow of highly specific although historically outmoded instantiations of authoritarianism. Such an economy of valuation arguably only makes sense with reference to the outlay of a theory of power that spectralizes its constitutive hostility to the anarchy of paradox and that logic's undisciplined representations. Hence, what are today standard expectations for paradox arguably lose justification the moment power begins to assume different guises, or to secure itself via an alternate machinery. One overriding question posed by this book concerns the diminished relevance of thought that sows paradox with redemptively political horizons.

Others have noted that many schools of especially deconstructive theory retain various Cold War problematics, memorializing them in their trademark vocabularies and assumptions. Those relics have been at times mirthfully maligned, perhaps most acerbically by Marxist thinkers. For instance, Terry Eagleton's 1984 *The Function of Criticism* satirizes "the Yale School" for projecting Frankfurt School anxieties about political totalitarianism onto a multitude of realities, conflating all manifestations of ideology and power with interwar fascism.[21] In a similar vein, Žižek's 2001 *Did Somebody Say Totalitarianism? Five Interventions in the (Mis)Use of a Notion* charges deconstructive brands of ethics with "shamefully exploit[ing] the horrors of Gulag or Holocaust as the ultimate bogey for blackmailing us into renouncing all serious radical engagement." Importantly, Žižek singles out semiotic analysis as deserving particular blame for those depoliticizing effects: for manipulating a blurring of political forms and purely philosophical notions in ways that excuse a textualist retreat.[22]

However, we have already seen Žižek and other Marxist thinkers to be far from immune to such conflations. If anything, Žižek's special bent for discerning the "symptoms" of capitalism in seemingly innocuous phenomena generalizes paradox onto all of contemporary existence, even while that quality yields almost mystical dividends. Yet what matters here is that Žižek's impulse to incriminate semiotic analysis alone is far too narrow. More accurately, a dense mix of factors coalesced beginning in the 1970s to erect paradox into something more than either a diagnosis or tool of critical unmasking: into a transformative ethos capable of rehabilitating rights (and theory) despite their many tragic failings.

Dissenting from Marx, the Cold War, and Rights-as-Utterances

Quarrels within factions of the left provided the impetus for some thinkers to espouse rights, as rights offered a foothold for critiquing both Marx and Marxism's midcentury incarnations. The Lacanian theorist Claude Lefort is one such figure who adopted rights as a platform for distancing himself from, and in the process chiding apologists for, Soviet Marxism. While illustrating why rights still today can serve as a wedge separating Marxism from other theoretical stances, Lefort's reclamation of rights was also motivated by impulses gaining broad traction across the left in the postwar decades—and that have since represented default positions for many. Most immediately, Lefort's insistence on the "symbolic" and declarative or enunciative fiber of rights routes their logic (and their paradoxes) through a linguistic frame, reconceiving rights as "utterances." In many ways, that privileging of the symbolic and rhetorical dimensions of rights, as suggested, is an artifact of the Cold War and totalitarianism's political theater, a climate no doubt occasioning many aspects of Lefort's thought. Yet while the cauldron of postwar Europe seeded the language of paradox with antitotalitarian resonances, Lefort simultaneously adheres to more classical views (traceable to Rousseau) regarding rights' inherent ungroundedness and indeterminacy.

Lefort's 1980 essay "Politics and Human Rights" (published in English in 1986 in *The Political Forms of Modern Society: Bureaucracy, Democracy, Totalitarianism*) construes rights according to terms that Lefort simultaneously leverages to indict the French left for failing to better diagnose and thereby confront the many abuses of Soviet power. For Lefort, those failures are foreshadowed in the early Marx's own overly categorical rejection of rights. As Lefort alleges, Marx was mistaken about rights on multiple levels—mistakes that later sanctioned the crimes perpetrated under his thought's twentieth-century auspices. Gesturing sweepingly, Lefort outright equates totalitarianism with the abuse of human rights, deriding it as "built on the ruin of the rights of man."[23] At once, he zeroes in on specific passages of "On the Jewish Question" (1844) to discover hints of Soviet Marxism's later degeneration. Like many, Lefort takes Marx's famed text as a touchstone—although here to justify his repudiation of the brands of rights skepticism usually ingrained within Marxist theory.

Marx's central blind spot, for Lefort, is ironic: Marx himself falls into the "trap" of ideology. That trap inures Marx, first, to the many salutary sociopolitical gains procured by rights and, second, to the ways rights are, in practice, "embedded in a social context."[24] On the one hand, Lefort thus rebukes Marx for overstating the individualizing and hence atomizing orientation of rights, neglecting their social, communal bearings. But on the other, Lefort complains that Marx wrongly discounts some rights in favor of others—in particular disregarding those rights protecting freedom of speech and opinion. Marxism's materialism overlooks these more "symbolic" aspects of rights—aspects that for Lefort are absolutely essential to comprehending totalitarianism's workings. From one angle, Lefort thereby understands totalitarianism to wage its warfare on the terrain of the symbolic, violently "totalizing" truth and meaning (and, like other instantiations of power, running roughshod over fractures, tensions, discontinuities, and other sites of paradox). Yet Lefort's "symbolic" is also of a psychoanalytic derivation, and it is notably that absent center that totalitarianism disobeys. With this charge, Lefort lends primacy to speech as a uniquely potent bulwark, even while evincing a characteristically Cold War obsession with censorship. As such, it is within this Cold War milieu that rights could semiautomatically encode the paramountcy of speech as a vital rampart against a domino effect of rights infringements.

This premise that "rights are not simply the object of a declaration, it is their essence to be declared" is one that Lefort explicitly labels a paradox—in a passage unpacking what he calls a "triple paradox" of rights.[25] One such paradox is that "it is impossible to detach the statement from the utterance," suggesting that rights have little meaning apart from their enactment as performative speech acts. But that tripartite paradox is furthermore identified by Lefort as the latticework distinguishing democracy from totalitarianism. These reflections on rights' interwoven paradoxes are, perhaps not surprisingly, in part prompted by the perennial quandary of what "anchors" rights, or of their foundations. In reproaching Marx, Lefort therefore concludes that Marx was *also* wrong about rights' eighteenth-century origins and especially rights' role in power's "disincorporation," in "depriv[ing it] of a fixed point." And it is this guiding insight that compels Lefort to infuse rights with what are today a set of predictable properties. As Lefort explains, a society committed to rights will be "uncircumscribed," organized by "multiplicity" as well as "modes of communication" that are "indeterminate" and geared to elude "the orbit of power."[26] Notably, these are the very sorts of paradoxes a philosopher like Jeremy Bentham deplored, fearing that they would unleash constant anarchy. Yet in Lefort's hands, the indeterminacies plaguing rights are recast as liberatory, among other things for their capacity to besiege authoritarian manifestations of power.

Lefort's rebranding of rights as preeminently linguistic claims leads him to define rights along other lines today axiomatic. Lefort is deliberate about the fact that the "declaration" of rights is what causes "an essential mutation [to become] apparent," just as he applauds rights for ensuring that "the duality of speaking and hearing in the public sphere is multiplied instead of being frozen in the relation of authority." Far from neutral is therefore the precise modality of discourse that Lefort associates with rights: discourse that is centrifugal, fragmentary, multiple, self-pluralizing, and so on. In particular those aleatory properties are what guard rights against the legal reification that we saw to disturb Arendt, as Lefort instead insists on "the irreducibility of the awareness of right to all legal objectification, which would signify its petrification."[27] No doubt, these are high hopes for speech as a first line of defense.

Lefort exhibits comparatively high hopes for paradox, the multifarious dynamics of which are essential to his reasoning. In adumbrating his "triple paradox" of rights, Lefort inscribes those paradoxes within rights' governing logic, including within the distinct types of speech rights make available. On the one hand, Lefort thereby partakes of common reasoning that exalts paradox as transformative and rejuvenating. In his thinking, paradox marks not a liability or problem but instead is something to be reveled in: to be pursued, promoted, and inhabited, given that paradox is nothing short of the life force of democracy. But on the other, Lefort's conceit that such paradox-inflected speech will frustrate the censoring appetites of political absolutism works to weaponize that quality. Paradox becomes more than a trip wire or buffer; it is understood to actively sabotage centralizing forms of power.[28] As Lefort's discussion of rights concludes, "It is the image of the engulfing of the particular within the social space which is destroyed" by that ammunition of paradox.

As if that were not enough, paradox functions for Lefort as a type of threshold separating totalitarianism from its democratic inverse or antithesis. Much as rights are receptacles of paradox and therefore invaluable, Lefort imagines paradox to guard the perimeter insulating democracy from totalitarianism—which is to say that a single algebra *both* endows rights with their resistant potential *and* demarcates the boundary segregating democracy from its antagonists. Here, too, this move to enshrine paradox as a borderland dividing yet connecting ostensibly opposing phenomena is a methodological commonplace. As chapter 1 saw, paradox has been the horizon of modernity, offsetting a modern consciousness from its purported antecedents and betrayals. As the signature of the aesthetic, species of paradox similarly insulate the literary or poetic from other modes of discourse. It is therefore tempting to interpret Lefort as recruiting these established cartographies and mapping them onto the landscape of the Cold War, much as a not so subtle subtext in thought like that of Mikhail Bakhtin and Georg Lukács is precisely to extrapolate from the formal features of Greek or epic genres to venture claims about political absolutism. Whereas for Bakhtin those allegedly premodern literary forms "express the centralizing tendencies in language," "know[ing] only a single and unified world view, obligatory and indubitably true," the novel with its polyglossia and "openendedness" engenders a bold vision of human freedom and "spontaneity" that, not accidentally, vindicates *The Dialogic Imagination*'s own plea for rights: "the right to be 'other' in this world."[29] Yet whether pervading art or modernity or democracy, those paradoxes thus venerated all require some form of dangerous totalization to posit as their foil, negation, and menace.

For Lefort, paradox is thus the linchpin *both* opposing *and* connecting totalitarian and democratic forms, acting as a pivot around which they together rotate. What this also means is that a logic of paradox ultimately reveals those ostensibly competing structures to be mirror if inverted images. Whereas democracy thrives on paradox, totalitarianism, the reasoning goes, must abolish, dominate, or contain that quality and everything it telegraphs (rights, speech, individualism, freedom, and so on). Such a symmetry might seem to render Lefort's notion of democracy derivative: only comprehensible under the threat of absolutism's venomous intolerance of paradox. But there is simultaneously a sense in which paradox becomes all-enveloping, seeing how its well-greased axis renders democracy at continual peril of gyration—of seamlessly morphing into its lethal other. No doubt, that was the whole point for many midcentury thinkers: to forewarn about democracy's vertiginous proximity to, and capacity for surreptitiously mutating into, political evil. Nevertheless, the logic of paradox can seem to operate as its own master trope, capable of uncracking the linked riddles of democracy and of totalitarianism in a single algorithmic code.

It is also crucial to observe how Lefort's recuperation of rights hinges on historically specific assumptions about the ontology of totalitarian power that, for all intents and purposes, became largely obsolete along with the Cold War. As Lefort conceives of totalitarian power, it "ceases to designate an empty place: it is materialized in an organ (or, in extreme cases, an individual) which is supposed to be capable of concentrating in itself all the forces of society." Similarly does power "reject" "the very notion of social heterogeneity,"[30] and it further demands "cohesion," "integrity," "transparency," "total knowledge," and a unitary image of the "the People-as-One," often denoted through organicist symbolism of a human body. Contrary to power's "engulfing" designs, then, rights and their claims are centripetal, dispersing, and, in Lefort's terms, "ineffaceably external to power."[31] Lefort's reasoning further imagines power's consolidation of symbolic meaning to occur in a precise correspondence with its material exertions of brute force. So on the one hand, Lefort takes totalitarianism to task for a refusal to respect the randomness, indeterminacy, and other workings of politics, wrongly imposing fixity, presence, transparency, mimetic identity, and resolution where none exists. But on the other, Lefort's thinking posits a notably precise symmetry connecting symbolics and politics, in thinking that falls victim to near identical explanatory errors as those he attributes to centralized political systems. Whereas he understands flawed if not violative strategies of representation (symbolic and linguistic) to solidify power, Lefort's own arguments can seem to assume a one-to-one correspondence between the symbolic plane and the concrete structures assumed by real-life political institutions.

By trumpeting the unanchored status of rights, Lefort evokes another received philosophical basis for yoking democracy to paradox then redolent within the general Cold War atmosphere. By underscoring their dearth of foundations, Lefort saddles rights with a legitimation deficit—although one that, rather than a sheer encumbrance, is characterized by Lefort as productive. Importantly, that emphasis on rights' ungroundedness for many would have brought to mind Rousseau's reflections on democratic paradox. And even though Lefort does not cite that inheritance, his thought has often been assimilated into such a genealogy. As we have seen, Rousseau is commonly recognized as the first to have grappled with such a "paradox of democratic legitimacy" in posing the question: "What makes a people a people?"[32] As *The Social Contract* relates:

> For a nascent people to be capable of appreciating sound maxims of politics and of following the fundamental rules of reason of State, the effect would have to become the cause, the social spirit which is to be the work of the institution would have to preside over the institution itself, and men would have to be prior to laws what they ought to become by means of them. Thus, since the Lawgiver can use neither force nor reasoning, he must of necessity have recourse to an authority of a different order.

As Rousseau suggests, democracy must fictitiously posit the preexistence of a People, even while that gesture retroactively brings such a People into being.[33] Akin to other nonmimetic and antifoundationalist representations, this uncertainty underlying democracy both threatens and enables its practice, rendering any representation of the People chronically open-ended. With his reflections on that "nascent people," moreover, Rousseau can seem to anticipate what has been hallowed as an adjacent paradox of democracy: the People's exclusionary architecture. Yet unlike the thinkers considered in the last chapter, Rousseau's heirs have frequently taken those paradoxical exclusions to be propagative and fertile: rather than a debility, the very portal of democracy.

Other theorists during the Cold War were overt in recruiting Rousseau to parse that midcentury context, navigating questions akin to those posed by Lefort and arriving at similar answers. Even then, Rousseau was credited with prescient insight into those components of politics—namely, abundant paradox—that totalitarianism cannot tolerate and instead must master. In a 1957 essay titled "The Political Paradox," Paul Ricoeur thus enlists Rousseau to decry crimes of Soviet Marxism that came to a head in the failed 1956 Hungarian Revolution. Praising Rousseau for inaugurating "the basic question of political philosophy," Ricoeur effectively redraws Rousseau's problematic in directions that have since become orthodox.[34] Like Lefort, Ricoeur sees himself as correcting a Marxist tendency to limit political evil to economic alienation, missing its symbolic dimensions. In contrast, the "reality of ideality" first identified by Rousseau sows politics with "absolute [...] contradiction," thereby rendering matters of legitimacy perennially yet fruitfully indeterminate. It is specifically political "evil" for Ricoeur that cannot live with and instead seeks to submerge political uncertainty by manufacturing "untruth"[35]—as Ricoeur basically blames the brutal Soviet response to the Budapest uprising on the need to manage, contain, and overcome paradox. Paradox, once again unearthed as the political's hidden design, is simultaneously isolated as the main quality separating one political form from another. What reasoning like Ricoeur's and Lefort's ultimately does is to locate disagreements over the significance and value of paradox at the inception of all modern politics.

Two quick examples can display this stamp of the Cold War's lasting imprint on contemporary theories of radical democracy. First, the 2016 volume *What Is a People?* (compiling short essays by Alain Badiou, Pierre Bourdieu, Judith Butler, Jacques Rancière, and others) is a case in point. An introduction by the Marxist theorist Bruno Bosteels opens by canvassing the reasons for that volume's investment in the category of the People. Bosteels's prefatory remarks rely on numerous moves we've just considered, holding them out as prevailing if not indisputable wisdom. In so doing, Bosteels spells out the usual assumptions according to which apparent failures or liabilities are revealed to be democracy's very essence. As he observes of democracy's "necessary exclusion," the exact "divisions and exclusions that keep the people from ever being one are very much part and parcel of the category's uncanny political efficacy."[36] Bosteels admits that, for the uninitiated, this might seem a "theoretical inconsistency or shortcoming" or even an "impediment"; however, that "gap," or "distance of the people from itself," in fact represents "the real efficacy of actual politics": the People's "true political effectiveness."[37] Contra the impulse to unify or consolidate meaning, democracy's promise lies with "the force of [its] paradoxical tension."[38] With "efficacy" encoding quite a lot, Bosteels does not hesitate to assimilate Marx into this brotherhood descending from Rousseau, explaining that such a lineage "also announce[s] the Marxist critique of the limits of modern politics."[39]

Second, Bonnie Honig's 2011 *Emergency Politics: Paradox, Law, Democracy* pays tribute to paradox within its very title. Although challenging the "apocalyptic" fatalism engrossment with Carl Schmitt and Giorgio Agamben has induced within political theory,[40] even Honig's reservations about Schmitt verify the centrality of paradox to democracy. Like many, Honig contextualizes her stance by pitting two different ways of handling paradox against one another. While critiquing a Schmittian focus on "the paradoxical state of emergency," she instead celebrates "the most fundamental and fecund paradox of all: democracy's *paradox of politics.*"[41] *Emergency Politics* thereby mobilizes a polarity we know well and will revisit. But in the process, paradox comes to devour virtually everything bearing on the political. Although Honig's critique of biopolitics jettisons one mode of reckoning with systemic paradox, paradox is nonetheless the crux of her argument, as she replaces "emergency paradox" with merely another incarnation of that all-consuming quality (i.e., "fecund paradox").

Even more questionable, Honig explains that her chief goal is to expand the explanatory compass of paradox, which she scolds other political theorists for artificially constricting. Rather than exclusive to the emergency, paradox for Honig is "a feature of daily democratic life."[42] However, Honig's mundane, nonexceptional variant of paradox still requires as its predatory double certain usual suspects: liberalism, legalism, rationalism, normativity, universalism, and so on. As Honig clarifies: "the paradox of politics does not elicit from us justification or confront us with the need for legitimation. [It] is not soluble by law or legal institutions, nor can it be tamed by universal or cosmopolitan norms. [...] Thus, the paradox teaches us the limits of law."[43] While pledging a garden variety anti-legalism, Honig's reflections assign still further labor to paradox: the pedagogical (i.e., paradox "teaches"). Those expectations for the edifying effects of encounters with paradox have also been overriding—arguably revolutionizing the humanities over the latter decades of the twentieth century (as chapters 4 and 5 discuss). But while superficially affirming the merits of the ordinary and "everyday," Honig's insistence on insolubility and untamability simultaneously etherealizes those spaces and everything they might be expected to enable, mystifying the coordinates of decision-making within many if not most actual legal and political forums.

While Lefort remains widely read, his influence pales in comparison to a thinker like Jacques Derrida, although their accounts of rights share much in common. While Derrida's theory of the relations between law and diverse guises of justice (forgiveness, hospitability, testimony, and more) are elaborated over the course of a long career, the basic parameters of his thinking were fashioned amid Europe's midcentury political fallout, causing his thought to retain multiple Cold War preoccupations. Whereas Lefort emphasizes the speech-based and symbolic tenor of rights, rights are patterned by Derrida on a deconstructive semiotics—and consequently suffused with all the paradoxical qualities of writing.

The extent to which Derrida's theories of law and justice are modeled on a deconstructive philosophy of textual language has been widely noted. That textualism also animates Derrida's conception of rights, imbuing rights with the many variants of paradox that for Derrida pervade writing. *Différance*, play, supplementarity, deferral, absence, postponement, indeterminacy, the trace: each such term crystallizes a modality of paradox. *Différance*, for instance, indexes how textual "meaning" is detoured through the ceaseless, irresolvable movements of the signifier and is therefore predicated on gaps and adjournments. Analogous tensions inflect Derrida's notion of the sign, which "represents the present in its absence" and therefore "is deferred presence."[44] In effect, Derrida envisions a crisis of legitimacy to haunt all representation, given how randomness and indeterminacy saturate the most basic units of textual language. Resembling other discourses of paradox, Derrida's semiotics thereby redeem what might look like deficiencies (i.e., "absence") to divine within them meaning-making virtuosity. Along such lines does deconstruction's critique of "metaphysics of presence" explain that apparent lacuna to be prolific: the impossibility of metaphysics for Derrida "extend[s] the domain and play of signification infinitely."[45] Relatedly does Derrida's description of "the movement of *supplementarity*" carry out a parallel conversion: "The *overabundance* of the signifier, its *supplementary* character, is thus the result of a finitude, that is to say, the result of a lack which must be *supplemented*."[46]

These and other features of textual language are, beginning in Derrida's early career, transposed onto matters of ethics—and in terms that, as above, meditate on the circumstances of the Cold War. Derrida's "Violence and Metaphysics" (published in French in 1964) in particular was a conduit for the phenomenology of Emmanuel Levinas and his grammar of Otherness and alterity, and in Derrida's account, multiple indicia of Otherness are cognate to *différance* precisely in their mutual defiance of "totalitarian" and "authoritarian" systems of thought.[47] Hence, "Violence and Metaphysics" memorably indicts "the entire philosophical tradition" for its beholdenness to totalitarian habits of thought, as Derrida comprehensively implicates Hegelian dialectics, phenomenology, ontology, structuralism, and especially the "Greek domination of the Same and the One" within "the origin or alibi of all oppression in the world."[48] All attempts to conceptualize or systematize are thus condemned as totalitarian "philosophies of violence."[49] In contrast, Derrida applauds the supposed immunity of Levinas's theology of Otherness to such conceptualist veins of thought. As he avers, Otherness refuses categorization, flouts legal codification, and emerges with no more than a *"trace"*—features that create striking homologies between "Otherness" and textual language. That Otherness cannot be immanently or completely known means that it will productively elude "metaphysics of oppression," evincing an anti-legalism not so distant from the versions considered in chapter 2.[50]

While present early in his oeuvre, the late 1980s and especially 1990s witnessed a growing focus by Derrida on politics and law that continued until the end of his life, including in the 2001–3 seminars published as *The Beast and the Sovereign*.[51] These later stages also find Derrida emphatic in declaring that deconstruction has all along been oriented toward matters of politics, democracy, law, and justice. As he submits in *Rogues: Two Essays on Reason* (2005), "the thinking of the political has always been a thinking of *différance* and the thinking of *différance* always a thinking of the political."[52] Throughout his writings, Derrida thus anoints many of deconstruction's trademark vocabularies (the gift, the undecidable, the incommensurable, the incalculable, singularity, heterogeneity, impossibility, aporia) as "at least obliquely discourses on justice."[53]

For some, the inaugural and therefore most important statement of this orientation is "Force of Law: The 'Mystical Foundation of Authority,'" a lengthy publication in a 1989–90 symposium issue of the *Cardozo Law Review* collecting essays from the colloquium "Deconstruction and the Possibility of Justice." "Force of Law" opens by submitting that "a deconstructive line of questioning is through and through a problematization of law and justice. A problematization of the foundations of law, morality and politics."[54] Yet while "Force of Law" is a bracing compendium of those diverse bearings, the seeds of Derrida's interest in law and rights germinated much earlier. As the first interlude addressed, Derrida investigates the nexus between "right" or "rights" as early as 1976, partaking of reasoning that becomes the scaffolding for his later work on legal-political questions.

"Declarations of Independence," a lecture translated into English in 1986 in the journal *New Political Science* and later included in the 2002 volume *Negotiations*, was written to commemorate the bicentennial of the United States Declaration of Independence.[55] Invited by his hosts to place that document into dialogue with the UDHR, Derrida cautions that "no previous work had led [him] along the path of such analyses."[56] Perhaps to be expected given deconstruction's basis in semiotics, Derrida frames his insights by foregrounding the textually inscribed or written status of rights, in the process extrapolating from his semiotics to decipher rights. On the one hand, this approach allows Derrida to stay within his assigned parameters, restricting his analysis to those two declarations. There is also little question that Derrida's Cold War milieu would have made his emphasis on the "right to writing" (i.e., on rights as anticensorship protections) semiautomatic. Yet on the other hand, it is that conjunction—"the right to writing"—that enables Derrida to transfer all of the deferrals, ambivalences, undecidabilities, and other paradoxical qualities of textual language onto rights, subjecting rights to the same economy of signification as a text.

The implications of this move and the swift relays it ingrains are hard to overstate. Such textualist patterning has subsequently been brought to bear upon virtually every phenomenon deconstruction has laid its hands on. In effect, that move installs a kind of conveyor belt within Derrida's theory, distributing his semiotics onto the vast plane of justice, politics, ethics, and more. But for now, we can again note the extent to which this intercourse is licensed (if not fully demanded) by the peculiar intellectual climate of the Cold War, which both rendered rights an ideal outlet for Derrida's semiotics and allowed the linguistic turn to collude with then-rampant fears about the censoring designs of totalitarianism.

Something equivalent transpires via that lecture's examination of the "signature," in reasoning also indebted to J. L. Austin's distinction between performative and constative speech acts. Reflecting on the Declaration of Independence, Derrida credits the "performative" nature of the "signature" with *both* constituting rights *and* vesting them with—or "propagating"—a chain of ambivalences otherwise characteristic of textual language.[57] Derrida even cites historical uncertainty regarding the official status of the Declaration's real-life signatories to establish such indeterminacy, asking whether Jefferson signed as an individual or instead was deputized by the people. What Derrida thereby does is to generalize those uncertainties tied to Jefferson's role as ambassador of the People to draw far-reaching conclusions about the "necessary undecidability" of rights. Historically specific (and arguably irrelevant) debates about Jefferson's legal-political status as signatory are thereby merged into (and confused with) a deconstructive theory of a text's "signatures" (i.e., residues and traces), all the while permitting Derrida's arguments concerning the Declaration to be globalized to apply to *all* claims to rights. While this sort of gesture is a calling card of deconstruction, such transit could only be secured by a semiotics riven with thoroughgoing paradox.

Permeated with the many paradoxical features of writing, rights become comparatively prolific in their meaning-making potential—and precisely due to their unending undecidabilities. Derrida is deliberate in this turn to inject rights with properties equivalent to those animating a written text: explicitly referring to rights, he emphasizes their "overdetermined temporality," "obscurity," "fabulous retroactivity," and "structure of the trace."[58] These protolinguistic qualities are exactly what allow rights to be incorporated into the same explanatory scheme as the abundantly profuse and inexhaustible properties of other written language.

By highlighting the uncertain authority of Jefferson's signature, Derrida further taxes rights with a legitimation crisis on par with writing. In ruminating over the "fabulous" nature of that signature, "Declarations of Independence" evokes long-standing debates about the paradoxical truths of fictions, activating aesthetic criticism's storehouse of tools for redressing art's fragile validity. As we saw in the interlude, Derrida quotes Francis Ponge's poem "Fable"—"By the word *by* begins thus this text / Of which the first line says the truth"—in order to liken the fictionality of rights to the liar's paradoxes of literature. And precisely in purloining the cache of aesthetic theory does Derrida find sanction for rights' embrace. Indeed, Derrida's reasoning is actively piratic of a justificatory framework crafted to defend the preeminent value of art, which he repurposes to explain away parallel worries about the ungroundedness (and, one might wonder, the liberal humanist derivation) of rights. Just as the indeterminacies of rights and of art thus become homologous, the charlatan workings of paradox come along to recuperate what, at first blush, might appear a detriment (rights' tenuous claims to truth), acclaiming that very shortfall of legitimacy as the source of rights' "overabundance." As for art, the foundationless foundations of rights (which simultaneously become cognate to the absent presence of the "signature") can be transmuted into something worthy of veneration.

These themes in "Declarations of Independence" demonstrate "Force of Law" to be much less pivotal than often surmised. Nevertheless, the latter reads as a road map to the full implications of Derrida's theory of law and justice, and along lines that simultaneously capture a deep grammar of paradox's imprint on deconstruction. In the same breath glossing the maneuvers central to justice and to deconstruction, Derrida conflates those twinned pursuits, and it is precisely a shared economy of paradox that subsidizes such elisions. It is a "paradox" that the deconstructibility of law "makes deconstruction possible" (in a series culminating with the assertion "deconstruction is justice").[59] Relatedly is justice cast as the "experience" of the "impossible" and of "aporia": qualities that issue metatheoretical commentaries on deconstruction.[60] One lengthy section catalogs "aporias" of justice concurrently presented as deconstruction's defining features: the haunting of justice by "the ghost of the undecidable"; the messianic horizons of the "*a-venir*" or to-come; justice's "absolute alterity"; its fundamentally "unrepresentable" status; and how it exceeds "calculation, rules, programs, [and] anticipations." These reflections render the projects of justice and of deconstruction virtually indistinguishable—while consecrating paradox as their common métier.

Even more important, that symbiosis derives from Derrida's insistence that both deconstruction and justice, being incited by the "allure" of paradox, must be conceived by way of a "style."[61] Insofar as those twinned pursuits are entwined, they are joined by—as well as made manifest through—a common modality, genre, and stylistics. One angle on Derrida's unique mode of delivery is that his writing itself endeavors to arouse an "experience" of that mutual style, giving life to the logic of paradox—or to the many rhythms, torsions, undecidabilities, ambivalences, deferrals, and impossibilities that are just as much the sinews of justice as of deconstruction. Thus does Derrida's enactment of the style of justice inextricably mount a defense of deconstruction, within "Force of Law" and elsewhere. As Derrida submits, deconstruction is needed precisely because of "the absence of rules and definitive criteria" that partition law from justice. Yet that observation simultaneously mulls the rhetorical if not tropological devices required to effectuate deconstruction: a method that outwardly strives to elude conceptualist, normative, and other systematized habits of thought. So what masquerades as a discourse on justice ultimately undertakes what is a protracted rhetorical performance of deconstruction's main itinerary.[62]

What are the ramifications of delimiting justice by way of a style or stylistics? Within literary criticism, "poetics," a label already examined in chapter 1, has frequently been applied to deconstructive practices of reading. For Jonathan Culler (recalling a thinker like Hayden White), a poetics above all aims to illuminate the "experience" of literature, rather than to extract clear lessons or content from a text. Culler's 2015 *Theory of the Lyric* thus categorizes lyric poetry by way of five elements that are also visibly pertinent to Derrida's writing: the complexity (and frequent reflexivity) of the lyric's enunciative address; its purport to be a nonmimetic event; its ritualized gestures; its invocation of a recalcitrant other; and its conceit of repetition or iterability.[63] Along with such features, a poetics is frequently denominated by what it refuses, namely its resistance to hermeneutic or "interpretative" modes of reading. Rather than the pursuit of substance or content, a poetics brackets subject matter, subordinating those inquiries to the study of the formal, linguistic, and other dynamics that allow meaning to emerge—or to asking what renders the literary *literary* (or justice *justice*, or rights *rights*). This is exactly Derrida's approach to denominating the parameters and terrain of justice (and of deconstruction), with his conceit that justice cannot be fathomed either legalistically or via other substantive or normative criteria. Derrida instead sidelines all such determinations regarding content, deeming justice recognizable through its stylistic, formal, rhetorical, and other experiential components alone. Naturally, something analogous becomes true for rights.

In turn, a text like "Force of Law" is wildly self-conscious about its stylistic, rhetorical, and formal devices, which it magnifies through metatheoretical self-commentaries and by conducting the exact moves cited by Derrida. Self-explicating, Derrida effectuates the very "double movements" and "suspense" that he heralds as the complementary odysseys of justice and of deconstruction.[64] He similarly accentuates how his essay begins and ends "in media res"—a liminal condition that seemingly inoculates deconstruction and justice alike against the lure of "origins." At other points, Derrida ventriloquizes his critics, asking "Why does deconstruction have the reputation, justified or not, of treating things obliquely, indirectly, with 'quotation marks,' and of always asking whether things arrive at the indicated address?"[65]—only to carry out such evasions. In his signature fashion, Derrida circles around insights without stabilizing them; ventures propositions only to undercut them; and dilates sites of aporia and ambivalence, dwelling within what he terms the infinite openness of the *a-venir*. The frequent "on the one hand" and "on the other"'s that propel his writing foretell not mere contradiction or duality but an unending project of overturning and complication. First and foremost, these sphinxlike, meandering, recursive proceedings of "Force of Law" serve to aesthetically dramatize the rhetorical and other features that Derrida assigns to justice, clarifying why justice (like Derrida's prose) will defy objectivization, prediction, and calculability.[66]

It is hard to dispute that paradox represents one central figure within a deconstructive poetics.[67] But while it is one thing to conceive deconstruction as a poetics, it is another to define justice accordingly. Nonetheless, this is exactly the implication of Derrida's construal of justice as an "experience": it privileges style and form as that domain's main indicia. In effect, justice for Derrida can be neither grasped nor ascertained apart from its (notoriously interstitial, evanescent) quasiliterary workings. As we have seen, there are valuable reasons one might seek to insulate justice from legalism's chronic errors. Among others, Derrida counterposes justice to the aridity of the law's rule-bound, mechanistic, rationalist orders of knowing, insisting that justice can be neither definitively "calculated" by standards nor verified by positivistic measures. Similarly, justice for Derrida is neither a goal nor a destination but rather an ongoing process without resolution. These are all incredibly fertile propositions. Hence, an antinomianism is one label for Derrida's theory of justice (and of rights, hospitality, forgiveness, testimony, and so on) that registers this wish to relegate it to an unprofaned realm beyond the law's tainted purview.

But all of this can nonetheless cause that sphere to appear quite narrow, with its distinguishing features coming into high relief only against the detritus of law's broken edifice. Once again betraying such thinking's reactionary derivation, the perils of law, conceptualism, metaphysics, clarity, rationalism, presence, resolution, and so on and so forth can seem fully necessary to give shape, weight, and meaning to justice, even though that quality possesses a singular capacity to deconstruct judgment-based orders like law. A particular irony therefore surrounds how a legal invention (and an individualistic, possessive, humanistic one at that) like rights can be reconstellated to purge it of everything associated with law. Yet beyond Derrida's peculiar flavor of anti-legalism, it is a familiar logic that he enlists to convert ostensible deficiencies (i.e., the incalculability of rights) into a reservoir of bottomless value. Whether attributed to the climate of the Cold War, or Saussure, or aesthetic criticism, such reasoning is organized by a negative economy of valuation that metamorphosizes sites of apparent lack, failure, and absence into sources of bounty and even resplendence.

Derrida's Levinasian idiom of Otherness suggests another genesis of what is ultimately a redemptive vision of rights—a vision that here too makes sense not *despite* but rather *because of* their paradoxes. With its messianic tenor, Derrida's thought clearly taps into theological genres of apology that similarly commute legitimation deficits, such as the one confronting rights, into fonts of justice and ethics. The muse for Derrida's essay "Violence and Metaphysics," Levinas's *Totality and Infinity*, is in fact an eschatology informed by Jewish theology (Levinas's later work is even more indebted to Talmudic hermeneutics). As Derrida describes Levinas's "metaphysics of the face,"

> The foundation of metaphysics—in Levinas's sense—is to be encountered in the return to things themselves, where we find the common root of humanism and theology: the resemblance between man and God, man's visage and the Face of God. [...] Presence as separation, presence-absence as resemblance—[...] a resemblance which can be understood neither in terms of communion or knowledge, nor in terms of participation and incarnation. A resemblance which is neither a sign nor an effect of God. Neither the sign nor the effect exceeds the same. We are 'in the Trace of God.'[68]

This enigma of human access to the divine is recast by Derrida as its own representational paradox, and that move permits Derrida to model (like justice, like rights) what might appear a matter exclusive to spiritual faith or to belief on the "traces" and other remainders inherent to writing. Later chapters examine why still other schemes for negotiating paradox adapted from theology have acted as bedrock assumptions across much theory. But what Derrida does is to layer those theological vectors of paradox onto the dilemmas of rights, generating another warrant for their rehabilitation that simultaneously inscribes rights' unrealized promise within a messianic temporality.

These diverse intellectual-historical branches of paradox that deconstruction interleaves have certainly enhanced its own allure, at the same time as their roots have enabled the wide exportability and transport of deconstruction's main problematics. Whatever can, like justice and rights, be patterned on a deconstructive semiotics or the enigmas of god or the fugitive truths of art will be readily absorbed into—and saved by—such an itinerary. Any representation seen to lack an origin, center, presence, or foundation, or to be cognate to a text's interstitial relays of signification, can be submitted to this intellectual equipment that transforms apparent lacunae into something grace-like in their profusion. Indeed, one reason such methods of reading have cultivated arguably too many homologies lies precisely with how those evanescent "traces" of meaning redeem whatever they are imagined to bless.

The above ventures a set of critiques advanced with greater depth in later chapters. But for now, one such emerging concern involves whether deconstruction has morphed into a neoformalism. Much as Derrida's own analyses thrive on analogical transfers and substitutions across disparate domains (allowing rights and writing to be digested via a single metric), analogous reasoning has deciphered a truly encyclopedic range of topics, revealing itself to be abundantly exportable. It should go without saying that the terrain at once separating and connecting structuralism with poststructuralism, or formalism from its detractors, is murky and sometimes nonexistent, as in an oeuvre like Lacan's, who we examine next. But deconstruction's formalist leanings can seem to run roughshod over certain of its founding commitments, and glaringly so given Derrida's own recurring complaints about law's mechanistic, summary imposition of overly categorical rules. That deconstruction would congeal into an all-encompassing framework capable of being formulaically reproduced again and again, at risk of sacrificing all nuance and particularity, certainly reeks of a (self-)betrayal. While these issues will for us recur, it is important here to observe how the ambidextrous logic of paradox brokers those conversions, precipitating endless such relays and ensuing elisions. And perhaps especially when paradox is elevated into a master trope or figure will its logic thus self-propagate to engulf an ever-expanding scope of inquiries.

We can further pause to briefly probe other consequences of this privileging of style. One oft stated function of such a priority is precisely to extinguish normative, calculative, objectivizing, instrumental reason—or at least to quarantine justice therefrom. However, there is a way in which deconstruction succeeds all too well, vacating the fine-tuned and other context-specific criteria necessary to navigate the rocky topography of justice, at least in the real-world. While a wayward style purports to sidestep such rule-bound judgments and determinations, little question exists whether such thinking imposes its own hierarchical regime of valuation— enforcing what Amanda Anderson might call a crypto-normativity.[69] Even while insisting that justice remain incalculable, Derrida is quite explicit about what falls outside of that rarefied category. Despite being gestural, his thought interdicts all sorts of intellectual faculties, argumentative styles, and propositions that refuse to comply with such edicts, including with what can start to resemble a game of rhetorical hide-and-seek and dissimulation.

Inhuman Rights and the Ethics of Otherness

So far, redefining rights as utterances or linguistic claims has offered one avenue for their recuperation, although not without collapsing paradoxes unique to rights into the distinguishing features of textual and other written language. A focus on the "inhuman" has provided another unexpected auspice for such an embrace—and one that similarly places enormous weight on rights' constitutive paradoxes. While the notion of the "inhuman" clearly grapples with egregious human rights violations and atrocity, as a conceptual prism it simultaneously works to extricate rights from humanism's dark sides to refract them through a nominally post- or antihumanist light. As within deconstruction, this emphasis on the inhuman has been wedded to, and helped to popularize, a discourse of Otherness and alterity: bywords, here too, encompassing matters of justice and ethics. Yet in blending psychoanalysis with deconstruction, theories of the inhuman typically begin with paradoxes deemed formative of the subject, all the while merging those psychic fractures into a post-Saussurean conception of the splitting of the sign—and thereafter displacing those paradoxes onto the many conundrums besetting rights. Theories of the inhuman accordingly layer yet another stratum of paradox onto those already considered, creating still further homologies (between the psyche and discourse and rights) that both reinforce the explanatory economy of paradox and have paved additional pathways for such thinking's dissemination.

Appeals to paradox populate Jacques Lacan's thought and especially his ethics, including a section of *Seminar VII: The Ethics of Psychoanalysis* titled "The Paradox of *Jouissance*." Especially telling, however, are prominent moments within Lacan's oeuvre that plumb the nature of "rights" and of "right," a line of inquiry Lacan takes up well before other like-minded theorists descended on rights en masse. Lacan himself is overt in connecting that quandary of rights to the inhuman, thereby incorporating rights into the lineaments of the "ethics" he elaborated largely during the late 1950s and early 1960s. This problem of right(s) surfaces at two key junctures in particular: within Lacan's influential discussion of Antigone in *Seminar VII* and his relatively brief 1963 "Kant avec Sade." Both of these discussions also lay bare the Cold War genesis of the inhuman as well as the decisive role of rights in forging that analytic.

Seminar VII famously reads Antigone's deed (of burying her brother Polynices in violation of Creon's decree) as placing her on the "edge" or "limits" of humanism. For Lacan, precisely because she defies Creon and his totalitarian rule does Antigone embody the "enigma" of the "inhuman," an enigma that inspires an almost allegorical lesson in the philosophical status of right and rights. Conversely, Creon is cast as not only the paragon of an authoritarian leader but also a Kantian spokesperson for practical reason and its universal validity. It is Creon's belief that he can "promote the good of all as the law without limits" that consequently leads him to "[cross] over into another sphere."[70] Given "law"'s associations with the symbolic for Lacan, such references are allusive; but there is no doubt that law and everything it telegraphs loom large in Lacan's thinking.

For Lacan, the paradoxically invaluable "inhumanity" of Antigone's resistance to Creon lies with factors foundational to poststructuralist theorizations of ethics ever since. Not coincidentally, that moment in Lacan's thought also marks what is frequently identified as his initial pivot toward poststructuralism. First, Lacan understands Antigone's deed to exile her to something of a no-man's-land or liminal zone beyond the jurisdiction of the formal law and its purport to universality; this is just as much why her actions bring her to the frontiers of humanism. This zone, second, is demarcated by Lacan as "the field of the Other." He explains: "Antigone's position represents the radical limit that affirms the unique value of [Polynices's] being without reference to any content, to whatever good or evil Polynices might have done, or to whatever he may be subjected to." Lacan's discourses of otherness are notoriously slippery, and in *Seminar VII* they increasingly gauge those phenomena eluding the sociolinguistic symbolic order. In reasoning widely extended, Lacan (thus recalling Derrida) condemns the imposition of content or criteria upon Antigone's deed as infidelity to all that she presages, having released herself from those conceptualist shackles. Given that law would label Polynices a criminal or enemy, Antigone's actions necessarily exist beyond or outside the legalistic order, which is simultaneously the order of the symbolic and its signifying powers. Hence, Antigone's deed "is not developed in any signifying chain or in anything else."[71] Third, Lacan labels this a "paradox" that specifically implicates "rights"—albeit "a right that emerges in the language of the ineffaceable character of what is."[72]

Lacan's succinct "Kant avec Sade" renders explicit certain of *Seminar VII's* more gestural links between paradox, ethics, rights, and the specter of totalitarianism. Similarly propelled by a critique of Kantian universalism, the essay levels that critique in terms that conduct a simultaneous meditation on authoritarianism. Published in French in 1963 (on the heels of *Seminar VII*) but not translated into English until 1989, these reflections were intended by Lacan to preface a new edition of the Marquis de Sade's *Philosophy in the Bedroom.*[73] Yet Lacan introduces Sade by noting his thought's surprising affinities with Kant, treating their inversely mirroring philosophies as referenda on the perplexity of how and why rights logic worked to assist totalitarianism.[74]

Lacan's discussion of Sade rotates around what he calls the "Sadian paradox": that Sade self-consciously grounds his perverse philosophy in the rights of man.[75] That gambit, for Lacan, decries the illusory and egoistic tenor of rights, characterizing rights as (in Lacan's terms) "reducible to the freedom to desire in vain"—and thus echoing the skepticism of certain of Sade's late eighteenth-century contemporaries.[76] At once, Lacan argues that Sade's clever upending of rights logic ultimately exposes those aspects of Kantian universalism that are similarly liable to manipulation, a risk residing in particular within universalism's purity of form.[77] As Lacan comments,

> Let us say that the nerve of [Sade's] diatribe is given in the maxim which proposes a rule for *jouissance,* bizarre in that it makes itself a right in the Kantian fashion, that of posing itself as a universal rule. Let us enunciate the maxim:
>
> "I have the right of enjoyment over [*le droit de jouir de*] your body, anyone can say to me, and I will exercise this right, without any limit stopping me in the capriciousness of the exactions that I might have the taste to satiate."
>
> Such is the rule to which it is claimed that the will of all could be submitted, if only a society's constraint were to make it effective.[78]

Much like Sade himself, Lacan cloaks Sade's thought in the rational universalist idiom of rights—although only to disclose that veneer to be deceptive. By parroting rights talk, Lacan highlights the boundless thrust of such rhetoric, much as the conceit of a rule "that is valid for all cases" lends itself to distortion. Albeit in complicated ways given his ethics' relationship to the symbolic, Lacan thus accedes to a variant of the anti-legalism explored in chapter 2, here in order to adumbrate the perilous proximity of democracy to totalitarianism. As Juliet Flower MacCannell explains the "paradox" of the intimacy between those seemingly opposing forms for Lacan, it "goes to the heart [...] of the deadlock in democracy's susceptibility to totalitarianism: how can the people that rules itself with absolute freedom find itself perpetually threatened with rule by dictatorship?"[79]

Both of Lacan's texts on rights further emphasize the linguistic dimensions of paradox (of right and of ethics). Lacan describes Antigone's singular relation to Polynices:

The unique value involved is essentially that of language. Outside of language it is inconceivable. [...] That purity, that separation of being from the characteristics of the historical drama he has lived through, is precisely the limit of the *ex nihilo* to which Antigone is attached. It is nothing more than the break that the very presence of language inaugurates in the life of man.[80]

While characteristically cryptic, Lacan parallels the paradoxes of democracy and of rights to those of subjection, under the aegis of the inhuman fusing those dual vectors of paradox. Just as "Kant avec Sade" baldly states that the problem of right is a matter of "that which occurs in any intervention of the signifier," Sade's perversion of Kant is for Lacan a lesson in overarching questions wrestled with by psychoanalysis, for instance as he claims that Sade's maxim "unmasks the splitting, usually conjured away, of the subject."[81]

Later thinkers have unearthed the midcentury subtexts for Lacan's discourse on the inhuman to directly analyze the phenomenology of the camp and the Holocaust. As for Lacan, debates about rights underpin those reformulations of the inhuman. Representative in this regard are Jean-François Lyotard's commentaries, developed in his 1993 Oxford Amnesty Lecture "The Other's Rights" and included in the 1993 book *On Human Rights*. In contending with rights, Lyotard also makes recourse to another strategy we have seen before: he dialectically juxtaposes two countervailing species of paradox. Reminiscent of the modernization-modernism dyad structuring many accounts of modernity, Lyotard instead contrasts "two sorts of inhuman": the negative inhumanity of the system and an affirmative inhuman replete with almost cabalistic resonances. That latter "infinitely secret [inhuman] of which the soul is hostage" hinges on another move we've also encountered repeatedly: it ransoms a site of deadly paradox.[82] With that opposition, Lyotard can further aver that the inhuman's "two sorts" cannot be reconciled or harmonized through the dialectic's "well-ordered" operations,[83] distancing himself from Hegelianism.

Lyotard's theory of the inhuman complies with what we can by now recognize as standard conventions of rights theorization in still other ways, although he manipulates them to find support for his impressionistic theory. Positively citing Arendt, for instance, Lyotard rewrites her classic remarks to vindicate his own stance. His Oxford Amnesty Lecture thus maintains:

Arendt defines the fundamental condition of human rights: a human being has rights only if he is other than a human being. And if he is to be other than *a* human being, he must in addition become an *other* human being. Then "the others" can treat him as their fellow human being. What makes human beings alike is the fact that every human being carries within him the figure of the other.[84]

The interpretive liberties Lyotard takes should be obvious. Evoking otherness, Lyotard commingles that typical designation for an ethics with Arendt's very different account of exclusion as a paradox compromising specifically *legal* rights. Similarly glaring should be how Lyotard treats that problematic of otherness-exclusion as all-governing. But even more worrisome is how that prism of the inhuman renders such dynamics of legal-political exclusion-othering interchangeable with the fractures internal to the subject, as Lyotard essentially amalgamates psychoanalysis with Arendt's famed reflections. While an undercurrent in Lacan's thought, Lyotard's analysis fully thrives on such false equivalences, manifest in a question like: "What is this figure of the other in me, on which, it is said, my right to be treated as a human being rests?"[85] While an allusion to the self-othering of the subject inaugurated by language (or returning to Lacan, by the "intervention of the signifier"), two separate registers of splitting (the decoupling of the sign and division of the subject) are wholly elided, in ways that furthermore permit Lyotard to present them as fully prior to—or a strange foundation for—rights. Rights, language, subjectification, and ethics are thereby subsumed indistinguishably within one and the same explanatory matrix.

But that is not all. Lyotard's inhuman literalizes still further elements of Lacan's reasoning. Rather than being confined to the symbolic order, those mechanisms of othering play out for Lyotard on the level of actual speaking and communication practices. Quite datedly, "The Other's Rights" goes so far as to assert that strictly *human* language "governs the formation of the figure of the other," which for Lyotard is something animals lack. For Lyotard, animals are instead trapped within "homogenous" (or we might say, premodern) communication and implicitly denied the opportunity for rights and ethics. In contrast, precisely "the strangeness of the other," especially when "dialectical," will "escape any totalization,"[86] and in ways imagined to immunize certain expressions of speech from such mastery.

Lyotard's vision of rights thus gives free rein to other preoccupations of Yale school theory (he taught there for years). Composed during the heyday of trauma studies, "The Other's Rights" construes rights not merely as linguistic claims but specifically as vehicles of witnessing and testimony,[87] and it is precisely such speech in extremis that activates the inhuman's redemptive potential. Not so far from biopolitical thinkers like Giorgio Agamben, Lyotard thereby divines within the "abjection" of the camp consummate if gnostic meaning. In one sense, witnessing involves "lack[ing] language to excess";[88] yet that very lack ushers in the "good inhuman" facilitative of ethics, otherness, and rights. Lyotard finesses this distinction through the language of theology. Explaining that the "Latin *sacer* (sacred) expresse[s] the ambivalence of the abject," Lyotard avers that it is "precisely when we think we have reduced the abject or the sacred to transparent meanings that it becomes most opaque and returns to us from without like an accident."[89] At base, the inhuman and abjection are thereby characterized as linguistic phenomena: circumstances in which speech falls apart or is threatened, epitomized in the "ordeal of being forgotten" hazarded by witnessing.[90]

In a way, Lyotard valorizes such a breakdown of speech—an impulse later considered in trauma theory. However, in Lyotard's hands that instinct becomes exceptionally troubling. In one sense, Lyotard's reasoning partakes of an emphasis on unspeakability and incommunicability that we might associate with Kierkegaard and the predicament of his "knight of faith." But those failures are actively lauded by Lyotard as insignia of Otherness and, in turn, of an inhuman ethics. As Lyotard puts it, the Other "announces to me something which I hear but do not understand."[91] Language jeopardized by total eradication is thus revered by Lyotard due to more than its precariousness; rather, he regards such speech rendered inarticulate (here, by genocide) as pregnant with preeminent yet esoteric meaning. At the same time as a theological grammar of paradox mortgages what is actually a tragic failure of representation (the testimony of the Holocaust's victims), converting it into something quasimystical, the ethics of the "good inhuman" become strangely contingent on the "bad inhuman" responsible for that violent erasure. Although Lyotard's reasoning makes it hard to tell apart reverence for the sacred duty of the witness from almost voyeuristic fixation on the underlying atrocity, it is crucial to recognize that less hyperbolic versions of his transferences are common.

In fact, the inhuman has offered as a relatively common framework for distilling the paradoxes of rights,[92] including within Judith Butler's work. Over her career, Butler has been a visible and dedicated—and, moreover, successful—advocate for a range of human rights issues. However, her theorizations of rights are underwritten by multiple of the premises considered here. Relying on a deconstructive-psychoanalytic semiotics, Butler's *Giving an Account of Oneself*, for instance, builds on Jean Laplanche's conception of the "irrecoverability and foreclosure of the referent" and the subject's resultant "disorientation" and "dispossession in language" to develop an ethics of rights.[93] Butler delineates her own discourse of the inhuman accordingly, specifying that "the 'inhuman' is, rather than the opposite of the human, an essential means by which we become human in and through the destitution of our humanness."[94] Precisely the implosion of the centered, self-present, integrated subject—along with the decoupling of the identitarian sign—is thereby extolled as the birth of the ethical relation at stake in rights. Once again, it is the breakdown of meaning and representation that, far from a liability, is touted as the fountainhead of justice.

At once, theory like Butler's is the apotheosis of other permutations of intellectual devotion to paradox. As we have seen, redemptive aspirations for paradox typically stem from an admixture of diverse ingredients, which that logic of paradox reconciles. This blend is prone to contribute to a kind of methodological syncretism, of which Butler's thought is particularly emblematic. Reasoning like Butler's quite self-consciously harmonizes multiple (and, according to some, antithetical) schools of theory and their allegiances. Marrying deconstruction to psychoanalysis to Foucault, exactly such ecumenicism frequently spawns Butler's central recognitions. That ecumenicism, this book argues, is transacted more than anything by a shared arithmetic of paradox.

At times, a spirit of catholicism like Butler's has elicited metatheoretical self-commentary and justification, which the logic of paradox, not surprisingly, also tends to orchestrate. As the introduction briefly noted, Thomas Keenan's *Fables of Responsibility* illustrates diverse reasons the logic of paradox often becomes both synthetic and transfigural: reasons that *Fables of Responsibility* self-consciously rehearses, and within the context of a theory of rights. Affirming the usual tenets of rights theory, rights for Keenan index a "structuring paradox" of democracy that lies with their status as "auto-ungrounding" and therefore aporetic linguistic claims. As for many, that account of rights enables Keenan to recuperate what might appear a detriment or void and instead to celebrate rights' very dearth of foundations as the life force of their emancipatory politics. In fact, an explication of Lefort's thought is what inspires Keenan's distinct apologetics. Keenan clarifies: "Rather than bemoan this loss of foundation, or criticize those who point to it as disingenuous or nihilistic, we can see in it the necessity of the political."[95] For Keenan just as much as for Lefort, paradox basically *is* politics; to revisit this chapter's epigraph from *Fables*: "Let us practice the peculiar bias, the slant, of paradox and approach these questions obliquely.

Politically." With such remarks, Keenan lends noteworthy precedence to exclusionary paradox, actively promoting "the experience of the truth of the paradox" as a recipe for "the transcendence of exclusion." No doubt, these statements are unabashed in brandishing such thinking's aestheticizing texture.

Even more instructive are Keenan's reflections on his intellectual debts, as Keenan unpacks the factors that allow him to assimilate especially Foucault into a deconstructive heritage (i.e., de Man) frequently allergic to such critiques of power. Above all, it is the dynamism of paradox that Keenan thanks for allowing that incorporation, sanctioning what might otherwise be viewed as methodological duplicity or error. Laying out the groundwork for this rather undeconstructive alliance, *Fables of Responsibility* also acknowledges up front the common impulse to condemn Foucault's thought as overly paradoxical, for instance citing a 1984 *Newsweek* obituary that dubbed him an "opaque, paradoxical French philosopher-historian."[96] As Keenan notes, *Newsweek*'s complaint was echoed by thinkers as diverse as Jürgen Habermas, Nancy Fraser, Clifford Geertz, and Charles Taylor, who all charged Foucault with being excessively paradoxical. But Keenan's response to those accusations is especially revealing, given that it crystallizes *both* that property's then shape-shifting meanings *and* its growing status as a unifying creed. Keenan plainly accedes to those critics' basic charge: "We can endorse these conclusions, take them at their word, but not the reasoning that leads to them."[97] And in challenging "the reasoning" but not the thrust of that underlying diagnosis, Keenan knowingly recalibrates the significance and valences of paradox. He admits to a received ground for disparaging Foucault—"his thought is paradoxical"—and instead recaptures it as a virtue—"his thought is paradoxical." What for others is a damning epithet is espoused by Keenan as the crux of theory and its politics: an "experience of paradox" that for Keenan globally sums up the spirit of theory.[98] More than the connective tissue linking de Man to Foucault, paradox effectuates a type of transubstantiation.

One could, of course, push back against such reasoning. What masquerades as ecumenicism neutralizes meaningful points of disagreement and divergence, papering over intellectual schisms. Besides attesting to the metamorphic energies of the logic of paradox, Keenan's thinking displays its frequent role as a radical leveler, one that blurs qualitative and other distinctions even while possessing the aura of more sophisticated, "difficult" vision. Paradox-inflected metrics like Otherness and the inhuman can thus appear to precipitate an avalanche of loose parallels and casual convivialities, enfolding nearly anything and everything capable of being deciphered as a failed or foundationless representation (the subject, rights, language, and so on) into what we are seeing to be an incredibly comprehensive and elastic conceptual schema. Even theory insistent on the irreducible and unresolvable can thus seem bent on cogitating a wealth of far-flung realities via what is really a single algorithm. Such reasoning itself becomes totalizing, notwithstanding its anti-totalitarian lineage. But to recall Kuhn, precisely this ability to dispose of phenomena that are in fact anomalies and outliers—or to accommodate problems that should be experienced as a challenge—is the definition of what makes a paradigm a *paradigm*. And when justice and ethics are that paradigm's ultimate horizons, its master tropes will perhaps inevitably become sacramental.

Aestheticizing Paradox and Radical Democratic Theory

So far, we have gotten a taste of how the logic of paradox can work to aestheticize, implicit in Keenan's appeal to "experience." Whether incited by challenges of democracy, justice, ethics, rights, or something else, that turn to aesthetics rescues apparent failures, just as in chapter 1 a poetics of modern*ism* salvaged modernity from its wreckage. This tendency of reasoning through paradox to metamorphosize otherwise lethal impasses into phenomena worthy of veneration borrows prodigiously from aesthetic criticism, appropriating that tradition's storied grammars of paradox (explored in the first interlude). In different ways, Lefort, Derrida, Lacan, Keenan, and the other thinkers in this chapter all conscript such an arsenal of moves to reckon with intractable quandaries of law and politics, which allows them to extol various crises of legitimacy as, lo and behold, a given phenomenon's sine qua non. Yet when genres of paradox purloined from literary critics offer the playbook for distilling otherwise sullied political and legal matters, one arguably understandable symptom is the aestheticization of those surrounding domains. Here again, such thinking also imagines those alternate spheres of aesthetics and politics to operate in concert, if not to be organically enmeshed, with the further effect of mystifying aspects of political existence better left transparent.

Perhaps the chief contemporary evangelist for such an "aesthetics of politics" is Jacques Rancière, whose theory directly advocates a comingling of those arenas. Within Rancière's corpus, moreover, paradox is the main conduit for that merger. Not surprisingly by now, Rancière's discussions of rights are where he sets forth the grounds for such a fusion of aesthetics and politics with exceptional deliberateness and lucidity. Especially overt is Rancière's short essay, "Who Is the Subject of the Rights of Man?," published in a 2004 special issue of the *South Atlantic Quarterly* and thereafter included in *Dissensus: On Politics and Aesthetics* (2010).[99] Like many of his interlocutors, Rancière's account of rights proceeds via the staging of quarrels with seminal thinkers and texts in the rights theory canon, taking particularly pointed aim at Arendt, Agamben, and Lyotard. In terms that echo some of the preceding chapter's arguments, Rancière accuses each of differently ontologizing paradox: of reducing the exclusionary paradoxes of rights (or the structural limits to human rights universalism) to a fatal "ontological destiny" or "trap."[100] Whereas Arendt mistakenly turns rights into an empty "tautology," Agamben dangerously consecrates the Holocaust as rights' "hidden truth," universalizing that eventuality.[101] What this further means for Rancière is that those theories are fundamentally "depoliticizing": they discount the real if untapped promise of rights. Whereas Arendt and Agamben wrongly restrict politics to a narrow and finite sphere (that can be juxtaposed, respectively, with the private or "bare life"), Rancière insists that politics cannot be thus delimited. As should be clear, those critiques are very much within the spirit of this book. As chapter 2 argued, Agamben and Arendt *do* endow the paradoxes of rights with problematically concrete, determinant force that renders that diagnosis foreordained, fixed, and fatal.

However, the larger conceptual framework supporting Rancière's objections is just as pernicious as reasoning that ontologizes paradox. Above all, Rancière charges Agamben and Arendt with failing to understand the nature of paradox and what paradoxes do. Given that for Rancière (like Keenan) politics basically *is* the staging of paradox, it is this neglect that amounts to a failure to grasp the subtleties of politics as an iterative process. In contrast, Rancière puts forward his own (by now recognizable) theory of those workings of the political, while affirming the usual view that paradox is constitutive. Just as familiar is other scaffolding of his theory of rights: his entire theory rests on an opposition between two competing approaches to paradox, one that Rancière deems correct and the other misguided. As we can guess, Rancière's favored approach is a conspicuously aestheticizing one. Whereas he chides Arendt for treating paradox as static, frozen, and immutable, Rancière instead celebrates the protean, self-complicating, dynamic energies of paradox. As he explains, those transformative energies are what place both the claims and the subjects of rights under ceaseless renegotiation, rendering politics fertilely inconclusive and open-ended.

Beyond Rancière's trademark insistence on an "aesthetics of politics," what compels that view? First, Rancière, too, regards exclusion and its paradoxes as primary and decisive. Importantly for Rancière, however, a radical politics productively harnesses that liminal, shifting boundary between inclusion and exclusion, thus rendering politics an ongoing "*process of subjectivization.*" Like Joan Scott, Rancière cites Olympe de Gouges as an avatar of such a politics, given how de Gouges was "caught in the pincers of [an] alleged double bind [yet] manage[d] to insert a third possibility." For Rancière this "double relation of exclusion and inclusion inscribed in the duality of the human being and the citizen" productively enables subjectification via rights, which occurs within "the interval between identities."[102] In Rancière's thinking, once again, ostensible limits of rights therefore become the very elixir of the political. Or as he elsewhere puts it, "The people is a supplementary existence that inscribes the count of the uncounted, or part of those who have no part."[103] Inherently contestatory, both rights and their subjects are perpetually (re)constituted through their own disputation and reenactment, entailing that neither rights nor their constituencies can be conclusively known, pregiven, or set. Further reminiscent of his predecessors, this focus on subjectivization derives for Rancière from a vision of rights as linguistic claims: as enunciative, "litigious," and contingent on "who has the ability to see and the talent to speak."[104] It is specifically a conception of rights-as-utterances that, in another routine sleight of hand, thus renders their claims boundlessly self-regenerating.

Rancière's central term for this collusion between aesthetics and politics is "dissensus." Rancière's oeuvre is littered with formulations of that notion, which also elucidate his anti-instrumentalist view of agency (of politics and of theory). Rancière explains that a "paradoxical form of efficacy [is] at issue in aesthetic rupture," arguing that "If there exists a connection between art and politics, it should be cast in terms of dissensus, the very kernel of the aesthetic regime: artworks can produce effects of dissensus precisely because they neither give lessons nor have any destination."[105] In what might appear a coded defense of aesthetic autonomy, or of "art for art's sake," Rancière clarifies that the ultimate workings of dissensus will be incalculable, unverifiable, and unresolvable—or, like other aestheticized experiences, resistant to closure. Second, that peculiar efficacy of dissensus emanates from experiential rupture and estrangement, other weathervanes of the aesthetic within much criticism of art and literature. One might therefore conclude that Rancière's purportedly novel vision of political agency merely reproduces a predictable conceptual landscape as well as vocabulary.

Rancière's reasoning also quotes standard dictionary definitions of the word *paradox*, evident in his description of dissensus as "a division put in the 'common sense': a dispute about what is given, about the frame within which we see something as given."[106] But while sloganizing a logic fully definitional of theory, Rancière simultaneously magnifies the "sense" aspect of common sense. A chapter titled "The Paradoxes of Political Art" thus describes aesthetic rupture:

> Let us call it the efficacy of *dissensus*, which is not a designation of conflict as such, but a specific type thereof, a conflict between *sense* and *sense*. Dissensus is a conflict between a sensory presentation and a way of making sense of it, or between several sensory regimes and/or "bodies." This is the way in which dissensus can be said to reside at the heart of politics, since at bottom the latter itself consists in an activity that redraws the frame within which common objects are determined. Politics breaks with the sensory self-evidence of the "natural" order.[107]

A passage like the above plays fast and loose with succeeding conjugations of "sense," if anything languishing in those confusions. Sense is "common sense" (i.e., a matter of reason) and denotes bodily-affective-visceral engagement simultaneously. This is certainly a politics suffused with all the vitalism that troubled many midcentury theorists of totalitarianism (including Lefort), even though Rancière insists that genuinely politicized sensory experience will be fissured by fractures and divisions (rather than aimed at presence or the People-as-One). Along the way, "sense" consequently migrates in ways characteristic of other empty, floating, unmoored signifiers, occasioning a certain play and deferral. In effect, those fluctuating valences of "sense" become tropological, guaranteeing that such a notion's meanings will mutate and proliferate—and, we might say, exactly because "sense" is both a vector and condensation of paradox. On one level, that is often the main point within reasoning such as Rancière's: to embrace those vagaries as a means to dodge rationalism's errors, to espouse such motility as an escape hatch from the snares of legalism. But as a source of rejuvenating paradox, that axis of dissensus becomes arguably too well oiled, allowing Rancière to move swiftly and seamlessly between spheres (art and politics) that, more accurately, are *dis*joined by meaningful differences—and therefore should not be analogically transposed.

To conclude with the significance of all this for rights, Rancière's title "Who Is the Subject of the Rights of Man?" is clearly a red herring. Rancière poses that question precisely to underscore not only the impossibility but also the undesirably of an answer. For to resolve that question would be to betray the essence of politics: to do away with paradox, to quell the indeterminacies that are the wellspring of the political. The paradoxical exclusions afflicting rights, plain and simple, must remain unresolved, although for markedly different reasons that those ventured by thinkers like Arendt and Agamben. And it is precisely when those paradoxes are *both* aggrandized *and* aestheticized (as they are for Rancière) that what might appear the ruination of rights becomes infinitely redemptive. All the while, the logic of paradox comes along to apologize for and, in the process, to divert attention from real-world derelictions and failures (whether of rights or of democracy or of agency in general)—with the further effect of obviating any need for moral reckoning. Thus can the dance of paradox become endlessly consoling, even while hovering on the edge of a normative chasm. Akin to the "liar's paradoxes" of art, so, too, is rights' "ultimate lack of legitimacy" thus exalted by Rancière as the "first [...] paradoxical condition of politics."[108]

Conclusion

Rancière is overt in spelling out the literary-aesthetic warrants supporting his faith in rights—faith not *despite* but rather *because of* rights' ever abounding paradoxes. Those aesthetic rationales underwrite a lot of other theory equally enamored of rights and their myriad paradoxes. Yet whether lending precedence to semiotics, or to the divided subject, or to totalitarianism, or to testimony, theory reliant on aesthetic subtexts akin to those broadcast by Rancière buys into what is ultimately a redemptive spirit of paradox. To be sure, such thinking often gives due credit to the endlessly creative, fertile, world-building capacities not only of art but also of a construct so aspirational as rights. But when the distinction between art and politics is fully collapsed, one result is a strikingly homogenous, monochromatic economy of valuation. More importantly, is it not the case that there are noteworthy differences separating the crises of legitimacy plaguing art or language or selfhood from those of political coexistence? How to tell those variations apart? In such ways can the logic of paradox appear to engulf if not completely erase the countless factors necessary to distinguish one scene or typology or register of paradox from another. Those distinctions, this book argues, matter.

There is surely something beguiling about how the logic of paradox can seem to uncrack so many enigmas, dissecting so many unrelated puzzles. But such reasoning is also overly sanitary in what it eschews, guaranteeing that certain inquiries and recognitions will remain off the table. Just as chapter 2 asked whether scapegoating paradox can excuse withdrawal or inertia, redemptive yearnings for paradox can induce something oddly similar, insulating theory from the vexing intellectual labor required to disaggregate divergent sites, species, and manifestations of agency. The agency of art, of politics, of rights, of subjectivization, of dissensus—and of theory—all become one and the same, delineable according to the same recurring algebra. But agency (or "efficacy," in Rancière's parlance) is a lot more complicated: far from uniform or generalizable or easily repeated. In turn, paradox does quite the opposite of what theorists like Rancière (and Joan Scott, and David Scott, and so many others) with their insistence on "irresolution" like to imagine: the logic of paradox more accurately comes along to resolve deep quandaries that should not, in truth, be put to rest. Indeed, "paradox" is really the only valid response to Rancière's query: Who (or what) is the subject of the rights of man? A paradox, end of story.

4
—

THE POLITICS OF EXCLUSION

Do the exclusionary practices that ground feminist theory in a notion of "women" as subject paradoxically undercut feminist goals to extend its claims to "representation"? —Judith Butler, *Undoing Gender* (1990)

The ventriloquism of the speaking subaltern is the left intellectual's stock-in-trade. —Gayatri Spivak, "Can the Subaltern Speak?" (1988)

So far this book has delved into somewhat specialized debates about rights, modernity, and the history of aesthetic criticism. But the habits of thought exemplified therein have not been confined to the echelons of high theory or even to the academy. More accurately, the intellectual developments they spawned came to reverberated throughout the university, only thereafter to migrate into and transform public culture. In many respects, it is hard to overstate the influence of these styles of thought that, I have argued, are administered by paradox and its claims to deeper understanding. One central avenue along which that faith traveled to become socioculturally and politically ubiquitous (and eventually anodyne) was a "politics of exclusion." The many innovations in higher education and beyond charted below have been near uniformly framed as matters of "giving voice to exclusion." Over the past decades, that impetus to unearth sites of exclusion (and their paradoxes) has governed innumerable political, educational, and other policies and initiatives. As a mandate, it has spearheaded radical social movements, overhauled the liberal arts, incited curricular and pedagogical reforms, shaped prevailing defenses of the humanities, and revolutionized public discourses surrounding realities like gender identity and trauma.

There is no question that all of this entailed a series of overwhelmingly positive changes. In certain ways, theory has been wildly successful in bringing about the advances it sought, ushering in comprehensive legal, political, social, cultural, educational, and other transformation. Those shifts, we will see, were both incubated by conviction in paradox and served to render such a mind-set doctrinal—again, far beyond the reaches of the ivory tower. However, it is also true that the logic both underlying and popularizing the imperative to give voice to exclusion bred some more troubling tendencies, which at times have even eclipsed such a politics' emancipatory vision. While what follows canvasses diverse instantiations of such a directive, it simultaneously confronts the impasses often attendant to a methodological privileging of exclusion and its corresponding paradoxes of "representation."

Whereas earlier chapters investigated the reasons exclusion has functioned as a kind of "master paradox," this one examines how and why that focus claimed increasingly mass appeal during the same decades that witnessed the explosion of theory onto the Anglo-American academic scene. To be *para* or contrary to a *doxa* (or a dicta, orthodoxy, dominant, rule, norm, law) is by definition to be excluded therefrom—a dynamic onto which theorists have widely cathected. That sense of positionality and orientation has also piloted countless sociopolitical struggles and initiatives: virtually every single contemporary social justice movement since the 1970s. To be sure, it is a clear fact that oppressed populations are excluded in myriad ways, whether economically, legally, politically, culturally, geographically, physically, or more. Yet while exclusion has offered a rallying cry in the fight for social justice, a near identical logic has been enlisted to explain other sites and vectors of marginalization, such as the foreclosures of traumatic memory and plight of the humanities relative to more practical, quantitative, scientific disciplines.

On the one hand, we have already seen why the excavation of exclusionary paradox has been crucial to diagnosing and mapping the anatomy of power and oppression, just as it has been indispensable to the activity of critique. But on the other, the theory era generated a whole storehouse of tools for simultaneously venerating the very exclusions being castigated as oppressive, some also considered previously. Within social justice movements, it has been commonplace to protest structures of exclusion, all the while championing the elevated insights awakened by that predicament—and often in the same proverbial breath. In some cases, this ambivalence makes a lot of sense; for example, with reference to the tenuous empirical status of art or even to humanists' feelings of diminishing relevance. But when transferred to concrete matters of activism and politics, those rehabilitative instincts create multiple double binds. For one, heralding exclusion as prophetic saddles that category with all the complex baggage of a negative theology—arguably mandating an antinormative posture. As a governing edict, exclusion has also been prized for its presumed resistance to integration and inclusion (i.e., to selling out), and the remit of theory has often been imagined to hinge on such irresolution and impossibility—ironically, on the impossibility of its own stated goals. So while giving voice to exclusion has been a call to arms in the battle for social justice, the principal logic overseeing that agenda—the logic of paradox—has often mortgaged the very political ambitions imagined to galvanize contemporary theory.

The material below scrutinizes these and other dynamics, while also examining additional sources of an exclusion-based politics. As within disputes over rights, left intellectual enthusiasm for paradox was fanned by a blend of the Cold War, student protest and the counterculture, post-Saussurean linguistics, literary-aesthetic criticism, theories of a radical democracy, a preoccupation with twentieth-century atrocity, and more. But still other tributaries feeding not only dedication to paradox per se but intellectual engrossment with the exceptional and excluded are vital to understanding what transpired within the peculiar ecosystem of the late-twentieth-century university. For instance, also fomenting a preoccupation with paradox has been theology, although less exclusively in the mold of a Carl Schmitt or Robert Cover than of Soren Kierkegaard and Pauline dispensations of grace. Relatedly has a theatrics of performance and the "performativity" of language placed a celebratory spin on exclusion, given the fertile absences and indeterminacies understood to beset all representational practices. And while a Cold War climate helped to ingrain the equation between paradox and justice, that link was independently subsidized by emerging critiques of racial oppression. Critical race theorists have also looked to the saving graces of paradox, although as a vehicle for extracting the possibility of creative reenvisioning from chronic suffering. Drawing on W. E. B. Du Bois's seminal notion of double consciousness, a condition deemed a "paradox" by Du

Bois himself, many theorists of race have recruited an optics of paradox to convert the trials of persecution into gifts of epistemic bounty, in reasoning that intersects with that studied in the preceding chapter.

A panoply of issues, agendas, and debates have thus been steered by a politics of exclusion and accompanying efforts to "give voice" to everything summoned by that category. Given this breadth, the inquiries begun here also extend across the next chapter, starting with an overview of the sheer range of sociopolitical and intellectual movements arrayed under such a banner. While those missions remade higher education and especially the liberal arts as we know them, their enabling logic has had the unintended effect of exacerbating many humanists' enduring crises of confidence and legitimacy. At the same time, however, it is true that many humanists have long rhapsodized perceptions of their own exclusion to the margins; hence, a logic of paradox has fully coordinated the genre of the humanities defense. To look ahead, this book's penultimate chapter next considers how a politics of exclusion reengineered the humanities classroom and pedagogical philosophy, in part by instilling a confessional or testamentary ethic corroborated by trauma theory.

Notwithstanding these developments' overridingly positive impact on virtually all domains of contemporary life, this chapter nevertheless asks: what factors allowed some strains of such reasoning (versus others) to dominate? Why have certain more pernicious dimensions of the logic of paradox become pronounced, and why can they seem to detract from a robust and applied practice of theory? Was it inevitable that things would end up this way?

Giving Voice to Exclusion

One way to narrate the changes that ricocheted throughout the academy with the onset of the theory era would maintain legal and political rights as its protagonist. In the preceding chapter, disagreements over rights served to dramatize the seismic shifts that shook the left intellectual landscape with the advent of deconstruction, Lacanian psychoanalysis, the linguistic turn, and their theoretical counterparts. Whereas critical thinkers had long presumed certain paradoxes of rights and law to be structural (and sometimes lethal), poststructuralism inaugurated a different repertoire of responses to, and underlying assumptions about, paradox. In particular, it engendered multiple rationales for exalting paradoxes historically deemed ontologically fatal as the very locus of rights' emancipatory promise. While I've stressed the competing assumptions informing these contrasting approaches to rights, those approaches are however married within much contemporary theory—and even can be within a single scholarly analysis. Hence, it is far from unusual for a given thinker to level damning charges against rights only to thereafter incorporate them into a messianic justice-to-come that revels in the paradoxical condition of their ungroundedness and indeterminacy.[1] That those divergent approaches sit comfortably together evidences the extent to which paradox has functioned as an all-encompassing and conciliatory explanatory prism.

These tensions have also caused rights to remain a recurring battleground, characterized by some as a litmus test revealing deeper political-ideological fault lines such as those separating a "liberal" from a "leftist" orientation.[2] Even while theory became institutionally entrenched, certain thinkers like those associated with critical legal studies (CLS) and many humanities fields doubled down on their established critiques of rights. If anything, the burst of popularity experienced by rights on the heels of the Cold War (encapsulated in rights' prominent inscription within newly post-Soviet Eastern European constitutions) was seen to confirm the fear that rights are fatally hostage to capitalism, liberalism, legalism, and so forth, much as an outpouring of work on *neo*liberalism meant something similar for many humanists a few decades later.

But for others, rights have continued to offer a platform for staging intellectual-political departures and feuds, brokering schisms akin to those studied in the last chapter. This has been true within both the legal academy and various humanities fields. Whereas some theorists found grounds for reclaiming rights in the new crop of theory that sprouted along with poststructuralism, rights also experienced changed fortunes due to historical turning points like the cessation of the Cold War. However, separately indicative is just how speedily the primary targets of rights skepticism and critique migrated from totalitarianism to liberal rationalism to legalism to (neo)liberalism. Whereas fixation on censorship under authoritarianism became largely obsolete, neoliberalism was ascendant, so a critical armory cast in the mold of midcentury totalitarianism was readily transferred onto more contemporary guises of power. Meanwhile, a rising generation of theorists studying race, gender, empire, and other nodes of oppression recruited established models for conceptualizing both power's basic design and technologies of dispossession to reckon with those diverse sites of injury. Almost across the board, theorists therefore continued to indict power for (and thereby define it vis-à-vis) hostility to contradiction and paradox. With equal uniformity, the disclosure of lurking paradox and contradiction has remained strategy number 1 in the arsenal of power's critique and unmasking.

Given this broad agreement over the anatomy of power, it might seem ironic that rights would be a sticking point. Within the legal academy, for instance, many founding texts of critical race theory (CRT) actively set out to salvage rights from the CLS critique of rights that has been one of that movement's pillars. As a project, moreover, rights both crystallized and cemented CRT's main complaints about CLS. Mari J. Matsuda's 1987 "Looking to the Bottom: Critical Legal Studies and Reparations" is a case in point. For Matsuda, CLS's categorical rejection of rights betrays the elitism, abstraction, and historical amnesia of that movement. One especially incriminating badge of that privileged self-enclosure is a neglect of the crucial role played by rights in aspirational law-making, such as traditions of African American constitutionalism since and during slavery.[3] Other landmark texts of CRT like Patricia Williams's 1991 *The Alchemy of Race and Rights* adopt a similar stance. Placing the recuperation of rights at the forefront of her argument, Williams defends "an expanded frame of rights reference" and the imperative to become "multilingual in the semantics of rights."[4]

The many factors prompting this split over rights are certainly worth further reflection. At least within the legal academy, especially early CRT did not imbibe the thoroughgoing antinormativity that would come to dominate many if not most work on structural oppression across the humanities. Legal academics working on race were thus less readily seduced by the pessimism—or, in our terms, the impetus to ontologize paradox—that has since assumed the status of an honorific in some recent scholarship. But one might also attribute that willingness to "go normative" to a reaction against inclinations then taking hold within critical legal circles, such as the religion of symbolics proselytized by some CLS thinkers (and considered below). That relish for cultural experimentation and play itself reeked of a certain luxury, at the expense of attention to real-world losses as well as gains, past and present. Yet regardless of their stimuli, these strains of CRT are an important counterpoint to the romance of failure and impossibility that has elsewhere prevailed, suggesting how and why a politics of exclusion need not shun more pragmatically oriented horizons of the sort proposed in this book's final chapter.

For these reasons, skirmishes over rights also risk obscuring the more profound accord then setting in within theoretically minded circles—in law schools and beyond. During the 1980s and onward, theorists of all inclinations and irrespective of their position on rights, increasingly converged on a politics of exclusion and corresponding onus to route political agency through the metabolics of paradox. Fixation on the ultimate ideological stakes of rights can therefore submerge the flowering and entrenchment of an even more significant and exhaustive consensus then underway within the left intellectual milieu. While spurred by eclectic motives, nearly all left-leaning theorists during the same era that saw theory's ascent were fast acceding to the singularly edifying, critical, and resistant energies of a distinctively redemptive, if not inherently salvific, spirit of paradox. Hence, even within movements fully chartered by rights skepticism like CLS did a liberatory ethos of paradox become overriding.

The near universal appeal of the call to "give voice to exclusion" was one reason for this seeming armistice. During the 1980s and 90s, exclusion became the standard bearer under which seemingly endless campaigns for social justice were regimented and aligned. Indeed, that basic mission unites contrasting social movements otherwise steeped in discord to this day, and it has similarly transcended theoretical factions (linking Marxism to deconstruction to "old-school" humanism). Of course, precisely because calling out practices of exclusion and their attendant paradoxes levels a powerful critique has that objective been compatible with more normative and humanistic ends. So as theorists lined up behind the onus to lend representation to historically silenced perspectives, it was at the beginning by no means narrowly wedded to the antinomian, antinormative mind-set that has mostly triumphed. Rather, over the years that mandate to rectify exclusion has operationalized a strikingly motley and inharmonious set of goals and projects.

For instance, early feminist work on law like Catharine MacKinnon's was organized by such an agenda. MacKinnon's 1984 speech "Difference and Dominance: On Sex Discrimination" (published in the 1987 volume *Feminism Unmodified*) endeavors not only to expose "gender neutrality" to be a fundamentally "male standard" but also wrestles with the limits of feminisms convinced of women's "difference." While promoting the superiority of her "dominance model," what "difference feminism" for MacKinnon nevertheless gets right is "a very important problem: how to get women access to everything we have been excluded from while also valuing everything that women are or have been allowed to become or have developed as a consequence of our struggle either not to be excluded from most of life's pursuits or to be taken seriously under the terms that have been permitted to be our terms." One barrier to the successful challenge of patriarchy therefore lies with its historical toll on women's voices. MacKinnon clarifies:

"when you are powerless, you don't just speak differently. A lot, you don't speak. Your speech is not just differently articulated, it is silenced. Eliminated, gone."[5] Equating patriarchy with the censoring of women's speech, MacKinnon presents the recovery of those "eliminated" voices as a crucial step to combatting women's oppression.[6] Even MacKinnon (far from an acolyte of either poststructuralism or paradox) thus conceives power in terms of a devouring of resistant speech, just as she exalts that excluded speech as a prelude to empowerment.

Not coincidentally, some of the most barbed rejoinders to feminism have requisitioned an almost identical conceptual framework—one that denounces structures of exclusion erected on the silencing of certain voices—to lodge their complaints. Rebukes to feminism launched by CRT scholars, including intersectional theory of the sort pioneered by Kimberlé Crenshaw, put forward parallel diagnoses of, as well as remedies for, the omissions not only of CLS but also of the style of jurisprudence promulgated by MacKinnon, Robin West, and other "second wave" feminists. Recalling MacKinnon's logic, Crenshaw understands the principal errors of both feminism and, ironically, a lot of antiracist scholarship as "problems of exclusion." Cautioning that those problems "cannot be solved simply by including Black women within an already established analytic structure,"[7] Crenshaw instead proposes changing the parameters of what voices count, since "exclusion is reinforced when *white* women speak for and as *women*."[8] Echoing such reasoning, Angela P. Harris's contemporaneous work on "Race and Essentialism in Feminist Theory" construes its interventions analogously: as Harris's prologue succinctly puts it, "the voices in which we speak."[9] Relatedly does Matsuda's call to "look to the bottom" ultimately advocate "consciousness-raising dialogue."[10] But striking is that *both* feminism *and* its detractors understood their errands in overlapping terms: as lending representation to voices suppressed (whether wittingly or not) within a given dominant. That project, moreover, was not inherently antinormative for many of those thinkers.

Beyond being framed as problems of exclusion, these arguments were choreographed by a (to us) recognizable method of staging paradox and contradiction. Thus does Harris read, first, MacKinnon's work to display "the very existence of feminism [to be] something of a paradox" and, second, Patricia Williams's thought as another lesson in "self-contradiction" and "paradox."[11] Such an itinerary similarly guides Crenshaw's landmark 1989 "Demarginalizing the Intersection of Race and Sex," in which Crenshaw extends that method to analyze momentous episodes from history. Crenshaw, too, blames feminism's errors on a failure to admit to contradiction, attributing that movement's inadvertent exclusions to an undue quickness to "rationalize the contradiction[s]" haunting feminism's pretense to speak inclusively.[12] While leveraging a stock definition of power (here, of feminism), Crenshaw also champions the eye-opening potential latent in the very paradoxes that shore up yet are camouflaged by power's hegemony. Specific events in history thus provide "Demarginalizing the Intersection of Race and Sex" with a tutorial in paradox, for instance as one passage analyzes Sojourner Truth's life and her 1851 speech, "Ain't I A Woman?" Crenshaw explains that Truth "us[ed] her own life to reveal the contradiction" between myth and reality, enacting a "personal challenge to the coherence of the cult of true womanhood."[13] For Crenshaw, the fact that Truth embodies one of feminism's constitutive exclusions is what grants her such agency, even while the provocation of Truth's speech is imagined to flow from a disclosure of paradox—in an agency suggested to be just as readily available during Truth's life as during the late twentieth century. Crenshaw's reasoning clearly mirrors that of other revisionist historians we have encountered, whether evident in Joan Scott's paean to Olympe de Gouges or David Scott's to Toussaint Louverture (explored in chapter 1).

Few scholars housed in the legal academy (excepting maybe Crenshaw) have superintended the intellectual formation of theory to the degree of a figure like Judith Butler. Relatedly, few theoretical texts have met with the cult status or proven so iconic as Butler's 1990 *Gender Trouble*—and, in many respects, rightly so. However, Butler not only packages her critiques of feminism in almost indistinguishable wrapping but also adheres to parallel assumptions as the above. Commonly viewed as a founding text of queer theory, *Gender Trouble*, too, anchors its reconceptualization of gender in outcries against the fundamentally exclusionary nature of feminism, even though "exclusion" for Butler carries additional associations I'll momentarily unpack. Yet Butler's spin on that recurring critique of exclusion leads her to an adamantly *anti*normative place: a place what follows interrogates.

This is in part because one ambition of Butler's genealogy of gender is to demonstrate the exclusionary character of *not only* feminism but in essence of *any and all* attempts to represent, especially those concerning "identities" conceived as either coherent or stable.[14] Butler's charge regarding feminism's "essentialism" therefore pertains broadly to the very category of the "subject:"

Juridical subjects are invariably produced through certain exclusionary practices that do not "show" once the juridical structure of politics has been established. In other words, the political construction of the subject proceeds with certain legitimating and exclusionary aims, and these political operations are effectively concealed and naturalized by a political analysis that takes juridical structures as their foundation.[15]

Such a statement clearly evinces the anti-legalism that is today second nature, given how Butler does everything short of conflate *all* power with the "juridical." But for now, Butler's affinities with a thinker like Crenshaw should be apparent. Following an almost identical sequence of moves as Crenshaw, Butler, first, identifies power as enabled by "exclusionary practices" that it vigilantly "conceals" and, second, discerns within those exclusions a liminal yet insurgent agency. As she explains: "The feminine as the repudiated/excluded within [a] system constitutes the possibility of a critique and disruption of that hegemonic conceptual scheme."[16] Once again, it is specifically the problem of exclusion that inaugurates the opportunity for not only critique but also an illimitable if interstitial agency that, given its camouflage, is deeply paradoxical.

Importantly, this methodological privileging of exclusion is by no means a relic of thinking today surpassed along with other infatuations of the 1990s. Many if not most of the examples scattered across this book display such reasoning's imprint on nearly all theorizations of class, race, disability, gender, species, and more.[17] Indeed, problems of exclusion also provided a central spur for the remaking of the university and especially the liberal arts that gained momentum largely beginning in the late 1970s, giving birth to germinal fields as well as reconstituting preexisting ones. Science and technology studies, feminist, gender, and sexuality studies, American studies, Africana studies, Indigenous studies programs: each of these departments or programs and accompanying undergraduate majors would not exist but for the rousing decrees and corresponding projects of *self*-reckoning investigated here. My own home institution rationalizes the conversion of "women's studies" into an FGSS program by citing such a remit: "But particularly throughout the 1980s, women's studies was outgrowing the exclusive concerns of heterosexual, white, middle-class women."[18] Exposing women's studies as exclusionary is cast as antecedent to that field's capacity to lend equal representation to nonhegemonic, nondominant, here nonbinary expressions of gender. Clearly, any attempt to deny the unrivaled value of such intellectual and social havens for students and faculty alike should be a nonstarter; in a slew of such ways did systemwide recompense for the exclusionary practices enforced by the power structures of the university launch truly irreplaceable shifts and advances.

Thus were not only brand-new departments and fields created but entire disciplines overhauled by efforts to give voice, here to the many sites of exclusion historically shoring up those elite centers of knowledge production and their hierarchical assumptions about merit. The "canon wars" that engulfed language and literature studies during the 1980s and '90s were fought on exactly this terrain. Naturally—and appropriately—those defending the recovery of silenced voices were successful, prompting sweeping curricular reforms that simultaneously expanded the research and scholarly archives of many academics. Forgotten authors were brought to life, spawning their inclusion on syllabi and a wealth of novel scholarship. Yet those recovery expeditions were also fated to induce bitter fights—and for reasons that are structurally inevitable. Given that the canon wars required implicating one's own colleagues and their areas of expertise within the crimes of exclusion, accusations of "exclusionary practices" had to be internally directed, frequently becoming quite personal (still today). Louis Menand thus describes the developments set in motion by the tidal wave of theory as a rise of "anti-disciplinarity": of diverse brands of self-directed censoriousness and recrimination. As Menand recounts, "academic activity [...] began flowing toward paradigms that defined themselves essentially in antagonism toward traditional disciplines" and that "justified themselves as means of accommodating what the old paradigms were leaving out."[19] Exclusion has been *the* primary label for talking about those many things historically "left out." But contrary to Menand's assessment, that climate of internal self-reproach is far from exhausted but rather alive and kicking in many humanities departments and fields; as we will see, the whole thrust of a politics of exclusion is to know no stopping point or natural terminus.

In large part, the dominant spirit within many humanities fields continues to be one of disciplinary self-flagellation paired with ongoing efforts to dredge the many burial grounds on which those fields are erected. These efforts, as before, have empowered the lives of both students and faculty while often motivating real-world change, meting out results that are unquestionably positive. However, those exercises have not been without their own blind spots and contradictions. Like many English departments, for example, the University of Chicago's issued a faculty statement addressing the Black Lives Matter protests of early summer 2020 that divulges certain tensions frequently accompanying such initiatives. That statement

outwardly confesses to literary studies' complicity with racial and other injustice, acknowledging that the university has long furnished opportunities
for some but is "a site of exclusion and violence for others." It continues to
spell out exactly why the study of English literature is implicated within
such insidious legacies:

> English as a discipline has a long history of providing aesthetic rationaliza-
> tions for colonization, exploitation, extraction, and anti-Blackness. Our
> discipline is responsible for developing hierarchies of cultural production
> that have contributed directly to social and systemic determinations
> of whose lives matter and why. And while inroads have been made in
> terms of acknowledging the centrality of both individual literary works
> and collective histories of racialized and colonized people, there is still
> much to do as a discipline and a department.[20]

One assumption underpinning statements like the above is that "giving
voice" through college-level syllabi and course offerings, websites, and hiring
initiatives will provoke concrete sociopolitical results. Or as John Guillory puts
matters, "If social construction was the Archimedean lever by which the
world itself—the world as culture—was to be dislodged from its normative complacency, the effectiveness of this lever was largely dependent
on the strength of the analogy between literary representation and social
construction."[21] Gestures of atonement like the above can therefore seem
to presume their own trickledown theory of sociocultural change, or that
progress on the level of cultural production will near automatically precipitate improvements on the practical, material levels of law, politics,
and economics. To be sure, if any real-world example might confirm that
consciousness-raising campaigns by academics can and do produce notably
measurable effects it would be BLM, given how that movement popularized
arguments regarding structural oppression that arguably originated within
theory. Nevertheless, the enormous weight placed on symbolic gestures
like the above can create the impression of their independent sufficiency,
at risk of chilling investment in other crucial components of principled
engagement and action.

For historians, corresponding reforms piloted by a symmetrical justificatory logic worked to reorient that field, in Judith Surkis's terms, "other-
-wise." As Surkis describes intellectual history, that subdiscipline had long
been "perceived as elitist and exclusionary," and hence beset with a "power
problem." Efforts to expand the intellectual history canon therefore chal-
lenged not only the hierarchies implicit to its primary archives of sources

and materials but also the philosophies of progress that have chaperoned intellectual history. As elsewhere, those rites of contrition often played out dramatically in the classroom, for example leading to demands for a reinvention of the "core course." But key, once again, is that history's distinct mode of self-admonishment was motored by parallel goals and an overlapping set of warrants as those that revamped other humanities and social science disciplines.

The next chapter delves at length into the factors that caused pedagogies aimed at giving voice to exclusion to radicalize the dynamics of the humanities classroom, and along lines especially pronounced within fields like literary studies and programs like FGSS. For now, it is important to note that the global imperative to "give voice to exclusion" also introduced lasting reforms into less predictable places like law schools. The legal storytelling movement, for example, promoted the world-altering role of narrative as exactly such a recipe for, as Richard Delgado submits, "show[ing] us the way out of the trap of unjustified exclusion."[22] Visible crusades to combat patterns of bias within law school testing and evaluation were similarly supported by such reasoning, central to a study like Lani Guinier's *Becoming Gentlemen* (initially published in 1994). While Guinier assembles statistical evidence geared to empirically show how practices like the Socratic method exacerbate gender disparities, she also defends the need to tell stories about the "crisis in identity" that law school inflicts on many female students. Praising those stories' for shedding equal light on how the same structural factors cause women to "feel excluded" from legal practice later in their careers,[23] Guinier indicts the legal system for, in essence, almost interchangeable crimes as those leveled by literary critics against the traditional canon: for enforcing exclusions that, left unmitigated, will only compound preexisting sociopolitical entitlements and exceptions.

It may be overkill to reiterate that the net effects of these attempts to ferret out bias and exclusion have been uncountably positive—altering public opinion irrevocably and infinitely for the better. Far from a fringe phenomenon, "theory" and its institutional footholds have been indispensable to reshaping the cultural *and* political apparatus, whether manifest in how BLM rendered arguments regarding structural oppression dinner table fare or the normalization of support for transgender rights and gay marriage. In one sense, this raises questions about why so many humanists continue to fixate on perceptions of their own persecution and irrelevance. But regardless,those very successes should be enough to clear the floor for earnest self-appraisal, aimed among other things at differentiating the potential downsides of such developments from their clear benefits. Are not certain guises of a politics of exclusion more (versus less) salutary than others? Will not any agenda by definition discount certain resources and recognitions that might instead prove profitable in alternate scenarios? Indeed, the sheer scope of diverse initiatives branded as efforts to "give voice to exclusion" should itself give pause. What allowed appeals to exclusion to operationalize such a wide spectrum of causes, prompting MacKinnon to deploy basically the same ammunition against patriarchy as Butler enlists to chastise MacKinnon-style feminism? As a mind-set, why has such a politics invited mass propagation; what features of that reasoning laid the groundwork for this contagion?

The most obvious answers to these puzzles lie with such reasoning's simple correctness. Today, it risks trivialization to point out that power excludes society's downtrodden in myriad ways. But that wisdom's now commonsensical flavor simultaneously problematizes both its politics and its yield—or the precept that dedication to exclusion necessarily equals a left-leaning, progressive, or critical ideology. Within the legal academy, for instance, relatively centrist work often begins with exactly such a premise that law is invariably constituted by its outliers, exceptions, and extreme cases, and most legal scholars do not exactly cite Cover or Schmitt in support of those recognitions. As Ronald Dworkin describes attempts to theorize discretion, it, "like the hole in a doughnut, does not exist except as an area left open by a surrounding belt of restriction."[24] Yet nearly any conceivable legal rule or standard will involve some measure of discretion, so one could technically limn the paradoxical "doughnut holes" bedeviling virtually any legal matter. Clearly, caveats like Dworkin's also illustrate why reading for exclusion need *not* culminate with anti-legalistic assertions regarding law's fundamental irrationalism or foundational oppressions.

Dworkin's observation captures additional factors that have contributed to a methodological focus on exclusion: the incredible versatility of such patterns of thought. Just as one can quite possibly find a doughnut hole within any legal rule, virtually any dominant or goal or norm or practice or system will gratify analysis geared to divulge the exclusions enabling its genesis or fulfillment. What is at base the incredibly mundane flavor of this logic has accordingly enhanced its rote recyclability. Insofar as nearly anything can be explained as at least partly oxygenated or determined by what it excludes, analysis devoted to the mining of exclusionary paradox will similarly possess almost endless flexibility as well as generalizability. Precisely because such a politics can be grafted onto in essence any issue or

movement or problematic—including reactionary and conservative ones—
has it orchestrated so many theaters of activism and debate.

Even more important is the proclivity of such reasoning to become
redemptive. Part of an exclusionary politics' magnetism involves how it
transforms the locus of critique (paradox) into something to be venerated
(paradox)—and due to more than that quality's propensity to unmask or to
consciousness-raise. For many, the predicament of exclusion—and its many
variants such as Otherness, alterity, singularity, hybridity, and difference—
has bordered on talismanic: expected to harbor privileged and more sophisticated understanding. Given exclusion's frequently *political* referents,
that deeper insight has above all been imagined to illuminate irreplaceable
matters of justice and ethics. In "looking to the bottom," for example, Matsuda concludes that the "victims of oppression have distinct normative
insights." As she argues, "adopting the perspective of those who have seen
and felt the falsity of the liberal promise" is therefore vital to rethinking
the relation between law and justice.[25] Whereas Matsuda defends the normative purchase of such excluded vision, that the experiences of suffering
and victimization attendant to exclusion will catalyze modes of heightened
comprehension has been a near uniformly acceded to proposition. Not far
afield from other reasoning in which the exception is expected to disclose
vital truths about larger legal-political realities and structures (e.g., Schmittian political theology), the exemplary awareness wrought by conditions
of sociopolitical marginalization and disenfranchisement has similarly (if
paradoxically) been imagined to bestow more profound, more complex,
fully foundational understanding. That logic sacralizing the exceptional
insight of the outcast has been subsidized by other intellectual sources beyond
those already considered.

The Sacrament of Paradox

Once such source is theology. In promoting a "multiple" (versus "double")
consciousness, Matsuda attributes such an imperative to W. E. B. Du Bois.
Du Bois's thought was indispensable to naturalizing recuperative hopes
for exclusionary paradox in areas like early critical race theory and its
contemporary offspring. *The Souls of Black Folk* is regarded as one of "the
definitive texts of the African American literary tradition"; especially its
opening passages have been pored over as near oracular in their wisdom.[26]
Besides being utterly foundational to contemporary theorizations of race, Du
Bois's meditations on the mixed byproducts of a double consciousness hallow

exclusion as the vessel of an emancipatory politics. However, these redemptive horizons implicit to Du Bois's thinking—horizons broadened by many of his heirs—are exactly why a politics predicated on the idealization of exclusionary paradox can, perhaps unexpectedly, become self-undermining. Given understandable reverence for Du Bois, it is surely charged to read *The Souls of Black Folk* as an illustration of intellectual tendencies that can prove counterproductive or disabling. Yet the very facets of Du Bois's thought that have empowered so very many are a case in point demonstrating why overly enthusiastic desires for paradox can inadvertently work to encumber if not derail a social justice–oriented politics.

One reason Du Bois's famed notion of "double consciousness" has organized uncountable scholarly efforts to address racial and other trauma involves how that notion extracts albeit ambivalent value from the psychic fractures induced by chronic oppression. For Du Bois, the "unreconciled strivings" and "warring ideals" of double consciousness, rather than wholly pernicious, bestow upon the recipient an uncanny clairvoyance. As Brent Hayes Edwards describes, double consciousness is "at once a deprivation [...] and a gift (an endowment of 'second-sight' that seems to allow a deeper or redoubled comprehension of the complexities of 'this American world')."[27] That more sophisticated awareness has further been conceived to engender forms of exceptional skill, genius, and creativity. In a type of call to arms, Du Bois thus laments the crimes of exclusion in terms that simultaneously conduct a metamorphosis we have observed quite widely: a locus of chronic blight is revealed to yield an epistemic harvest bearing particular fruit for matters of justice and ethics.

Crucially, Du Bois enlists the exact term *paradox* to distill these dynamics. A mere two paragraphs after his oft recanted discussion of double consciousness, Du Bois comments metacritically on his own project: "The would-be black *savant* was confronted by the paradox that the knowledge his people needed was a twice-told tale to his white neighbors, while the knowledge which would teach the white world was Greek to his own flesh and blood."[28] This appeal to paradox is multiply significant. In one sense, it speaks to *The Souls of Black Folk*'s consciousness-raising ambitions, or what Henry Louis Gates Jr. characterizes as that text's "revelation of black life not only to other 'black folk' but also to white folk, to those who have no experience within or of the Veil."[29] Du Bois thereby construes his attempt to lend representation to certain excluded or submerged truths as a paradoxical one, imperiled by double binds. At once, that paradox encompasses the psychic dualities and divisions experienced by the truth teller, whose efforts to divulge paradox are fated to become self-referential (hence, that allusion's metacritical resonances). One might take this insistence on duality and division as quintessentially modern(ist), encapsulating why modernity and paradox have so often been yoked together. Yet *The Souls of Black Folk*'s paradoxes are nested one within the next. Just as Du Bois's mission involves a giving voice to paradox, or to registers of "knowledge" equally foreign to both of his dual audiences, the underlying content of that "revelation" lies with the epistemic profit of encounters with paradox. Du Bois's project of "telling" is therefore fraught precisely because he must navigate a maze of such interwoven dualities.

Any reader of *The Souls of Black Folk* will be struck by the religious references crowding that text, and there is little question that theological genres of wrestling with paradox are among those from which Du Bois draws. Whether his opening reference to Saint Paul's letter to the Corinthians ("For now we see through a glass, darkly") or the Forethought's citation of Genesis, Du Bois situates *The Souls of Black Folk* within distinct Judeo-Christian traditions of justification and apologia. Suggestions of revelation and divination have in turn dominated academic studies, especially of what Gates calls the text's "fundamental style,"[30] for instance leading Robert Stepto to categorize it as a "book of prophecy" and others as a gospel of racial uplift and awakening.[31] On the one hand, this portentous spirit is what compels Du Bois to don the mantle of a "spokesman of a movement for social equality,"[32] as well as such a voice.

But on the other, the conventions of alternate religious genres of paradox, namely those grappling with phenomena like self-sacrifice and martyrdom, are simultaneously requisitioned by Du Bois to decipher the strangely ennobling effects of suffering. In this sense, too, the grammar of paradox carries out a conversion, in particular condensing the enigma of how pain and loss could be preludes to grace and redemption. Recalling a thinker like Kierkegaard, religious sacrifice has been widely conceived to pose such a "monstrous paradox," which for Kierkegaard is exemplified in Abraham's willingness to give up Isaac.[33] Yet in his discussion of Abraham, Kierkegaard also negotiates an authenticatory deficit or shortfall mirroring the one Du Bois confronts, given the prospect that the experience of double consciousness will be "Greek" to his own people. Much as Kierkegaard's lexicon elucidates why, with certain manifestations of faith, "the single individual [will be] quite unable to make himself intelligible to anyone,"[34] Du Bois's insistence on paradox does something similar: it highlights the constitutive barriers to his revelatory project, or the fact that Du Bois strives to convey elusive truths structurally disposed to defy communication (if not to be dismissed as outrageous).

Beyond the above, at stake within Du Bois's appeal are still additional vectors of paradox commonly operative within religious discourse and especially Judeo-Christianity. Du Bois's statement of paradox is notably accompanied by a biblical allusion that likens his quandary as truth teller to the martyrdom of Christ. Quoting John 6:35, "Whoever eats my flesh and drinks my blood has eternal life," Du Bois locates his own trials of bearing witness within a distinctly apostolic lineage of spreading a gospel (here, of racial deliverance). Yet that early Christian evangelism was also the genesis of the Eucharist, and it is an explicitly sacramental conception of paradox that inflects his account of double consciousness and its second sight. Indeed, double consciousness is implied to achieve something analogous to the symbolism at issue in the ritual of the holy Communion—with its multiple layers of transfiguration. Because while the Eucharist reenacts the paradox that salvation could arise from the agony of Christian martyrdom, it simultaneously relives the miracle of transubstantiation—or that the divine could become human flesh and blood. Interchangeably does Du Bois's allusion thus harness these two mysterious yet ultimately redemptive tenets of belief. So by infusing double consciousness with those twinned paradoxes basic to Christian theology, Du Bois ultimately likens that awareness to other dispensations of grace, which redeem human existence not *despite* but *because of* the existence of manifold suffering—human and divine. However, what ensues is that, insofar as double consciousness is an avenue to a provisional deliverance, it only makes sense within a forsaken world wracked by all-pervasive, incurable negativity and oppression.

To be sure, other foundational thinkers within African American letters (and other prominent strains of Christianity) take things in notably different directions, instead of espousing a cosmology that might appear to condone or to apologize for suffering viewing it as an unambiguous scourge at all costs to be abolished. Although a lot more could naturally be said about Du Bois and his legacy, what matters to us here are the theological—and, in fact, ritualized if not sacramental—conduits of paradox that his thought harnesses. Such a relationship to paradox animates a substantial body of contemporary work on racial and other trauma, including recent theory invested in resistance deemed fugitive, vagrant, or otherwise elusive. No doubt, these religious roots of Du Bois's thought might also be taken to explain the vast attraction of his coinages, given how his language conspicuously taps into recognizable sociocultural codes and associations. However, that lineage itself raises questions about whether those yearnings for grace-like salvation do not make significantly more sense within theology or religion than in lived struggles over race and politics. Given those otherworldly horizons, such a redemptive economy of paradox can seem to risk inscribing urgent demands of action in the here and now within such a messianic (and mystifying) eschatology.

There are other reasons these messianic frontiers of paradox can excuse (if not encourage) a retreat from the pragmatic and normative aspects of political action. The methodological privileging of exclusion implicit in Du Bois's notion of double consciousness derives less from a sense of structural-ontological permanence (as within a lot of critical race theory) than from traditions of theology that come to grips with suffering by deeming it precursory to the conferral of illumination and grace, as we have seen. But this logic ends up entrenching the assumption that injustice will be foundational in its own right. Whereas Du Bois wrests forms of elevated awareness from that fallen state, such a cosmology nevertheless depends on a world ransacked by omnipresent, unmitigable fallibility and sin. So what the divinatory genius of double consciousness arguably does is to render exclusion and its paradoxes something one neither *can* nor frankly *would want to* do away with. This is why conviction in structural oppression (ontological paradox) and in an antinomian grace (redemptive paradox) often coexistent quite harmoniously within contemporary theory.

This sort of ambivalence further suggests why a politics grounded in such thinking hazards becoming impaled on paradox and its worship. Despite the outrage coloring allegations of exclusionary practices like those canvassed here, such reasoning's redemptive strains can appear to hinge upon (if not glorify) the very conditions of injustice critique aims to eradicate. A kind of holy grail, exclusion must remain mercurially impervious to inclusion or incorporation, since those ends would forsake the excluded's exceptional claims to more profound and potentially saving understanding. Resolving exclusion would furthermore be to falsify the contaminations on which any emancipatory politics is, at base, wholly predicated. So while a politics of exclusion often fulfills a cautionary role for theory, staving off the combined threats of rationalism, liberalism, legalism, and more, such reasoning proceeds in a strangely symbiotic relationship to the exact ills that it recriminates, seeming to rely on them for simultaneous authorization and replenishment. Regardless of how vigorously such a politics protests a given injustice, it evinces absolutely no wish to return to a prelapsarian world, since such a universe would ultimately forfeit the opportunity for justice, ethics, politics, or grace.

The Aesthetics of Exclusion, or the Semiotics of Paradox

For Du Bois, the theological texture of paradox is inextricable from his writing's lyrical, metaphorical, and other such qualities. Memorably, each chapter of *The Souls of Black Folk* opens with dual epigraphs, one a written quotation (mostly from the English literary canon) and the other bars from a musical score (largely from Black spirituals). Song thus overlays Du Bois's philosophical reflections, although those notes and chords are deprived of lyrics. While thereby effectuating a kind of historical recovery, lending an imprimatur to and preserving a silenced archive, Du Bois simultaneously evokes "The Sorrow Songs" (one chapter's title) to endow his own voice with testimonial gravity.

Whereas Du Bois's lushly poetic writing gives voice to a rich culture long denied legitimacy, such an aestheticizing impulse has broadly shaped the politics of exclusion. Earlier chapters argued that, for many and especially for theorists ensconced in literature departments, the grammar of paradox would summon multiple episodes from the history of aesthetic criticism. But those protoliterary undercurrents, we have also seen, increasingly permeated the novel brands of theory that flourished beginning in the late 1970s—and that remain prevalent still. Whereas chapter 3 examined the logic according to which distinct paradoxes of rights came to be aestheticized, such a spirit has similarly overseen the many efforts to "give voice to exclusion," whether in the classroom or the streets, investigated here. However, that impulse—an impulse, of course, far from uniform but that nevertheless consumed left intellectuals—can help us grasp further reasons why a methodological orientation toward exclusion becomes limiting. With its prioritization of form and style, that mind-set has often contributed to a creed of "politics as process" prone only to reinforce the antinormative, antipragmatic dispensation of theory.

Two case studies can demonstrate why an emphasis on style, process, and a poetics of political agency became epidemic, widely embraced as the métier of theory. First, Butler's *Gender Trouble* is a text this book has returned to, in the first interlude for its Wildean tribute to the imitative and in this chapter as a garden variety statement of an exclusion-based politics. As with Du Bois, one cannot possibly do justice to the intellectual or political transformations for which Butler deserves credit. Although *Gender Trouble* exploded onto the scene during deconstruction's heyday, Butler also contravenes certain deconstructive pieties, spiking an acceptable cocktail of Derrida and Lacan with an account of juridical power adapted from Foucault. Indeed, one angle on the magnetism of Butler's thought lies precisely with how it hybridizes theoretical approaches some have deemed inimical. That eclecticism, by many accounts, is the face of theory today, as we already observed with rights. It has become pro forma to critique rights by citing a Foucauldian conception of disciplinary power while, in the next breath, invoking the open-endedness of paradox as an escape hatch from total negativity. Butler does something similar vis-à-vis the theory of representation that emerges across *Gender Trouble*. Yet whereas we have already well studied certain ingredients of Butler's variant of an exclusionary politics, other frequent rationales *both* for lending primacy to crimes of exclusion *and* for heralding those exclusions as redemptive-creative are made visible in her theory.

While spurred by complaints about feminism's "exclusionary practices," *Gender Trouble* simultaneously celebrates the meaning-making and insurgent potential latent in other comparatively exclusionary phenomena. This is because Butler's conception of exclusion issues in part from post-Saussurean linguistics (paired with J. L. Austin's theory of performative utterances). So while exclusion is a *political* problem, Butler's articulation of its dynamics is nevertheless patterned on a semiology, and a shared logic of paradox can elucidate how and why. Whereas for Butler nondominant genders experience a chronic crisis of legitimacy, for Ferdinand de Saussure it is instead language that is subject to such a legitimation deficit, given the arbitrary relationship between signifier and signified. Fundamentally ungrounded, the sign (versus gender) is what possesses no natural or necessary correspondence to its alleged referents, hence explaining why language, too, must be understood as a social construct. Yet that crisis afflicting language is not a liability but rather endlessly generative, given how the gaps and remainders (i.e., exclusions) attendant to that unmooring of the signifier are exactly what proliferate meaning. But this Saussurean semiotic framework is one that Butler extends to *all* gestures of representation, in thinking thus able to exalt those gestures' "foundational" exclusions as "necessary failures": "That language inevitably fails to signify is the necessary consequence of the prohibition that grounds the possibility of language and marks the vanity of its referential gestures."[35] Those failures are also acclaimed as subversive, since they "in their multiplicity exceed and defy" the representational orders to which they are nonetheless bound. Throughout, Butler develops diverse "figures" (her term) to index these slippages and ambivalences haunting all discourse. One, for instance, is the "etc.," which Butler considers "a sign of exhaustion as well as of the illimitable process of signification itself."[36] Yet the bottom line is that Butler essentially enlists Saussure to warrant a transfiguration we are seeing to be part and parcel of reasoning through paradox: Butler relies on semiotics to transmute a seeming lacuna into an inexhaustible windfall.

That semiology holds a comprehensive authority for Butler, providing the template for her interlocking theories of gender, politics, agency, "representation," and more. To begin, its imprint on Butler's diagnosis of feminism's problems is palpable:

> The feminist "we" is always and only a phantasmatic construction, one that has its purposes, but which denies the internal complexity and indeterminacy of the term and constitutes itself only through the exclusion of some part of the constituency that it simultaneously seeks to represent. The tenuous or phantasmatic status of the "we," however, is not cause for despair or, at least, it is not *only* cause for despair. The radical instability of the category sets into question the *foundational* restrictions on feminist political theorizing and opens up other configurations, not only of genders and bodies, but of politics itself.

Butler's charge against feminism is telling: feminism is guilty of nothing short of misunderstanding how language works. Just as neglect of the "indeterminacy" and "instability" of language leads to that movement's "gross misrepresentations," the conceit that feminism could speak for all women is traced to a fundamental blindness to the "ambiguity and openness of linguistic and cultural signification."[37] Whereas erroneous assumptions about the nature of representation are thus identified as what predisposed feminism to squander its potentially emancipatory politics, those mistakes simultaneously set feminism up to become oppressive, duping feminists into advancing an inadvertently "coercive and regulatory" conception of womanhood.[38]

This same "ambiguity" and "indeterminacy" of representation about which feminism was misguided (occasioning its faulty politics) is inextricably lauded by Butler as what "opens up other configurations" of politics and identity together, enabling the subversion of dominant norms. Butler is explicit that the "etc." and "necessary failures" intrinsic to the meaning-making faculties of language *also* administer sociopolitical agency, or that "the question of *agency* is reformulated as a question of signification and resignification work" (Butler's italics).[39] Such reasoning lends a noticeable priority to the symbolic. Yet Butler's overarching (and quite valid) point is that projects of political representation must both welcome and maneuver the unavoidable indeterminacies plaguing any and all attempts to "represent" (and, by extension, any and all politics, insofar as politics is ultimately a matter of representation). In turn, "representation" becomes, in a certain sense, impossible without undergoing an attempted negotiation with—or else (like feminism) unwittingly running roughshod over—the sorts of paradoxes that inhere within the most elemental arbitrariness and instability of the sign. Politics thus involves a protracted if paradoxical dance with the exclusions upon which all representations are invariably parasitic.

So what reasoning like Butler's gives us is another basis for venerating not only the derivative nature of all identity but also sites of exclusionary paradox: here, those that create the conditions for any emancipatory attempt to alter the coordinates that dictate political speech, representation, and meaning. As a result, there are poignant ways in which Butler's thinking is not so far afield from the political theology of Schmitt and Cover. Butler, too, inscribes politics (and its dynamics of exclusion) within a negative theology of failure and impossibility: an antirationalism wherein limits to representation and to knowing are viewed as abounding with consummate value. Indeed, Butler finds a kind of infinitely regenerating if inscrutable agency within those very representational misprisions, residues, and other failures.

At first blush, there is a certain optimism to such thinking, with its bent for transmuting sites of apparent lack (i.e., sociocultural marginalization) into reservoirs of "illimitable" allowance. But under closer scrutiny, the very assumptions Butler inherits from semiotics end up undercutting whatever emancipatory vistas might be suggested by her theory. Most immediately, this extends from how that lens of semiotics works to collapse diverse legitimation crises into one another, as the very different hurdles besetting political action versus gender identity versus ordinary speech acts are subsumed within—and can be digested vis-à-vis—a single economy of representational paradox. Butler herself (rather than her many acolytes) overtly effectuates that work of leveling and generalization, as we have seen by paralleling the (negative and positive) valences of *political* exclusion to a (post-Saussurean) theory of the sign: to the inchoate meaning lying in wait within *all* attempts to signify. As elsewhere, these conflations render such a logic eminently appealing: applicable to nearly any subversive representational practice (or, for that matter, to performative speech acts in general). But at the same time, such thinking absolutizes an explanatory framework one might confine to *some* representational dilemmas or to *some* claims to inclusion or to *some* juridical structures, erasing the granular distinctions that are ordinarily the bread and butter of all political action and decision-making. Hence, one might conclude that the antinormativity often associated with theory such as Butler's resides less at the level of policing certain content than of fidelity to form—or to a poetics of paradox. Yet with all vectors and planes of representation rendered fungible, it is hard to dispute that such reasoning commandeers its own basic ability to draw distinctions between one exclusionary practice versus another.

Such reasoning can work to stymie its own politics in further ways. This routing of politics through a semiotics, recalling Du Bois's investment in a messianic eschatology, guarantees that the project of giving voice to exclusion will know no resolution. Just as a theology of exclusion renders suffering a baseline yet enabling condition, Butler's variant of deconstructive semiotics makes that condition's remedy neither viable nor entirely desirable. After all, within post-Saussurean linguistics, it is impossible to eliminate the gaps and residues that comprise language—which for Butler, of course, are brimming with untapped creativity. So while such a politics contemplates an unending cycle of successive exclusions and their uncovering, that activity nevertheless rests on the premise that it *must* remain unending and unfulfilled. To clarify: this is very different from saying that critique should be without cessation or terminus, which of course is accurate. By contrast, what models of agency like Butler's do is to render all action hostage to an obsessive awareness of its ultimate impossibility—even while that impossibility is circularly idealized as agency's only cradle. In the process, such thinking interdicts a whole slew of principles and objectives that one might expect to outfit a leftist, progressive politics—goals like inclusion, rights, incorporation, recognition, success—lest critical theory enter the benighted company of feminism. Just as the union or "identity" of signifier and signified is a pipe dream, a long set of parallel political objectives are categorically eschewed. In a manner of speaking, then, it is not just that norms work to tyrannize or repress; instead, the very positing of norms or universal principles becomes functionally naïve and futile—even while a distinct logic of paradox acclaims that very futility for proliferating meaning.

While these tensions will continue to absorb us, this unmooring of discourse from its real-world referents can also lead to modes of autonomization—and not only of discourse but also of the politics of theory. As Toril Moi argues, theories of meaning inherited from Saussure by definition *must* bracket certain determinations that are usually central to debates about agency, including factors like intentionality, action, and responsibility.[40] Yet rather than merely sidelined or held in abeyance, those evaluative signposts are more accurately leveled, along with their context-specific and adjudicatory rudders. Insistence on the basic lack of correspondence—or sheer randomness governing the relation between—representation and reality clearly obviates the need to assess the accuracy or fit of that connection; those links plain and simply do not matter. To a degree, Butler's debt to Saussure makes good sense within a theory of *gender*, given how gender bears no set correspondence to what appears "natural," biological, or the substance of "sex." However, the recurring instinct to extrapolate from theories of gender or of language or of art—an instinct, this book argues, that defines theory—in order to venture global observations regarding politics or rights or a radicalized agency elides crucial divergences that separates those discontinuous domains. Besides a deceptive fungibility, those symmetries write off the possibility that either one's methods or one's solutions might vary from one theater of politics to another, baffling inquiry into the nexus between a given problem and the best-suited analytic—or between question and answer. Hence, theory can proceed on autopilot, and the answer will always be the same. And whereas theory becomes ensnared in a kind of formalist feedback loop, that internal reflexivity can begin to look a lot like solipsism.

Notably, Butler's insights are cut from a mold that was being broadly cast at the time of *Gender Trouble*'s publication. Intrigue with the interstitial agency of resignifying practices was in the general air at that moment in intellectual history. Matsuda's 1987 "Looking to the Bottom," for instance, includes among the ambivalent rewards of a Du Boisian multiple consciousness a uniquely "transformative skill" over language.[41] In thus amalgamating Du Bois with certain tenets of deconstruction, however, Matsuda cites not Butler but rather Henry Louis Gates's theory of "resignification," soon thereafter elaborated in *The Signifying Monkey* (1988). Analyzing texts ranging from African myth to contemporary literature, *The Signifying Monkey* probes not the vagaries of gender but instead the "ambiguity of figurative language," which entails "the open-endedness of every literary text." For Gates, it is therefore the process of reading literature that involves "uncertainties of explication" nevertheless enabling "disclosure" that is "never-ending" and "dominated by multiplicity"[42]—intuitions at one point inspired by a discussion of the Yoruba god Esu. Gates describes Esu—in a description that could be mistaken for an account of modernity—as a "figure of doubled duality, of unreconciled opposites" and thus "the epitome of paradox."[43] Cognate recognitions arise from Gates's analyses of contemporary fiction, as passage after passage of *The Signifying Monkey* avers the epistemic harvest of paradox. Not coincidentally, Gates counts "paradox" among other types of "figurative" language (simile, metaphor, allusion, personification, idiom), lest there be any question about his reasoning's literary-aesthetic fiber. Yet with this continual traffic between recent novels and Yoruba spirituality, it is also hard to miss the slippages between aesthetic and theological registers of paradox, albeit in analogical transfers that only enhance the power of such enthralling reasoning.

To be sure, there are important cases where a deconstructive cognizance of the exclusions riddling all language has *not* barred types of pragmatism, including on the political stage. Renowned among such appeals, for instance, is Spivak's call for a "strategic essentialism,"[44] although Spivak later forswore such a prospect. But notwithstanding selective willingness to own group identity for the strict purpose of coalition-building, there are ways in which Spivak herself refuses to entertain alternatives to an exclusion-based politics. As much as for Butler, Spivak's ethics actively depend on the positing of an excluded Other—or, we could say, on resignation to the subaltern's never being able to speak. Even though Butler and Spivak differently avow this "radical dependency" again and again across their careers, if anything foregrounding their own inescapable complicity, a certain paradox of derivativeness carries out its own alchemy within their respective theories. Hence, it is not so much that those conversions become tautological, or that theory is piratical on the very injustices it decries. Rather, that impulse to exalt the contingency of theory can ingrain a corresponding reluctance to account for one's praxis and other practical commitments in an independent or affirmative language—or, put differently, to do so outside the protection of another negative theology.

The Politics of Parody

This inclination to denominate the radicalized agency of theory vis-à-vis a figural style took hold across humanistic disciplines, including within thought less outwardly enamored of the intricacies of Derrida or of Saussure. In the left legal academy, Duncan Kennedy and Peter Gabel's dialogue "Roll Over Beethoven" thus pays homage to what was for law scholars a relatively short-lived mood, in a piece published as part of a 1984 *Stanford Law Review* symposium on critical legal studies. In a lengthy back-and-forth, Kennedy and Gabel's essay opening that symposium is a manifesto for an aestheticized-spiritualized politics routed through the meandering play of paradox. Gestural, the dialogue begins with an appeal by Kennedy to "essential, metaphysical/spiritual paradox" and an accompanying allusion to Kierkegaard, rendering "Roll Over Beethoven" another laboratory in the physics that synthesized diverse ingredients of paradox into an electrifying yet cohesive politics. "Roll Over Beethoven" also marks a transition within CLS thought, especially for Kennedy, whose early structuralist work is dedicated to what he terms "the method of contradiction." That superficially drier writing, however, is not without its elements of subversion. An essay like "Form and Substance in Private Law Adjudication" performs what is essentially an extended parody of conventional legal reasoning: a tour de force in which Kennedy mimics mainstream legal scholarship precisely to demystify its stock argumentative assumptions and moves.[45] Satirizing legal positivism, Kennedy unmasks contradiction precisely to debunk the formalist myth that legal reason involves the neutral application of abstract, unbiased rules. Eight years later in "Roll Over Beethoven," deconstruction's impact on Kennedy is palpable, having only fed the appetite for rhetorical and other experimentation.[46]

Above all, "Roll Over Beethoven" is a debate regarding the factors capable of prolonging the vitality of radical social movements, which prompts Gabel and Kennedy to wrestle with the difficulties both of giving voice to the popular and of protecting that voice from co-optation. Along the way, they inventory various of the landmines a progressive politics must sidestep; many of those (to us, well known) hazards have been widely anathematized. Kennedy and Gabel warn against misappropriation "by a dominant discourse" and worry that "all utopian descriptions [will] be taken over and falsified to legitimate oppression and flight and alienation."[47] This is exactly the fate that, in the eyes of CLS, befell rights, dramatizing the need, as Gabel puts it, to "undercut [theory] the minute that it becomes frozen in the same way that rights discourse becomes frozen."[48] "Roll Over Beethoven" similarly parlays the then-rampant concern that all rationalist, "philosophical," "conceptualist" modes of thought will prove not only complicit or corrupt but also liable to manipulation. For thinkers housed in the legal academy, such anxieties regarding the liberal suffocation of left progressivism have understandably loomed large, although that preoccupation was exceptionally acute during the late Cold War era. Indeed, we just saw Gates analogously speculate over whether the complex rhetorical figures found within Fon and Yoruba myth were devised "as if to protect [their] own codes from (mis)appropriation."[49]

Nevertheless, for Gates, Kennedy, Gabel, Butler, and countless others, one strategy for outflanking such liberal-legal-rationalist takeover has involved a vagrant, erratic, forever-on-the-move rhetorical style and spirit.

Numerous features of "Roll Over Beethoven" set out to enact, and in the process to theorize, such a discursive mode geared to resist liberal-legalistic-rationalist-authoritarian-conceptualist plunder. Metacritical and theatrical, Gabel and Kennedy's dialogue mulls the types of speech necessary both to consciousness-raise and to channel the popular voice. As Kennedy reflects: "What I think we need to do is look for ways of talking, ways of responding, ways of doing things in which the goal is not to convince people by lucidity.... But rather to operate in the interspace of artifacts, gestures, speech and rhetoric, histrionics, drama, all very paradoxical...."[50] In particular are the codes of "paradox" thus touted as defense mechanisms against ideological infiltration as well as the unwitting if inevitable domestication feared by CLS.

Similarly is a negative dialectics imagined to conjure such a discursive "interspace." Throughout, Gabel and Kennedy mimic a pseudo-Platonic (or, we might say, Wildean) catechism, with their restless questioning itself modeling the "mode of talking, writing, and doing organizing stuff which gets you out of th[e] dilemma" of philosophizing versus "pure negative critique."[51] Rather than oscillating between contradictory poles, however, Kennedy and Gabel more accurately effectuate the slippery, peripatetic movements of what they call "total indeterminacy."[52] Experimental if not transgressive relative to other legal scholarship, that exchange also self-consciously applauds the parody we have seen to accompany a methodological prioritization of style. Much as for Butler, those tactics subvert more than conceptualism, instead working, as Gabel relates, to "continually [pull] the rug out from under anything at all."[53]

The joke is another rhetorical device promoted by Kennedy and Gabel for its alleged immunity to being hijacked. In many respects, the dialogue itself delights in the "jokey, colloquial things" that "can defend the integrity of [...] communication." Yet Gabel and Kennedy are also overt in explaining why the logic of a joke is to self-inoculate against opportunistic cooptation. As Gabel comments, "they can't take over a joke, which has its momentary unveiling that can't be captured by the other side. Whereas any philosophical discussion can be captured."[54] Here, too, evocative of *Gender Trouble*'s discussion of drag (see the first interlude), it is tempting to mine the many affinities connecting Butler's account of that resistant practice with Kennedy and Gabel's version of parody. Like "Roll Over Beethoven," *Gender Trouble* revels in the "subversive laughter in the pastiche-effect of parodic practices," noting that such "laughter emerges in the realization that all along the original was derived."[55]

Yet one signal feature of parody and jokes involves their contagion: jokes breed humor that begs to be prolonged and repeated. Clever jokes summon their own retelling, and the more infectious that glee (and more delicious their feats of unveiling), the more likely they are to self-propagate. Paradigmatic expressions of resignifying agency, successful jokes elicit subtle (re)iterations that take on a life of their own, proliferating unexpected associations as they travel. While mirthful, however, specifically parodic humor often tends to be contrarian—which, of course, is why theorists have gravitated toward such genres. Most jokes do not exactly translate into affirmative principles or agendas, instead ruthlessly undercutting the common sense on which they prey. Many jokes therefore relish the outsider, excluded awareness that they marshal, akin to how Butler imagines the performance of parody to rejoice in its own counterfeicy. That said, it is also true that mimicry often equals mockery, whether of bourgeois complacency or of power or, for that matter, of one's immediate interlocutors. While thus at risk of becoming cartoonish, many jokes are furthermore contingent on the perception of a hostile status quo that they set out to embarrass—and can consequently hover on the fringes of the mean-spirited. So although it's tempting to idealize the improvisatory exuberance of these sorts of appeals, a substantial majority of jokes deal in hyperbole, embellishment, caricature, or even knowing distortion—like the logic of *para doxa*, seeming to require outsize, overdrawn villains.

Another mode of contagion is alluded to in Kennedy and Gabel's title and epigraph that quotes Chuck Berry: "I got the rockin' pneumonia / Need a shot of rhythm and blues." Like Du Bois thereby eroding boundaries between high and low, "Roll Over Beethoven"'s mood also works to harness the charisma of aesthetic experience. In fact, rock 'n' roll provides that text's arguably central emblem for the aesthetically-spiritually-experientially charged politics that Kennedy and Gabel celebrate as vital to successfully radicalized social movements. Amid intellectual excitement over Derrida, phenomenology's influence especially on Gabel is also unmistakable, given his petitions for perceptual intensity and immediacy. Whereas Berry's title stages a plea to overthrow the stodgy, rule-bound constraints of classical music à la Beethoven, the prospect of "having music at the meeting" is held out as the secret to an emancipatory politics within the dialogue. Relatedly is the basic nature of the dialogic mode suggested to activate the phenomenologically charged, alive, rhythmic vibrancy of the participatory engagement summoned by the experience of popular music. Coupled with references to Kierkegaard, those energies simultaneously become quasi-spiritual, much as Gabel heralds what he terms the "intersubjective zap" and "sudden experience of connectedness."[56] Here again, aesthetic and theological registers of consciousness-raising fuse into a single ethos.

The contemporaneous intellectual movements of which Butler, Gabel, and Kennedy are progenitors naturally met with divergent fates and fortunes. Whereas an influence like Butler's has resounded far beyond gender studies to render her a paragon of a public intellectual, CLS became all but marginalized within most law schools, so much so that Allegra McLeod can categorically lament "the scarcity of ruthlessly critical thought in US law schools, with rare exception."[57] Yet the vision of "politics as process" that unites those thinkers is one of their legacies, even while it is surely cut from the same cloth as more recent theory like Jacques Rancière's. Far from merely a glimpse of deconstruction's thrilling early reception, their conception of political agency as an aestheticized style remains authoritative. To return to *Gender Trouble*, Butler is overt in defining "gender" as "*a corporeal style*, an 'act,' as it were, which is both intentional and performative, where '*performative*' suggests a dramatic and contingent construction of meaning." As Butler clarifies, "Sartre would perhaps have called this act 'a style of being,' Foucault, 'a stylistics of being.'"[58] Here again hearkening back to the texture of specifically modern(ist) self-fashioning (whether apotheosized in Wilde or the lionization of a dandy-esque Baudelaire) examined in chapter 1, that worship of style can however appear mere steps away from other guises of formalism—including in the pejorative sense of that term. Not coincidentally, Butler was inspired to parlay that charge head on in the preface to the 1999 edition of *Gender Trouble*. As she explains, "If in some of its guises poststructuralism appears as a formalism, aloof from questions of social context and political aim, that has not been the case with its more recent American appropriations"[59]—an assertion this book disputes. Yet one might expect CLS thinkers to be particularly leery of such formalist quicksand, given that movement's grandfathering into a legal realist tradition dedicated to critiquing *legal* formalism, a project springing from awareness of how the rote, mechanical application of ostensibly abstract, neutral rules tragically severs law from concrete, particular concerns, like those bearing on matters of social justice.[60]

Whether formalism or something else represents the best label for these tendencies, the maxim of "nothing but style" (to evoke Wilde) does require numerous abdications. For many, that has been the main agenda: to elude the conceptualist-categorical-legalistic habits of thought regnant within other disciplines, to self-inoculate theory against the unwitting seductions of mastery or dominance. But it is nevertheless worth asking whether those ends have not been achieved too antiseptically: whether a wholesale moratorium on rationalism, instrumentalism, normativity, and so forth is as emancipatory and radical as it is often imagined to be.

Before moving on, it is also necessary to grasp why this premium on style emanates from a preoccupation with exclusion—and is therefore basic to many humanities fields' chromosomal makeup. Myriad phenomena have been projected onto that (non)place of the excluded-exceptional: (in)justice, oppression, consciousness-raising, critique, elevated truth, creativity, genius, prophecy, and more. But by definition, the excluded will (like drag or a joke or the hole in a doughnut) occupy a roving, itinerant, conditional location relative to the putative existence of an inhospitable status quo. To recall Dworkin's metaphor, it is impossible to zero in on the intermediary space of exclusion without first identifying its surrounding rule or dominant. Radically contingent, that absent center will also vacillate in relation to those embedding structures, all the while remaining empty of independent, determinable substance or content of its own. One impetus for methodologically prizing exclusion is precisely this refusal to be pinned down—because if exclusion could be stabilized or arrested or predicted, it would lose its subversive potential. In another exemplification a negative theology, exclusion cannot *but* be delineated within reference to everything it is not—a quandary that has begotten critical vocabularies (incalculability, indeterminacy, indecision, untranslatability) scrutinized further in the next chapter. Whatever politics is modeled on such devotion will be analogously compelled to self-justify through the subterfuge of absent presence—and without recourse to values or commitments capable of being freely or self-sufficiently asserted. Politics, too, thus becomes captive to a negative (and derivative and defensive) economy of valorization: fated to defend itself with reference to everything it jettisons and disavows.

Reasoning that came along to navigate various justificatory crises— How to affirm gender identities defiant of biological verification? How to excavate and authenticate histories expunged from the official record?— can therefore risk exacerbating the very conditions of failed or tenuous legitimacy to which that logic responds. To be sure, a politics governed by aesthetics and style may be charismatic, creative, and even intoxicating. Chameleon in its adaptability, such thinking can also give the impression of a self-replenishing theory forever on the move. As we have seen, its aestheticized argumentative style can appear to inoculate theory against ideological seizure or profiteering, just as playing rhetorical hide-the-ball will surely outfox one's opponents. These are the sorts of factors that have led many to espouse the protean, subtle, elastic technicities of paradox. But that mutability, while alluring, can itself hasten a given argument or view's irrelevance. It is hard either to contest or to evaluate the merits of reasoning that refuses to align itself with tangible, clear, unwavering positions or criteria or goals—and some potential interlocutors might not bother to try. So the eternally iterating, vagrant politics of theory guarantees not so much the upper hand as its consignment to the margins—although, of course, the very margins long claimed as the sole province of theory.

The Bonfire of the Humanities

An analogous reverence for exclusion has orchestrated many popular defenses of the humanities. Much as projects of giving voice to exclusion have supervised the humanities classroom (as the next chapter considers), that ethos has long authored humanists' self-images. At first blush, this investment in exclusion and its paradoxes might seem far from surprising, given the prominent role played by that logic in fields like literary criticism and theology. But popular justifications for the irreplaceable value of a humanities education have also trafficked in highly overdetermined views about exclusion's many paradoxical rewards. The conceit of humanists' exile to the margins has consequently acted as a pillar of the genre of the humanities' self-defense—although one that itself rests on highly questionable foundations.

As within political movements aimed at confronting exclusionary practices, this logic has been recruited by humanists to ward off a suite of perceived threats, perhaps above all humanists' own irrelevance. On the one hand, exclusion has named what is held out as the humanities' increasingly dire predicament: expulsion (perhaps permanent and fatal) from the dominant centers of knowledge and power within both university and society. But on the other, it has simultaneously been routine to vindicate the humanities' existence by citing to such exclusion, trumpeting that plight as the locus of their superior worth. Given public views about the superfluity of many humanistic fields, it is understandable that academics would internalize such suspicion to develop an identity complex, weaving it into their own self-rationalizations. But in so doing, contemporary defenses of the humanities borrow from multiple other traditions (i.e., literature and art), where an optics of paradox has managed various legitimation crises—deploying an analytic repertoire that will therefore strike us as quite familiar.

To begin, it is no secret that humanists have a hard time justifying themselves—if they are even so willing. It is similarly true that those challenges to effective self-advocacy have only escalated in recent years. Virtually any attempt to craft a persuasive case for the liberal arts can therefore seem to flounder on successive double binds. As Helen Small notes, even classical defenses for the humanities typically ended up either promoting self-quarantine, inadvertently diminishing the humanities' relevance, assuming a pious tenor, or all three.[61] Yet these dilemmas become newly exaggerated when disputes over whether and why the humanities "matter" are on the table, causing pressure to demonstrate that one "matters without mattering" in an instrumental or pragmatic sense to intensify humanists' natural feelings of insecurity. As Robert J. C. Young explains, those pressures have often unleashed a spiraling dialectic of uselessness and usefulness that itself stultifies humanists' ability to self-promote in an uncompromising manner. Similarly for Small, this same conundrum injects many such statements of "value" with a degree of pluralism verging on incoherence.[62] One consequence is that even congratulatory appraisals of the humanities tend to be mired in a thicket of qualifications and provisos, the net effect of which becomes undermining. Indeed, the substantial volume of writing that weighs and contrasts alternate visions for the liberal arts might be independently taken to evidence the depths of resistance to the onus to self-rationalize—or, frankly, to engage in any form of rationalization at all.

It makes complete sense that humanists' fears about exclusion would skyrocket in recent years, given the very real perils encroaching on their livelihoods. The primary culprit has undoubtedly been the neoliberalization or corporatization of the university (only accelerated by a pandemic). In recent years, alarm over this onslaught against higher education has therefore risen to an often fevered pitch—and, in many respects, rightly so. For Terry Eagleton, we are witnessing the "slow death of the university."[63] Or as William Deresiewicz maintains, college is "selling its soul to the market," becoming the "neo-liberal arts."[64] For still others, the language of a "war," "assault," and "attack" best registers that menace, as the sheer stealth and multitude of predators currently stalking the humanities can appear catastrophic. Whether austerity measures like slashed budgets, ghosted departments, evaporating graduate programs, belt-tightening academic presses, or fights over academic freedom and faculty governance, the range of battle lines is frightening, and precisely this looming blitz can cripple humanists' capacity to advance arguments attesting to their worth and purpose. As Wendy Brown observes of the growing demand for compliance with market-based metrics, it "paradoxically weakens the capacity of liberal arts scholars to defend the liberal arts at the moment of their endangerment."[65]

That said, it is also the case that versions of these perils and of humanists' ensuing fears can be traced to their earliest beginnings. Others have developed genealogies tracking the disdain many humanists can seem to experience when faced with the need to assemble a reasoned case exonerating their existence. Reflecting on aesthetic criticism, Doris Sommer accordingly asks when and why art's purposelessness became the watermark of its authenticity, speculating over whether that mind-set should be attributed to Theodor Adorno and World War II, or to the New Critics' "abandoning ethics for the sanctuary of formalism," or to the revolutionary 1960s, or instead to poststructuralism's fortress.[66] While certain of these candidates are perhaps misplaced, it has nevertheless been de rigueur to blame "the midcentury Ivy League establishment" for developing various philosophies all differently condoning either the humanities' elite privilege and/or their autonomy. Just as customary has been the view that "mount[ing] a defense of the social value of literature or literary study [will be] seen as not just unnecessary but as a kind of utilitarian capitulation to a philistine public," as Evan Kindley comments about Stanley Fish's oeuvre.[67]

While these ambivalences may thus be in part relics of midcentury elite enclosure and high French theory, they are also symptomatic of conviction in paradox—a conviction, we have seen, wired into the humanities' genetics. That spirit of paradox has *both* decreed the recurring conventions of the humanities' defense *and* can shed light on certain of its limits, including that genre's proclivity to become self-sabotaging. Like political initiatives piloted by the critique of exclusionary practices, almost all defenses of the humanities take that exclusion for granted; insistence on chronic disenfranchisement thus acts as a baseline supposition within many if not most arguments regarding the humanities' key merits. But what simultaneously occurs by way of this justificatory logic, as we also know, is that the ambidextrous workings of paradox come along to ransom what might appear a curse, revealing an ostensible debility to be, lo and behold, the nucleus of the humanities' most abiding value. Hence, humanists have not only venerated their exclusion but also conscripted an apologetics of paradox commonplace within some humanistic fields in order to redeem that apparent crisis and lack. It has thus been customary for humanists to rhapsodize their own persecution, all the while installing a volatile mixture of outrage and martyrdom at the core of their identities.

One understandable side effect of this love affair with the margins has been an oppositional mind-set. As elsewhere, it is hard to make claims decrying exclusion without singling out an unsympathetic majority for blame. Following suit, many justifications for the humanities begin by hypostasizing a parade of foes (some real, some imagined). Demonized has been a predictable lineup of adversaries, some classical (science, philosophy, reason), some more contemporary (legalism, (neo)liberalism, normalization, totalization). Whether seen as internal to the academy or as barbarians at its gates, these villains have played a crucial part in fashioning many humanists' existential warrants, offering foils to their virtues while rendering an organizing narrative of strife and embattlement integral to many fields' self-understandings. And while indulging fantasies of self-sacrifice, those tales of beleaguerment have also encouraged rampant anathematization—including of the very publics to whom humanists purport to minister. But the further reality is that this penchant for reprobation that is pervasive within some disciplines is notably self-serving, even while such a mood risks fanning the very flames of public misgiving that humanists decry.

Within this perennial saga, certain enduring creeds have crystallized a vision of the humanities as *para doxa*. One taps into a larger antiestablishment wariness of the institutional structures housing the liberal arts: an anti-institutionalism that has rendered the modern university, as Young puts it, "at permanent variance with itself."[68] That antagonistic stance toward one's fellow academic travelers, also perhaps understandably, has led some to magnify if not overplay their feelings of vexation. As Jennifer Fleissner argues of literary studies, it has frequently endowed such enmities with monumental importance—and much larger proportions than by humanists' supposed rivals.[69] Relatedly have incommensurable divides been imagined to place humanists in stark competition with contrasting knowledge structures like those of economics and the sciences. Although today positivistic and quantitative fields and professional schools often do vie with the humanities for scarce resources, that polarized landscape must be situated within a much longer history. A parallel schism underpinned the "Humanism/ Scholasticism" split of the Early Modern period (as Small explains), with later echoes in the "two cultures" controversy of the early 1960s.[70] Indeed for Bruno Latour, the instinct to erect partitions segregating contending spheres of expertise is the very architecture of modern knowledge—and one producing silos Latour deems *the* primary incubator of modern paradox.[71]

Menand similarly blames the "humanities revolution" for deepening such perceived rifts, fueling a generalized climate of internal suspicion.[72] So it is no wonder that the slow gutting of the humanities would cause age-old jealousies to flare.

Another edict that has captured many humanists' sense of vocation albeit through its own logic of negative displacement—anti-instrumentalism—encapsulates why specifically a cult of paradox has encumbered humanists' capacity to self-defend. That nostrum has assumed varying shapes and guises, some indebted to aesthetics and some to theology. As Peter Brooks opines in the 2014 *Chronicle Review*: "To submit to the measures of usefulness proposed in most of the schemes of evaluation [...] would betray what we do, which is not directly instrumental."[73] Or as Butler inveighs (describing Adorno's theory of the lyric): "to communicate nothing is precisely to refuse the structures of communication that ratify society, and so the most 'critical' potential of the lyric is expressed when communication is refused."[74] Or we can recollect Jacques Rancière's argument that "'aesthetic efficacy' means a paradoxical kind of efficacy that is produced by the very rupture of any determinate link between cause and effect."[75] These statements are powerful precisely because, like the category of exclusion, they marshal yet confuse prohibitions with inverted expressions of value. And while interdicting the "instrumental," such reasoning simultaneously works to embargo an array of adjacent concepts like "evaluation," "use," "communication," "cause and effect," and even "society." Yet while masquerading as a catalog of the alleged crimes perpetrated by practical-pragmatic disciplines (and therefore dire threats impinging on the humanities' future), prophylaxes like those tied to the creed of anti-instrumentalism also marshal a series of claims about the humanities' exceptional merits. Hence, this justificatory logic, too, ultimately borrows from the generic conventions of a negative theology, allowing blessings and sins to inhere within the self-same faculties. As a result, the fundamentally derivative status of edicts like anti-instrumentalism can seem to perform on a type of dissimulation, if not an active obfuscation of values that should instead be "communicated" in "measurable," "determinate" terms precisely in effort to persuade the same "society" Butler offhandedly dismisses.

So although presented as a badge of undue hardship, humanists' exclusion has simultaneously been hallowed for, among other things, enabling privileged access to the slant, singular vision of paradox. As elsewhere, those designs on the *para doxa* are believed to forestall a web of temptations and hazards, whether rationalism, complicity, normativity, essentialism, unity, power, or more. However, what such reasoning unfurls, predictably by now, is another negative economy of valuation that structurally impedes humanists' ability to promote their own contributions without direct reference to what they are not: without offsetting their value against everything scapegoated as their calling to resist. While explaining many humanists' feelings of alienation, this dependence on a logic of inverted valorization also displays those sentiments to be at least partly self-engineered. Allergic to stipulating their worth without opportunistically pitting it against that of various competitors, certain humanities fields can seem bent on unremitting villainization, including of the bourgeois public. It should be no surprise that this impetus to construct almost Manichean hostilities as a mode of self-reassurance can backfire, evident in the tendency of some to deride the exact audiences they aspire to sway. A genre that one would expect to defray or ameliorate public suspicion can consequently lend it fodder, whether due to actual bad-mouthing or muddled decrees like the anti-instrumental.

At once, these reactionary alibis divest the humanities defense of an independent integrity. Another feature of a negative theology, we know, is to stifle assertions of positive, affirmative, concrete, self-sufficient value, and indeed many have observed that humanists can be hard-pressed to self-advocate in terms that are not defensive or otherwise bootstrapped by assumptions about their putative adversaries. However, this conundrum is just as much a signature of the logic of paradox as a hang up of some humanities fields. Regardless of the issue at hand, reasoning through paradox tends to neutralize constructive, prescriptive, practical statements of content or truth or purpose—this being, as we also know, the frequent source of its attractiveness. Yet as ambassadors of the *para doxa*, humanists have rejoiced in what is more accurately a justificatory abyss—and an abyss fully destined to swallow up whatever principles or goals one might put forward. A kind of poison pill, the logic of paradox can seem to be near automatically triggered by certain veins of argument. Nevertheless, the net result is that the humanities defense can leave humanists unable to describe what they do except in apophatic language.

This negative economy of valorization confiscates a number of important intellectual and other resources. Insistence on ideals like "necessary failure" artificially restricts the analytic tactics, rhetorical modes, and larger objectives deemed permissible as horizons for theory, as later chapters submit. Just as the politics of exclusion discounts ends like incorporation, unity, and identity, it favors certain assertions as well as rhetorical styles.

Thus have humanists been leery of optimums like standards, prescriptions, foundations, universals, criteria, or other normative measures, in part a matter of the qualitative (versus quantitative) bent of most humanities fields. But notwithstanding that divide, frequently taboo have been registers of discourse that aspire to lucidity, clarity, stability, objectivity, transparence, and intelligibility. Juxtaposing the humanities with quantitative disciplines can thus appear little more than a ploy providing active license for indirection and indecision, including for the liminal, fugitive reasoning espoused within certain brands of theory. Yet besides these effects, perhaps the greatest problem is that such aversion to rational, persuasive communication can foreordain the very fears that for many humanists loom largest—which is again to say that many humanists can seem to actively conspire with their own relegation to the margins.

Another explanation for why humanists tend to double down on the logic of paradox involves how the humanities defense often piggybacks on theories of democracy, and in particular those that extol democracy's foundationless foundations and other legitimacy deficits. Whereas humanists brandish their own exclusion, theorists of democracy instead laud the exclusions constitutive of the category of the People, celebrating that indeterminacy as democracy's very wellspring, as we saw in chapter 3. The remainders understood to haunt *all* democratic representations are, in such thinking, embraced as the locus of that political form's enduring resilience. Thus have humanists cast their lots with democracy, similarly framing their own tenuous legitimacy as their abiding promise. But in so doing, humanists do more than take cover under what is in fact a justificatory failure, circularly romanticizing their lack of a public voice as a prime vindication. In annexing their elite plight to that of the democratic populace, they also pretend to share a fate akin to that of other excluded and oppressed populations. Beyond being disengenuous, those presumed links excuse—if not revel in—what is at base a troubling dereliction of responsibility.

Naturally, this cross-collateralization of theories of the humanities and of democracy descends from a storied tradition that confers special responsibility for the cultivation of civic life upon the liberal arts.[76] The prospect that humanists' vocation is to mold a democratic citizenry—and especially a critical, reflective, responsive one—has united thinkers of all leanings (humanist and posthumanist together), even while they may disagree regarding the ends and tactics supporting that mission. Whereas for someone like Sommer the genetic nexus between the humanities and Latin *humanitas* has been tragically severed, for others (as we just observed) that affinity primarily inheres within the aestheticized and itinerant agency of radicalized social movements. Notwithstanding these splits, humanists' claims to be guarantors of public life have saddled the humanities defense with dilemmas mirroring those of democracy.

Hence, that allegiance can ironically seem to aggravate whatever ambivalence humanists organically experience toward their prospective audiences. As Spivak notes, all conceptions of culture depend on a begged community, or "the formation of collectivities without necessarily prefabricated contents."[77] Characterized by Brown as "another variation on Rousseau's paradox," rationales for the humanities, as for democracy, rest on a fabulation: they must fictionally posit an engaged public that their energies strive to retroactively bring into being.[78] In turn, one might conclude that the mutual liar's paradoxes vexing humanists and democracy together involve more than their ungrounded claims to truth but also the chronically fragile nature of their basic authority, including the authority to address a potentially fickle, indifferent constituency.

Yet whereas the exclusionary and precarious People of democracy is exalted as (at least theoretically) that political form's continuation and cradle, humanists have adopted a significantly more mixed attitude toward their prospective publics and reception thereby. Many today express growing qualms about whether those publics even continue to exist. Still, the ruse of humanists' ostracism by the exact audiences to whom they purport *both* to give voice *and* to minister remains a bedrock of the humanities defense as a genre. And that fantasy structure of rejection by a recalcitrant Other can seem, beyond addictive, to induce a certain incoherence and indecision. Torn between adulation and belittlement, humanists can appear immobilized by more than warring impulses, even while the logic of paradox glorifies that internal division. These ambivalences also lay bare the extent to which some humanists' claims to be emissaries of democracy are, when all is said and done, a form of wishful thinking.

Hence, many pleas for the humanities only redouble the legitimation crisis to which that genre ostensibly responds. This chapter has argued that such a syndrome is far from unusual or unexpected, given the centrality of paradox to the humanities defense. In a way, humanists have happily imbibed a version of Plato's remonstrance, accepting the view that, like poetry, their relevance is, at best, peripheral and paradoxical. Sometimes even delighting in that predicament, the humanities defense has been choreographed by various negative theologies that divine within sites of failure and lack an infinite bounty. But this economy of valuation has been accomplice to many forfeitures. Having eulogized the margins, humanists are all too comfortable with that tangential relevance—even alchemizing their own fears of transience into a source of paramount value. So in flaunting the supposedly elevated vision of the outcast, the humanities defense ultimately sanctions a mode of cop-out. Indeed, the margins also offer a readymade pretext and shelter, whether for reluctance to tarry with the center or to undertake those thorny normative and practical decisions that the charisma of paradox fails to explain away. The incalculable, wayward spirit of paradox can thus begin to resemble something closer to protective armor, shielding humanists from the many challenges of democracy rather than anointing them its only guardians.

Conclusion

This chapter has canvassed the many spheres in which a politics of exclusion took hold along with the prospering of theory in the Anglo-American academy. The sheer number of agendas clothed in virtually identical garb is one indicator of that mandate's force and purchase, while also capturing why the innumerable sociopolitical advances it inaugurated have been irreplaceable. However, this chapter has also asked whether a methodological privileging of exclusion creates certain impasses, stemming among other things from a politics divided about its own stated goals; such thinking's tendency to fan humanists' chronic embattlement; and a mood of noteworthy cynicism. Yet there is simultaneously a way in which parading one's own exclusion is all too easy, offering an alibi for the tough choices and difficult action that underlie any real-world application of theory.

This chapter has also studied the exhilarating conversions conducted by reasoning through paradox: reasoning that discovers exclusionary limits to be bastions of limitless renewal. However, that logic is just as likely to broker an inverse relay, causing values worth safeguarding to be ravaged by its intoxicating machinery. Especially when rote and unthinking, the contrarian play of paradox does not discriminate: it is just as prone to decimate one normative structure as another, to run roughshod over one principle as the next. And when that happens, it should go without saying, the good will not always triumph, coming out on top. Perhaps, then, the politics of exclusion has backfired for humanists in exactly such ways—causing us to mistake our gifts for failings and to throw ourselves onto a purifying bonfire fated to destroy rather than to win our salvation.

5

—

THE PEDAGOGY OF PARADOX

C onsciousness-raising projects of "giving voice to exclusion" also came to govern ideas about a humanistic pedagogy. Just as efforts to recover silenced voices and thereby atone for exclusionary practices piloted innumerable social justice and reform initiatives, they helped shape the dynamics of the liberal arts classroom, across disciplines and syllabi and universities. As Peter Brooks exhorts, teachers of literature should be "mouthpieces of others," striving to "allow the voice of the other to develop its full force."[1] Brooks's appeal also points to the new terminologies—Otherness, alterity, hybridity, singularity, multiplicity, difference—that both escorted and were spawned by the novel educational approaches to which humanists increasingly adhered amid the revolution in the humanities. The need to bear witness to marginalized perspectives and especially to experiences of victimization has been a bedrock of liberal arts teaching philosophy ever since, across higher education and beyond.

Along with such pedagogical advances arose now-authoritative ideas about the ethical and therapeutic benefits of encounters with paradox. The same period during which a politics of exclusion electrified the humanities classroom also saw the efflorescence of trauma studies, including a mounting focus on confession, witnessing, and testimony. Motivated by its own variant of an exclusionary politics, trauma theory is a textbook case of a school of thought coordinated by faith in paradox. By emphasizing the limits and foreclosures bedeviling traumatic remembrance, early trauma theorists in particular fully defined trauma by way of—routing it through—its experiential, conceptual, representational, and other failures and dilemmas. Such thinking explains trauma by way of a formula by now well recognizable: as an excluded viewpoint struggling to gain representation after being silenced by different oppressive structures (including those of the psyche). Although some later work on trauma would shed these preoccupations, especially Yale school trauma theory enlists a familiar optics of paradox to contend with suffering, injury, and victimization, in the process culling redemptive insights from those painful if not horrifying circumstances. Although reminiscent of reasoning we have observed far and wide, trauma theory simultaneously amplifies the explanatory compass of paradox. In both equating trauma with its aporias and valorizing those representational barriers, it often divines within trauma almost allegorical lessons regarding the "crises of truth" broadly afflicting speech in an era of atrocity.

Like the preceding chapter's examples, trauma theory and the humanities classroom offer forums for contending with the mixed and sometimes damaging bequests of left intellectual faith in paradox. On the one hand, it should go without saying that the momentous changes ushered in by innovations like trauma studies have been overridingly positive. In its infancy, trauma theory revolutionized ideas about mental health, taking stigma and reexplaining it as an illness beyond the victim's control. Developments in pedagogy have been similarly transformational, no doubt helping to remake the larger sociocultural landscape. But on the other, certain more worrisome tendencies of the reasoning shepherding these advances have dominated, and what follows asks why. While testaments to the real-world changes precipitated by everything associated with theory, both trauma studies and pedagogies rotating around various crucibles in exclusion offer a window on the hazards of intellectual absorption with paradox, including how it can anesthetize politics and thought together.

For its proponents, the rise of the humanities classroom devoted to witnessing about exclusion entailed a hyperpoliticization of that space. The politics of exclusion were imagined to transform the classroom into a workshop in the microphysics of power, which could combust at any moment to reveal any old speech act or scene of reading to be a reenactment of historical bastions of entitlement and their enabling violations. These elementary particles of a radicalized liberal arts have been exalted for revealing day-to-day exchanges between teachers and students to be brimming with emancipatory potential. But the educational encounter was just as much turbocharged by the elision of pedagogy, testimony, therapy, and sociopolitical consciousness-raising—an elision that has required even instructors to comply with those autobiographical and confessional directives. The epistemic fabric of paradox has provided the connective tissue harmonizing these contrasting imperatives (soul-searching and social justice) for the awakened classroom. In the process, it has also indulged humanists' yearnings to claim eminently political if not world-altering stakes for their educational missions, mollifying the sorts of crises in confidence and legitimacy examined in the last chapter.

At the same time, both a reborn humanities pedagogy and the prospering of trauma as an infectious grammar are stories of the mainstreaming of paradox: of how paradox came to be normalized within public discourse and popular awareness. This chapter therefore inquires into the conditions that allowed for that domestication: what about the logic of paradox permitted something like trauma (or, for that matter, the idiom of paradox itself) to be recast as a run-of-the-mill, mass-marketable sensibility? Why is paradox today evoked as a kind of quick-fix therapy? Clearly, this contraction of paradox into its own orthodoxy traduces everything one might expect from such an ethos, again prompting questions about why that reasoning's less salutary aspects would prevail over, even colonizing, other of its orientations. Ironically, then, even while a fusion of pedagogical and therapeutic hopes for paradox radicalized higher ed, certain methodological instincts impelling those shifts simultaneously reined them in, curtailing their ultimate horizons.

Some explanations for this taming naturally lie with the truth claims of paradox. Long promoted as savvier and more sophisticated, mastery at the game of paradox has also served to credentialize, encoding not so much intellectual proficiency as savoir-faire and elite wherewithal. Sometimes, pedagogies of paradox have also fostered a feel-good equation between "difficulty" or "ambiguity" and moral discernment, just as they can reward modes of villainization with deeply polarizing repercussions. In what follows, trauma theory offers a paradigmatic demonstration of why preoccupation with exclusionary paradox can derail normative inquiry as well as principled critique. Among other things, the frequent identification of trauma with regard to its speechlessness and disintegrating fractures depletes that analytic of moral and normative weight and precision, all the while obscuring matters of agency, responsibility, and choice. Ironically, precisely because cries of paradox possess an incredible veto power, we will see that logic—once again—to be ripe for opportunistic exploitation.

The Politicized Humanities Classroom

One feature of reasoning through paradox that can begin to explain its pedagogical sway involves how it creates synergies between content and method—causing subject matter (the discovery of paradox) and the tactics eliciting such awareness (inhabiting paradox) to become one and the same. While efforts to lend representation to exclusion revamped the content of syllabi and research agendas alike, those reforms were facilitated by a critical method that simultaneously revolves around the staging of paradox. So even as humanists sought to impart lessons divulging both the larger structures enforcing exclusion and its experiential wounds, they relied on strategies geared to enact those dynamics in the classroom. No doubt independently satisfying, this simultaneity of content and method has fueled expectations regarding the generalizability of those teaching approaches, or that such pedagogies could be just as applicable to one problematic or field or political-moral quandary as to another. As such, a supposed flexibility of method has sanctioned the impression that the upshot or yield of any given pedagogical encounter will travel with comparable ease, far beyond the classroom's rarified space and into real-world arenas. This illusion of near automatic transit between advances in higher ed and actual political activism was nourished by a blend of ingredients, some by now well known. Here again, a collision of the linguistic turn, the symbiosis of defenses of democracy and of the humanities, a deconstructive ethics, and a broad faith in symbolics together inseminated a politics of exclusion within the liberal arts seminar room and lecture hall.

Yet when it comes to teaching philosophy, additional rationales for aggrandizing the classroom's perceived political stakes were circulating in the 1980s intellectual air. Some such warrants are implicit in the celebratory accounts of globalization that flourished along with germinal subfields like postcolonial theory. Just as globalization was imagined to entail dizzying interconnections linking distant places, lives, and events, discourses of the global naturalized assumptions about other kinds of traffic. Not only were the classroom's discoveries deemed cosmic in their relevance; they were imagined to flow naturally into other domains. At once, globalization theory generated a series of spatial metaphors widely recruited to limn the exuberantly transgressive character of such educational-political discovery. To explore one unexpected example, the legal scholar Cheryl I. Harris's influential "Whiteness as Property" opens with an autobiographical meditation on the choice of Harris's grandmother to "pass" as white for economic reasons, which enabled her employment at a department store in Chicago. Although in an American chronicle, Harris extols that decision in language borrowed from globalization theory. Harris explains that her grandmother "was transgressing boundaries, crossing borders, spinning on margins, traveling between dualities of Manichean space [...]; she could thus enter the white world, albeit on a false passport, not merely passing but trespassing."[2] The bywords of globalization theory here transfigure what might represent self-compromise into a visionary act of self-reinvention and defiance.

But even more important as a basis for convincing humanists that the classroom could be an exemplarily political forum was the collapse of political awakening into a mood of therapeutic soul-searching and self-discovery. Pedagogy, politics, witnessing, and therapy thus became tightly wrapped up in one another, conjoined through a recurring explanatory matrix that has resonated across a notably diverse spectrum of thinkers. By anointing ordinary student interventions with the freighted status of testimony (or, conversely, confessionals), pedagogy was injected with intensely personal significance. In many ways, the feminist mantra "the personal is political" therefore rang true as a justification for refurbishing the classroom and its dynamics, even while the immediacy of that space's results primed many to enlarge its consequences. But above all does trauma theory claim responsibility for this makeover of liberal arts pedagogy that imbued particularized experiences of suffering and pain with what were seen as undeniably political bearings. The duty to give voice to one's own individualized trauma— and to listen diligently to that of others—was therefore a primary impetus for this radicalization of higher ed, after which the classroom could be touted as a controlled experiment in the anatomy of power and its censoring machinations.

One the one hand, this process of politicization did in fact intensify the classroom's operations, although not in wholly desirable ways. Invariably, the burden of giving voice to exclusion assumes a different tenor and shape within the relative sanctuary of a humanities seminar versus struggle in the streets. The main actors in the classroom's dramas of exposure are obviously students, texts, conventional disciplinary formations, and teachers.[3] With teachers orchestrating those maneuvers, their ensuing reckonings often hit close to home. Thus did the seminar room's reconstitution as a theater of consciousness-raising invariably create certain dilemmas, many due to the dependence of an exclusion-based politics on the singling out of both scapegoats and victims. And while the close reading of texts could offer something of a safe haven, pedagogy's testimonial bidding nevertheless meant that students and instructors alike would ultimately be implicated as firsthand penitents and crusaders.

On the other hand, it is hard to escape the irony that such a pedagogy's most ardent defenders were generally domiciled in disciplines dedicated to variants of antinormativity, including to anti-instrumental creeds regarding humanistic inquiry. So while the liberal arts were recast as supremely political, the classroom had to maintain its status as a preserve exempt from the burden of offering clear-cut morals or rationales or policies supporting its existence. Whatever awakenings humanists sought to induce therefore had to be couched in antinormative, anti-institutional language. As before, various grammars of paradox have distilled what is merely the latest incarnation of the humanities' age-old predicament of "mattering without mattering," rationalizing how and why the payoff of a humanities education could be politically world-altering while nevertheless resistant to pragmatic or normative "translation." Hence, that optics came along to manage this latest chapter in the humanities' ongoing saga of tenuous legitimacy, although here to reconcile humanists' newly muscular agendas with a habitual conceit of exile and persecution. In so doing, however, those newfangled teaching philosophies allowed their practitioners to have their cake and to eat it: to claim the ethical-political high ground while obviating the need to take full ownership of their over-hyped ambitions.

That a romance of the global spurred this rebranding of the humanities is evident in the vocabularies that cropped up during the late 1980s and '90s. Alterity, in-betweenness, difference, Otherness, singularity, marginality, hybridity: these fashionable grammars, some freshly coined, all differently index species of exclusion, many tied to race. Examining one such popular terminology, "hybridity," can help to disentangle the congeries of influences that, while politicizing the classroom, also infused pedagogy with a palpable spirit of paradox. Like other discourses of exclusion, talk of hybridity gained traction precisely by placing a celebratory, recuperative spin on certain historical grounds for Othering. Yet despite again exemplifying how the algebra of paradox reaps rewards from apparent liabilities, the roots of that grammar are significantly more complicated. Another such source, for instance, extends from the Russian formalist Mikhail Bakhtin (recall the first interlude), whose influence also sediments late-twentieth-century appeals to hybridity with democratic, pluralistic, anti-totalitarian expectations. So what the semantics of hybridity thus do is to fuse those democratic links with the "newness" promised by globalized networks, border-crossing, and the jubilance of cultural heterogeneity and diversity.

Gloria Anzaldúa's 1987 *Borderlands/La Frontera* contains one influential rendition of these themes. In that experimental and itself boundary-crossing text, Anzaldúa reconstellates the term hybridity's pejoratively biological (and even eugenicist) insinuations to instead affix it to what she describes as the emancipatory "mestiza consciousness" of the borderland. Reclaiming a putative badge of "inferiority," Anzaldúa explains: "At the confluence of two or more genetic streams, with chromosomes constantly 'crossing over,' this mixture of races, rather than resulting in an inferior being, provides hybrid progeny, a mutable, more malleable species with a rich gene pool."[4] Crucially, the value of such "cross-pollination" ultimately stems from an internalization of paradox: "The new *mestiza* copes by developing a tolerance for contradictions, a tolerance for ambiguity. [...] She has a plural personality, she operates in a pluralistic mode. [...] Not only does she sustain contradictions, she turns the ambivalence into something else."[5] Striking first are the echoes of Du Bois; Anzaldúa similarly promotes *la facultad* of the mestiza as a recipe for transmuting "intense pain" into "continual creative motion."[6] Second, the pluralism thus touted is reminiscent of the "tolerance for ambiguity" often cited as the threshold separating democracy from totalitarianism—and crucial for Bakhtin.

Anzaldúa's tributes to contradiction are further illustrative in how they compel various levels of slippage between content and interpretive method (along with a symptomatic ability "to see the deep structure below the surface"). Anzaldúa actively conflates alternate registers of "plurality": namely, of identity and of a generic or stylistically "pluralistic mode."[7] Throughout, her writing therefore enacts the texture of the psychocultural pluralism she applauds, not only hybridizing English with Spanish but also blending journalistic and autobiographical meditations with historical data, poetry, and theory. In turn, Anzaldúa's personal journey of "leav[ing] home so I could find myself" becomes inseverable from her volume's plea for political awakening, much as the verse and legends punctuating that text inscribe Anzaldua's life journey within those larger records of collective and ritualized memory, vesting her unique travails with almost allegorical, certainly generalizable significance. When taught, *Borderlands/La Frontera* similarly invites participatory engagement, luring its readers on a parallel odyssey of self-discovery while beckoning a method of instruction (or rather of consciousness-raising) fully choreographed by confessional acts of bearing witness. Metamorphic, that "mixture" of rhetorical modes is presented by Anzaldúa as necessary both to forging and to occupying a hybridized and hence emancipatory political-cultural identity.

Like Anzaldúa, other proponents of hybridity such as Homi Bhabha exalt the "hybrid location of *cultural* value" (my italics), however theorize that location by way of a semiotic or "representational" frame. Thus has a fusion of post-Saussurean linguistics and psychoanalysis furnished another set of warrants for assigning monumental importance to the ordinary humanities classroom. Published at the apex of postcolonial theory's vogue, Bhabha's essays in *The Location of Culture* seed the term hybridity with a wealth of meanings. As for Anzaldúa, hybridity denotes a specifically globalized and (and, in Bhabha's hands, cosmopolitan) awareness.[8] It is also creative for both thinkers; as Bhabha relates in an allusion to Salman Rushdie's fiction, hybridity is what causes "newness [to enter] the world."[9] Similarly does Bhabha emphasize the political dividends of everything augured by a hybridized culture, stressing "the importance of the hybrid moment of political change" and its "historical necessity."[10] Yet Bhabha simultaneously recruits his own distinct amalgam of Lacan and deconstruction to treat the "displacement and disjunction" or "interstitiality" of a globalized world as cognate to the "difference 'within,' a subject that inhabits the rim of an 'in-between' reality." So for Bhabha, psychoanalysis cum semiotics is what permits an imbrication of the personal ("the splitting of the self") and the (geo)political.

Quotes like the foregoing capture why Bhabha's investment in a "representational model" for conceptualizing not only hybridity but also politics, agency, identity, globalization, and so on would incline him to regard the classroom as a microcosm of the political. The logic that for Bhabha governs the psychic economy of the colonial stereotype and its disciplinary gaze encapsulates these links. For Bhabha, that aperture of power is unstable and ambivalent rather than to mark a secure point of identification, and this very contradictoriness is what resistant practices of "sly civility" and "mimicry" exploit. In a seeming nod to Butler's account of drag, mimicry exposes colonial mastery to be "belated" and derivative, in effect turning that gaze back upon itself to reveal its counterfeit status and contingency on its disavowed Others. Moreover, it is Bhabha's emphasis on representation renders his conception of mimicry's subversive agency eminently generalizable, pertinent to *all* political action, as is evident in statements like: "politics can only become representative, a truly public discourse, through a splitting in the signification of the subject of representation."[11] In proper deconstruction fashion, Bhabha can thus herald writing as paradigmatic of a whole slew of ancillary phenomena. As he reflects, "the force of writing, its metaphoricity and its rhetorical discourse, as a productive matrix which defines the 'social' and makes it available as an objective of and for, action. Textuality is not simply a second-order ideological expression or a verbal symptom of a pre-given political subject. That the political subject. [...] Is a discursive event."[12] Such thinking reduces power and identity alike to "discursive events," just as all political action comes to be waged on the terrain of "enunciation," "the force of writing," "textuality," and enculturation.

This patterning of political agency on the relays governing the (psycho-analytic) "subject" as well as metaphysical truths about discourse spawns an osmosis wherein virtually any "representation" can be assimilated into a single, uniform analytic, in ways we have seen many times. In the pro-cess, that transport overruns whatever distinctions might separate one node or manifestation of power from another, merging all such "signs" and symptoms into a single conceptual schema. So even while day-to-day "discursive events" become high-voltage crucibles in political subjectifica-tion, all such events become both fungible and equivalent. To return to the classroom, even minor skirmishes over mundane discursive exchanges thus become replete with potentially colossal meaning, so much so as to rise to the level of political engagement. In fact, Bhabha is overt in assigning such revenue to the interpretive skills cultivated through the study of literary and other cultural artifacts. In his words, "To live in the unhomely world, to find its ambivalences and ambiguities enacted in the house of fiction, or its sundering and splitting performed in the work of art, is also to affirm a profound desire for social solidarity."[13] But key is that the linguistic turn serves up its own distinct if unexpected rationales for politicizing a liberal arts pedagogy, impregnating the commonplace scene of close reading with stakes capable of being deemed wholly planetary.

This worldly classroom ironically garrisoned against the risk of its own instrumentality brings us to another reason the spirit and grammar of para-dox has proven so very attractive.[14] Humanists' heightened conviction in the decidedly political payoff of their pedagogy, as suggested, created whole new burdens of justification—including the need to re- or better inoculate the humanities against what we can recognize as certain perennially lurk-ing perils. Naturally, threats like instrumentalism and rationalism became freshly pressing amid humanists' sudden grandstanding regarding their superior authority over a political education. In many ways, the allure of qualities like Otherness, singularity, and hybridity—and of the many aspirations projected onto those qualities—inheres within how they fulfill such a defensive, prophylactic function. Akin to other campaigns for exclusion, humanists could claim to give voice to Otherness while recusing themselves from responsibility for that voice's translation—hence, the mantra of untranslatability. Yet at the same time, modish vocabularies like unpredictability, indeterminacy, relationality, ambivalence, and indecision were conscripted to do double duty. Long staples of the humanities' defense, those bywords acquired inflated currency through such pedagogical philosophies enamored of their own political eminence yet committed to the doctrine that humanistic inquiry should not be calculable or pragmatic.

One unquestionably positive role played by those grammars has been both to caution against and to suggest tools for disarming "top-down" or authoritarian styles of pedagogy as well as the classroom's internal hierarchies and power structures. Grammars like "incalculability" thus recriminate against forms of rote indoctrination, or the instructor acting as sole purveyor of knowledge lorded over the students. Gayatri Spivak, a prolific commentator on the merits of a humanities education, reflects on the challenges of fostering a non-domineering classroom in exactly such terms. For Spivak, an education in the humanities should "[attempt] to be an *uncoercive rearrangement of desire*."[15] It should relatedly entail "learn[ing] from the singular and unverifiable," as well as "striving for a response from the distant other, without guarantees."[16] These endeavors should enroll the instructor, too, in an "apprenticeship as suturer or invisible mender," wherein even an education in human rights becomes "the 'activation' of dormant structures," rather than the external imposition of value.[17] Spivak is unabashed in avowing her thinking's debts to aesthetic criticism: she outwardly characterizes such a pedagogy as a "teleo-poesis."

Yet still another factor informing Spivak's vocabulary of Otherness and undecidability is the complicity understood to color all knowledge production, including pedagogy. Needless to say, foregrounding the snares of complicity itself aggressively raises the political amplitude of the everyday classroom. And indeed, Spivak does not sanitize or downplay the fact that an education in something like human rights occasions an "enabling violation" reminiscent of *both* the postcolonial encounter *and* the "strategic exclusions" "shoring up" all claims to "truth"—truth being a word Spivak qualifies with the "proviso" of scare quotes.[18] As Spivak (like Butler) insists, pedagogy has no choice except to negotiate the exclusionary paradoxes that enable any and all representational gestures, including pedagogy's own.

Hence, teaching will be productively hampered by its own necessary failures, central among which is the impossibility of definitively speaking for the excluded/Other. But those "margins" and other double binds are for Spivak ultimately generative as ever-present reminders of the inescapability of one's own implicatedness and ensuing need for contrition. Albeit through the back door, even here a call for confessionalism enters the picture.[19]

The deconstructive bent of theory like Spivak's has occasionally warranted a celebration of "destruction" and "transgression" as independent pedagogical imperatives. Thus does Brooks advocate "naysaying" and a "negative dialectics," inveighing "[f]ar from teaching virtue, we in the humanities advocate immersion in the destructive element."[20] Importantly, such a vision of a humanities classroom exempt from conformity to social mores has by no means been confined to deconstructive circles. Hence, the Marxist critic Terry Eagleton (skeptical of deconstruction) can analogously maintain that "[a]ll emancipatory theory [...] has built into it a kind of self-destructive device, and moves under the sign of irony."[21] A mainstay, calls to transgress even today underlie rationales for emergent fields like the digital humanities, eager to self-brand as foremost "about breaking stuff."[22]

Whether fueled by pseudo-Nietzschean disdain for bourgeois morality or something else, insistence on the transgressive classroom has above all been partner to a vision of humanists as gadflies and critics. But even here, such pleas for dissidence have typically gone arm in arm with a mood of post-countercultural soul-searching and confessional bearing witness, whether to one's own complicity or to personalized experiences of persecution. bell hooks's 1994 *Teaching to Transgress: Education as the Practice of Freedom* reads as an instruction manual in the logic knitting together negative critique within the testimonial culture administering the humanities classroom ever since (and, no doubt, as a harbinger of the "experiential learning" widely espoused today). Like other scholarship of its moment, *Teaching to Transgress* is a manifesto for "rethinking," "deconstruction," "antagonism," and the need to repudiate "accepted boundaries."[23] In hooks's vision, that oppositionality facilitative of a "radical pedagogy" is a necessary component of a classroom geared toward experimental "excitement," "flexibility," and "spontaneous shifts in direction." Thus promoting an immediacy aroused by "the passion of experience," hooks further emphasizes that such immersive, firsthand learning stems from conversations wherein "everyone's presence is acknowledged" and "students [are] seen in their particularity as individuals."[24] Hence, hooks outwardly characterizes such a pedagogy—including its performance within her own scholarship—as a form of "testimony" and "bearing witness."

One and the same activity, teaching, therapy, consciousness-raising, and confession are thereby together imagined to actuate the "complexity" that hooks, like others, champions as a "privileged standpoint."[25] As she clarifies: "This complexity of experience can rarely be voiced and named from a distance. It is a privileged location."[26]

Although packaged as rebellious, it is above all pain—including hooks's own—that such a pedagogy seeks to unearth. The primary locus of the "experience" that hooks (and many, many others) acclaim is victimization—or, we might say, the many deleterious effects of society's exclusionary practices. Newly sanctified as the holy grail of a liberal arts education, access to the "particular knowledge that comes from suffering," including its "splitting" of the victim's selfhood, is thus commended as intrinsically edifying and, for many, ethical. Yet as before, pedagogy (undergoing suffering) and subject matter (suffering) become coextensive. And while it should go without saying that such an exercise has been life-changing for many, its enabling logic also encourages what, within this book, has been a recurring syndrome: a formal generalizability of the signs of suffering expurgated of any content beyond pain's sheer reality. Such thinking prizes the sheer attempt to uncover and linger with the hardships of society's excluded irrespective of those lesson's truth content or moral-normative fiber, with that responsibility to inhabit victimhood and its "complexity" embraced as pedagogy's foremost objective.

Such a medley of pedagogy, self-awakening, critique, and testimony has, as one might expect, found extensive theorization by trauma studies scholars, who we turn to shortly. Indeed, trauma theory disseminated still other rationales for the confessional classroom, including expectations regarding its inherently ethical accruals. In reflecting on one of her graduate seminars, Shoshana Felman recounts the circumstances revealing that class to be an "uncanny pedagogical experience as my own 'life-testimony.'" Felman's "story of how I myself became a witness to the shock communicated by the subject-matter" is one she enlarges, first, to explain why a teacher's job will be unfailingly paradoxical.[27] And second, Felman is moved to venture sweeping statements about how "teaching in itself, teaching as such, takes place precisely only through a crisis: if teaching does not hit upon some sort of crisis, it does not encounter either the vulnerability or the explosiveness of an (explicit or implicit) critical and unpredictable dimension, it has perhaps not truly taught."[28] Like Bhabha and other of their contemporaries, especially early trauma theorists were already primed by the disciplines that housed them to globalize the reach of trauma, both cross-culturally and transhistorically.[29]

But for now, Felman's idiom is further representative in how it configures teaching, testimony, and experiential crisis to be interwoven activities: in Felman's premise that the classroom in extremis should induce dramatic and unhinging "encounters" for teachers as much as for their progeny.

Far from last, we should note that hooks's plea for a transgressive pedagogy is itself motivated by larger recognitions concerning the exclusionary architecture of language. Unlike deconstructive thinkers such as Spivak and Bhabha, however, hooks explains language as a live battleground, a field composed of political antagonisms in miniature. Such attunement to the exclusions secreted within the building blocks of communication similarly served to transform the classroom into a singularly political arena. Indeed, hooks does shy away from actively endorsing "antagonisms in the classroom," as she notes in a statement reminiscent of Audre Lorde's famed commentary on the "master's tool":

> To heal the splitting of mind and body, we marginalized and oppressed people attempt to recover ourselves and our experiences in language. We seek to make a place for intimacy. Unable to find such a place in standard English, we create the ruptured, broken, unruly speech of the vernacular. [...] We take the oppressor's language and turn it against itself. We make our words a counter-hegemonic speech, liberating ourselves in language.[30]

In her own rallying cry, hooks subscribes to bold expectations for such "counter-hegemonic" discourse, which she also conceives as a medium of combined "healing," "recovery," "liberation," "intimacy," and more.

While powerful, hooks's description of that disrupted yet reconstituted speech raises more questions than it answers. In hooks's formulation, not just any old speech act carries the potential to become "counter-hegemonic"— and thereby to corroborate a given speaker's marginalized, oppressed standpoint. Relatedly, not just any old speaker or subject position possesses that insurgent potential. So a certain irony, first, ensues from the fact that hooks's ingredients for linguistic self-liberation are far from uniformly available across viewpoints and groups—and simply because not all students (or teachers) can claim to be excluded. Second, it is hard to avoid the conflicting impulses riddling such an argument. hooks's emancipatory speech is imagined to be at once self-emptying of subject matter and coherence, *and* deeply personal, *and* decidedly political. What results, here too, is another image of the classroom as supremely political yet nevertheless released from the strictures that ordinarily orient political debate and action, within any conceivable definition of a public sphere. Such thinking's transgressive edge, of course, springs from this refusal of mainstream conformity, whether it is dismissed as tyrannical or simply numbing. But third, a certain romance of the uncensorability and ungovernability of such resistant speech also haunts hooks's thinking—a romance even more pronounced in trauma studies. There is consequently a way in which such a classroom's politics extend directly from the bracketing, if not evacuation, of graspable, measurable truth content from the very speech that pedagogy purports to recover.

Pedagogy, Ethics, and the Savoir-Faire

Conviction likes hooks's in the saving graces of "complexity" has been another widely shared article of faith within the radicalized humanities classroom. For many, a cluster of what I've described as conceptual cousins to paradox (alterity, ambivalence, ambiguity complexity, difficulty, difference) have been taken above all to signal matters of justice and ethics—an ethical remit that, while supervising the college classroom, has also been promoted as crosscultural. A 2013 CNN op-ed by the literary critic James Dawes showcases the steps that not only enable such thinking's globalization but cement the common assumption that sensitivity to paradox offers a failsafe recipe for ethics. In that brief editorial, Dawes sets out to address the cognitive deficits that account for the perpetration of mass atrocity, and Dawes in essence cites the epistemology of paradox. While focused on the psychology of Syrian rebels affiliated with ISIS who did terrible things, Dawes broadly maintains that perpetrators are trained "to think that the world is painted in black and white, not shades of gray"; they are captive to either-or, friend-enemy, pure-impure, Manichean and binaristic habits of thought.[31] With that assessment, Dawes applies a recurring framework we have seen to digest an incredibly wide assortment of legal-political-ethical issues. Whereas power and oppression are blamed on hostility to paradox, Dawes ties ethics and justice to an embrace of that quality.

To be sure, much is accurate about Dawes's diagnosis of radical evil, just as history is replete with corroborating evidence. However, the ability to abridge such reasoning to fit the sound-bite format of an op-ed betrays just how much it simplifies matters. Indeed, the CNN "story highlights" capture that undue tidiness, as a blurb summarizes Dawes's logic: "The same steps used for creating monsters can show how to stop atrocities." A deceptive symmetry connects remedy and scourge, as the germs of evil are perfectly mirrored in a startlingly forthright cure. As elsewhere, various synonyms for paradox—in this instance, "ambiguity and uncertainty"—condense the mystery of why evil and ethics can seem to possess an uncannily intimate, if not genetic, similarity. That connection also guarantees the pedagogical and consciousness-raising harvest of those ethical qualities, which Dawes holds out as innate defense mechanisms against cruelty and wrongdoing. He is clear about that profit, submitting that all parents should teach their "children" that "there aren't easy solutions to complex problems" as well as "to seek out 'the other.'"[32] It is this alloy of Otherness, ambiguity, and uncertainty that invites globalization, subsuming a humanities education and international human rights tribunals within the same all-encompassing explanatory schema. The humanities classroom is once again revealed to be teeming with cosmic significance, and pedagogy a drill in the fashioning of a global citizenry.

This chapter proceeds to unpack other of the assumptions underwriting defenses of paradox like Dawes's, some of which he adopts from trauma theory. Yet that answer to radical evil—an answer that has fully curated the theory canon—should feel far too neat and consoling. Because is it really true that respect for "uncertainty" will always, invariably trump evil? Is paradox really the algorithmic formula for ethics? Are there not cases wherein paranoid doubt and overwhelming complexity will fester, skewing an actor's empathetic radar along with principled commitments such as to human rights? Put differently, are there not myriad cases when a *surplus* of moral "ambiguity and uncertainty" should be blamed for a perpetrator's psychological hang-ups, for condoning (if not encouraging) unjust actions? Either way, does it really make sense to proclaim a faculty like attunement to paradox in and of itself a vessel of justice? Even if one accepts that "ambiguity and uncertainty" *can* enhance an ethical sensibility sometimes, don't those qualities require supplementation with other intellectual resources? It seems a lot more accurate to say that something like moral complexity *may* be productive or even essential but that it is independently too whimsical and flimsy to hang a whole theory of justice upon. With these and other distinctions muddled if not sidelined entirely, it is no wonder that something as vexing as mass atrocity can be boiled down to paradox and competing attitudes toward everything that quality is imagined to telescope.

With such reasoning, Dawes (like so many others) repackages an ethics forged under the aegis of post-Saussurean linguistics into a globally marketable strategy for battling abuses of human rights. While this hat trick is made visible within the brevity of an op-ed, it is the intellectual air we all breathe: the humanities' primary if not sole habitat. Instilled within teaching philosophy, our research methods, our truth-producing procedures, our canons, sand more, Dawes's insights simply *are* our most cherished ideas about the humanities. However, it is one thing to recognize that hatred of difference can stoke the flames of atrocity; it is another to glorify difference as the single-handed equipment of ethics. While it analogously may be true that all representations are contingent upon their exclusions, it is another matter to hail those remainders as a redemptive master code capable of unraveling the mysteries of the just and of the political. One could argue something similar about the "splitting" and "in-betweenness" of the subject, acknowledging that elusiveness of selfhood without beholding within it intimations of truth verging on celestial.

The next section turns to trauma studies—an interdisciplinary juncture similarly founded on the mandate to bear witness to excluded truths, especially the repressions of trauma—to probe these therapeutic and pedagogical expectations for paradox at greater length. For now, it is worth further contemplating how this all can play out within the ordinary classroom. As we have seen, radical pedagogies are often centrally operationalized by the imperative to dismantle hierarchies of expertise and authority; but those leveling effects can know no stopping point. While deputizing the excluded voice, that priority by definition demotes and de-authorizes other perspectives, including quite possibly those of the teacher. While not without its benefits, this dynamic can be exacerbated by the fact that giving voice to exclusion has often been synonymous with a politics of authenticity—hence, its compulsively autobiographical, confessional mode. The axiom that one must experientially inhabit (if not embody) a given subject position in order to lend full expression to its truths can thus instate surrogate hierarchies of authority over what has been the humanities classroom's number 1 endeavor. So even as claims to exclusion arrogate superior insight, they become especially unassailable when pitched in a firsthand, auto-disclosing register.

Thus can the testimonial classroom seem to activate, if not thrive upon, a certain disarray. When unveiling "crises in truth" is the pedagogical gold standard, who or what should do that witnessing? Are students expected to confess? Or, like Felman, is the teacher? Or should that exercise be safely confined to texts, characters, and episodes from history? In an experiential classroom predicated on allegorical readings of its own interactions, those lessons will perhaps inevitably become *both* universalized *and* intimately personal—for thinkers like Anzaldúa and hooks and Spivak, this being exactly the point. But within a classroom's limited radius, who will accept to play the part of foe-antagonist? What world views or subject position will be thus prostrated and scorned? And what about the ensuing atonement: can it be jointly owned, or will the classroom descend into a blame game? In short, what happens when outing exclusionary practices is the preeminent badge of one's radicalism? Given how the politics of exclusion can seem to invite performative scapegoating, those dynamics can easily go awry. And while it's one thing to point fingers at texts (Herman Melville and Tony Kushner were my students' culprits last spring), can those proxies for collective contrition remain so tidily localized? How much class time should be devoted to character assassination of Kushner for *Angels in America*'s alleged elitism and insufficient inattention to race? (Last spring, I allowed those attacks to devour a full fifteen minutes.) What are the effects of such exorcisms on students who find meaning or purpose within a given work of literature?

There is no question that ordaining the humanities classroom as a theater of recompense for deep legacies of silencing has ushered in uncountable gains—gains that have resounded throughout public culture to motivate historic sociopolitical advances. (It's not entirely off base to remark on the whiteness of Kushner's roster of characters as an angle on structural racism.) But those efforts to exact penance for exclusionary practices have not lacked their censoring effects, among other inhibiting the classroom's acceptable range of interactions. Even more, they have normalized a certain exhibition of moral remorse—rendering pro forma gestures of self-abnegation that, when ritualized, becomes trivializing. At least in my classrooms, students arrive already well adroit at broadcasting their complicity—and relying on those displays to condone whatever questionable comments might follow. They have already internalized hypercognizance of, including the imperative to pay lip service to, the landmines of complicity, sidestepping them with proficiency. So while the humanities classroom risks becoming an exercise in group self-monitoring, it's not so clear that ethical or nonegoistic desires drive students to comply with those enhanced protocols. Rather, their knack for pantomiming caution over moral implicatedness and its hazards can minimize if not belittle the very offenses ostensibly under scrutiny.

Just as troubling are the vectors of privilege that can facilitate such skill. It is not accidental that newly inflated hopes for paradox arose alongside academic intrigue with the global, cosmopolitical, and other fantasies of borderless circumnavigation. To return to Bhabha, *The Location of Culture* indeed assigns a highly specific location to the "culture" thus hypostasized. In one sense, Bhabha's project is to refute the derogatory ideas about cultural stasis, backwardness, and homogeneity long displaced onto the global South to rationalize the civilizing mission, including to this day. However, the ensuing mystique of hybridity ends up reinforcing the very stigmatizing logic Bhabha purports to unravel, in effect re-relegating the non-Euro-American world to a condition of premodernity. Others like Simon Gikandi have questioned "the unprecedented valorization of culture" in "postcolonial theories of globalization" like Bhabha's.[33] For Gikandi, not only are such overly enthusiastic renditions of globalization as Bhabha's woefully out of touch with the rampant suffering of the global South, but they are plainly inaccurate, since they miss the fact that "citizens of the postcolony are more likely to seek their global identity by invoking the very logic of Enlightenment that postcolonial theory was supposed to deconstruct."[34] Mistakenly "valoriz[ing] alienation rather than local identity,"[35] this worship of an internationalized culture of fragmentation and displacement is further attributed by Gikandi to the elite educational systems that produced a particular generation of intellectuals.

Within the arc of this book, it should be obvious that Bhabha's conception of cultural hybridity is overflowing with a spirit of "tantalizing contradiction" (Bhabha's phrase). [36] Yet, like other conduits of paradox, hybridity, too, hinges on the positing of anathematized foils—foils that should by now be readily identifiable. Bhabha juxtaposes hybridity with, and thereby demonizes, liberal identity politics, assimilation ("The time for 'assimilating' minorities to holistic and organic notions of cultural value has dramatically passed."), recognition, and what Bhabha derides as "the exoticism of multiculturalism [and] the *diversity* of cultures.[37] He simultaneously explains cultural hybridity by way of a familiar economy of negative valorization. Hybridity is offset against everything it is not: "organic," "holistic," "original," "pure," unitary ("Cultures are never unitary in themselves"), "continuous," "constant," "nationalist," "authentic," and so on.[38] Not coincidentally, these are the very qualities that the body of theory Bhabha draws from has long condemned as *both* pre- or antimodern (Bakhtin, Lukács, and innumerable others) *and* perilously totalizing-totalitarian (Lefort, Bakhtin, Lukács, and so on). In Bhabha's hands, however, that stock inventory of antitheses and foes serves mainly to decry a deficit or failure of hybridity—or to project inadequacy and underdevelopment onto the, here, insufficiently globalized non-Euro-American world.

It should, in turn, be far from shocking that Bhabha would characterize his project as a "postcolonial translation of modernity."[39] Purged of (yet parasitic on) the usual litany of premodern pathologies, hybridity is instead enrobed with an array of quintessentially modern(ist) insignia: ambivalence, antagonism, displacement, contradiction, repetition, duality, and, of course, paradox. Similarly does hybridity denote a cryptomodern(ist) sense of time out of joint, as Bhabha champions the "in media res," shorthand for a liminal capacity to circulate with dexterity between otherwise incommensurable worlds and cultures. Smooth and unencumbered geographical transit is, once again, the paradigm for an emancipatory politics and consciousness— although a paradigm, also customarily, gratifying the illusion of seamless mobility between those separate planes and spheres. Throughout, Bhabha is at pains to demonstrate that modernity is far from a strictly European bequest but equally extant within "the subaltern history of the margins of modernity" and evidence of "a colonial contramodernity at work in the [...] matrices of Western modernity that, if acknowledged, would question the historicism" long lending ideological sanction to empire.[40] Yet whether or not Bhabha's multiple modernities thesis holds water, key are two things. First, Bhabha's yearning to recover a colonial modernity "of the margins" imbibes the modernity-as-paradox thesis hook line and sinker, ratifying the customary view that paradox represents an elevated way of knowing. Second, Bhabha's vision of hybridity actively depends (as Gikandi suggests) on the denigration of the local, homogenous, cohesive, stable, unified, and so on—qualities Bhabha derides as a lapse of everything "translationally modern." Here too the myth of a hybridized culture outright requires the phantasmic backdrop of enslavement to a "totalizable" worldview, although perpetuating the very Othering logic Bhabha purports to take apart.

Albeit along different lines from hooks's counterhegemonic speech, Bhabha's globalized-hybridized cultural subjectivity is clearly far from uniformly available across nationalities, classes, geographies, and other such variables. Rather, it is contingent on a prototypically modern(ist) ability to abstract from one's sociocultural, religious, political, and other loyalties and attachments—refracting them through the critically self-alienating dispatches of paradox. To be sure, one might counter these assessments by crediting worthy figures like Du Bois or Frantz Fanon with responsibility for such emphasis on psychic ambivalence, disintegration, and fracture. Yet as an instruction manual for the radicalized humanities classroom, hybridity and its paradoxes should leave us deeply troubled. Because such an education in the quagmires of paradox also bestows a kind of savoir-faire, one presumably including know-how in the arts of nuance, poise, and discretion. That ability to dance the dance of paradox without falling out of step has rightly been framed as cognizance of one's own "guilt" (Althusser) and complicity

(Spivak). But the translational irony and self-relativization that pedagogies of exclusion cultivate are also lessons in diplomacy—or their own badge of elite sophistication and wherewithal. No doubt, the ability to give voice to paradox is today what grants access to power, allowing one to interface with countless vectors of privilege. Fluency in that language of paradox is arguably *the* primary marker of what it means to be an initiate—as Bhabha suggests, indeed separating a globalized intelligentsia from the "authentic," "unitary," "pure" cultures presumably transcended and fled.

The Therapy of Paradox

This privileging of the excluded voice was also fertilized by trauma theory and its parallel endeavor to bear witness to silenced truths: the many repressions and foreclosures attendant to trauma. The flowering of trauma studies within the academy, along with its subsequent evangelism as a gospel of popular self-help, actively worked to ratify and to naturalize the pedagogical innovations being contemporaneously implanted within the humanities classroom by sources like globalization theory and an ethics of Otherness. Few theoretical developments have proven more transmissible—within higher education or culture at large—than the discourse of trauma, even prompting trauma theorists to remark upon that contagion.[41]

Given the enormous diagnostic weight carried by the basic label of trauma, many have tracked its proliferation, among other things investigating how academic trauma studies came to sponsor a public culture of witnessing and confessionalism. There is no question that, in both lay and scholarly arenas, the language of trauma has confiscated other approaches to comprehending injury and loss to become its own "empire."[42] Importantly, the decade that saw trauma standardized as a clinically recognized diagnosis also coincided with the medical community's mounting focus on, and efforts to validate, the psychic tolls of pain, in an attempt to take pain seriously that helped to turn pain management into a human right.[43] Ever since, these liaisons between public and academic discourses of trauma have shaped classrooms, law courts, film and television, memoir, news reportage—and on all levels.[44]

Trauma theory's conferral of epistemic authority on the logic of paradox is one factor that fueled this transport. In many ways, especially its early incarnations are a catechism in the rudiments of paradox as an explanatory schema. Conversely, trauma studies has been perhaps the most influential field disseminating a religion of paradox both within and beyond the walls of the academy, ingraining that grammar and its peculiar therapeutics as a kind of household awareness. On one level, trauma theory reproduces the main features of reasoning this book at length has studied, and like other politicized (and poeticized) projects of giving voice to exclusion, it has assumed all the gusto of those initiatives. But on another, trauma theory furnishes its own warrants for the education-political impetus to rectify circumstances of sociocultural silencing and erasure, beyond those considered before. Even though trauma theory has often generatively underwritten a progressive politics over its evolution, that discourse has metastasized to produce significantly more murky results, becoming self-undermining if not potentially destructive. Saturating popular culture, appeals to trauma can invite ready manipulation, and more than anything does that vast circulation of "trauma talk" raise far-reaching questions about what disposed its (albeit watered down) devotional of paradox to monopolize popular, academic, and legal ideas about psychic abuse and injury.

At first blush, trauma studies might seem the last place reverence for the contrarian play of paradox would take hold. However, trauma has consistently been *both* defined *and* called into question with regard to its many paradoxes, including its alleged refusal of present, full, and integrated representation. This footprint is prominent in the field's founding texts. While merely one entry in a then growing scholarly focus on political and other violence, Elaine Scarry's pathbreaking 1985 *The Body in Pain* (influenced more by Marx and Freud than Derrida and Lacan) introduced now unquestioned assumptions about the dire impact of suffering and victimization on speech and language. That Scarry is a rather conventional humanist (and less a student of poststructuralism) itself illustrates how comprehensively the logic of paradox has shaped scholarship across the humanities.

To recall chapter 3's discussion, for Scarry pain is largely an anomalous condition, a view on some level distinguishing her from Yale school theorists who instead pattern trauma on the constitutive foreclosures of language, the divided subject, and so on. Nevertheless, Scarry understands pain with primary reference to its representational hurdles, and in particular its resistance to linguistic and other verification. For Scarry, this "unsharability" renders pain "at once that which cannot be denied and that which cannot be confirmed."[45] For the sufferer wracked by a reality defiant of empirical proof or validation, pain therefore induces cognitive dissonance and isolation. The most real thing to the victim, the "world-destroying" effects of pain, elude communication. Like many, Scarry proceeds to endow those representational obstacles with substantial political import, treating them as the raw material of power—and drawing monumental conclusions about power's anatomy therefrom. Although the experiential fabric of pain is Scarry's starting point, *The Body in Pain*, as we saw, is preoccupied with larger representational dilemmas: with pain's referential "instability," "invisibility," and the legitimation crises those dynamics pose. The fact that a conceptual failure—the ineffable nature of pain—would furnish deeper insight into something as consequential as power is therefore one paradox lying at the heart of Scarry's theory.

Yale school trauma theory only enlarges the scope and significance of the sorts of representational blockages identified by Scarry, discerning within them consummate meaning. Trauma theory is strewn with statements like the following from Felman, who surmises "that testimony is the literary—or discursive—mode par excellence of our times, and that our era can precisely be defined as the age of testimony."[46] This impulse to generalize (if not universalize) the lessons of trauma—extrapolating from the isolated scene of witnessing to draw sweeping conclusions—is omnipresent within early trauma theory in particular. Many have looked to the defining attributes of trauma as a referendum on what Lawrence Langer terms "the age of atrocity."[47] But while symptomatic of the general mood of reckoning that consumed many academics in the 1980s, license to globalize a diagnostic centered on individual suffering simultaneously comes from the schools of theory that together gestated trauma studies, which congealed in ways that have lent trauma its comprehensive explanatory purchase. As we noted, both of trauma theory's main parents—psychoanalysis and deconstruction— encourage modes of formalist patterning and ensuing analogical transfers across disparate domains—such as from politics to aesthetics and back again—that have similarly been characteristic of trauma studies. Especially within its inaugural formulations, the psychic economy of trauma is there- fore modeled, first, on the deferrals, remainders, and aporias understood to haunt *all* signification and, second, on the repressions and foreclosures intrinsic to the psychoanalytic subject. Precisely these analogues allow trauma to be deemed a "mode par excellence."

Within trauma theory, a deep grammar of paradox, as elsewhere, fulfills a plethora of discontinuous and overdetermined functions, many recognizable. Indeed, that welter of paradox has itself enhanced trauma's diagnostic currency, although not without producing a cluster of nested paradoxes that can feel inordinately difficult to separate. A given paradox plaguing traumatic remembrance often annexes countless others, even while the appearance of paradox acts as a weathervane foretelling trauma's episodic emergence. As we have observed before, that concatenation of self-propagating paradox is, at least to a degree, a result of the blurring (and confusion) of negative with affirmative species of that property. Precisely the tragic impediments to witnessing—or, we might say, trauma's paradoxes of giving voice to its own excluded status—have been placed by trauma theorists in a decidedly redemptive light. Relatedly, it is by conceiving trauma as a paradoxically *necessary* failure of representation that glimpses of elevated insight capable of being venerated as fully ethical have been divined within the untold horrors of the twentieth century.

The negative aspects of these paradoxes coloring trauma should be obvious, given that the Holocaust was the main reference point for that field's pioneers. Like other ruminations on global modernity, trauma studies was borne out of the onus to reckon with unspeakable calamity and devastation, and the grammar of paradox registers that unthinkability. For critics like Felman and Cathy Caruth, the central yet "peculiar paradox" of trauma consequently concerns how its "truth" is "bound up" in an invariable "crisis in truth."[48] Those limits to the human comprehension of something as horrendous as genocide, however, have simultaneously been deemed generative by many, much as chapter 3 considered with Jean-François Lyotard. Caruth describes trauma as a "radical disruption" that "unsettles" and "brings us to the limits of our understanding."[49] As she asks of trauma theory's basic endeavor, "How does one listen to what is impossible?"[50] Such a query stages a paradox indexing more than the reasons why phenomena like mass atrocity confront the mind with realities that *cannot* be grasped or fathomed; it also problematizes whether trauma *should not* be intellectualized or granted expression. With the language of paradox marshaling a type of caution, trauma theory's project of venturing into psychologically and emotionally scathing territory has bred an understandable insistence that human knowing will run up against certain "necessary failures" (recalling Butler) and other impediments (recalling formulations of the sublime).[51]

Naturally, these cognitive hurdles have been understood to beset efforts to depict trauma in art, literature, and narrative. Richard Kearney thus chronicles the "paradoxes attached to every attempt—fictional or documentary—to tell the story of the Holocaust," while simultaneously submitting that "stories may, paradoxically, come to the rescue of truth" concerning trauma.[52] Assessing the explosion of fiction about trauma, Anne Whitehead differently asks whether "the term 'trauma fiction' represents a paradox or contradiction," since an excess of narrativization can inadvertently stifle or "destroy" traumatic memory.[53] Sarah Clift instead ventures a caveat: "Ultimately, literature cannot reveal. The insanity of the effort to do so turns on an elaborate paradox."[54]

While underscoring the perils accompanying attempts to fathom something like atrocity, the language of paradox simultaneously elucidates the phenomenological-experiential texture of trauma, including of theory bent on voyaging into those psychic depths. In its defiance of representation, trauma has therefore been categorized by way of qualities like its evanescence, incompleteness, aporias, and other enigmas, in reasoning that enshrines paradox as a telltale sign of both its underlying existence and its fleeting disclosure. Caruth comments on the peculiar time lag that is part of traumatic remembrance: "in trauma the greatest confrontation with reality may also occur as an absolute numbing to it, [and] that immediacy, paradoxically enough, may take the form of belatedness."[55] Relatedly does Whitehead explain trauma with regard to "the striking paradox that while its re-enactments are disturbingly literal and precise, they nevertheless remain largely unavailable to conscious recall and control."[56] With great regularity, first, trauma is thus deciphered as a "process of disintegrating perception" (Scarry) or "an experience that is not fully assimilated as it occurs" (Caruth); and second, it is deemed fundamentally impervious to "integration" (whether psychic, legal, epistemic, or representational).[57] Commenting on this, Stef Craps rightly observes the distinctly poetic fabric of trauma for many theorists, who "often favor or even prescribe a modernist aesthetic of fragmentation and aporia as uniquely suited to the task of bearing witness to trauma."[58]

At the same time, the centrality of paradox to accounts of trauma points to trauma's frequent tendency to function as a vehicle of critique. Trauma's status as an excluded or failed representation has imbued it (like other suppressed voices) with a critical, dissident edge, including relative to an observer's pretense of epistemic mastery and rational self-ownership. Indeed, this critical thrust is one reason an anti-legalism animates much trauma theory. Whereas on the one hand its paradoxes indict the legal system for an epistemic animus to the inscrutable elements of trauma, those very features are, on the other, acclaimed for stymying legal oversight and capture. Hence for a thinker like Felman, trauma is fundamentally incommensurate with the evidentiary, rationalist, and proceduralist regimes of knowing associated with legal process. Felman anathematizes the legal system's incentives to impose "closure" and thereby to "master and subdue" trauma by submitting it to a "totalizable" version of events.[59] As she clarifies, "the site of memory is an unintegratable, residual unconscious site that cannot be translated into legal consciousness or legal idiom," and similarly decries law's "[use] as a straightjacket to tame history as madness."[60] In such thinking, not only does law risk distorting traumatic remembrance by inflicting cognitive violence on the witness; it also means that trauma is by definition excluded from or beyond law's circumference. Precisely that exceptionality has been understood to endow trauma with its disruptive, revelatory force. That trauma's elusive truths occupy a space akin to other excluded representations is, plainly put, what procures its critical, ethical, just orientation.

That dissidence is for many also why trauma becomes transformative. "Fundamentally creative," the impossible kernel of traumatic remembrance is thereby seen to yield explicitly pedagogical dividends—hence, its influence within the revolutionized liberal arts classroom. In a reading of Claude Lanzmann's *Shoah*, Caruth notes: "It is precisely in the struggle to make sense of this refusal that the possibility of a truly pedagogical encounter emerges, an encounter that, by breaking with traditional modes of understanding, creates new ways of gaining access to historical catastrophe for those who attempt to witness it from afar."[61] In the same passage, Caruth further proceeds to laud trauma's consciousness-raising prospects as so collectivizing as to become fully transcultural. Recalling Dawes, Caruth surmises: "In a catastrophic age, [...] trauma itself may provide the very link between cultures."[62]

Far from last, trauma's very likelihood of being silenced (and thereby delegitimized) is often presented as what awakens its elevated understanding. Like other sites of exclusion, trauma is seen to reside within the margins of the *para doxa*, and thus to bequeath to its victims the more complex, sophisticated ways of knowing—including over the historical circumstances breeding injustice—enabled by exile from the dominant. In this vein does Caruth describe trauma as "the greatest confrontation with reality," heralding trauma's "enigmatic core" (or for Felman "ungraspable kernel") as a locus of exemplary meaning.[63] It is surely tempting to seize upon the theological registers of paradox coursing through this reasoning, given how forms of incomprehensibility and incommunicability are near to being sanctified. As within theology, it is exactly the inability to speak or to articulate the essence of something vital that summons the language of paradox and, moreover, converts apparent lacunae into fonts of almost clairvoyant recognition.

This urge to find renewal within the wounds of trauma—and to enlist the grammar of paradox as such an optics—is far from a hangover of deconstruction at Yale. Rather, those etherealizing moves continue to coordinate trauma theory's uptake within fields like critical race theory, as we have seen. Whereas chapter 4 saw Du Bois's notion of double consciousness to metamorphosize the pain of racial persecution into a well of creative genius, Yale school trauma theory crafts separate rationales for such transfigurations, even while those lineages are often entwined. Hortense Spillers's thought has acquired new purchase along with Afro-pessimism, for theorists like Alexander Weheliye and C. Riley Snorton because, even amid the appalling violence of racial oppression, Spillers envisions a utopian beyond.[64] Not surprisingly, the physics of paradox are what open up such frontiers for Spillers. For instance, Spillers's landmark "Mama's Baby, Papa's Maybe: An American Grammar Book" (1987) begins in autobiographical fashion by citing the foundational status of (Spillers's own historical) exclusion, which is cast as a paradox: "My country needs me, and if I were not here, I would have to be invented."[65] Spillers's project therein is accordingly to excavate distinct archives of exclusion: the "lacunae" and "relative silence of the record" of the "corpus of law that underwrites enslavement."[66] The method overseeing that enterprise is also not unusual, as Spillers ultimately exposes law's "transactions" to be "riddled" with "contradictions, accident, and surprise" as well as "antitheses."[67] The workings of paradox thus fulfill a prototypically critical (and anti-legal) function within Spillers's celebrated essay.

Along with that intransigence, the "play of paradox" ushers in an "insurgent ground" that Spillers construes as unmistakably redemptive. And that insurgency is key given how it directly extends from an embrace of lethal paradox: from what Spillers calls "claiming the monstrosity." (It is surely tempting, here too, to hear echoes of Kierkegaard in this "monstrous paradox" of insurgency.) That "play" also inaugurates an unprecedented manner of writing: a "hieroglyphics of the flesh," in a coinage that has understandably been oft recanted. It is thus an explicitly linguistic paradigm for theorizing trauma that facilitates the possibility of such transformations, or as Spillers puts it, "representational potentialities" and "a new *semantic field/fold*" that "might rewrite after all a radically different text for female empowerment."[68] Whatever materialism might seem to inhere within Spillers's "flesh" is consequently eclipsed by this emphasis on texts and writing. As a species of paradox, moreover, that image of "stand[ing] in the flesh" is theologically freighted—once again hearkening to Du Bois and his corresponding "paradox" of "knowledge" alien to "his own flesh and blood." Thus does Spillers's flesh that "break[s] in upon the imagination" layer semiotic, literary-poetic, and theological registers of paradox onto one another, and those synergies are what spawn the liminal space of almost queer ungendering that Spillers claims for Black womanhood—a space she heralds as capable of eluding the "traditional symbolics" legislating gender identity.

One other recent text can further delineate the doctrinal status of this blend of trauma theory and reasoning best described as indebted to Du Bois. Christina Sharpe's *In the Wake: On Blackness and Being* (2016) pays similar tribute to the insurgency of paradox as a tactic for contending with racial terror in the aftermath of slavery. Sharpe also takes particular aim at law, condemning "the ongoing state-sanctioned legal and extralegal murders of Black people" while also inscribing contemporary antiblack violence within "the long time of Dred and Harriet Scott."[69] While thereby magnifying the enormity of structural oppression, Sharpe, like Spillers, nevertheless contemplates an approach to living within otherwise "un-imaginable" times that derives from "becoming undisciplined." Sharpe's metaphor designed to underscore these tensions is that of "the wake" and what she terms the vocational ethic of performing "wake work." In reflecting on her book's portfolio of examples, Sharpe explains that she selected texts

> that do not seek to explain or resolve the question of this exclusion in terms of assimilation, inclusion, or civil or human rights, but rather depict aesthetically the impossibility of such resolutions by represent-ing the paradoxes of blackness within and after the legacies of slavery's denial of Black humanity. I name this paradox the wake, and I use the wake in all of its meanings as a means of understanding how slavery's violences emerge within the contemporary conditions of spatial, legal, psychic, material, and other dimensions of Black non-being as well as in Black modes of resistance.[70]

Continuing, Sharpe clarifies that her "metaphor" of the wake and "se-miotics of the slave ship" are useful precisely because they can harbor an "entirety" of "meanings." At one point, Sharpe spells out those resonances, not coincidentally within a parenthetical: "(the keeping watch with the dead, the path of a ship, a consequence of something, in the lines of flight and/or sight, awakening, and consciousness)."[71] While suggestive of a ritualized mourning, even the negative valences of paradox morph into something freeing and creative. In recognitions that pay further homage to Du Bois, Sharpe welcomes the reenvisioning enabled by the pain of "this exclusion," or for her being "positioned [...] as no-citizen." As she avers, "if we are lucky, the knowledge of this positioning avails us particular ways of re/seeing, re-inhabiting, and re-imagining the world."[72]

These discussions of Sharpe and Spillers clearly return us to the enormous value such thinking has possessed for so many. That a logic of paradox continues to remain a blueprint for contemporary theorizations of race testifies to its restorative and incisive nature, which has not diminished with time. However, that very persistence returns us to the question of what has allowed that basic explanatory framework to endure: to remain constant and unyielding notwithstanding the passage of time and across far-flung locations, to be just as conducive to grappling with the Holocaust as with the contemporary faces of American racism. Here, too, one answer would be to concede that such reasoning is nothing short of correct. Indeed, documenting the mutual architecture of ostensibly distant and unrelated phenomena is often the core point of work on structural oppression like that addressed above. Yet it is also hard to escape the ways such reasoning exceptionalizes trauma when deeming it alien to the universalizing remit of systems like law, an irony compounded by the fact that trauma's decisive features are frequently conceived in ways that become universally recyclable from one scene of injury to another. Analysis that alchemizes a lever of critique (paradox) into a redemptive cure (paradox) just as applicable to one manifestation of trauma as to the next can therefore seem to play fast and loose with more than specificity and context. Paradox starts to appear a one-size-fits-all remedy fated to obscure more than it tells us.

Given all of this, it might seem inevitable that critiques of trauma theory would be pitched in terms that mobilize, and thereby ratify, that diagnostic authority. And no doubt, many rejoinders to trauma theory have accused that body of thought of either redoubling the paradoxes afflicting trauma or instating their own. Ruth Leys's *Trauma: A Genealogy* thus sets out to unravel "the tensions and paradoxes that have continued to trouble the field," many of which for Leys lie with trauma's purportedly antimimetic nature.[73] Dominick La Capra's interventions in trauma studies have often directly pivoted on disagreements over the nature of paradox, which La Capra charges Yale school thinkers of fundamentally mishandling. As La Capra rightly notes, one need not "becom[e] compulsively fixated on or symptomatically reinforce[e] impasses" resulting from "paradox and aporia"; "the disclosure of an aporia [...] is not the ultimate goal of analysis or the invitation to an endless repetition."[74] But even amid these caveats, La Capra is troubled not so much by the equation of trauma with paradox as by the impulse to exalt paradox as an end in and of itself. That trauma is paradoxical remains undisputed.

Trauma and the Empire of Paradox

As should be clear, trauma theory often wears its claims to jurisdiction over ethics and justice on its sleeve. As Didier Fassin and Richard Rechtman note, trauma has regularly been imagined to "[articulate] an ethical truth that [lies] beyond individual judgment,"[75] or that is unassailable. Yet the very features enshrined as watermarks of trauma (i.e., its many paradoxes) can produce their own impasses, especially with regard to the justice-related concerns long an impetus for trauma theory.

This, most immediately, is because trauma is often denominated in terms that artificially constrict the range of injuries qualifying as trauma—a purview that, we know, the logic of paradox decrees. That narrowed scope is doubly ironic given how those very same codes of paradox can encourage a universalization of trauma's structural and formal logic. Nonetheless, trauma is consistently classified along lines that extol its exceptional and its excluded status—hence, its consignment to a region of crises and extremes. For some, this exceptionalism stems from an etiology of trauma that is event-based, or that roots trauma in unique, isolated occurrences rather than in systemic conditions (like those accompanying structural oppression).[76] Yet that etiology is just as much a byproduct of trauma's patterning on a semiotics, which suffuses trauma with all the indeterminacies, deferrals, and foreclosures besetting textual language as well as other failed or threatened representations. While those qualities immunize trauma against oversight by rationalist, rule-based, and objectifying orders like law, such a fabric simultaneously barricades trauma against efforts to render it graspable, stable, or assimilable such as into "normal" ways of seeing. This also explains why the sporadic, unreliable character of traumatic remembrance has been viewed not only as the bellwether of its unpredictable emergence but also as the source of its antinomian, grace-like ethics.

We can take further stock of exactly why this exceptionalism circumscribes the caliber and expanse of injuries that will conform to trauma's identifying markers and thereby merit that label's validation. One link between trauma theory and the educational missions explored above is a shared reliance on representational models for contending with suffering and its mercurial yet insurgent agency. As with other vectors of exclusion, one result has been a privileging not so much of the voice as of the *voicelessness* of trauma, or what Caruth calls trauma's attempt to "articulate the difficulty of articulation."[77] As Felman argues of Albert Camus's *The Fall*, it "enacts the Holocaust as a radical *failure of representation*, in both senses of the word: failure of representation in the sense of *making present* the event; failure of representation in the sense of truly *speaking for the victim, whose voicelessness* no voice can represent."[78] We can quickly grasp why such premises dovetail with those of a thinker like bell hooks. Whereas hooks identifies "expressionless" and "unruly speech" as evidence of a speaker's marginality, so do unspeakability and "voicelessness" become insignia of trauma, including its prerogative over justice and ethics. It is trauma's shattering of language and ensuing muteness that is thus configured as near redemptive, but such thinking also bars wounds that might be speakable or find successful verbal and other acknowledgment from rising to the level of trauma. Injuries that disobey trauma's rarefied codes thus risk falling outside that category's limited radius.

Analogous assumptions have informed discussions of witnessing: the very indiscipline, insubstantiality, and evanescence of memory are what have been taken to establish testimony's legitimacy. As Dori Laub explains: "Massive trauma precludes its registration; the observing and recording mechanisms of the human mind are temporary knocked out, malfunction. The victim's narrative—the very process of bearing witness to massive trauma—does indeed begin with someone who testifies to an absence, to an event that has not yet come into existence."[79] Clearly another paradox of trauma, this "absence" or lack of cognizable truth content—including the inability of its origin and sources to be fully named—is for many what reveals trauma to be Trauma. Consecrated along with trauma's ephemerality and expressionlessness is thus a matrix of for us standard properties: aporia, adjournment, deferral, unverifiability, fracture, unrepresentability, alienation, deracination, hiddenness, fugitivity, ambivalence, ambiguity, and so on. Yet that conceit of trauma's impenetrable, recalcitrant kernel withholds that label's imprimatur from memories that *are* somehow coherent or concrete or easy to recall. As has been widely notedly, that exceptionalism can similarly discredit psychic injuries that might be ongoing, endemic, and/or fully present within and accessible to the contours of a victim's day-to-day experience (rather than buried in repressed realms of the psyche).

It is essential to recognize that these properties here policing the precincts of trauma are ones observed to conduct parallel gatekeeping functions many, many times before in this book, although within alternate (if overlapping) inquiries. In its own negative theology, the epistemic contours of trauma come into view only against the backdrop of its antitheses, as qualities like integration, cohesion, resolution, unbrokenness, organicism, intelligibility, tangibility, wholeness, harmony, presence, and so on are deemed alien to genuine trauma. Yet as earlier chapters examined, an almost identical constellation of terms as those overseeing the parameters of trauma has simultaneously secured the boundaries of categories like modernity, poetry, democracy, the humanities, justice, and more—segregating those idealized domains from their (albeit prerequisite) foils and inversions. And as elsewhere, the relief of those contrasts is for trauma entirely necessary to bring its distinguishing features into view, to illuminate its preeminent value. While this negative economy of valuation works to ransom trauma not *despite* but paradoxically *because of* its crisis of truth, it is hard to escape the Manichean world view that such thinking fosters.

These protocols have not been confined to graduate exams or humanities classrooms but can (de)credentialize certain nonconforming manifestations of trauma within public settings, including the courtroom. The sheer influence of trauma as a diagnostic has naturally entailed the standardization of its powerful authenticatory equipment, and clearly one strategy for discounting a witness is to poke holes in their testimony. But the aporetic data of trauma can actively furnish a pretext for such invalidation—albeit one that opportunistically turns trauma theory on its head. For instance, the notion that inarticulacy and elusiveness represent the core signs of trauma can invite disingenuous tactics for discarding evidence of trauma, such as for a cross-examining attorney bent on undermining the testimony of a witness. As Christina Fogarasi asks of high-profile trials, pointing to trauma theory's investment in symptomatic modes of analysis, "If symptomatic readers require a survivor's silence to help prove the event, what happens when [certain traumatic] narratives exist on the surface, plainly and immediately stated by the survivor?"[80] As Fogarasi suggests, the prospect that trauma is solely recognizable through its expressionlessness is just as likely to provide a basis for refuting a speaker as for corroborating the testimony of a fragile witness. Hence, the very features imagined to protect trauma from manhandling by law can seem highly susceptible to unscrupulous manipulation, and especially when testimony happens to elude the conventions sanctified by trauma theory—or, for that matter, fulfills those conventions so completely as to in fact be reduced to silence. So beyond how trauma's codes can disallow the protections and privileges offered by that label to injuries that contravene the fleeting, interstitial logic of paradox, many definitions of trauma play quite directly into the hands of power in real-world forums like the legal system. Ironically, trauma theory's own criteria can thus impose the very distortions that it accuses law of inflicting on traumatic memory.

Second, it is this representational model convinced of trauma's excluded, exceptional status that sets in motion a universalization of the formal logic of trauma. Recalling the above, another spin on the edict that trauma "precludes [...] registration" is to say that it wipes out its own content and subject matter. While clearly a real facet of syndromes like repression, that focus on the fundamental inarticulacy of trauma is nevertheless what allows it to be submitted to the formalist patterning widely pursuant to reasoning through paradox. Yet as a result, matters of degree, context, intentionality, subject matter, and so on also become functionally irrelevant—whether to an examiner seeking to ascertain trauma's traces or for other legal, political, and documentary purposes. As with other vestiges of exclusion, this vacancy of cognizable, determinate content (whether empirical, normative, or otherwise) is ultimately what permits trauma's explanatory grid to be grafted onto a host of wildly divergent injuries over geography and history together— however not without eliding crucial grades and distinctions. Indeed, such elisions are present even in Felman's simple description of the Holocaust as a "failure of representation," since that failure is implied to pertain just as much to mass atrocity as to the isolated act of bearing witness. A certain collapse of scale—here, a conflation of the Holocaust as a cataclysmic event with the molecular problem of testimony—renders those very different phenomena digestible by way of a single and recurring analytic.

On the one hand, I've already suggested why such emphasis on the formal signposts connecting both collective with individual trauma and one episode of historical trauma to another can be intentional, especially for thinkers aiming to document the titanic reach of oppression that is, lo and behold, structural. But on the other, an exclusive focus on the symmetries joining disparate traumas can become blinkered and reductive, allowing the label trauma to become generalizable in a cursory, unthinking manner. A substantial literature has therefore indicted especially early trauma studies not only for its diagnostic imperialism but specifically for being Eurocentric, classist, male-centered, and otherwise biased, whether due to trauma's roots in psychoanalysis or otherwise.[81] Nonetheless, when all traumas become interchangeable and equivalent, permitting that label to be programmatically applied, those slippages do more than to trivialize the underlying injuries;[82] they also saddle trauma with significant antinormative baggage guaranteeing that it will short circuit differential and prescriptive analysis. So besides how the heuristic of trauma privileges certain injuries over others, it places a moratorium on certain types of inquiry. Indeed, the very features deemed definitional of trauma can seem to

CHAPTER 5

stonewall the deliberative effort to distinguish (not to mention hierarchize or prioritize) measurably different traumas.

Further compromising the politics of trauma is accordingly what we might term a crypto-normative antinormativity. Why is this the case? That the traumatic injury itself cannot be fully "claimed" or substantiated (one of Caruth's books is titled *Unclaimed Experience*) certainly robs such injuries of whatever specificity, weight, and gravity comes from validation in speech and other representation. Yet identifying trauma through its refusal of namable or "present" bearings further effaces any given scalar metric that might differentiate one trauma from the next, leveling indicia that might be tied to severity, frequency, context, magnitude, longevity, and degree. With all traumas rendered fungible, such formalist evacuation of substance and content is by no means confined to trauma alone; rather, such thinking can neutralize much wider matters of intent, volition, and agency—in other words, nullifying the sorts of calculi needed to assign responsibility, blame, and punishment to a perpetrator.[83] The same conflations that impede the localization of trauma can, in consequence, thwart the allocation of guilt and accountability, interfering with the ability to condemn traumatizing behaviors. To be sure, this instinct to decipher trauma with respect to those unremitting deferrals, foreclosures, and other paradoxical failures (i.e., its formal logic) that mirror the features allowing meaning to surface within a text arose out of a valuable desire to insulate trauma from legal over-reach, distortion, and misunderstanding, just as those qualities do in fact capture many aspects of trauma's experiential fabric. Precisely those evanescent signs and traces are imagined to inoculate trauma against mastery and co-optation. But the problem is that this formalist bracketing of cognizable truth and meaning, when mapped onto trauma, cannot be restricted to the traumatic core. Rather, that logic will bleed into and dictate the (non) interpretation of broader circumstances surrounding the scene of injury, licensing larger diagnostic avoidances and failures. Far from remaining confined to the memories of the trauma victim, insistence on unverifi-ability and indeterminacy can sandbag the ascription of both proof and fault to the harmful actions responsible for traumatic injury. With such moral, evaluative, and evidentiary rudders engulfed in a deluge of paradox, it is perhaps inevitable that analysis will lose sight of the concrete pursuit of justice, even while razing such differential yardsticks surely expedites trauma's globalization.

Like other contemporary theory, trauma studies has rested on a deep anti-legalism, one that villainizes law *both* as inherently inimical to trauma *and* for perpetuating the societal and other background conditions that breed such injury. Yet at the same time, trauma is often theorized in terms that are parasitic on the legal order. Like other sites of exclusion, trauma is thereby conceptualized through a framework that can seem to require the infringements of law, first, to make its psychic economy visible and, second, to trigger traumatic remembrance (with all of its ethical potentiality). Exactly this derivativeness has (like the parody of drag, like the humanities) been venerated, but through a logic that ironically handcuffs trauma to the legal system. Trauma theorists, including not only Felman but also Sharpe and Spillers, thus endow the legal system with a strangely paramount authority over trauma.

Such a symbiosis informs Felman's influential account of Hannah Arendt's *Eichmann in Jerusalem*—a text that for Felman itself contains many "paradoxes." Reading Arendt's reportage against the grain, Felman argues that the Eichmann trial forged a global yet unprecedented faith in testamentary versions of truth (versus the statistical and documentary evidence amassed in Nuremberg) predicated on the shock of the encounter. That premise compels Felman to contrast two competing modes of evidence: testimony (the province of trauma) versus legalistic and empirical proof. Yet by affiliating trauma with the former, Felman conspicuously juxtaposes testamentary evidence and its capacity to "transmit" (versus prove) with the deadening, dehumanizing modes of knowledge allegedly prized by law. Once again, traumatic witnessing gains shape and significance in direct yet inverse relation to everything it is not.

For parallel reasons are law's proceduralist (and hence for thinkers like Felman, innately domineering) orders of truth simultaneously a catalyst for the surfacing of traumatic memory, here too arguably required to disclose trauma's otherwise inscrutable fabric. For Felman, one specific episode in the Eichmann trial that involved not only the inarticulacy of traumatic speech but also the literal collapse of a witness exemplifies such tensions. That incident in which K-Zetnik, a survivor who had actually seen Eichmann in Auschwitz in the flesh, fainted at the very moment he was tasked with identifying Eichmann is interpreted by Felman to offer paradigmatic insight into the "truth" of trauma, prompting Felman to deem that scene a "necessary failure." Yet the significance of that "truth" foremost concerns the "epistemological abyss," "cognitive rupture," and "ungraspable kernel of collective memory"—or the fact that trauma's essence lies within its inherent unknowability. So although K-Zetnik's breakdown is taken to crystallize why the unbreachable silence of trauma becomes illuminating and productive,

Felman simultaneously explains the law's crass incursions as precursory to and enabling of that revelation. Contradictorily, trauma's tenuous validity from an empirical and objective standpoint is, once again, what procures its clairvoyance. So notwithstanding Felman's pointed complaints regarding law's chronic mistreatment of trauma, her reasoning shackles trauma to law's edifice. Wholly contingent, trauma's exclusion from law is what transacts its insurgency, and in reasoning that (as for many others) allows Felman to divine within trauma near allegorical lessons regarding power and its anatomy.

Still additional factors can lead some formulations of trauma to undercut the very justice-related aims that sparked that body of theory. As elsewhere, the notion that trauma and its wounds are by definition impervious to cure embargoes a continuum of clinical, intellectual, and political responses to trauma. As Leys explains of that field's dominant wisdom, "victims of trauma cannot witness or testify to the trauma in the sense of narrate and represent it to themselves and others: all they can do is perform the experience as if it were literally happening all over again."[84] That the traumatic kernel will on some level resist integration into consciousness, thriving on its own elusiveness, has been a staple of trauma studies. When coupled with trauma's exceptionalism, or its configuration as yet another failed and excluded representation, that wisdom ingrains an antipathy to more than healing: it also writes off the prospect that the traumatic memory might be made integral or whole or fully present to cognition, individual or societal. Recalling the double binds we have seen to bedevil other projects of giving voice to exclusion, this directive can end up mortgaging trauma theory's stated goals (i.e., justice) to a religion of impossibility and failure. As before, the basic attempt to lend mimetic or verifiable representation to trauma becomes not only futile but fully undesirable (not to mention how it disobeys trauma's own logic), given that such an eventuality would extinguish trauma's ethical "truth" and its critical edge. So just like other roving nuclei of exclusion, trauma's absent center must remain inaccessible in order to preserve its edifying and resistant harvest. In a mind-set only redoubled by trauma theory's anti-legalism, whatever faint resolution law might afford is castigated as the imposition of a taming, normalizing straightjacket (to draw upon Felman's language) on trauma.

The next chapter proceeds to further question this etiquette, while proposing alternate approaches to psychic injury. For now, the worry is that trauma theory recriminates a whole spectrum of political, psychic, sociocultural, and other resources that might instead facilitate trauma's recovery and larger redress. Beyond how such thinking can seem to discount any psychic wound amenable to either healing or recuperation for a dearth of genuine trauma, trauma theory withholds the possibility of self-ownership, self-trust, and perceptual wholeness, coherence, and integrity from its victims. In one sense, this is because trauma's defining features merely amplify the experiential disembedding and fracture broadly acclaimed as modernity's signature, so to tame trauma could betray a yearning to recover a delusionally (and dangerously) premodern condition. And in another, it is because such thinking also burdens trauma with the same perennial crisis of legitimacy widely deemed the cradle of art, justice, ethics, and more. As should be abundantly clear, especially early accounts of trauma are modeled on a near identical economy of negative valorization as the many other examples gathered in this book.

Yet the reflex to define trauma with reference to its obliteration of stable, lucid, and other evidentiary markers ultimately disposes trauma to misappropriation along the very lines as are liable to materialize within a hostile courtroom. This reactionary weaponization of trauma is a growing phenomenon, and theories that equate trauma with its myriad paradoxes lack adequate mechanisms for counteracting such a syndrome. Debates over free speech can clarify why the axiomatics of trauma theory are prone to tie theorists' hands. The fact that, as Joan Scott puts it, "these days, free speech is the mantra of the right, its weapon in the new culture war," certainly epitomizes an extremist arrogation of a stance historically associated with a left-leaning, liberal politics.[85] But that rebranding of First Amendment speech rights as a conservative crusade also demonstrates exactly why certain doctrines foundational to trauma theory (and to theory as an intellectual formation) lend themselves to ready distortion. Critical thinkers have rightly cited phenomena like the corporatization of speech rights (for Wendy Brown apotheosized in the *Citizens United* decision) and media-fueled tyranny of "fake facts."[86] However, illiberal politics simultaneously hijacks a creed of uncensorability highly reminiscent of the adulation of unruly, inarticulate speech shaping much trauma theory (and, we saw, influential humanities pedagogies). Although that premium on contentless speech has conventionally been imagined by theorists to defray both the imperialism of normative reason and ideological capture, it is more accurately illiberalism that today profiteers from such thinking—here again, turning the methodological privileging of those qualities on its head. Fights over speech rights consequently lay bare more than just a shifting of the ideological landscape that leaves critical thinkers marooned; those fights are also indicative of a strategic seizure of the analytic-argumentative arsenal long deemed exclusive to both theory and democracy. With its mounting cries of radical constructivism, illiberal politics sets loose a fusillade of paradox, indeterminacy, and contradiction—qualities that (as theorists have long acknowledged) indeed armor such a politics against counterattack, and quite effectively.

However, there is a sense in which trauma theory, in highly representative fashion, conceives of paradox solely as a fail-safe shield that will safeguard trauma from various forms of totalization. But that logic of paradox, as theorists also know well, can simultaneously operate as an agile sword—and one that is just as likely to be brought back to bear upon trauma (and upon theory). Hence, the issue is not only that many accounts of trauma scramble calculations of moral blameworthiness and intent by reducing everything to paradox, which they do. In addition, trauma's chameleon logic can offer a playbook for skeptics. In fact, the codes and conventions of trauma can seem unduly susceptible to such commandeering, even while a certain methodological purity of trauma artificially restricts the range of tactics permissibly enlisted to fend off such maneuvers.

These syndromes become especially pronounced in the face of xenophobic and racist speech. What some albeit controversially deem a main guise of contemporary racism—microaggressions or aversive racism—often exploits the very representational indeterminacies, furtiveness, and delays that trauma theorists have at times extolled. As the next chapter addresses, aversive racism is often (again controversially) explained as subtle, confusing, and unintentional (rather than explicitly aggressive), which can cause "attributional ambiguity" in its victims—indeed, making an offender's volition, ill will, and responsibility tricky to corroborate.[87] Whether manifest in verbal epithets or other nonviolent behavior, aversive racism frequently assumes a low-grade, casual, or cavalier veneer, which likewise compounds the barriers to confirming, documenting, and repudiating those offenses. A mode of gaslighting that destabilizes its victims' grasp of objective reality, aversive abuse defensively cloaks itself in open-endedness, incalculability, and equivocation. Ransacking its targets with uncertainty and indecision, aversive acts of racism thereby foist self-blame back upon the victim. So beyond the experiential unhinging induced by this ambiguity, such discrimination enlists a spirit of paradox to cunningly indemnify itself against legal and other censure—warding off legalism in exactly the ways trauma theorists have long claimed paradox achieves for trauma.

Aversive bias is therefore a prime example of the ways injustice today actively capitalizes on paradox—creating a haze of unverifiability that insulates abusive practices from moral and other denunciation. To elaborate, aversive assaults (whether tied to race or other vectors of exclusion) are frequently damaging for a victim precisely because they indeed displace agency into a web of adjourned, evasive traces, multiplying gray areas to make those affronts harder to pinpoint and condemn. In a parallel manner do those abuses exploit the time lags of deferred comprehension—although, again, to derail a victim's moral certitude and compass. Like other paradox-riddled phenomena, aversive bias inhabits a liminal zone, although a zone in which the distinctions between overt aggression and inadvertency are elided. But the point is that these sorts of abuses not only weaponize paradox but also do so in service of outcomes long promoted by theory: to vacate various evaluative barometers and other criteria; to neuter law; and to subvert normative judgment. Of course, theorists have usually recruited such a set of tactics to unmask and decry oppression, whereas illiberal speech today inverts that agenda to rationalize and condone objectively offensive and unjust behavior. But the basic strategies remain eerily the same.

As before, the effects of all this are far from purely hypothetical or abstract but can mete out decisive consequences in various real world settings. In their indeterminacy, for instance, aversive assaults commonly prey on loopholes within law, eluding legally punishable categories to occupy the margins of formal definitions of hate speech, defamation, and discrimination. Something not so far afield can occur in the classroom, wherein the very curricular and other reforms prompted by outrage against exclusion can, however, inadvertently reentrench the same exclusions such a politics was designed to overcome. As Jeannie Suk Gersen cautions regarding trauma theory's impact on the topics covered in law school courses, areas of law "once marginalized from the curriculum because of their perceived unimportance [can become] at risk of being remarginalized because of their perceived weight."[88] While complicated interactions are clearly at play in such an example, the full repercussions of the confessional classroom and its mainstreaming of trauma are far from clear or decided. To the contrary, the rhetorical and argumentative moves long championed by theory can appear newly ripe for the picking, including by nefarious actors.

The Banality of Paradox

In recent years, the language of paradox has also become a prominent face of the self-help industry. A quick search of Amazon.com turns up a lengthy list of lucrative trade paperbacks attesting to that quality's status as a pop-psychological elixir: *The Paradox of Choice: Why More is Less* (2004, inspiring 330 reader reviews on Amazon.com); *All Joy and No Fun: The Paradox of Modern Parenthood* (2014, with 261 Amazon reviews); *The Chimp Paradox: The Mind Management Programme to Help You Achieve Success, Confidence and Happiness* (2012, 116 reviews); *The Progress Paradox: How Life Gets Better While People Feel Worse* (2003, 100 reviews); *The Time Paradox: The New Psychology of Time That Will Change Your Life* (2008, 95 reviews); *The 8-Hour Sleep Paradox: How We Are Sleeping Our Way to Fatigue, Disease and Unhappiness* (2016, 94 reviews); *How to Be a Person in the World: Ask Polly's Guide to the Paradoxes of Modern Life* (2016, 75 reviews); *Vitamin K2 and the Calcium Paradox: How a Little-Known Vitamin Could Save Your Life* (2013, 441 reviews); *My Dog: The Paradox: A Lovable Discourse about Man's Best Friend* (2013, 504 reviews); *The Polio Paradox: What You Need To Know* (2002, 137 reviews); *The Winner's Curse: Paradoxes and Anomalies of Economic Life* (1991); *The Plant Paradox: The Hidden Dangers in "Healthy" Foods* (2017, 867 reviews).

As these popular titles suggest, paradox not only claims a mass-marketable appeal but is proselytized as its own common sense. Consumerism has swallowed its gospel, preaching a religion wherein paradox is the answer to all of contemporary life's problems. A stock ingredient of the self-help manual, that language surely registers a dizzyingly complex world. But those paradoxes also disburse various therapies: behavioralist programs for juggling the many dilemmas of contemporary life. One might observe that, in so doing, the language of paradox taps into lurking paranoia: anxiety over the perils hidden within even the most mundane phenomena (sleep, economic fortune, healthy food). Or, at once, one could note how it conjures a managerial ethos of boardroom governance and corporate dispute resolution, along with an illusion of nonpartisanship. This merchandisability might expose that language as quintessentially neoliberal, or perhaps instead betoken a twenty-first-century "culture of narcissism," as Christopher Lasch famously characterized "diminishing expectations" in the wake of the 1960s.[89] Promising not only consolation amid disappointment but savvy and sophistication, paradox sells.

This quick-fix and widely attractive side of that logic is one that can also overtake the classroom. Paradox is a language in which our students today are already fluent, and they no longer experience the discoveries elicited by such reasoning as terribly surprising. One or two generations ago, the revelations of paradox were surely mind-bending and even unprecedented, whether they shed light on the constructivism of truth, the repressions formative of the subject, or the exclusions enabling privilege. But those intuitions have become banal: mundane features of our students' intellectual geography. The very quicksand critics and theorists devoted vast energies to unearthing thus risks becoming a mere curiosity: a muddle to blithely steer around. Indeed, those quagmires of paradox can seem quite easy to skirt, evident in our students' deft performances of self-abnegation. But this is also because the lessons of paradox have become habitual—something our students imbibe long before arriving among us.

In many ways, it makes total sense that paradox would orchestrate so many features of a phenomenon like trauma. As chapter 1 observed, it is hard to fathom the truly unthinkable catastrophes of global modernity without recourse to some grammar of paradox and contradiction. But the extent to which trauma studies can seem overrun by paradox also exemplifies the analytic impoverishment prone to set in when paradox is elevated into a gnostic regime of knowing. It is that aura of privileged understanding that finds domestication in the self-help manual, with its wager of therapeutic know-how and self-discovery. Yet within that popular genre, it is also true that appeals to paradox foremost serve as palliatives, coddling self-involvement and neutering real moral-political difficulty. Less troubling than the routinization of paradox, then, is its propensity to anesthetize, whether as a rote distraction or to dumb things down. Given the enormous good effectuated by the politics of exclusion—both in the classroom and in the streets—it is certainly wrong to deem this entirely a tragedy. But it is also hard to miss how the siren song of paradox can breed complacency, soothing us even amid devastation.

Interlude

A DIFFERENT KIND OF THEORY

As the autumn of 2018 found me completing a draft of this book for the first time, a graduate seminar titled Theory and Method afforded a chance to experiment with certain of its arguments. That seminar's efforts to assess the "state of the profession" drove us first into foundational texts and thinkers, as we immersed ourselves one week in inaugural statements of the linguistic turn and the next in defenses of "interpretation" as a historically materialist enterprise. All the while taking those inquiries as a point of entry into the predicament of theory today, we asked: is there a difference between criticism and interpretation? How should one denominate "the aesthetic," or literary form, or for that matter style? Can and should art and politics be linked; if so, how? Often, we felt anxiously implicated within the legacies of the traditions we sampled. Within the halls of English and Comp Lit and language studies at Cornell, deconstruction and its technicians remained objects of reverence, and so lapsing fidelity to Derrida or de Man was no light or laughing matter. With the Avital Ronell affair dominating the media as the semester opened, concerns over the ethics of the theory era similarly felt far from abstract or removed. To the contrary, the matter of whether theory had forsaken certain of its guiding commitments was, at times, intense and personal. Amid all of this, paradox naturally appeared to me the writing on the wall sanctioning the caprice of the charismatic thinker.

Our foray into the dossier of theory was followed by more contemporary thinkers and developments, many claiming to launch "new" methodologies. In general, we welcomed the complaints leveled by these internal critics, just as their diagnoses of theory's ailments often resonated. How could one not agree with thinkers like Rita Felski or Eve Sedgwick that theory had succumbed to a surfeit of critique, negativity, paranoia, and suspicion—romanticizing those qualities, no less?[1] Relatedly, how could one dispute that certain energies of theory had "run out of steam"?[2] But while sharing certain such reservations, many of us simultaneously felt dissatisfied by what were being touted as post-theoretical or postcritical alternatives. Whether arrayed under the banner of affect studies or new materialism or a reconstituted formalism, these clarion calls to redress theory's missteps left us wanting. One reason for that discontent involved how those purportedly newfangled approaches seemed to repeat the exact moves and assumptions that they claimed to repudiate. For instance, we were sufficiently convinced by Toril Moi's concerns about the dissimulations wrought by post-Saussurean semiotics that we thereafter despaired when Eugenie Brinkema modeled her formulation of affect on a textualist-linguistic paradigm, refracting affect through a stale heuristic that failed to do anything terribly new or surprising. In other cases, we were alarmed by the dismissiveness, speed, and even vehemence with which these voices of dissent were shot down. (Afterward, shaken by such animus, a few students told me that they "didn't want to work on theory" in their dissertations.) That impulse to shame and prostrate theory's detractors felt trite if not petty, especially when backed by uninspired rejoinders like the trotting out of a well-worn dialectic.[3] So while partly convinced by the need for a methodological self-reckoning, we left the semester even less clear about what its terms should look like than when we began.

Other aspects of our dissatisfaction revolved around matters of style. In canvassing one after another attempt to call theory on its hedged bets, we repeatedly seized on the demeanor, modality, tenor, and mood of those pleas. On one level, the manifesto seemed to have regained fashion, with its bold, visionary pronouncements of radical openings and departures. However, this recourse to the manifesto also seemed ironic, given that genre's associations with the avant-garde. Rather than in service of insurrectionary transgressions, many of its contemporary envoys enlisted the manifesto to rebuke the instinct to épater le bourgeois. Further jarring was the use of that genre to promote what some have disparaged as a new minimalism, incrementalism, ascesis, and modesty (labels that at the same time gave us substantial pause).[4] Nevertheless, that the grand, exhortatory rhetoric of a manifesto would advocate something like a downsizing of theory, or the espousal of clarity and commonsense, seemed a discordance symptomatic of our current juncture.[5]

Uniting many of these emergent approaches was an appeal to something like the basics: to the elementary, fundamental, and/or heretofore understudied building blocks of theoretical labor. Newly espoused have been values like simplicity, clarity, ordinariness, surfaces, the obvious, description, plain meaning, straightforwardness, attention, realism, and so on. Sometimes aimed at denouncing theory's cult of difficulty as a sham, others sought to actualize those commitments on the level of rhetoric, tone, and style (i.e., enacting minimalism or restraint within a manifesto's parameters). But here, too, these attitudinal-discursive maneuvers left us uneasy. For one, they seemed to replay a highly familiar gesture—namely, to identify a problem and then latch onto its binaristic inverse as not just a contrapuntal strategy but ultimately a panacea. Hence, we worried: just because reading to unmask and demystify has its limits, surely that does not automatically render surfaces replete with untapped meaning.[6] And even if critique and suspicion have been ravaged by their excesses, that does not require a total about-face, such as to convert affirmation into the balustrade of a whole new methodology. Regarding this book's project, even if an all-consuming vortex of paradox has fettered theory, that should not absolve us of the duty to develop a stand-alone case for whatever might replace it. So despite worthy impulses, the reasoning underlying too many recent battle cries felt disappointingly pat and categorical, especially in its reliance on either/or, polarizing thinking that worked to empty out a vast middle ground: a ground comprised of gray areas demanding granular, fine-tuned evaluation.

In a certain sense, we were struck by the rhetorical sleights of hand underlying these anthems to the plain or straightforward or uncomplicated. At risk of downplaying moral-normative complexity, many adopted a feint of common sense. The "of course you've always known this" drift of their logic seemed to casually renaturalize the exact phenomena theorists had spent decades vigilantly debunking. Although held out as forward-thinking, those calls to innovate fell back on the very moves long castigated for smuggling in, dissembling, and shoring up power and its accomplices. While casting a weary eye on certain knee-jerk equations (i.e., between suspicion and intellectual sophistication), to instead flaunt a veneer of sober levelheadedness or to baldly cite the pragmatic facts of life felt another matter. That pretense of the natural or purely realistic further struck us as self-minimizing, belittling of the full import of its own incitement. To issue bold decrees in the name of the taken for granted was oddly deflationary, giving short shrift to those ideas.

Like others, our initial instinct was to praise thinkers like Eve Sedgwick for what looked like a near-impossible balancing act. At once, however, we sensed that our frustrations were indicative of a wider paralysis. While gripped by so many complaints about theory's shortfalls, we nonetheless felt immobilized in our efforts to chart an escape route. Although our readings had successfully shattered countless disciplinary nostrums, we suffered a failure of imagination even when facing a blank slate—an asphyxiating inability to breathe without a stock repertoire of interrogation, unmasking, and unsettling. Having hit this roadblock itself seemed important to mark and to take stock of. It was easy to lament the threadbare attire of theory (still donned long after it stopped being haute couture), but how to cloak our arguments within different intellectual garments?

This sense of malaise made me nervous, since I was striving to undertake the very sort of project that raised my students' hackles, and often vehemently so. I, too, was trying to develop an alternate theory that required thinking and writing in a different mode: a mode long demonized as theory's unyielding enemy. While I had no problem promoting the integrative (one of the final chapter's terms of art), that itinerary seemed to depend on an altered tone, posture, and attitude. Before even trying to stipulate the substantive goals of an integrative criticism, then, I was faced with a conundrum: how to write accordingly? What should an integrative style look and sound and feel like? What rhythms should it follow, and by obeying what tempo and pacing? What sorts of analytic moves and surrogate vocabularies should become its lodestars? What imaginative horizons might it enact? Given my hope to lay bare a growing vacuum, what would it mean to occupy an intellectual space currently foreclosed by theory? But even more confounding, how to practice a different kind of writing and reasoning without alienating my readers?

These sorts of questions will never—and probably *should never*—feel easy. For me, they have persisted in refusing clear-cut or gratifying answers. Despite striving to reorient theory's compass toward more expansive bearings, I did not want to revert to the dry, analytic thinking that once drove me from law and into the arms of the humanities. It seemed important to retain some handle on the exuberant and spontaneous play inspired by encounters with literature and art and everything they promise. However, I also balked at the default assumption that paradox and indeterminacy were the sole lessons to be thus derived. Contrary to freeing, that valorization of paradox, we have seen time after time, produces its own gridlock. But my attempt to sever the rote equation between intellectual savvy and paradox-laden complexity created a separate double bind: how to outfox paradox without trying to beat it at its own game, thereby conceding that game's authority?

Over time, I rewrote, and then rewrote, and then yet again rewrote from scratch what follows, more times than I ever hope to re-rewrite any piece of scholarship again in my entire life. At first, I, too, tried on the conventions of the manifesto, only to be taken to task by my interlocutors. Thereafter, I adopted something closer to the matter-of-fact stance that caused my graduate students to cringe, performing the gambit of renaturalization that rightly triggered their allergies. The version initially submitted with my manuscript for review instead took refuge in a discussion of a single literary text. Given my training in literary studies, I was comfortable letting literature coax my reasoning, allowing me to blame any uncomfortable moments on fidelity to the literary. Moreover, I do believe in the capacity of literary experience to shape us in unpredictable ways, chaperoning our quests for insight into what really matters. However, I came to recognize this strategy as its own avoidance mechanism: one that shirked the burdens of the very intellectual resources I aimed to defend. On the one hand, these successive struggles felt endless, debilitating, and disconcerting—a loss of confidence in my own ability to write or even to think. But on the other, they occasionally did feel fruitfully proportionate to the magnitude of my endeavors. Insofar as paradox has indeed operated as something like a paradigm, of course every sentence would be encumbered by the full weight of that tradition (as one friend put it). I was knowingly shedding the protective armor of theory (as my husband explained), so of course every assertion if not individual word would leave me vulnerable and naked.

I completed this book during two summers that made the anxieties of fall 2018 look like child's play, and that climate induced its own crises of confidence in this project. How could scholarship matter when the world was coming to an end? Pandemic, looming fascism, economic collapse, violent crackdowns on peaceable protest, climate catastrophe, the end of the postal service, a rigged election, toilet paper and refrigerator shortages, hiring freezes, salary cuts, sickness and dying, and on and on and on. Are we not staring down the barrel of a death sentence, one bearing down on not only the profession but other taken for granted aspects of contemporary life? If so, is it not true that mere squabbles over method, beyond diversionary, represent a full-fledged dereliction of duty?

6

WHAT HOLDS THINGS TOGETHER
Toward an Integrative Criticism

The wonder is that any book so composed holds together for more than a year or two [...]. But they do hold together occasionally very remarkably. And what holds them together in these rare instances of survival [...] is something one calls integrity, though it has nothing to do with paying one's bills or behaving honourably in an emergency. What one means by integrity, in the case of the novelist, is that conviction that he gives one that this is the truth. [...] One holds every phrase, every scene to the light as one reads—for Nature seems, very oddly, to have provided us with an inner light by which to judge the novelist's integrity or disintegrity. (72)
—Virginia Woolf, "A Room of One's Own" (1929)

S everal key passages in Virginia Woolf's classic appeal for a women's literary tradition, "A Room of One's Own," invoke an unexpected ideal: "integrity." A property Woolf identifies as allowing "famous" artworks to "survive," integrity is simultaneously described as irradiated through the act of criticism. In one sense, integrity for Woolf is therefore "judged" or evaluated by the critic, who in reading "holds every phrase, every scene to the light." But in another, Woolf characterizes integrity as "remarkable" and hard-won: something accessed and inhabited only by those writers endowed with a rare "conviction" and "genius." One of patriarchy's crimes, as Woolf later explains, is consequently to "interfere with the integrity of a woman novelist," making her "unable to distinguish between the true and the false."[1] Such a statement clearly acknowledges the epistemic injuries wrought by oppression: how exclusion censors and undermines the experiential realities of its victims. Yet with that linkage, Woolf also speculates over the truth claims at stake in art and literature—and in terms that elude a familiar romance of art's derivative, non-evidentiary, indeterminate, unpredictable value.

This is surprising, given everything for which Woolf and her oeuvre have been taken as representative (modernism, queerness, interiority, epistemic dislocation). So it is hard to imagine her advocating "truth" in any absolute, objective way. Instead, she infuses those reflections on aesthetic integrity with associations more experiential if not existential. One verb that recurs throughout—"hold"—telegraphs those more phenomenological senses of integrity, including how they shape criticism, creativity, and the lifespan of the artwork. In the passage above, one manner of holding—as in "one holds every phrase [...] to the light"—is conceived to shepherd criticism as a practice. Far from muscular or domineering, the reading process Woolf thus envisions involves something like patient receptivity or attunement. At once, a different manner of "holding" is suggested to oversee writing. As Woolf remarks of those few existing female authors, "what genius, what integrity it must have required in face of all that criticism, in the midst of that purely patriarchal society, to hold fast to the thing as they saw it without shrinking." In this instance, "hold" connotes fortitude and perseverance: confidence in the worth and authority of one's vision notwithstanding paternalistic skepticism.

Taken together, these variations on the verb "hold"—a strikingly simple, straightforward, active, and yet tender verb—elaborate on what one might further call integration or even an integrative criticism. While ruminating over the dimensions of integrity in art, Woolf puts forward a series of what read like definitions. As she explains of some novels, "what holds them together [...] is something one calls integrity." And later, "What one means by integrity, in the case of the novelist...." Whereas in the epigraph above integrity at first implies a type of resilience amid modernity's disintegrating currents, that property acquires prescriptive and even normative associations as Woolf proceeds: it serves to marshal criteria that one can "judge." As an insignia of momentous art, integrity therefore summons another derivation of the root "integ" (or "whole"): the state of being integrated or of integration. Here, too, contrary to a prototypically modernist emphasis on epistemic fractures and disembedding, Woolf concentrates on the sinews that bind the disparate parts of an otherwise sprawling literary artifact like a novel, or on those elements that render an artwork full and connected and present and alive and resplendent and whole.

There are all sorts of reasons these appeals integrity will evade our available critical categories. Naturally, one knee-jerk response would be to dismiss Woolf's musings as essentializing, moralizing, sentimental, naïve. Perhaps reeking of elitism or conservatism or nostalgia (and, of course, certain aspects of Woolf's legacy are thorny), integrity is not what one would ordinarily associate with either the gender-bending subversions or aesthetic experiments for which she remains iconic, with their breaking of boundaries, nonlinearity, protean adaptability, and so on. Indeed, it would not be entirely off the mark to deride the prospect of integrity as fundamentally antitheoretical: a dereliction of those tenets most core to criticism and theory. Whether smuggling in fantasies of the self-present and autonomous subject or of unitary, harmonious ways of knowing, a value like integrity transgresses all sorts of theoretical pieties. In one sense, that sacrilege stems from the ways integrity flouts almost everything usually associated with modernity: that modernity represents a condition of mounting and incurable paradox, that it entails an unhoming and rupture of the "integrated cultures" (to recall Lukács's *Theory of the Novel*) modernity by definition supersedes, that it sows chronic alienation.

Notwithstanding (or, more accurately, precisely because of) these tensions, an "integrative criticism" aimed at grasping "what holds things together" promises one avenue for stepping outside of paradox as an all-encompassing conceptual prism. In such a spirit, this chapter extrapolates from Woolf's meditations on integrity to sketch one potential avenue for escaping the hall of mirrors that reasoning through paradox can create.[2] Although other exit routes are no doubt available, varying senses of "integrity," "integration," and the "integral" will here spur a succession of attempts to practice a different kind of theory—a theory with something more than paradoxes to offer.[3] But first, a few other prefatory words are needed.

This book has compiled a veritable rap sheet of worries about paradox as a framework for making sense out of the world. Chief among those complaints concerns how the logic of paradox can sever theory from its practice, obviating the onus to account for theory in its lived application—and oftentimes actively subverting attempts to do so. This cultivated resistance to a praxis theorizable in affirmative, serviceable, constructive terms could of course be blamed on myriad factors, some considered below (and some having little to do with paradox). However, perhaps the biggest problem is that, when paradox is the answer to almost everything, its logic ceases to tell us how to act. Whether in the face of divergent circumstances or tough choices between contrasting agendas, the uniformity of thought ingrained by paradox causes us to lose sight of the specificity of our critical objects, in the worst case reducing critique to a semiautonomous and mechanical exercise. Relatedly is the self-expurgating vacuum often produced by that logic prone to cancel whatever prescriptive arguments might be on the table, stymying the assertion of goal-oriented, actualizable ends for theory. Paradoxes, we have seen, are geared to neutralize substantive propositions, rather than to facilitate reasoning aimed at the positing of practical game plans or normative goals. However, the net result of these and other prophylaxes has been to dupe us into deserting many commitments foundational to theory, of greatest concern sacrificing the pursuit of social justice on an altar of unrelenting paradox. Having allowed the *para doxa* to devour too much, we have forgotten many of the pursuits and ideals most dear and indeed integral to theory. In this respect, one might conclude that criticism has not been critical enough, operating on autopilot to arrive at near-identical diagnoses (paradox) and solutions (paradox) regardless of the occasion.

This chapter's primary goal is therefore to consider various surrogates to paradox, opening up expanded horizons for theory and, in the process, retrieving resources, values, and recognitions too tidily expunged. Much as Woolf's appeals are multidirectional, the interwoven valences of integrity and the integrative that I'll play upon are gestural, more than anything devised to clear a conceptual space long placed under erasure. For instance, one meaning of integration is to include or to incorporate. Abandoning the "either/or" logic promoted by thinkers like Theodor Adorno as theory's sole métier, this chapter instead explores manifestations of the "both/and." That itinerary of the both/and extends to reasoning through paradox; rather than a wholesale abdication of paradox or some grand about-face, this chapter argues that paradox, too, requires supplementation with, and assimilation into, more variegated and complex modalities of thought as well as objectives for theory. I have tried to stress that reasoning through paradox is not inherently "wrong" or diversionary or pernicious; rather, the problem lies with its uniformity of style and application—or with the fact that such logic gets deployed even when it is neither on point, nor illuminating, nor productive. Indeed, this book has contemplated many scenarios wherein insistence on paradox becomes downright destructive, whether in providing an ideological alibi or itself laying siege to critical thinking. Hence, this chapter hopes to reorient the compass of theory by better attuning it to the interplay between sites of analysis where paradox does actually exist versus those just as much informed by something like hints of _non_contradiction.

Types of integrity and integration are also among the intellectual assets and pursuits that this chapter recuperates. The methodological interdictions accomplice to paradox have frequently translated into political bans: the either/or has embargoed a whole range of sociopolitical projects seen, among other things, to entail inclusion or integration. Those dictates, we know, are simultaneously decreed by a matrix of other well-known priorities, such as the privileging of residues and remainders; of deferrals and delays; of marginal, liminal, threshold spaces; of repressions and absences; and of other locales of literal and figurative exclusion or exceptionality. Whether within a text, archive, or political contest, vectors of exclusion (versus inclusion) have been negatively valorized, expected to be brimming with (albeit fugitive) meaning. However, those premiums can occlude the integral, just as a focus on the lacking and impossible diverts attention from phenomena that are present, full, actualizable, and effective. Such a mind-set can simultaneously inure us to the interactions between the usual sources of paradox and that quality's provision hiatus, or between situations indeed awash with paradox and those better characterized by noncontradiction. Critical awareness of these junctures and interfaces, I'll argue, is absolutely crucial to the drawing of distinctions: to differential analysis aimed at assessing the qualitative and quantitative discrepancies separating one instance of a particular syndrome or structure or phenomenon from another. Such comparative and evaluative analysis, although often pilloried within influential schools of theory, is vital to the implementation of theory as a cognizable (and self-accountable) practice.

But how exactly to tell when ideals like inclusion and integration are worthwhile pursuits in a given scenario versus risk casting a damaging smokescreen over reality? Precisely those instances when "things come and then provisionally hold together," I'll submit, can operationalize such tricky labors of differentiation. (Yet, as Woolf cautions, those instances of holding together can be quite rare.) Noncontradiction, harmony, coherence, stability, unity, clarity, resolution, perseverance, continuity: these sorts of factors tend either to fall below the radar of theory or to be roundly excoriated. This omission is also not surprising, given what we have observed to be a corresponding preoccupation with discontinuities, clefts, and fissures; splitting and rupture; conflicts and antagonisms; failures and impossibilities;

and naysaying and de(con)struction. But that myopic focus either overlooks or outright condemns instances where things can and do come together—whether to function productively and relatively well or even to succeed.

These allergies in part stem from prevailing assumptions about the *agency* of criticism and theory. When theorized, that agency, we have seen, tends to become near-synonymous with the chameleon logic of paradox. So whereas agencies deemed liminal, fugitive, interstitial, vagrant, incalculable, impossible, inchoate, indeterminate, and so on are acclaimed, that reasoning discounts (if not entirely censors) guises of agency that are "effective" and capable of being affirmed accordingly, whether that effectiveness is understood to reside in causality, intentionality, healing, restoration, trust, confidence, predictability, self-realization, progress, or something more. This chapter asks: what would it mean to assess agency not in terms of its vagaries but instead of its actualization, and how to register such dynamics without reinscribing fantasies of mastery or transcendence? Could alternate models for deciphering effective agency enable us to discuss and/or study phenomena like the above that otherwise baffle our established analytic arsenal? And to reiterate, how to distinguish between exertions of agency that are truly salutary versus those that are harmful, predatory, and/or overbearing? The very qualities Woolf's reflections herald—harmony, completeness, fullness, plenitude, survival, conviction—can help us undertake such an endeavor. Those qualities, I'll submit, can be bellwethers of practices and activities we want to endorse—and possibly even to celebrate.

Far from last, the "holding together" alluded to by Woolf is also suggestive of a phenomenal fabric that challenges our usual premises regarding the birthplace and anatomy of the critical spirit. This chapter's plea for an integrative criticism therefore returns to—and reenvisions—the scene of (self-)distanced reading so often allegorized as a laboratory for both critique and modernity. That scene installs doubt, division, objectivization, privation, fragmentation, and rampant paradox at the heart of modern knowing and, precisely in so doing, is exalted as the nativity of justice, ethics, democracy, and so on. Yet Woolf's proverbial "room of one's own" summons an alternate ecology of perceptual engagement, one this chapter develops in order to question the "strategies of containment" and other strictures governing what is imagined to be critique's idealized genesis.[4] What would it look and feel like to inhabit a critical space overseen by a less homogenous and mutually reinforcing array of protocols and faculties? To supplement the fractures of paradox with modes of experiential immersion, attunement, and harmonization? Such a question is partly underwritten by concerns that a cognitivist bracketing of absorptive (i.e., insufficiently mediated) habits of perception and engagement has itself impinged on theory's translation into a livable practice. But it is true regardless that if we want to recover a wider constellation of intellectual horizons for theory, our starting place should be to reconsider the architecture of knowing that balustrades critique, asking about the tools and truths that it does (versus does not) make available.

At first blush, it may seem odd that something like experiential fullness and absorption could commission a more robustly evaluative and prescriptive theory—but that is exactly what this chapter proposes. As I'll continue to underscore, there are certainly other paths and priorities that might work just as well to replenish what this book has characterized as a sorely anemic intellectual diet. So while prospects like integrity, harmony, presence, noncontradiction, and so on have I'm sure triggered many allergies, the collision course of antipathies and aversions that follows is also intentional: perhaps necessary to clear the floor for what is best conceived as a reoccupation of the foreclosed conceptual habitat of theory. Whereas Woolf's fictional room offers a rather playful motif for that intellectual abode repudiated by theory but that this chapter strives to re-access, such an endeavor is essential to retrieving many resources long disavowed, irrespective of how we understand those resources or such an arena.

Importantly, this chapter's debts to Woolf are *not* a windup to another excursion into aesthetic theory like that of the first interlude. It does *not* advance yet another genre argument rooted in a paean to literature's "singular" or otherwise exemplary capacity to sustain indeterminacy and ambivalence.[5] While debates about the literary have underpinned many of this book's arguments, its closing examples are deliberately culled from history, politics, film, journalism, theory, and finally literature—and precisely to challenge the seductive mystique of everything we have seen to be projected onto the exceptional and excluded. This chapter's heterogeneity of examples is further designed to demonstrate why the vistas of an integrative critical practice—with this chapter's insistence on context-specific differentiation—are by no means confined to one intellectual mode or field or inquiry. Instead, this book has investigated the overarching preoccupations that administer how and why and what we read for *across* the humanities: or with the analytic conventions ordaining what it means to be a student of theory as an intellectual formation.

De-Ontologizing Paradox, Disability Studies, and the Limits of Anti-legalism

This book has advanced multiple explanations for why it can be hard to talk about, not to mention rationalize, certain expressions of agency—including the agency of theory. Whether to suggest autonomy, intentionality, free will, or the self-governing subject, agency has been the sort of notion carefully qualified through scare quotes or prefixed with admonitory labels ("instrumental," "calculative," "developmental"). Something to be wary of (rather than pursued in unambiguous or straightforward terms), theories of agency instead route that notion through the technicities of paradox, including an apologetics of failure and ephemerality we have seen to be inherited from traditions like literary criticism and theology. At once, however, properties like contradiction and paradox are often vested with propulsive if not absolutized force, commonly regarded as the main engines driving modernity, capitalism, law, oppression, and more—and ensuring that such systems and their processes will be insatiable and relentless. This reasoning, I have suggested, ontologizes properties like contradiction to deem them "a total social fact," dwarfing all else.[6] Along with talk of agency per se, a host of related terms like ability, capacity, self-determination, and self-possession have also been suspect—and, here too, in a certain sense for good reasons. But what are the conceptual shortfalls and costs of this moratorium on discussing something like the effective agency one might expect to be integral to a praxis? What does that opprobrium prevent us from taking account of? What happens to our ideas about the lived application of theory when refracted through (and circumscribed within) discourses of itineracy, liminality, interstitiality, indeterminacy, impossibility, irresolution, subversion, and more? While those grammars allow us to reflect upon agency through a less than transparent (or self-honest) back door, do they not etherealize agency in ways that leave it both hampered and worrisomely (if strategically) incomprehensible?

One field understandably founded on a critique of specifically liberal conceptions of human agency is disability studies. In its efforts to unmask "ableism" as an exclusionary ideology that stigmatizes less-than-fully-capacitated bodies, disability studies has also interrogated a slate of other "exceptionalist" benchmarks like normalcy, health, bodily integrity, fitness, and so on, and to ends typically coupled with more comprehensive insights into the tentacles of juridical and disciplinary power. Clearly, the vast majority of these critiques of ableist bias and its impact on something like the legal system are enormously productive, leading to irreplaceable sociopolitical advances. However, certain enabling warrants subsidizing those critiques are nonetheless a demonstration of why reasoning that totalizes fatal paradox will short-circuit inquiries into the nature of effective or cognizable agency. As a result, the actual history of disability rights activism, and especially the gains ushered in by the 1990 Americans with Disabilities Act (the ADA), can seem to represent something of a fly in that field's ointment. The ADA is in many respects the apotheosis of successful movement-based political advocacy propelled by constructive and strategic objectives beyond sheer opposition to discrimination. In a kind of roll call of the resources anti-legalistic skepticism regarding rights wrongly discards, the ADA's history can thereby illustrate why a diagnosis of structural oppression need not end up in either the trap of ontological fatalism or the escape hatch of an antinomian "right to have rights"-to-come.

Many of these liabilities inform Jasbir Puar's *The Right to Maim: Debility, Capacity, Disability*, a widely read book that exemplifies the oversights of reasoning that substantializes lethal paradox. In one chapter titled "Crip Nationalism," for instance, Puar dresses down the ADA for a collection of predictable errors. One of the ADA's main problems for Puar is its beholden-ness to rights logic, or its "standardization of what disability is in human rights regimes"—a refrain reverberating throughout Puar's book. Voicing a stance arguably even more doctrinal within anticolonial thought (Puar's other main audience) than disability studies, Puar's suspicion of rights is just as much mandated by her reliance on biopolitical theory. Puar subscribes to the maxim (shared with a thinker like Agamben) that legalization, or the juridical codification of categories of exclusion, inevitably creates a road map for future oppression. Puar censures rights and law alike for "unwittingly impos[ing] definitions, evaluation, and judgment about what disability is,"[7] all of which she derides as inherently normalizing. Still another problem with the ADA for Puar is its tendency to be narrated as a success story. Puar construes her study accordingly, as "about what happens after certain liberal rights are bestowed, certain thresholds or parameters of success are claimed to have been reached."[8] Not surprisingly, those illusions of success become especially nefarious when they paper over structural contradictions such as those produced by the invidious exclusions of disability. Puar thus com-plains that the ADA "uses capitalist logic to solve a problem largely created by capitalism," much as "neoliberal regimes of biocapital produce that body as never healthy enough, and thus always in a debilitated state in relation to what one's bodily capacity is imagined to be."[9] Rather than a testament to the viability of progressively minded activism, the ADA becomes a cautionary tale bearing far-reaching, if not universal, lessons.

Actively globalizing her book's theses, Puar describes disability as its own fable or allegory of modernity: an "ableist modernity" that projects "incapacity" onto modernity's "Others." Held out as a paradigmatic instance of "exclusion," disability becomes emblematic of other, related "states of exception" on which neoliberalism, capitalism, structural oppression, and modernity all depend. Singling out capitalism in particular, Puar warns that it possesses an "unflinching need for social pariahs available for injury, excluded from the economies that hail certain bodies as worthy of being objects of care, however compromised this inclusion must be." Those axes of exclusion-debilitation are consequently "not just an unfortunate byproduct" of capitalism, but "required for and constitutive" of it.[10] Once again, exclusion functions as a kind of master paradox condensing capitalism's structural violence—or an antifoundationalist foundation only entrenched by the legal codification of rights principles.

Corollary to this move to ontologize exclusionary paradox is Puar's premise that sociopolitical programs to integrate or "include" will merely reinstate newly treacherous technologies of abuse and marginalization. Puar bewails that the ADA

> transposes and thus dilutes a systemic critique of structures of employment into a liberal identity politics focused on inclusion and recognition. It ironically desires assimilation of people with disabilities into some of the very structures that debilitated them initially. [...] The ADA does not so much challenge prevalent constructions of the organization of labor that might be debilitating as it minoritizes the otherwise inadequate labor contributions of bodies deemed disabled by insisting on their incorporation into work spaces that are modified especially for them.[11]

Assimilation, inclusion, recognition, incorporation: Puar's rhetoric evokes those terms as if they were self-evident crimes. And Puar can do so in part because her thinking castigates each of those aims as inherently "liberal" and thus contaminated.

Nothing so far in Puar's analysis should strike us as terribly new or surprising. Yet *The Right to Maim*'s critiques simultaneously lay down trip wires that are incredibly common, and it is this minefield that works to sabotage the conversion of theory into a constructive, prescriptive, habitable practice. Puar's book accuses the discourse of disability (versus debilitation) of untold offenses: it is a badge of "white privilege," "neoimperial," a "privileging of the human," and so on. As elsewhere, those sweeping charges are clearly meant to disclose the conspiracy between seemingly far-flung realities of oppression, in another meritorious effort to capture the enormity of structural injustice and discrimination. But when guilty of so very many violations, the logic of disability starts to resemble an overdrawn if not caricatured scapegoat. Puar's indictments further depend on vast conflations, which merge manifold sites of historical malfeasance into a single, towering monolith that indeed eclipses nearly everything. Representative of a lot of work on neoliberalism, Puar's brand of critique quite cursorily collapses qualitatively and quantitatively distinct aspects of capitalist modernity into a unitary and hegemonic phenomenon—obliterating whatever material gradations might separate one guise of exploitation from another. Such broad brushstrokes similarly nullify whatever factors might fruitfully distinguish settler colonialism from racism from antiqueerness from disability: Puar treats those manifestations of bias as one and the same. Though well-intentioned, such radical leveling impedes (and even criminalizes) the very sorts of scalar determinations that would enable the disaggregation and differential assessment of disparate sites of institutionalized violence.

What ensues is that conclusions like Puar's predicated on the denial of granular and other variations can end up forfeiting their own critical acumen. Uninterested in nuances and degrees, Puar's allegations become just as all-encompassing as the appetites she abhors in capitalism. But especially worrisome is how those categorical pronouncements confiscate numerous of the analytic tools necessary to render critique more than an abstractly philosophical drill. While the trepidation regarding tools like "evaluation" and "discrimination" and "judgment" underlying such reasoning extends from valid reservations, the resulting prohibitions are far too broad, given how they also blacklist the sorts of calculi and corresponding evaluative assessments that inescapably steer practical action and decision-making in any live legal or political forum. Put differently, critical inquiry also needs to magnify the *dis*similarities not only that differentiate one unique situation from the next but also between colonialism, anti-queerness, and disability as imbricated yet nevertheless meaningfully discrepant machinery of oppression—and precisely so that each separate node in that larger edifice can be most carefully isolated, critiqued, and dismantled. Lumping together (versus disarticulating) these kinds of deviations can thus have the unintended consequence of masking or obscuring the workings of important levers of injustice—not to mention discouraging if not occluding opportunities to intervene. Feeding fears that there is "no exit," an exclusive focus on continuities and homologies can thus breed resignation and inertia, obstructing the actualization of one's theory in a cognizable practice.[12] Can one not agree (and even set out to prove) that oppression is structural without treating its diverse matrices and instantiations as wholly fungible? Or without discerning in their covert interconnections another master narrative? Would our critiques not be *even more* pointed and well received if they took stock of these discrepancies and other fluctuations, and precisely so that we can tailor our answers and our strategies to the messy complexities of action in any given arena?

Such absolutism of method clearly compels deterministic outcomes, and in ways prone to spill over and infect meaningful debate over a spectrum of ancillary issues. Indeed, it is not only with respect to rights that Puar confronts her readers with a *choix forcé*. Throughout the book, the many harms Puar imputes to the discourse of disability redouble and resurface as not so subtle attacks on anyone foolish enough to support rights, law, normative analysis, inclusion, recognition, and of course disability. Puar dismisses those ends as wholly bankrupt, refusing to entertain the prospect that some of their channels might enable viable and even salutary action under some circumstances, whereas be revealed as sullied or counterproductive in others. With these sorts of nuances sidelined, either one is on Puar's side or not, and if not one will be cornered into exposure as elitist, white, antiqueer, imperialist, ableist, privileged, and so on. Given this penchant for villainization, Puar can seem far more interested in outing and shaming her potential interlocutors than in actually finding forward-looking and realistic strategies for remedying the conditions of injustice her study purports to uncover. Yet such holier-than-thou posturing also hinges on a blame game we have seen many times before: a game in which the trump card of crying (here, ontological) paradox is sure to win.

Ironically, Puar's thinking can therefore seem trapped in a prioritization of the symbolic. Indeed, scoffing at something like the ADA makes sense only if one turns an indifferent eye on the very real material-practical gains and protections that piece of legislation has brought about for innumerable people. But such misprisions are actively encouraged—if not required—by the logic of paradox. Puar overtly locates herself within a tradition of left dedication to the "either/or," but it is also true that the basic ability to stage and thereby brandish a hidden paradox depends upon the positing of warring antinomies. Hence, the reflex to construct a balkanized landscape is hardwired into reasoning through paradox—which is to say that Puar's bent for hyperbole and polarization is neither rare nor, relatively speaking, all that extreme. Yet Puar leaves us with a starkly Manichean worldview, in which intellectual-political stances can be neatly slotted into the properly critical (i.e., Puar) versus the reprobate (i.e., everybody else). By now it should be clear why such a tidy moral universe also creates straw men; marshals faulty assumptions about reality (i.e., conceiving certain goods like rights as scarce and finite); and falsely casts coextensive options as mortal enemies.

I'll shift momentarily to explain why things do not need to be this way, including why such sanctimony is not inevitable. But it is first important to observe that Puar's either/or swagger—with its militancy and puritanical tone—is not remotely unusual today. Comparable forms of disciplinary mortification and policing have become standard intellectual fare. As earlier chapters observed, the politics of exclusion has found frequent direction inward. For decades now, successive theoretical "turns" have launched their debuts with often gladiatorial flourish, outing the exclusionary biases of their blameworthy predecessors. A preoccupation with the unwittingly exclusionary practices even of one's coconspirators has authorized at times colorful internecine warfare, conducted via performative exorcisms that can seem contrived more than anything to convince their ringleaders of their outsider (and hence ethically superior) status. But that impetus to trumpet one's marginalization at the hands of one's confederates has also, perhaps unavoidably, bred infighting that can be mean-spirited. It may be excusable to enjoy the gamesmanship of a David Kurnick, who with panache unmasks particular critics' inattention to the "contradictions" and "symptomatic places" of their "fantasy structures."[13] But those "dramas of exposure" (in Eve Sedgwick's terms) are too often conducted via character assassination, parody and caricature, trivialization, and other smear campaigns, many discerning sins like apolitical "ascesis," modesty, or weakness within what are in fact minor differences.[14] Too much theory today justifies its existence through moralizing belittlement of interlocutors who, for all intents and purposes, are on the same side. This book has argued that captivity to a style of thought rotating around the dramatization (and outing) of paradox has reinforced these instincts, causing displays of one-upmanship to be mistaken as a badge both of more than vigorous critique and of sophisticated thinking.

Even efforts to shed certain proclivities of theory have not been immune to these brands of argumentation, including a craving for blood sport. Such efforts can also seem to proceed through pendulum swings: to legitimize a given position by hypostasizing bipolar alternatives, where the negative relief of one pole can be adopted as a wholesale substitute for the other.

This instinct is also an artifact of the logic of paradox, with its frequent tendency to divine saving virtues within the inverse relief of a given scourge. However, even theory with which this book shares many sympathies has not shirked such habits (along with other ammunition of paradox). Hence, affirmation is imagined to come solely at the expense of critique; generalization to entirely replace a focus on singularity; surface reading a surrogate for depth; attachment-distance; therapeutic-critical; weak-strong; and so on. While rhetorically fetching (and sometimes accurate), otherwise fertile attempts to traverse challenging methodological roadblocks can seem to remain strangely hostage to the snares of the either/or. Given this disciplinary geography, it might feel unavoidable that so many household feuds would become bitter and divisive. But false antitheses are not only too easy; they seduce us into hoping for panaceas. So notwithstanding a sense of whiplash, particularly worrisome about this mind-set is how it erases a unifying and common ground. That vast intermediary space composed of an unending sequence of muddy gradations and degrees also cries out for theorization: for analysis aimed at assessing its terrain, with an eye to its suitability for intervention. However, the prospect that ostensibly countervailing alternatives might work in concert or be enmeshed in ways that require meticulous parsing and disambiguation—in other words, the spirit of the both/and—largely remains discounted.

Returning to the ADA can suggest one path toward less deterministic and more situationally alert practices of criticism. The ADA has naturally elicited a whole gamut of theoretical responses, some significantly less cynical than Puar's. Two more affirmative appraisals of that law—James LeBrecht and Nicole Newnham's celebrated documentary *Crip Camp* and Lennard J. Davis's *Enabling Acts: The Hidden Story of How the Americans with Disabilities Act Gave the Largest US Minority Its Rights*—can shed light on some of the territory that Puar-style critique wrongly obscures, while also modeling a more integrative criticism. Generically, LeBrecht and Newnham's film and Davis's history could not be more different. *Crip Camp* superimposes a heady spirit of countercultural dissidence onto the ADA, feting the bold, boundary-crossing lives and choices of the groundswell activists who helped to achieve that act's adoption. *Crip Camp*'s aesthetic also fits the bill; parts could be mistaken for a documentary on Woodstock. Enlisting mirthful humor, rousing music, and at other times transgressive play, it de-exceptionalizes disability while harnessing the exuberantly consciousness-raising ethos of 1960s-style protest. Yet whereas *Crip Camp* possesses something of a "feel good" aura that also fosters sympathetic identification, Davis's powerful study is informed by a realism that refuses to gainsay the many tradeoffs and compromises either leading up to the ADA's initial passage or dogging its subsequent enforcement.

Other salient differences between these two texts are worth noting. Given a film's compressed length, *Crip Camp* naturally paints in broad brushstrokes, whereas Davis burrows into detail regarding both relative arcana and the complicated forces, including the unexpected supporters, that united to back the ADA and shepherd its adoption. In so doing, Davis is explicit that his study sets out to correct certain myths about activism, such as that the disability rights movement arose "spontaneously" and with a "bang" versus a mere "whimper."[15] With the caveat "the devil is in the details," *Enabling Acts* immerses its readers in the nitty-gritty of history and context, memorializing the arduous and assorted labor that proved effective for the ADA. In another noteworthy divergence, Davis's history and the film marshal contrasting narratives concerning the principal actors and types of action that made the dreams embodied in the ADA a transformative reality. Whereas *Crip Camp* lionizes a select group of activists whose bonds were forged at a high school summer camp only to come to fruition in a type of manifest destiny, Davis's history ranges across a motley cast of characters, some with inglorious pasts and motives, precisely to tell a less easily romanticized or redemptive tale.

However, both are unafraid to describe the ADA as a relative success story: a prototype for effective political agency that begs for repeating. As such, both *Enabling Acts* and *Crip Camp* are frank about the momentousness of that legislation, including the magic of what has, generally speaking, been a victory for social justice. *Crip Camp's* overall mood is joyful; and Davis does not shy away from characterizing the ADA as a "powerful support of people and a clarion call for justice and fairness."[16] Both texts also devote substantial energy to documenting and evaluating those strategies that proved workable, again for Davis in order to demystify certain idealized fantasies about the mainly symbolic tenor of left activism. As Davis explains, the national demonstrations that mustered popular support for the act "were, and perhaps had to be, coordinated and orchestrated. Although they used grassroots sentiment, those demonstrations were more likely top-down affairs—in which organizers and planners" called the shots.[17] Instead of parroting a familiar anti-legalism, Davis treats law, legislative action, and the court system as thorny yet necessary spheres of intervention: forums that can serve *both* to crystallize *and* to render formerly nonexistent legal rights an actuality. Far from Pollyannaish or sanguine, however, Davis simultaneously wrestles with the ADA's many wrinkles and infelicitous bargains, continually checking the book's praise with concerted attention to the act's invariable shortcomings.

Importantly, both texts do subscribe to accounts of disability discrimination that dovetail in meaningful aspects with the theoretically mainstream wisdom espoused by Puar. All three thinkers, for example, establish parallels between different vectors of oppression to foreground their structural nature, linking disability especially to stigma tied to sexuality and race.[18] Yet those interlocking nodes in the circuitry of structural oppression are identified within *Crip Camp* and by Davis as simultaneous levers of solidarity and resistance and meaningful change. So the very institutional channels that Puar's ontologizing logic both immobilizes and dismisses as irredeemably fatal are recognized to be significantly more responsive, pliable, and productive. For *Crip Camp*, a focus on those overlapping patterns of discrimination contributes to an ethos of gender-bending subversion, including a celebration of being "crazy."[19] In contrast, Davis recounts the tactical alliances forged between the AIDS and disability lobbies, one "crucial concept" of which "was that there was not going to be a divide and conquer mentality."[20] However, neither in *Crip Camp* nor in *Enabling Acts* do those connections deliver strictly negative lessons about the dependence of rights and citizenship on categories of disposable lives, or what Puar would call a biopolitics of debilitation. Instead, mutual experiences of exclusion inspire the building of coalitions and pooling of resources. That collaborative and constructive attitude, for instance, is encapsulated in one episode documented in *Crip Camp* when the Black Panthers took responsibility for feeding groups of disability rights protestors during their legendary Oakland sit-in. Not so differently, *Enabling Acts* opens in a type of situation room filled with prominent congressmen and cabinet members who ultimately endorsed the bill, many of whom were personally impacted by disability in ways that elicited what Davis construes as bipartisan fellowship. In Davis's book, moreover, emphasis on such united fronts is part of a larger reluctance to spectralize power. He repeatedly clarifies that bias does not necessarily equal malice, for example pointing out that certain legal decisions of the 1970s and '80s carrying discriminatory effects nevertheless "weren't driven by animus toward people with disabilities as much as by misinformation or political conviction."[21] As a result, both texts reckon with exclusions that are presented as structural and institutionalized; however, they stop short of reifying or aggrandizing or otherwise ontologizing disability's allegedly incurable or foundational status. Awareness of imbricated lines of exclusion instead incites the historical actors those texts study to engage in forms of teamwork and strategic action.

In part, this emphasis stems from the fact that both texts adamantly reject an explanatory framework that seeks gnostic truths in the exceptionality (or, put differently, the exclusionary paradoxes) of disability. As Davis avers, "Far from being an odd and unlikely thing, disability is more the rule than the exception."[22] Both *Enabling Acts* and *Crip Camp* further present the injuries wrought by disability discrimination (and disability itself) as relatively amenable to cure and remediation. Hence, they both catalog numerous real-world gains and benefits procured for real people by the ADA, while similarly singling out concrete legal principles and larger social values that the ADA generatively worked to institutionalize. Both thereby refuse *either* to etherealize disability's wounds via a telos of impossibility and irresolution *or* to condemn legalization for rendering those wounds fixed and impervious to rectification. It is essential to observe why that impulse to normalize disability goes hand-in-hand with conviction in that locus of injustice's susceptibility to redress, reform, and improvement—in practical, symbolic, and material ways. Whereas *Crip Camp* describes the damage inflicted by prejudice in recognizable language (i.e., as being "sidelined," "excluded"), it nevertheless neutralizes those harms with meaningful antidotes like "freedom," "inclusion," "mak[ing] the world a better place," and even the value of legalism. As one activist explains, "We want the law enforced. We want no more segregation." Davis, too, commends the ADA for affording great "empowerment," which was effectuated by "highlight[ing] the rights of people with disabilities as civil rights."[23] So although his book concludes by balancing the ADA's limits against its gains, Davis unambiguously asserts that "we are so much better off that the ADA is there than if it were not."[24]

Davis also praises the ADA because of how it codifies, and seemingly vindicates, insights best understood as bequests of theory. In Davis's hands, those precepts ingrained within theory importantly do not subvert translation in the ways typically expected of them. The doctrines of theory are therefore neither congenitally resistant to operating as normative optimums nor incommensurate to legal acknowledgment and ratification for Davis. As he argues, one virtue of the ADA is that it deprived religious and medical authorities of the power to define disability, replacing those stigmatizing discourses with a "social model" predicated on the idea "that disability was socially constructed and done so in a political way." This constructivist view of disability is for Davis prominently enshrined in the ADA Amendments Act of 2008. Davis quotes from that bill:

> Although variations in people's abilities and disabilities across a broad spectrum are a normal part of the human condition, some individuals have been singled out and subjected to discrimination because they have conditions considered disabilities by others; other individuals have been excluded or disadvantaged because their physical or mental impairments have been ignored in the planning and construction of facilities, vehicles, and services; and all Americans run the risk of being discriminated against because they are perceived as having conditions they may not have or because of misperceptions about the limitations resulting from conditions they do have.

Davis acclaims this provision as the "heart and soul" of the Amendments Act—and exactly because it both affirms and formalizes the reality that "discrimination can be built into the environment" and is therefore not as much "about 'them'" as "about 'us.'"[25] The act's language, while identifying disability as "exclusionary" and structural, nevertheless frames that diagnosis to implicate everyone, regardless of demographics or identity or privilege. Yet particularly telling is how Davis relies on a constructivist model of identity to arrive at very different conclusions than most theory contending with the consequences of "legalism," including with the impact of rights' codification on structural oppression. Rather than, as is customary, concluding that juridification renders the arms of bias all the more invidious, Davis understands the ADA—and to reiterate, precisely because it naturalizes a social constructivist view of power—to set the stage for the mitigation of disability-based prejudice and injury. Davis's reasoning thereby captures why such a baseline proposition need *not* culminate in compulsory anti-legalism: for Davis, law is not a guidebook plotting future oppression. In *Enabling Acts*, law is instead a ready and willing servant to a left, progressive agenda—and, moreover, a highly responsive, workable, and empowering one. This is clearly a conception of the agency *both* of law *and* of theory that departs markedly from what we have repeatedly encountered. Indeed, one might take Davis to suggest that it is precisely the détente of law and theory that can achieve world-altering—if imperfect—outcomes like the ADA. As the final sentence of Davis's book asserts, there is a need to "thank" the ADA's assorted band of activists for producing "what is after all, a most enabling act."[26]

It might feel tempting to temper the cynicism palpably coloring a text like *The Right to Maim* by evoking the redeeming openness, indeterminacy, and irresolution that the logic of paradox has encoded for so many. However, conviction in those metamorphic energies of paradox can lead to just as negative if not defeatist positions as reasoning that ontologizes lethal contradiction—especially when those energies are transposed onto real-world legal-political opportunities and challenges. Faith in a transformative spirit of paradox has also been fueled by deep skepticism regarding prospects like legality, progress, inclusion, reform, and effective agency, whether that faith is subsidized by an antinomianism, antirationalism, posthumanism, aestheticized politics, or an ethics of the divided subject.

A final rendezvous with one of this book's touchstones, Joan Scott's *Only Paradoxes to Offer*, can elucidate at least some of many of the reasons redemptive expectations for paradox similarly hamstring attempts to describe the agency of theory in serviceable, concrete, prescriptive terms. Because although Scott exalts the emancipatory promise of paradox, her panoramic study of the French struggle for women's rights ultimately uncovers a lengthy record of pitfalls, failures, and double binds. Scott's analyses recurrently converge upon the disappointments of feminist activism: that movement's "nagging reminder[s] of [...] insufficient universalism" and other "problems" that "cannot be resolved."[27] Something analogous plays out within Scott's reflections on the lives of her individual protagonists: she emphasizes their "isolation," sacrifices (whether jail time or, for Olympe de Gouges, death), and lack of recognition during their lives. In a display of such thinking's reflexivity, Scott also cabins the takeaways of her own "theories" accordingly, warning that "they have not and cannot resolve the dilemmas [of feminism] or make them less intractable."[28] While on some level true, Scott nevertheless magnifies those letdowns, allowing them to cheapen, if not eclipse, that movement's achievements. These outsized proportions assumed by impossibilities, aporias, and limits, we have seen, is one insignia of an aestheticized conception of politics. Yet what emerges is that, even though Scott champions the charisma and theatricality of politics, the obsessively self-qualifying and self-minimizing tenor of that enthusiasm nevertheless dominates.

Hence, among the many referents of the "paradoxes" evoked in Scott's title (along with rights, exclusion, feminism, revisionist history) are feminism's self-betrayals. As she concludes about Jeanne Deroin: "Paradoxically, and unavoidably, [her] advocacy undermined the very woman in whose name she spoke."[29] One of Scott's main arguments is that feminism's apparent successes backfired in myriad subtle ways, ironically compounding the paradoxical terms enforcing women's exclusion to render them all the more obstinate and insidious. In an insight credited to Simone de Beauvoir, Scott is explicit:

> For the vote, instead of resolving the tension between the abstract undifferentiated individual and the individual self defined through difference, had heightened the conflict between the two. In the past the tension between them has apparently been resolved by taking both individuals to be masculine; that resolution no longer worked when women were admitted to the ranks of abstract individuals. [...] The acquisition of the vote had not solved the problem of women's subordination, but it had moved the locus of contradiction.[30]

As Scott similarly observes of women's suffrage, "having resolved one of the inconsistencies of republicanism meant erasing the fact that it had ever existed."[31] Not surprisingly, these dilemmas become even more acute for Scott when activism makes recourse to law, rights, or other formal legal, political, and institutional channels. So whereas for Puar the decoy of "success" is particularly pernicious, what Scott finds most irksome is "resolution." Resolution, rather than serving as an objective or guarantee, is repeatedly characterized by Scott as a ruse fated to perpetuate the central mechanisms of women's exclusion—precisely because that lure of resolution would necessarily require the silencing and suppression of the ongoing paradoxes attendant to women's subordination. As should be clear, Scott's version of anti-legalism is brokered less by Agamben and Foucault than by deconstruction's insistence on the infinitely generative irresolutions that plague all representational practices. The ever-mutating locus of political exclusion like that confounding feminism is consequently infused with a logic parallel to the traces that adjourn and otherwise displace meaning within a text. Both planes of meaning-making agency (of feminism and of writing) are thereby subjected to a shared signifying economy that inheres within those continual slippages and deferrals, which of course are commended for evading whatever stabilization, normalization, and closure might come with an endpoint like "inclusion."

Whereas for Scott resolution thus marks a kind of hoax, she extols its inverse—irresolution—as the crux of a radical politics. As Scott avers throughout her study, "it is in the nature of paradox to be unresolvable."[32]

As we know, many laudable motives underlie such a creed of irresolution and indeterminacy; among others, it forewarns against complacency regarding fates ranging from right-wing cooptation to the stagnation and malaise jeopardizing any social movement. But it is one thing to cite paradox as a caveat or red flag, and yet another to deem the attributes of that property the elementary particles of a philosophy of transformative agency. While no doubt inspiring, that logic mystifies agency in ways that bleed into and muddle the coordinates of real-world political action, shrouding (rather than illuminating) crucial ingredients at stake in the practical enactment of any given platform or agenda.

Yet why exactly does this lodging of agency in exclusionary paradox impale its theorization as a praxis? Another angle on commitments like Scott's is that they grant preeminence to the residual, marginal, and deferred—at expense of attention to the integral. Such thinking actively (and often intentionally) discounts a host of considerations that might ordinarily be seen as fundamental, essential, or basic to political and other concerted action. Along with irresolution, Scott's vision of agency is rooted, as we saw, in the consciousness-raising appetencies of the paradox-disclosing spectacle. But that emphasis places inordinate trust in the ability of purely symbolic gestures to effectuate lived and lasting change. However, are such intellectual-aesthetic discoveries really enough to incite principled and deliberate action in all circumstances and for all consequential political actors (whether good or bad)? Or to garner the fortitude and other resources necessary to sustain a given pursuit both within the day-to-day and for the duration?

Troubling is how the future-oriented telos of much theory is often coupled with downright hostility to the mundane dimensions of agency that unfold within the here and now. In a representative statement of such thinking, José Muñoz condemns the "lull of presentness" and "goal-oriented tautological present" as a lapse of the "critical" that is further indicative of "straight time."[33] But won't any praxis necessarily take shape within one such "goal-oriented present" or another? And how can theory promise change if it doesn't adopt feasible, visualizable goals? Or come to terms with the arduous, potentially lulling aspects of day-to-day struggle? Scott's dedication to the liminal agency of paradox is, in many ways, just as emphatic as Muñoz in gainsaying the resilience and unwavering conviction (not to mention goods like security, stability, tangibility, and continuity) indispensable to long-term and effective political action. But will theatrical stagings of paradox, regardless of how electrifying, really nourish the requisite stamina, whether over the long haul or amid real hardship? And what about the "holding fast" "without shrinking" even "in face of" adversity that Woolf can remind us of?

It is relatedly the case that truly difficult choices are unlikely to be either distilled or rescued by those fireworks of paradox. As we have seen again and again, the logic of paradox is not only ill-suited to, but can actively railroad, certain kinds of judgments and decision-making endeavors. While adroit at the preliminary (and undoubtedly important) labors of unmasking and unraveling, paradoxes are significantly less good at facilitating the goal-oriented calculations needed to guide any viable course of action. If anything, their logic risks dissolving crucial normative and practical levers of choice and evaluation into a force field of free and all-consuming play—in other words, expunging the very benchmarks and criteria that normally administer policy-based and other strategic determinations regarding how and when and why to act. Clearly, electing to prioritize one issue or tactic or crisis-ridden scene versus another underlies any well-considered practice, but hypercognizance of chronic irresolution offers little to no direction therein. More accurately, that mind-set risks rarifying the critical and adjudicatory equipment most vital to a habitable politics—indeed relegating the political to an extraordinary, if not otherworldly, to-come.

Scott's insistence on irresolution and insufficiency, we have seen, can be partly attributed to her thinking's basis in a semiotics, and that mise-en-scène further explains why such philosophies of agency can seem oddly impervious to the onus to translate their commitments into an applied and actualizable practice. Here, too, valuable concerns inform this allergy to self-instrumentalization—which, no doubt, offer one rationale for Scott's indebtedness to deconstruction. But that quarantine works to deprive Scott's theory of agency of important normative and analytic rudders, leading to the odd sense that theory like Scott's tells us nothing—even while claiming pertinence to virtually everything. Scott is unabashed about her study's generalizability, proclaiming globally: "political movements emerge at sites of difficult, sometimes unresolvable, contradiction."[34] Further evident in her frequently spatial imagery and language ("Post-suffrage feminism was constructed in the space of a paradox"[35]), that universalizing thrust also stems from a formalism of paradox: or a privileging of form and style.

Recall that for many thinkers the label formalism pejoratively denotes a disingenuous skirting of politics, whether under cover of a mechanical application of ostensibly neutral rules or a belief that the province of certain domains (i.e., literature) is apolitical and thus autonomous. We can also remember that many early uptakes of theory actively deployed that body of thought to protest the disciplinary dominance of various formalisms (whether in literary study or law), reacting against those disciplines' alleged indifference to the real-world consequences of their reasoning. Yet while a formalist exorcism lies within theory's own genetics, this book has repeatedly asked whether the logic of paradox transacts merely another version of such an all-too-comfortable syndrome. Because while it is one matter to trace how symmetrical contradictions align to buttress an oppressive structure, it is another to find within those same patterns an ethical, just, or creative exodus from what are in actuality stifling conditions of intellectual impasse and inertia.

Still additional factors can render philosophies of agency thus transfixed with their own irresolvable paradoxes counterproductive. One involves the perplexity of what activities do versus do not get redeemed through those prolific and infinitely reproducible formal patterns. Whereas properties that might appear integral to effective agency (progress, precedent, clarity, purpose, certitude, stability, norms) are denied such iterability and repetition, markers of insufficiency and disappointment are instead vested with near universal (i.e., ceaselessly mutating and self-replicating) authority. While razing vital evaluative signposts, such reasoning also trains us to be wary of instances when agency *does* prove feasible, measurable, salutary, or effective. This is a huge problem, insofar as we want to affirm any of our existing accomplishments as either meritorious or deserving of replication—or, put differently, to submit those gains to the same iterability and repetition thinking like Scott's noticeably withholds from practical, worldly, mundane affairs. Thralldom to paradox can consequently trick us into discounting (if not negating) gains and ambitions that we instead want to take eminently seriously. Whether those modest gains magically endure or simply beg for validation, the spirit of paradox can stifle such responses. For all of such thinking's frequent thrill, it can nevertheless rob us of the ability to rejoice in the plenitude and joy and empowerment and affirmation that oftentimes do indeed capacitate and extend from the realization of effective agency.

These conceptual lacunae become even more glaring when studies like Scott's are juxtaposed with other famous episodes from the annals of feminist activism—and episodes just as visibly tinged by failure and disappointment. Much as a preoccupation with indeterminacy and impossibility takes for granted gains that are far from certain, it can trivialize the very real roadblocks that have tragically thwarted the battle for objectives like women's equality and rights. The Equal Rights Amendment (the ERA) in the United States is a crucible in not only actual defeat but also the seductions of unreflecting devotion to a paradox-fueled vision of political change. During the state ratification process, growing momentum and wide bipartisan support for women's rights made that amendment's adoption look like everything short of a foregone conclusion. However, in a late-1970s story that is well known, conservative saboteurs, the most iconic being Phyllis Schlafly, expertly derailed its passage, even inciting five state legislatures to revoke their prior approval. That outcome has long been read as an admonitory lesson in the fragility of grassroots progressive politics—a tale today finessed as an omen of right-wing backlash in the twenty-first century. Nevertheless, the combined agility and ease with which Schlafly and her troops rebuffed the ERA can disclose further costs of unbridled faith in paradox, including excessive focus on the symbolics of political activism.

The particular tactics that *both* Schlafly *and* ERA activists on the ground did and did not deploy are quite revealing, especially since they ultimately led to that campaign's collapse. In many ways, the amendment's foot soldiers embodied the activist spirit idealized in theoretical circles still today. Yet, as Jane Mansbridge recounts in her classic study, *Why We Lost the ERA*, those crusaders made a series of errors, above all to be led astray by their own enthusiasm. According to Mansbridge, perhaps their biggest misstep was to pay insufficient attention to messaging, neglecting to spell out either the larger substantive or immediately tangible benefits that would result from the amendment's passage. In failing to translate their principles into publicly accessible terms, ERA activists misjudged public sentiment, believing that the symbolism of "rights in the abstract" would be enough to secure the vote.[36] This naïve faith in the primacy of symbolic change proved fatal for multiple reasons. Most immediately, activists' reluctance to lend sufficiently material or practical content to the ERA permitted Schlafly and its other reactionary opponents to hijack the popular conversation regarding its likely impact and meaning. In so doing, Schlafly essentially exploited left activists' exuberance, crucifying that movement on its neglect to make recourse to pragmatic or policy-driven argumentation. One implication of Mansbridge's study is that the ERA's frontline supporters were too confident in the payoff of a particular theatrics of consciousness-raising, at the expense of the strategizing and principled persuasion required to convince the public.

This vacuum created by ERA activists' failure to vest the ERA with a tangible agenda allowed Schlafly and her cohort to commandeer its associations, linking the ERA to then-extremist scenarios like the women's draft and shared public bathrooms. Even worse, ERA activists were actively caught off guard, at times fully buying into those narratives and even doubling down on such then-hyperbolic visions of the amendment's ramifications. For Mansbridge, precisely "the dearth of immediate benefits made feminists reluctant to compromise on issues of principle" and, moreover, "to exaggerate even its unpopular potential effects," including those concocted by Schlafly.[37] Unwilling to moderate or sugarcoat their emancipatory vision, the ERA's proponents were effectively impaled on overzealous activism for activism's sake. As Mansbridge relates, this posture set them up to accede to the very rhetorical inflation and absolutism that Schlafly conveniently used against them. Ambushed by their own ardor, ERA activists exhibited several other common tendencies examined above—either/or anti-accommodationism, ideological purity, and categorical thinking—and to that movement's great detriment.

The single-mindedness of activists' faith in the consciousness-raising power of abstract if symbolic ideals thus had the tragic effect of eroding public trust in the amendment. For Mansbridge, activists' failure to frame the debate in terms that would have endowed the ERA with immediately applicable content meant that "almost any move from principle to substance tended to hurt the amendment's chances," and was likely "to create an atmosphere of distrust."[38] A resistance to submit aspirational ideals to differential calculation, weighing one path against another, therefore partly caused the ERA movement to run aground on the same avoidances that today plague theory: an unwillingness either to tailor methodology to the situation at hand or to be selective in drawing from a diverse tactical tool kit. No doubt, these are also matters of the integrity of theory: of the fit between visionary principles and their realization in practice. For the ERA, a parallel refusal to redress exclusion through a strategic, viable plan of action led activists to lose touch with more than popular sentiment; that neglect stoked public anxiety and mistrust, making the ERA cause for suspicion rather than something to get behind.

Television serials like *Mrs. America* have played up parallels between the Trump presidency and the rise of Reagan-era conservatism. But the cunning of Schlafly's messaging can seem prescient for additional reasons, given how she successfully embezzled a left agenda through a mode of subterfuge today increasingly rampant. Schlafly was expert at maneuvering lurking paradox—rendering her (and not the ERA's activists) the most fitting avatar of a latter-day Olympe de Gouges. By fanning fears over outcomes that seemed outlandish like single-sex bathrooms, Schlafly and her crew staged dramatic enactments of paradox, laying bare the contradictions riddling activists' accounts of the ERA in order to undermine its popular following. By making the ERA look absurd, Schlafly created a public carnival that became a losing situation for the amendment's defenders, who were cornered into capitulating to paradox and its invariable upper hand. It is accordingly tempting to look upon Schlafly as an early architect of what has since become a stock right-wing gambit: fomenting paranoia precisely to besiege informed and rational civic deliberate. That she deployed such tactics during the same era that saw left intellectual conviction in paradox come of age only compounds these ironies.

Reclaiming the Foreclosed Conceptual Space of Theory

It is impossible to say whether something like the ERA could have met with a different fate had its ambassadors relied on a more pragmatic, less heady portfolio of tactics. But this book is foremost interested in how we analyze such incidents, whether our critical objects are the archives of history, literary-theoretical texts, or legal-philosophical constructs like rights. Reading in strict pursuit of contradictions, exceptions, ambiguities, and foreclosures is merely one available approach—which is to say that criticism need not end up in either an impossibly utopian or darkly fatalistic location. However, it is one thing to identify where that quest for paradox goes awry, and another to practice a different manner of criticism. This book closes with one experiment in reading more expansively and with a wider menu of goals in mind.

Two influential literary-theoretical texts from very different periods offer platforms for trying out such an alternate theory, while illuminating merely a few of the philosophical and practical resources and goals germane to what I've referred to as an integrative criticism. Both Woolf's "A Room of One's Own" and Claudia Rankine's *Citizen: An American Lyric* are extended outcries against historical sites of exclusion from citizenship and other sociopolitical and cultural life, and they have been oft celebrated for consciousness-raising along those very lines. Many of their themes reflect on the paradoxes produced by those exclusions—paradoxes also dramatized within their formal and stylistic features. Yet whereas those texts have in turn found interpretation via an optics of paradox, many of their core insights into exclusion and corresponding aesthetic components simultaneously refuse to gratify such a hermeneutics, placing into high relief the tensions between a habitual quest for paradox and analysis attuned to sources of what I'll describe as integrity and integration. Notwithstanding the many eruptions of paradox pervading both texts, *Citizen* and "A Room of One's

Own" converge upon perceptions of harmony and fullness and *non*contradiction, and within both texts are those recognitions suggested to escort theory's integration into a livable and applied practice. Among the many orthodoxies Woolf and Rankine's texts thus call into question are, first, that a methodology scaffolded by paradox exhibits the greatest fidelity to literary experience and, second, that paradox will augur the most robust, committed, critically alert political imaginary. While each differently gestures toward a constellation of values eschewed by theory, both texts, I'll argue, are above all instructive given how they open up a space composed of everything that theory has been unable or reluctant to fathom.

Woolf's essay and Rankine's multimedia lyric might initially appear to have little in common. Published in 2014, *Citizen* has acted as a standard-bearer due to its portrait of the unexpectedly treacherous guises of anti-Blackness during the glory days of the Obama presidency. Notwithstanding Woolf's fervent pleas for women's equality, "A Room of One's Own" instead defends a kind of aristocracy of great fiction—one predicated on its own privileges and omissions, including concerning race.[39] But despite these and other dissimilarities, both texts recurrently dramatize the conditions that allow "things [to] come together," while metacritically theorizing those phenomenal, sociopolitical, and other intimations of synthesis. That integrative spirit is evident in various of their central formal and stylistic features, again as different as they are. Woolf and Rankine both break down the artificial boundaries separating genres, blending fiction with memoir with theory with criticism with (for *Citizen*) visual art. That flouting of the partitions classifying literature is intimately tied to their parallel investments in other modes of integration, as they both set out to foster more integrative habits of knowing and participation.

It is important to stress that neither *Citizen* nor "A Room of One's Own" refutes or resists analysis aimed at the excavation of paradox, whether as a diagnostic, critical apparatus, or overarching *mentalité*. One could readily interpret either as fully a tutorial in numerous tenets instilled by paradox and its peculiar ethics. Many accounts of Woolf's oeuvre and life have lionized her for breathing new life into the subversive, outsider ethos of the *para doxa*, like Wilde revealing its nonbinary, queer spirit. This is just as much true of "A Room of One's Own," wherein the chameleon logic of paradox can seem to convert sociopolitical marginalization into insight and edification. Like Woolf's novels, its multiple narrators (a coterie of "Mary"'s) enact the fluid indeterminacy of such a "queer, composite being," echoing the usual link between psychic fracture and exclusion. Woolf's reflections on "the accumulation of unrecorded life" and "all these infinitely obscure lives [that] remain to be recorded,"[40] similarly offer a textbook formulation of the "politics of exclusion" that would stoke the canon wars half a century later. While decrying women's historical silencing, Woolf leverages that predicament to consciousness-raise, in the process marrying trenchant structural critique to a mood of giddy discovery. So there is no question that "A Room of One's Own" exemplifies preoccupations that remain definitional of theory.

Similarly has much of *Citizen*'s acclaim stemmed from how it portrays the tolls of oppression in terms that align with the axiomatics of much theoretical work especially on race-based injustice. Like Woolf's essay routed through a network of unnamed speakers, *Citizen*'s lyric both recounts and formally enacts a certain psychic splitting and self-loss, ratifying many codes of trauma studies. Along with its kaleidoscopic of discursive registers (journalism, poetry, fiction, memoir, theory), *Citizen* assembles a collage of narratively unrelated yet formally mirroring encounters with racism. The random connections between those isolated incidents rendered proximate through their arrangement in the text imitate the associative nature of traumatic remembrance, reminiscent of how accidental triggers prompt painful memories to surface. By failing to pinpoint or localize those incidents in place or time, *Citizen* also causes them to blur indistinguishably. While mimicking phenomena like delayed comprehension and cognitive vertigo, *Citizen*'s structural logic further generalizes each individual offense, configuring each successive incident as merely another node in a vast structure or edifice. Thus does *Citizen* present racism as both institutionalized and systemic.[41]

This enactment of the architecture of structural oppression via its formal and stylistic elements is surely one reason *Citizen* has been a lightning rod. That portrait, moreover, coincides with what we can recognize as other dominant wisdom regarding institutionalized racism: that it both camouflages and capitalizes on submerged paradox. As a meditation on its title, *Citizen* substantiates the view that understudied if not actively disavowed practices of exclusion are foundational to that institution, including to appurtenances like democracy and rights. On one level, these themes make *Citizen* eminently teachable. In my own classrooms, we examine how, over its course, *Citizen* accumulates a barrage of verbal and other aversive assaults in order to illustrate how they come to interlock within an overarching structure. That accrual of the low-grade yet constant background noise of structural bias also becomes a laboratory in, first, how racism is naturalized: built into the building blocks of language, perception, and ordinary social relations. And second, *Citizen*'s unending litany of assaults has the effect of redoubling injuries at risk of being minimized as purely abstract or intellectual, exponentially rather than incrementally multiplying their insidious consequences. This relentless aspect of *Citizen*'s formal arc is only intensified by Rankine's frequent use of deeply visceral imagery and metaphors. As one passage describes a passing insult: "You both experience this cut, which she keeps insisting is a joke, a joke stuck in her throat, and like any other injury, you watch it rupture along its suddenly exposed suture" (42). Within *Citizen*'s critical reception, we can readily imagine why such a quote would invite biopolitical readings wherein such a "suture" is taken to emblematize modernity's inescapably genocidal logic.

But other features of *Citizen* less clearly comport with—and instead complicate—such a hermeneutics of paradox and its routine lessons. For instance, one way to interpret *Citizen*'s onslaught of low-grade assaults would collapse them, in a testament to the epistemic texture and infinite web of racial subjection. However, other of its aesthetic and structural components instead serve to exaggerate the differences between its successive incidents, for instance as abrupt shifts from one snapshot of racism to another highlight the variations and degrees distinguishing those encounters. Sudden vacillations combined with uncanny adjacencies magnify qualitative and quantitative divergences that bear on matters like severity, intentionality, malice, duration, and so on. So although *Citizen* documents the grave harms inflicted even by inadvertent slurs, its organization simultaneously underscores the factors that separate and distinguish each of its segments, in the process also accentuating matters of agency, responsibility, choice, and sincerity—of perpetrator, victim, bystander, and reader together.

Just as not all offenses are held out as equal, *Citizen* amplifies and otherwise calls attention to the fluctuating reactions of its speakers (and presumably of Rankine's audience as well). Rather than to suggest a natural or automatic correspondence between a particular racist affront and a given riposte, *Citizen* repeatedly disarticulates that relation. Whereas some incidents thrust a speaker into a spiral of self-loathing and despair, others elicit momentous acts of solidarity, courage, and even empowerment. Other passages instead track a speaker's cycle of feeling as they initially succumb to and then metabolize anger, grief, shame, and disappointment. Placed into high relief, these sorts of deviations uncouple each individual entry from *Citizen*'s longer catalogue in ways that solicit evaluative assessment by the reader, concerning among other things the relationship (or lack thereof) between injury and response. So although *Citizen* cultivates emotions like rage over the lethal exceptions constitutive of American citizenship, it simultaneously summons normative judgments regarding the dicey matter of how and when to act in the midst of any given juncture in an oppressive system. Over its course, Rankine's speakers draw from a strikingly eclectic tool kit of strategies as they navigate the text's sequence of abusive encounters, and that heterogeneity itself invites differential analysis aimed at contrasting the relative utility of one such rejoinder versus another. In essence, *Citizen* spurs criticism to disaggregate and comparatively appraise the many incidents and reactions comprising its vast patchwork, suggesting that each such trial is cut from the same cloth yet nevertheless marked by salient discrepancies. Given how many passages announce their own implications for theory, the matter of how to understand *Citizen*'s formal architecture is inextricably a meditation on theory and its praxis.

There are similar ways in which *Citizen* can seem *both* to indulge *and* to unravel the usual nexus between trauma and properties like ambiguity and paradox. There is little question that *Citizen* besieges its readers with endless, incurable, and devastating paradox, even going so far as to induce a sense of futility amid that veritable leviathan of institutionalized racism. Throughout, it chronicles the many factors that cause systemic injustice to undermine its victims' perceptions of stability, confidence, and self-certainty. For Rankine's speakers, this utter persistence and ubiquity precipitate oft-theorized symptoms, such as to decenter, fragment, erode, and unmoor continuity of consciousness, knowing, and selfhood. Yet unlike theorizations of trauma resembling those the last chapter studied, there is a way in which Rankine's lyric refuses to come to grips with those psychic fractures and their ensuing paradoxes by redeeming or idealizing them. It does not embrace the "play of paradox" that for a theorist like Hortense Spillers ushers in an "insurgent ground" teeming with "representational potentialities."[42] Relatedly, it does not revel in the transfigural dynamics of paradox as a vehicle for metamorphosizing blight into bounty. Quite differently within *Citizen*, the protean, mercurial workings of paradox are shown to be part of the problem, and in fact one key technology of contemporary racism. Indeed, it depicts racist behaviors as parasitic on the very conditions of epistemic uncertainty often theoretically exalted, revealing them to be oppression's handiwork. Aversive racism in particular is suggested to succeed by opportunistically commandeering and thereby overwhelming its targets with a flood of unhinging paradox. While independently damaging to the victim, those bombardments are further suggested to be how racism cunningly armors itself, cloaking itself in the same haze of inconclusivity and unverifiability theoretically venerated, in order both to mask intent and to render those affronts harder to penalize. Far from an incitement to ethics, the admittedly paradoxical relays of psychic fracture and repression are not ennobling; rather, they consistently entrap *Citizen*'s speakers in states of stultifying indeterminacy and irresolution, wreaking havoc on things like perceptual self-trust, conviction, and integrity.

Many segments of *Citizen* therefore follow its speakers through protracted efforts to recover and restore the inverse of these paradox-riddled insignia typically deemed the watermarks of trauma. Yet far from being transported by trauma's ambivalent fruits, its speakers struggle to acquire affective and epistemic resources that have been violently shattered: to regain equilibrium, certainty, resolve, confidence, determination, and security. Such an arc arguably oversees the trajectory of Rankine's volume as a whole. *Citizen*'s closing passages are in many ways replete with expressions of plenitude, gratitude, contentment, and fulfillment, reflected in imagery like "the kiss the world offers," (154), "so soon we love this world," (155), and the final scene's description of a "sunrise [...], dragging the light in" (159). Small-scale odysseys of self-centering and reclamation are also related in numerous of *Citizen*'s compressed vignettes. Again and again, *Citizen* thus charts the steps—and quite methodically so—through which its speakers banish self-loss to agentively reassemble and reclaim a formerly disintegrated subjectivity.

This all raises the question of how to analyze these passages when things provisionally come and hold together—or when *Citizen* appears to welcome wholeness, noncontradiction, sufficiency, self-ownership, and integration, including the agentive pursuit of those faculties. How should we account for these clearings in the vast wilderness of paradox? How to explain its apparent attempts to reconsolidate and reoccupy the selfhood and community harmfully divided and dispossessed by institutionalized racism? How to decipher the almost normative tasks that it delegates to its readers, such as to compare and contrast the panoply of actions and attitudes adopted by its speakers? In ways that, here too, evade many categories made available theory, key passages in *Citizen* aspire and even appear to successfully actualize integrity of selfhood, perception, and knowing—and to ends that herald that perceptual fullness and plenitude as involving a lot more than a mere retort to oppression and its violence. Seemingly awash with independent value, these highly pregnant moments are clearly deserving of analysis; yet how do they square with *Citizen*'s eviscerating indictment of the manifold contradictions upon which the institution of citizenship depends?

Citizen's affinities with "A Room of One's Own" can help us begin to answer these questions. In echoes with Woolf's title, many scenes in *Citizen*'s montage encounter a speaker at home alone, wrestling in seclusion with agonizing physical and psychic damage. An intimate, private space (a bedroom) is similarly where *Citizen*'s final speaker awaits the sun. On the one hand, those confined spaces objectivize certain components of racial terror, whether the alienation wrought by trauma or slavery's literal captivity or instead forms of ostracism from public life. That domestic setting is also a reminder of the ways racism invades the intimate and the private, leaving nothing exempt from its reach. But on the other, these enclosures are suggested to provide nourishment and sustenance to *Citizen*'s many wounded speakers. Rather than pure symbols of subjugation, they can thus appear to encode the environmental conditions necessary to enable defiance of the snares of institutionalized oppression and its immobilizing paradoxes—and in the process to effectuate things like healing, self-integration, self-ownership, and the empowerment that is a prelude to action.

Woolf's titular motif—women's lack of "a room of her own, let alone a quiet room or a sound-proof room"—can help us further access these complicated links. Like many metaphors, Woolf's room condenses inconsistent meanings. On the one hand, as with *Citizen*, it lodges critiques, materializing the literal and figurative constraints enforcing women's subordination and exile from countless domains. Among other casualties, those exclusions are what Woolf blames for women's lack of a rich intellectual tradition, lamenting that "indeed literature is impoverished beyond our counting by the doors that have been shut upon women."[43] Along with frequent references to closing or barred doors, Woolf envisions women (mostly seated though often working) in many claustrophobic spaces: the "common sitting room" that limited women's "educat[ion] for centuries"; "the drawing-room or nursery"; the "bed-sitting-room" where the young "Mary Carmichael" writes her first novel; and simply being "kept in one room."[44] Those narrow, confining spaces reify the more abstract sociocultural barriers that deny women full access to rights, citizenship, the marketplace, and other such domains. And given that a room is merely one node in a larger edifice, that emblem's architectural referents could even seem to level critiques that are decidedly structural in their thrust and spirit.

But on the other hand, Woolf's title and everything it signifies also seem to prescribe a collection of normative goods and resources presented as indispensable to women's empowerment. It is most immediately suggestive of a type of haven for the aspiring female novelist: a refuge that might nurture and capacitate female creativity. But that sanctuary, returning to Woolf's reflections on "integrity," also kindles the self-conviction that Woolf identifies as withheld from women. So while conducive to an individualized undertaking like authorship, Woolf's room simultaneously conjures a matrix of legal-philosophical principles and optimums often deemed antecedent to any disenfranchised group's sociopolitical gains: objectives like independence, autonomy, property, education, rights, privacy, self-determination, dignity, and more.[45] With these resonances in mind, it is hard to escape the normative significance of Woolf's emblem: it marshals a prescription for what women require on an abstract legal and political level. Indeed, Woolf even connects that imaginary room to romantic and erotic freedom, surmising "For if Chloe likes Olivia and Mary Carmichael knows how to express it she will light a torch in that vast chamber where nobody has yet been." Quite a lot therefore hangs on Woolf's title, and that medley of associations *both* embeds negative critiques of patriarchy *and* affirmatively sketches the groundwork for women's uplift and equality.

Those normative stakes of everything telegraphed by Woolf's title play out in additional ways, including in the juxtapositions between the many diverse rooms described in her essay. Woolf emphasizes that the impact of any given room on its occupants is far from uniform or constant; instead, understanding the significance of any such space requires context-specific and comparative assessment. Contemplating the contrasting experiences of men and women upon entering any given room, she ponders why "rooms [can] differ so completely," whether to be "open on to the sea, or, on the contrary, give on to a prison yard."[46] No doubt, these sorts of reflections confront the irony that the very conditions imprisoning women might contain a recipe for their empowerment, in reasoning that subverts a simplistic equation between the domestic and captivity. But insofar as Woolf's title stages a paradox, that ambivalence begs for differential analysis and the drawing of context-based discriminations. Woolf's title leverages an abstract ideal the ultimate bearings and yield of which will only become clear upon its implementation—or when put into practice. While assigning a certain evaluative burden to the reader, the whole point is that the status of such an empty container will fluctuate situationally. And when divorced from specificity of content and surroundings, that symbolic room (i.e., unit in a larger structure) on its own tells us little if nothing.

In many ways, the implications of Woolf's room canvassed so far are unsurprising and even quite straightforward. But the phenomenological dimensions of that imagined space, including their relevance to the political objectives above, are more layered. Woolf's title here functions as significantly more than a mere metaphor inciting playful philosophical speculation; rather, it also indexes an aggregate of more material, practical, immediate, tangible, concrete, and other experiential furnishings and goods that Woolf characterizes as just as crucial to enabling a thriving women's literary tradition. As Woolf comments of great literature, "But when the web is pulled askew, hooked up at the edge, torn in the middle, one remembers that these webs are not spun in midair by incorporeal creatures but are the work of suffering human beings, and are attached to grossly material things, like health and money and the houses we live in.[47] Such a passage accentuates the corporeal substrate of otherwise conjectural notions, or the "material things" indispensable to literary production and political belonging alike. As Woolf writes, "The book has somehow to be adapted to the body." And throughout does "A Room of One's Own" insist that "the conditions in which women lived" cannot be bracketed or partitioned from the gestation of great ideas.[48]

However, that insistence on the bodily is only a fraction of what's at stake in Woolf's ruminations over integrity. "Integrity" is itself a construct with lofty philosophical connotations tied to autonomy and self-possession (i.e., "bodily integrity"), and we should certainly keep these links in mind. But Woolf's emblem also invites us to contemplate the perceptual ecology that might nourish the wider matrix of practical *and* philosophical ideals to which it alludes. In one sense, Woolf thus foregrounds the bodily-material embeddedness of ostensibly cognitive faculties, averring their importance to otherwise highfalutin notions like citizenship and rights. Rights and citizenship carry little meaning in the abstract, as Woolf suggests, detached from their real-world protection and enforcement.

But there are still other senses of grounding or embeddedness that Woolf's language of "integrity" demands that we take seriously. Such rootedness, first, seems to include the environmental conditions necessary to incur individual action and empowerment—or the circumstances capable of forging the integrity of selfhood and conviction that for Woolf are the backbone of authorship. We can pause to enumerate these conditions that presumably would be purveyed by such a dwelling. Offering reprieve from both the self-Othering inflicted by social marginalization and the incessant demands of subservience, such a stronghold is suggestive of qualities like resilience, continuity, predictability, fortitude, endurance, and stability—here, again, qualities carrying practical, economic subtexts. Just as important, however, those material resources are suggested to be enmeshed within a distinct perceptual fabric also necessary to procure experiential integrity: a fabric woven by features like presence, immanence, fullness, synthesis, harmony, completion, attunement, and, naturally, integration. It should be clear why such a fabric of knowing might breed results like self-trust, confidence, certitude, and, quoting Woolf, "conviction." Crucial, then, what Woolf's emblem seems to elucidate is how and why integration of knowing and experience are required to engender the conviction of selfhood (i.e., integrity) required to actuate principled action and engagement—whether at the writing table or in the streets.

Each of these dense interconnections above is for us enormously significant. Given this density, one might, to begin, take Woolf's room and everything it encodes as a striking counterpoint to the scene of reading often mythologized as the smithy forging modern critique and its refined operations. Woolf's emblem clearly prescribes a markedly different mix of ingredients than those usually imagined to fashion the critical spirit. Rather than the aloof, divided, self-abstracted consciousness enshrined as critique's factory and métier, that enclave implies a hard-won freedom from those badges of modern(ist) alienation and self-fracture. Catalyzed not by duality or fragmentation (psychic conditions long inflicted on subordinate populations), the ecology of critique Woolf conjures instead seems to transpire from a synchronization and harmony of sense, perception, knowing, experience, and, in turn, selfhood. Contra the itinerate, protean, elusive play of paradox, Woolf's image similarly seems to inlay the critical spirit within an abode furnishing guarantees like solidity, constancy, permanence, trust, and even normalcy, deriving if nothing else from such a room's ongoing, nonexceptional existence.[49] Insofar as Woolf's emblematic room thus offers a surrogate workshop in the critical spirit, that anatomy of critique certainly flies in the face of almost every orthodoxy regarding theory and its exceptional provenance.

Woolf's essay can therefore seem to envision the critical spirit to emanate from the exact conditions long singled out as critique's antithesis and (premodern, precivilizational) foil. Those conditions instead promoted by Woolf have, as we know, long been pilloried for jeopardizing, derailing, or otherwise impinging on the modes of critical discernment long claimed as theory's elevated calling. And from this angle, still other aspects of Woolf's appeals to integrity—what exactly is Woolf after?—can start to appear quite revealing, given how her image ultimately compels us to enter a space long repudiated by the intellectual formation of theory. The ecology of critique implicit in Woolf's title is certainly not incubated within the epidemic crisis, dissolution, and "problematization" long yoked to modernity as a consciousness, and it certainly does not romanticize that predicament. Relatedly, it does not glorify critique's ensuing vacuum of legitimacy, championing the ephemerality of those fragile if nonexistent foundations.

I've suggested that one way to make sense out of Woolf's iconic room is to read it as denoting a whole infrastructure of prescriptive goods and resources that might equip an alternate fabric of the critical spirit—although one usually reviled as the failure and dereliction of everything axiomatic in criticism and theory. But before returning to Rankine, Woolf's reflections simultaneously seem to do something even harder to grasp. I've tried—no doubt walking onto exceptionally thin ice—to affix that emblem to a constellation of almost normative prospects and proposals. But more than anything is Woolf's room a spur to reinhabit an intellectual terrain long foreclosed by theory yet that—as we have seen time after time—is absolutely crucial (indeed foundational) to theory's own self-image and chromosomal makeup. Put differently, Woolf's title above all begs to be taken as a placeholder for everything we are unable or reluctant to theorize: for everything missing and otherwise purged from theory and its environs. Those excised things surely include the many uncritical, antitheoretical Others the negative relief of which has allowed theory to acquire shape and purpose and meaning. Yet that emblem is also a repository of so many things we have tragically neglected to theorize, among others the fortitude and certitude motivating any feasible politics; the sinews that bind our theory to lived experience; and the perceptual awareness that harbors our most closely held convictions.

This is exactly why a notion like integrity can be so hard to talk about, at least not without running afoul of innumerable pieties and interdictions. However, Woolf's meditations also suggest why it is absolutely essential that we start to do so. Because another dimension of integrity lies with that quality's frequent role as a gauge measuring the difference between alternate claims to truth. Integrity is one metric for distinguishing truth claims that *are* worth supporting—from those that are not. It offers one angle on the gulf separating truths that *are* backed up by conscientious, thoughtful, principled, self-honest, and equitable considerations—versus those unmoored from such bearings. These evaluative dimensions of integrity also seem to underwrite Woolf's appeals to that notion. Yet those are the very sorts of distinctions that theory has had a hard time drawing, instead basking in its own perennial legitimacy deficits. Needless to say, a methodological inability to rigorously differentiate between countervailing truths—and with reference to some larger normative framework—can itself interrupt the lived application of any body of thought.

Central features of *Citizen* similarly beg to be understood as calls to reoccupy the sort of disavowed conceptual space summoned by Woolf's room. Attunement to "grossly material things" is another affinity connecting those two texts, and *Citizen*, too, strives to "[keep] the body front and center" (8). As for Woolf, however, that focus in *Citizen* serves less to assign some kind of paramount status to the body per se than to prompt a broader awareness of the partitions ingrained by strictly cognitivist and textualist modes of knowing. So although *Citizen*'s descriptions of bodily experience vivify the wounds of anti-Black violence, such passages simultaneously dramatize the perceptual-experiential cohesion, presence, and trust shown to enable action and engagement. So whereas cuts and illness concretize abstract psychic injuries, similarly do empowering, even pleasurable bodily sensations augur the instances of generative "coming and holding together" that orient Rankine's lyric. Indeed, those scenes of perceptual synesthesia and self-integration are repeatedly laden with overtly political implications, in particular by preceding, embedding, and otherwise verifying modes of social and political harmony and integration. The fleeting glimpses of bounty and conciliation that punctuate *Citizen* thus become referenda on the virtues of parallel vectors of sociopolitical enmeshment and togetherness, as those experiences serve *both* to actuate real sites of solidarity *and* to marshal almost normative precepts and goals. While impinged on by constant intrusions of psychic dissonance, even the fractures menacing Rankine's speakers only lend gravity and significance to those moments of respite from *Citizen*'s otherwise wrenching portrait of structural oppression.

Even many vignettes that incarnate aversive racism's intolerable tolls with particular vividness are thus either interjected with or build toward countervailing perceptions of bodily-experiential fortitude, wholeness, and fulfillment. Often, those eruptions of noncontradiction serve a notably adjudicatory and evaluative function—indeed clarifying when and how things can and should come together versus when they will fall drastically apart. *Citizen* opens with one speaker's flashback to a childhood memory in which a schoolmate informed her, "you smell good and have features more like a white person" (5). A kind of primal scene of racial subjection, the terms of that affront masquerading as a compliment reverberate throughout the volume, although frequently to prefigure a given speaker's haphazard efforts at self-reclamation. A segment shortly after the original epithet thus relates:

> An unsettled feeling keeps the body front and center. The wrong words
> enter your day like a bad egg in your mouth and puke runs down your
> blouse, a dampness drawing your stomach in toward your rib cage. When
> you look around only you remain. [...] [Y]ou pull yourself to standing,
> soon enough the blouse is rinsed, it's another week, the blouse is beneath
> your sweater, against your skin, and you smell good. (8)

Harsh and guttural sounds hamper the flow of Rankine's prose, intensifying
the visceral sensations aroused by such imagery: noxious smells, nausea,
chills, revulsion.

Yet those negative affects are ensconced within a larger progression that
crescendos toward self-recovery and repossession. It is not accidental that
many such corporeally charged moments in *Citizen* burrow inward, akin to
how the volley of sensations triggered by the "wrong words" bores into the
pit of the speaker's abdomen. Although recounting something painful, that
passage's overall trajectory enacts a recentering and rehabitation of perception in the most intimate, immediate, rooted sensations. In Rankine's terms
"pulling" together the self, the passage walks quite methodically through the
steps that bring about not only a perceptual rehoming but also other, less
amorphous badges of integrity—of selfhood and of knowing together. The
self-affirmation of "smelling good" carries distinctly epistemic implications
validating that speaker's perceptual authority and judgment. Yet such an
assertion simultaneously conducts what we might describe as a banishment
of the cognitive splintering and self-erasure perpetrated by the original assault: a working through of paradox. Such moments of perceptual synthesis
clearly function as rebuttals of the unverifiability and ambivalence that
act as ammunition within many cases of aversive racism. Indeed, *Citizen*'s
entire progression resembles a protracted effort to corroborate the otherwise submerged and indeterminate violence of those assaults. That violence
stems directly from such paradoxes, just as they are what strategically self-
immunize the underlying offense. As we have seen, precisely by breeding
attributional and other forms of ambiguity are aversive assaults suggested
to ward off moral and other censure.

At the same time, these scenes that reclaim the epistemic integrity of
the marginalized subject conspicuously fail to make recourse to a familiar
apologetics of paradox. Rather than to ransom the tenuous legitimacy that
comes with exclusion, they countermand that crisis with various moves to
reanchor both selfhood and perception. Recalling Woolf, *Citizen* can therefore seem to endorse an itinerary of selfhood that departs in countless ways

from the logic of negative valorization animating many theories of racial and other trauma. *Citizen*'s speakers are not christened with an uncanny clairvoyance that flowers from paradoxes of self-loss and division. Instead mourning those conditions, many of its segments respond by questing for something closer to a reoccupation of experiential intelligibility, coherence, presence, and clarity—and, by extension, self-conviction. Not accidentally does the above passage culminate with an exertion of effective agency: with the act of "standing" and facing "another week." Such a speaker's experiential self-mooring is thereby configured as a necessary prelude to other modes of action.

Similar odysseys of perceptual-psychic recentering and reassembly in the aftermath of racial trauma populate *Citizen*, also playing out within prominent of its formal features. This is one facet of Rankine's subordination of the lyric "I" to a second-person "you." As one verse reflects, "the worst injury is feeling you don't belong so much / to you—" (146). In some respects, that device epitomizes the sorts of warring tendencies that pervade *Citizen*, given how its beseeching "you" creates both immediacy and distance (like the pronoun "one"), both solidarity and alienation. Oftentimes accusatory, it inculpates the reader within the afterlives of slavery (much as many of *Citizen*'s snapshots occur in academic settings), while simultaneously cultivating intimacy. The many slippages and enjambments that surround and introduce that "you"' can also seem to amplify the self-dispersal, opacity, and fracture widely regarded as signatures of modern paradox. These effects of Rankine's second person speaker would clearly reward the application of trauma theory or a Du Boisian notion of double consciousness or an ethics of Otherness.

But from another perspective, that imploring "you," rather than apologizing for dispossession or loss, conducts one arduous feat of self-reincorporation after another. At certain points, this recuperative project is overt, such as in the verse below, where a process of self-hailing strives to localize what *Citizen* terms an "immanent you."

> To be left, not alone, the only wish—
>
> to call you out, to call out you.
>
> Who shouted, you? You
>
> shouted you, you the murmur in the air, you sometimes
> sounding like you, you sometimes saying you,

go nowhere,

be no one but you first—

Nobody notices, only you've known,

you're not sick, not crazy,
not angry, not sad—

It's just this, you're injured. (145)

With iterating and enjambed "you"'s, such a passage clearly negotiates self-erasure and dispersal. Yet those floating "you, you"'s also work to pursue and arrest an otherwise inchoate subject, exhibiting a yearning for something like self-identity. Building to a declarative statement regarding what "only you've known," that endeavor is cast as one with eminently epistemic consequences. While authenticating a state of injury, what also transpires is a lyric rescue and substantialization of a selfhood foremost imperiled by its protean liminality: a subjectivity ravaged by its lack of a stable, coherent, and viable identity. Rather than to esteem this fugitivity and elusiveness of selfhood, such passages from *Citizen* seem more accurately to decry the very conditions rhapsodized by theory. In such ways both steadying and solidifying experiences harmfully hollowed out by their marginality, a progression like that in the verse above also mounts toward an attempt to assign a label to that condition: to apprehend an experience of ineffability by affixing it with a concrete, authoritative diagnosis, stabilizing that unhinging state with such precision. Although *Citizen* wrestles throughout with what many would call the abjection of blackness, it simultaneously answers negation and denial with something like perceptual wholeness and abundance and conviction. In a strange way, it can thus seem to remediate abjection by actualizing self-presence, integrity, lucidity, and self-ownership. Hence, the question persists: which of these orientations within *Citizen* should one bless with interpretive priority? Should its encounters with fullness and synthesis outstrip its chilling portraits of psychic shattering and disintegration? What effect do those rendezvous with integrity and integration have on its trenchant critiques, as well as its many statements of outrage? Again and again, crushing despair is met by Rankine with what look a lot like practicable proposals for how to act: for how to translate awareness of such monstrosity into a constructive, serviceable, habitable practice.

Parallel to those glimpses of intimate, private self-reclamation, other sections of *Citizen* chart the forging of interpersonal bonds—and within locations understood to carry public if not fully political importance. One such episode occurs on public transportation and involves a shortage of available seating, revisiting Rosa Parks's legendary part in the 1955 Montgomery Bus Boycott. That scene's speaker, in response to racialized suspicion from other passengers, enters into an alliance with a stranger. Their connection is initially acknowledged only in unspoken and corporeal terms, as "shoulder to shoulder" "your cotton coat touches the sleeve of him" (132) and "you put your body there in proximity to, adjacent to, alongside, within" (131). Leading to a pact eventually cemented by the decision to "tell them we are traveling as a family" (133), that scene's arc builds from isolation to solidarity, from suspicion to trust, and from fracture to togetherness and inclusion. (Rankine's "within" is telling.) Memorialized in the symbolism of "shoulders" "touching," an experiential rootedness and conviction here again precedes and formalizes this compact, one freighted by Rankine's historical framing. While Rankine's sparse prose leaves much unspecified, the episode nevertheless depicts the background conditions that facilitate a judgement regarding something like integrity. Moreover, that integrity seemingly resides at the imbricated levels of the principled content warranting such an act of resistance in miniature; the unspoken motives and intent of those two fellow travelers; and the perceptual attunement that breeds such an accord. In turn, this allegiance brokered by a kind of perceptual harmony ultimately charts and climaxes with theory's conversion into action.

But how to explain such instances of cognitive-experiential integrity and integration, which orient many of Rankine's scenes even while being actuated formally and stylistically? How to put language to the sense of reconciliation and resolution that stems from such a scene—resolution that lies precisely with how its speaker transforms an incipient awareness of injustice into an exertion of effective agency? How to theorize the perceptual self-trust and wholeness that seem to secure conviction in a particular course of action? Far from isolated, sequences like the above recur throughout *Citizen*, as Rankine's speakers traverse the text's labyrinth of institutionalized racism—although only to discover something other than a total social fact. Many vignettes in *Citizen*'s montage converge not on immovable roadblocks or tragic lessons in erasure but on openings susceptible to intervention and empowerment. Yet how should we account for those albeit short-lived moments in which things do come together along lines that defy the axiomatics of theory? How to theorize those passages that appear to embrace agency and its fulfillment—and an agency at once causal, instrumental, and even pleasurable?

One way to assess these themes in *Citizen*—themes that, I have suggested, will quite likely oversee any political venture or plan of action—is to place them into dialogue with the many sources of paradox that also saturate Rankine's text. I have tried to argue—in terms meant to be relevant far beyond the purview of *Citizen* or of finite debates about the literary or for that matter of theory—that precisely the interplay between paradox and its abeyance, between epidemic fracture and momentary synthesis, between chronic uprootedness and insinuations of presence and immediacy, is crucial to the differential analysis too often shirked by many humanities and critical fields. We could certainly pause here—once final time—to rehearse the many worries that have rightly led so many to deride a prospect like "presence" as either naïve, idealized, an apologetics for power, or just plain wrong. But the point is that a text like *Citizen* does attune us to those provisional intermissions in the gravitational pull of paradox, and it repeatedly endows those clearings with the utmost importance. Those clearings also seem to display why acceptance of the limited harmony and conciliation that the world makes available is necessary to shepherd theory's (re)entrance into that world: to realize its lived application as a workable, meaningful, and potentially even revolutionary mode of engagement.

To conclude, there are still additional ways in which an integrative criticism might promise to replenish a depleted, strained theory. In reading both Woolf and Rankine over the years, I've recurrently been struck by the intimations of sufficiency and plenitude implicit in Woolf's emblem and that surface intermittently throughout *Citizen*, including its attempts "to end what doesn't have an ending."[50] Even though both texts monumentalize the excruciating violence of exclusion in their different ways, they are sustained tributes to the abundance overflowing within the here and now. There is a mood of adequacy, generosity, capaciousness, and fulfillment that both accompanies Woolf's spartan room and emerges throughout many passages in *Citizen*, to which I'll return. Neither idealizing the lacking nor taking refuge in a messianically deferred futurity, that presentism is far from a warning sign of complacency and quiescence, but rather returns us to the integral and basic, although without a suggestion of modesty or minimalism. More accurately, that sensibility is quite bold and visionary, and not only in eluding so many theoretical doctrines. Indeed, Woolf's conception of integrity is neither stripped down nor deflated nor concessionary, but rather the "holding together" and "holding fast" that Woolf promotes repeatedly culminate with assertions of "wonder," "rapture," and "reverence."[51] While an unobtrusive verb primed to escape notice, "holding" thus becomes the vessel of something like resplendence, just as it implies audacity, courage, and daring. In a related manner are the scenes of perceptual and self-integration that represent *Citizen*'s denouement overflowing with experiential attunement ("A breeze touches your cheek. As something should"), expectancy ("This brings on the moment you recognize as desire"), and almost overwhelming bounty ("Yes, and your mouth is full up and the feeling is still tottering").[52]

This brings me to one of my deepest concerns about the stultifying effects of paradox as a scheme for knowing and for making sense out of the world. More than anything, a thought experiment like this one ultimately asks whether that logic has not sanitized some of the richness and marvel and purpose from experience, whether of life or of politics or of literature, or at the very least throttled our ability to contemplate certain goods. It is no great secret that it can be difficult even for literary critics to put a label to (at least not without some embarrassment) phenomena like the bursts of splendor and satisfaction interspersed throughout *Citizen*. That avoidance certainly begs to be attributed to the constitutional unrest of theory, including the dependence of many humanists' self-images on a bottomless supply of exclusionary scapegoats. But while self-critical dissatisfaction can obviously be productive, compulsory discontent can also breed anxiety that becomes misplaced. And above all have expressions of clarity and coherence and integrity and resolve like those avowed by Woolf and Rankine elicited not rigorous theorization but instead doubt and skepticism, at times verging on the obsessive. This is worrisome, first, given the larger trust deficit today stalking democracy and, second, since conviction in the provisional sufficiency and completeness of one's own understanding is typically prior to action: a preliminary assessment regarding a given principle or idea or game plan and its fitness for implementation, for being brought to reality. This is part of the power of Woolf's room, with its poignant reminder that conviction and perseverance do not arise in a vacuum but instead are nourished by a broader infrastructure. So for me, there are real questions about whether the logic of paradox embargoes not only affirmation or construction as viable projects for theory but also our capacity to theorize the pursuits upon which just coexistence most fully depends. In short, that logic stymies a theory just as willing to account for its embeddedness, involvement, and application as for its exclusion, inconsequence, impossibility, and removal.

Such inklings of certitude, sufficiency, and fullness also overlay *Citizen*'s concluding scene, which occurs against the backdrop of "the sunrise [...] slow and cloudy, dragging the light in, but barely" (159). That scene finds its speaker in bed telling her partner about an exchange with a stranger in a parking garage prior to an appointment to play tennis. As she sums it up, "Our eyes met and what passed passed as quickly as the look away" (159). Within *Citizen*'s maze of microaggressions, that exchange is surely laden with racist overtones. However, the speaker explains that, rather than to "worry" her suspicions, she continued on to play tennis. Rather than aggrandizing that unnerving and offensive affront, Rankine's language relegates it to the "passed passed," with such repetition not only summoning the privileges of whiteness (i.e., the practice of "passing") but also denoting intentionality and choice.

Yet the speaker's stance toward that game is particularly telling. Assuming she played a match, her partner asks, "Did you win?" But the speaker rejects that adversarial stance in what are *Citizen*'s closing lines: "It wasn't a match, I say. It was a lesson" (159). Ambiguous, the phrase "being taught a lesson" certainly carries cautionary or even disciplinary resonances, especially given *Citizen*'s many parallels between sports and the legal system's institutionalized racism. Serena Williams's travails throughout have characterized tennis as another ordeal demonstrating the omnipresence of bias and discrimination. Nevertheless, *Citizen* leaves us with its speaker welcoming apprenticeship to that game's rules, despite their brokenness. As the finale of a taxing read, this gesture might be received as a sign of exhaustion or inertia or even futility. But with much left unsaid, the interjection of an emphatic "I say" again underscores the deliberate, overt tenor of that decision to reconstellate tennis as a "lesson," highlighting the agency claimed and inhabited in such response.

That choice further jettisons a mind-set that would reduce tennis to yet another theater of combat. There is accordingly a way in which this final speaker's combined attitude toward tennis and the parking garage incident repudiates the Manicheanism rampant within theory, and especially the stark either/or alternatives that demand the ontologization of structural paradox. Just as Rankine's speaker refuses to foist a deterministic interpretation on that game, she stops short of villainizing the stranger. To be sure, *Citizen* does conclude with that encounter, adding it to its long inventory of aversive and other assaults. But that final entry fails to compromise the sense of sheer beneficence and gratitude also animating *Citizen*'s terminal scene, which opens describing "the even breathing that creates passages to dreams" as the speaker's partner "wrap[s] his arms around me." Breath (like smell) is another embodied metaphor that circulates throughout the text, although usually to suggest asphyxiation, state-sanctioned violence, and other peril. Hence, such "even breathing" similarly recalibrates those negative associations. But that image does significantly more than either to issue another riposte to oppression or even to repossess a vital resource withheld from Rankine's speakers. Rather, it is within a state of reprieve from contradiction that *Citizen* leaves us: a state of harmony, fullness, stability, well-being, and equilibrium.

Far from sanguine or optimistic, such breaths of plenty amid a sea of devastation are what promise to revive the normative horizons of theory. In a world indeed ravaged by paradox, glimpses of noncontradiction can allow us to grab ahold of things when they are, lo and behold, going relatively well. Attunement to such factors can also help clarify when agency might prove serviceable, habitable, and effective. Precisely the interface between paradox and hints of integrity and integration can thereby foretell when and where critique will be productive, versus a disabling or damaging distraction. Such perceptual awareness can also lead to the drawing of meaningful and careful distinctions, including between our diverse array of critical objects, better tailoring our strategies to a more complex assortment of puzzles. Far from last, a wider tool kit and set of goals for theory might also enable us to trust—that is, to proceed with conviction—in the integrity of both our ideas and the project of their actualization. As both Woolf and Rankine suggest, foretastes of noncontradiction can be weather vanes pointing to the differences between varying claims to truth: between those backed by integrity versus those that fatally or disingenuously weaponize paradox.[53] Those albeit passing flares of synthesis and resolution can therefore begin to indicate how and when we should act, including how to go about constructively theorizing our ensuing practice.

Conclusion

What if faith in paradox has had the unintended effects of deadening thought, of depriving criticism of receptivity and responsiveness? What if that epistemology has ironically silenced the fullness and complexity of certain domains of experience, whether of politics, life, or literature? And what if it sets us up to gainsay some of the most vital resources that the humanities have on offer? This book has been motivated by a host of such worries: that obeisance to paradox prevents us from talking about things we dearly value; from theorizing principles and ideals we urgently need to promote; and from admitting those rare instances when things do in fact come and hold together, generating sustenance and purpose. Those shifting registers of integrity and integration are necessary to motivate, equip, and prolong a habitable, effective agency—including the agency of theory. The incredible sway of paradox has not only swallowed phenomena that aren't terribly paradoxical but caused us to squander if not actively eschew resources, faculties, objectives, and ideals that we should instead cherish and foster.

This account of those misspent horizons of theory has by definition been partial, being confined to a gestural chapter of a much longer book. What's more, I have proposed what I hope will be taken as merely one among many possible approaches to breaking the spell of paradox. An integrative criticism may offer one potential path to supplementing paradox with recognitions that its logic has foreclosed, but there are certainly others. In the end, it matters less what norms and agendas and values we propose than that we participate in some such activity: that we enter the fray of public debate, that we get behind and fight for something. Because, after the arduous labors of critique, and after the spectacular disclosures of paradox, there is also a need to theorize the constructive, goal-oriented, practical components of our engagements, intellectual and otherwise. And to better integrate those lived applications back into our theory.

Notes

Introduction: On Paradox

1 Wilde, *Dorian Gray*, 15.

2 Culler, *Literary Theory*, 4.

3 Wilde, *Dorian Gray*, 8, 20.

4 It has become a bit fashionable to ask whether the prevailing instincts within literary criticism and/or theory can best be summed up as a paradigm. However, Kuhn's formulation remains enormously helpful. For other reliance on Kuhn, see Moi, *Revolution of the Ordinary*; North, *Literary Criticism*.

5 See McCann and Szalay, "Do You Believe in Magic?"

6 Moi, *Revolution of the Ordinary*, 15.

7 Kierkegaard, *Fear and Trembling*.

8 The acknowledgments in Stephen Best's *None Like Us* open with a telling reflection. As Best writes: "A friend of mine (an editor at a major press) once gave me a bit of advice: every good book should be structured around a paradox." Best, *None Like Us*, 133.

9 Scott, *Only Paradoxes*; Brown, "Suffering the Paradoxes of Rights."

10 Bentham, *Anarchical Fallacies*.

11 Scott, *Only Paradoxes*, I, II.

12 Foucault, "Nietzsche, Genealogy, History," 95.

13 Russell, *Philosophy of Logical Atomism.*

14 Langer, *Age of Atrocity.*

15 Berman, *Modernism in the Streets.*

16 Žižek , *Did Somebody Say Totalitarianism?*

17 Fredric Jameson is also particularly prone to use those terms interchangeably. See Jameson, *Antinomies.*

18 Harcourt, *Critique.*

19 Lacan, *Ethics of Psychoanalysis.*

20 Butler, *Psychic Life*, 1.

21 Keenan, *Fables of Responsibility*, 138–41.

22 Searle, "Reality Principles."

23 Kuhn, *Structure of Scientific Revolutions*, 44.

24 Kuhn, *Structure of Scientific Revolutions*, 10.

25 Kuhn, *Structure of Scientific Revolutions*, 5.

26 Colie, *Paradoxica Epidemica*, 5–11, xv. It is telling that Colie's study was published in 1976, at the inception of an intellectual era this book investigates.

27 Latour, "Has Critique Run Out of Steam?"

Chapter 1: All That Is Solid Melts into Paradox

1 Berman, *All That Is Solid*, 13.

2 Marx and Engels, *Marx/Engels Reader*, 476.

3 Marx, *Economic and Philosophical Manuscripts.*

4 As Fredric Jameson clarifies, "the notion of contradiction is central to any Marxist cultural analysis." Jameson, *Political Unconscious*, 80.

5 Marx's account of alienated labor layers one paradox upon the next. As he describes it, "The devaluation of the world of men is in direct proportion to the increasing value of the world of things." In turn, "Labor's realization is its objectification." See Marx, *Economic and Philosophical Manuscripts.*

6 *Capital*, for instance, mines how "the absolute contradiction" intrinsic to modern industry "dispels all fixity and security in the situation of the worker." Marx, *Marx/Engels Reader*, 413.

7 Marx, *Marx/Engels Reader*, 406.

8 Mao, "On Contradiction."

9 Hiley, "basic contradiction."

10 Berman, *All That Is Solid*, 92.

11 Kornbluh, *Realizing Capital*, 122–23. For Kornbluh, the notion of "psychic economy" is the "crowning" example of Marx's personifications. *Realizing Capital*, 11.

12 Marx, *Marx/Engels Reader*, 413.

13 Marx, *Marx/Engels Reader*, 77, 317.

14 Marx, *Marx/Engels Reader*, 86.

15 Jameson, *Antinomies*, 6. Žižek is the poster child for this tendency to elide such distinctions. If anything, paradox carries greater analytic force than contradiction within Žižek's thought. See Žižek, *Sublime Object*.

16 Althusser, *Reading Capital*, 20.

17 Weber, *Political Writings*, xvi.

18 Weber, *Protestant Ethic*, 117, 119.

19 Freud, *Civilization*, 52.

20 Freud, *Civilization*, 38.

21 Nietzsche delves into the "workshop where ideals are manufactured" in order to lay bare the contradictory disconnect between "the cause of the origin of a thing and its eventual utility." *Genealogy of Morals*, 483, 513.

22 Ricoeur, *Freud and Philosophy*, 32.

23 Althusser, *Reading Capital*.

24 Rorty, *Contingency*, 39, 64.

25 Ricoeur, *Freud and Philosophy*, 19, 27.

26 Ricoeur, *Freud and Philosophy*, 27.

27 Althusser, *Reading Capital*, 16.

28 Ricoeur, *Freud and Philosophy*, 48, 27.

29 Althusser, *Reading Capital*, 16, 31.

30 Althusser, *Reading Capital*, 11.

31 Althusser, *Reading Capital*, 22.

32 Baehr, "Introduction," ix.

33 Baehr, "Introduction," ix

34 Harcourt, *Critique*, 27.

35 Koselleck, *Critique and Crisis*, 114.

36 Horkheimer and Adorno, *Dialectic*, 24, iv.

37 Foucault, "What Is Enlightenment?" 42.

38 Foucault, *Discipline and Punish*, 26–27.

39 Foucault, *History of Sexuality*, 33.

40 Foucault, *Discipline and Punish*, 82, 86, 76–100. As Talal Asad points out, genealogy therefore often proceeds with the unstated assumption that "hegemonic power necessarily suppresses difference in favor of unity [and] abhors ambiguity." See Asad, *Genealogies of Religion*, 17.

41 MacIntyre, *After Virtue*, 204–5.

42 Taylor, *Sources of the Self*, 11.

43 Taylor, *Sources of the Self*, 123, 227.

44 Butler, *Psychic Life*, 9. For Butler, such chronic self-Othering is importantly a precondition for ethics, as paradox effectively becomes a catalyst for ethics.

45 Lacan, *Ethics of Psychoanalysis*, 184, 192.

46 Berman, *All That Is Solid*, 21. Berman likewise concludes that "modernity can be said to unite all mankind. But it is a paradoxical unity, a unity of disunity: it pours us all into a maelstrom of perpetual disintegration and renewal, of struggle and contradiction, of ambiguity and anguish." Berman, *All That Is Solid*, 15.

47 Warner, "Uncritical Reading," 24, 20.

48 Koselleck, *Critique and Crisis*. For Habermas, it "separate[s] off" "spheres of knowing ... from the sphere of belief." *Philosophical Discourse*, 19.

49 Latour, *Modern*, 30.

50 Habermas, *Philosophical Discourse*, 128.

51 Koselleck, *Critique and Crisis*, 100.

52 Habermas, *Philosophical Discourse*, 16, 10.

53 Calinescu, *Five Faces of Modernity*, 10.

54 Berman, *All That Is Solid*, 16.

55 Berman, *All That Is Solid*, 328.

56 Calinescu, *Five Faces of Modernity*, 10.

57 Habermas, *Philosophical Discourse*, 8.

58 Rorty, *Contingency*, 78.

59 Calinescu, *Five Faces of Modernity*, 49.

60 De Man, "Literary History."

61 Berman, *All That Is Solid*, 159, 142.

62 Foucault, "What Is Enlightenment?," 41–42.

63 Lukács, *Theory of the Novel*, 32, 30.

64 Lukács, *Theory of the Novel*, 60, 41.

65 Lukács, *Theory of the Novel*, 84, 81.

66 Lukács, *Theory of the Novel*, 31.

67 MacIntyre, *After Virtue*, 22–125.

68 Taylor, *Sources of the Self*, 16.

69 Freud, *Civilization*, 38.

70 Ricoeur, *Freud and Philosophy*, 23.

71 Althusser, *Reading Capital*, 15.

72 Said, *Orientalism*, 3.

73 Spivak, *Critique*, 9, ix, 4.

74 Koselleck, *Futures Past*, 10

75 Asad, *Genealogies of Religion*, 18.

76 Asad, *Genealogies of Religion*, 19. As Hayden White similarly explains, "it is possible to view historical consciousness as a specifically Western prejudice by which the presumed superiority of modern, industrial society can be retroactively substantiated." White, *Metahistory*, 2

77 Asad, *Genealogies of Religion*, 23, 19.

78 Brown and Butler, *Is Critique Secular?*, 42.

79 Mahmood, "Religious Reason," 844.

80 Mahmood, "Religious Reason," 841, 844.

81 Keane, *Christian Moderns*, 6–7.

82 Keane, *Christian Moderns*, 21.

83 Hartman, *Scenes of Subjection*, 62.

84 Said, *Orientalism*, 8.

85 Asad, *Genealogies of Religion*, 52.

86 Chakrabarty, *Provincializing Europe*, 9, 7.

87 Chakrabarty, *Provincializing Europe*, 74.

88 *Chakrabarty, Provincializing Europe*, 6.

89 Chakrabarty, *Provincializing Europe*, 23, 45.

90 Chakrabarty, *Provincializing Europe*, 43; See Chakrabarty, "Postcoloniality and the Artifice of History," 21.

91 Chakrabarty, *Provincializing Europe*, 40.

92 Chakrabarty, *Provincializing Europe*, 254.

93 Scott, *Only Paradoxes*, 3–4.

94 Scott, *Only Paradoxes*, 17.

95 Scott, *Only Paradoxes*, 5.

96 Scott, *Only Paradoxes*, 11–12. Not coincidentally, Derrida is the one thinker found worthy of citation by Scott in this passage.

97 Scott, *Only Paradoxes*, 17.

98 Scott, *Only Paradoxes*, 4.

99 Scott, *Only Paradoxes*, 4.

100 Scott, *Only Paradoxes*, 16.

101 Scott, *Only Paradoxes*, 16.

102 Scott, *Only Paradoxes*, x, 4.

103 Scott, *Conscripts of Modernity*, 21.

104 Scott, *Conscripts of Modernity*, 129, 133, 163.

105 Scott, *Conscripts of Modernity*, 13.

106 Scott, *Conscripts of Modernity*, 129.

107 Scott, *Conscripts of Modernity*, 20.

108 See Appadurai, *Modernity at Large*.

109 Scott, *Conscripts of Modernity*, 170.

110 Scott, *Conscripts of Modernity*, 98.

111 Scott, *Conscripts of Modernity*, 189.

112 Scott, *Conscripts of Modernity*, 207.

113 Scott, *Conscripts of Modernity*, 20.

114 Scott, *Conscripts of Modernity*, 15.

115 Scott, *Conscripts of Modernity*, 46.

116 White, *Metahistory*, 4.

117 White, *Metahistory*, 37. In *Metahistory*, White develops his own account of modernity, here plotted according to a ladder of ascending literary-historical modes at the apex of which lies "irony," "a mode of thought which is radically self-critical."

118 White, *Metahistory*, 3–4.

119 Scott, *Conscripts of Modernity*, 163.

120 Scott, *Conscripts of Modernity*, 208.

121 Greenblatt, *Renaissance Self-Fashioning*, 1.

122 Greenblatt, *Renaissance Self-Fashioning*, 4.

123 Greenblatt, *Renaissance Self-Fashioning*, 3.

124 Greenblatt, *Renaissance Self-Fashioning*, 23.

125 Greenblatt, *Renaissance Self-Fashioning*, 18–19.

126 Greenblatt, *Renaissance Self-Fashioning*, 24.

127 Greenblatt, *Renaissance Self-Fashioning*, 32, 27, 31.

128 Baehr, "Introduction," xxxii.

129 Baehr, "Introduction," xxxii.

130 Gumbrecht, "Mythographer of Paradoxes." Those dual registers of paradox are symmetrical in their magnitude, even while they can only be fathomed through "the impossibility of their own mediation and reconciliation" (to again quote Gumbrecht). See also Johnson, *Intellectuals*. Johnson's first chapter on Rousseau is titled "An Interesting Madman."

131 Rita Felski asks about the "gender of modernity," exploring the complexities of feminism's relationship to ideas of modernity. See Felski, *Gender of Modernity*.

Chapter 2: Ontologizing the Paradoxes of Rights, or the Anti-legalism of Theory

1 See Brown, "Suffering the Paradoxes of Rights."

2 See Perugini and Gordon, *Human Right to Dominate*; Puar, *Right To Maim*.

3 See Mutua, *Human Rights*.

4 See the influential 2004 issue, "And Justice for All? The Claims of Human Rights," edited by Ian Balfour and Eduardo Cadava. Costas Douzinas's work on human rights offers another example of theory that defines human rights via their paradoxes; the first half of *Human Rights and Empire*, for example, is titled "The Paradoxes of Human Rights." Douzinas demonstrates how nearly every variant of theory necessitates the recognition that rights are paradoxical. See also Douzinas, *End of Human Rights*.

5 Balibar, "Is a Philosophy of Human Civic Rights Possible?," 311.

6 Rousseau, *Social Contract*, 71. Reinhart Koselleck focuses at greater length on Hobbes's formulation of the "logical paradox" underlying the social contract. See Koselleck, *Critique and Crisis*, 32.

7 Book titles like Bonnie Honig's *Emergency Politics: Paradox, Law, Democracy* or Chantal Mouffe's *The Democratic Paradox* evidence the depth of this dedication

to transformative paradox. See Mouffe, *Democratic Paradox*; Honig, *Emergency Politics*. In many ways, such thinking has been so thoroughly internalized as to oversee more mainstream legal scholarship like Bruce Ackerman's characterization of "constitutional moments" as "extraordinary" politics involving "rare periods of heightened political consciousness." See Ackerman, "Storrs Lectures." Among countless other examples, see Martin Loughlin and Neil Walker's edited volume, *Paradox of Constitutionalism*.

8 For the original quote, see de Gouges, *Le bonheur primitif de l'homme*, 23.

9 Fischer, *Modernity Disavowed*, 232–41.

10 See Waldron, *Nonsense upon Stilts*.

11 The text is largely a discussion of the 1789 French Declaration of Rights of Man and of the Citizen. See Bentham, *Anarchical Fallacies*.

12 Marx, *Marx-Engels Reader*, 42.

13 Marx, *Marx-Engels Reader*, 42.

14 Marx, *Marx-Engels Reader*, 43-44.

15 Baucom, *Specters of the Atlantic*, 55, 135.

16 Cheah, *Inhuman Conditions*.

17 Badiou, *Ethics*.

18 For Brown, *Citizens United* "more than merely unleashing market forces into democratic life" "advances neoliberal rationality's signature economization of law and politics." Brown, *Undoing the Demos*, 155–56. See also Brown, *In the Ruins of Neoliberalism*.

19 Puar, *Right To Maim*, 66.

20 Puar, *Right To Maim*, 87.

21 Golder, *Foucault and the Politics of Rights*, 50, 156.

22 Cohen, "Minimalism About Human Rights."

23 Kennedy, *Dark Sides of Virtue*.

24 The title of Ignatieff's 2004 *The Lesser Evil* also evidences this mind-set.

25 Ignatieff, *Human Rights*, 90, 95, 84.

26 See Brown, "'Most We Can Hope For …'"

27 Posner, *Twilight of Human Rights Law*, 23.

28 Posner, *Twilight of Human Rights Law*, 6-7.

29 Posner, *Twilight of Human Rights Law*, 12.

30 Posner, *Twilight of Human Rights Law*, 10. Posner cites both the *Iliad* and the intellectual historian Lynn Hunt's 2007 *Inventing Human Rights: A History*, a controversial study that recounts how the rise of novel-reading furthered human rights awareness. See Hunt, *Inventing Human Rights*.

31 Posner, *Twilight of Human Rights Law*, 148.

32 Given that Posner is on the faculty at the University of Chicago Law School, home to Martha Nussbaum, and the son of Richard Posner, who authored an albeit deeply dismissive yet nevertheless widely read treatise on "law and literature," this could make sense. See Posner, *Law and Literature*.

33 See Glendon, *World Made New*.

34 Historians have also set out to dispute overly flattering pictures of Roosevelt. For instance, Carole Anderson recounts how Roosevelt strategically abandoned W. E. B. Du Bois and the cause of the NAACP, threatening to remove herself from that organization's board when Du Bois sought to pursue African American civil rights as a matter of international human rights. See Anderson, *Eyes Off the Prize*.

35 Moyn, *Last Utopia*, 20.

36 Alston's comment is cited on the website of Moyn's publisher: https://www .penguinrandomhouse.com/books/234196/human-rights-and-the-uses-of -history-by-samuel-moyn/9781781689004/

37 See DeGooyer et al., *The Right to Have Rights*.

38 Tony Judt's *Postwar* estimates that Hitler and Stalin uprooted, expelled, and otherwise dispersed more than thirty million people. As Judt describes, in September 1945 the UN Relief and Rehabilitation Administration was still managing 6,795,000 people, with another seven million under Soviet authority as well as millions of homeless Germans. See Judt, *Postwar,* 29.

39 Arendt, *Origins*, 298.

40 Arendt, *Origins*, 297.

41 Arendt, *Origins*, 299-300.

42 Arendt, *Origins*, 302.

43 Arendt, *Origins*, 296-97.

44 Arendt, *Origins*, 295-96.

45 This is exactly the thrust of the accusation that Jacques Rancière, whom we'll engage in the next chapter, levies against Arendt. Rancière, "Who Is the Subject?", 302.

46 Arendt, *Origins*, 269.

47 Schmitt, *Concept of the Political*, 35.

48 Schmitt, *Concept of the Political*, 27. See also Strong, "Introduction," xxi.

49 Strauss, *Notes on Carl Schmitt*, 84.

50 Schmitt, *Concept of the Political*, 35.

51 Thinkers like Gayatri Chakravorty Spivak and Pheng Cheah enlist this language of the "enabling violation" to theorize rights. See Cheah, *Inhuman Conditions*; Spivak, "Writing Wrongs."

52 Schmitt, *Political Theology*, 13, 6.

53 Schmitt, *Concept of the Political*, 50-51.

54 Schmitt, *Political Theology*, 36.

55 As Cover further explains, the "infliction of pain remains operative in even the most routine of legal acts." Cover, *Narrative, Violence, and the Law*, 203, 236, 210.

56 Cover's other landmark text is the 1982 Supreme Court foreword for the *Harvard Law Review*, titled "Nomos and Narrative."

57 Cover, *Narrative Violence, and the Law*, 207-8.

58 Cover, *Narrative Violence, and the Law*, 208. Cover's critique of liberalism was packaged as a legal realism, and therefore also a characterization of legal positivism as a mechanistic application of legal rules.

59 Cover, *Narrative Violence, and the Law*, 209.

60 Schmitt, *Political Theology*, 13.

61 This section could easily include a discussion of Walter Benjamin's reflections on "mythical lawmaking" and "divine justice" in "Critique of Violence." See Benjamin, *Reflections*, 295.

62 Agamben, *Homo Sacer*, 174.

63 Agamben, *Homo Sacer*, 9.

64 Agamben, *Homo Sacer*, 10.

65 Agamben, *Homo Sacer*, 166.

66 Agamben imagines that he here remedies a lacuna in Foucault's thought, involving Foucault's failure to adequately theorize "the exemplary places of modern biopolitics: the concentration camp and the structure of the great totalitarian states of the twentieth century." See Agamben, *Homo Sacer*, 4.

67 Esposito notably vests his central principle, that of "immunization," with comparatively decisive status, calling it "the symbolic and material linchpin around which our social systems rotate." See Esposito, *Immunitas*, 2.

68 Agamben, *Homo Sacer*, 7.

69 Agamben, *Homo Sacer*, 130.

70 Weheliye, *Habeas Viscus*.

71 Agamben segregates testimony and other vectors of ethics from law and its adulterated channels. See Agamben, *Remnants of Auschwitz*, 12, 13, 20, 69.

72 Hamacher, "Rights to Have Rights," 349–50.

73 Hamacher, "Rights to Have Rights," 350, 351.

74 Hamacher, "Rights to Have Rights," 352.

75 Brown and Halley, *Left/Legalism*, 16. Costas Douzinas spells out other reasoning that often informs the theoretical opposition to legalism: "Codification transfers the responsibility of deciding ethically to legislators and resurgent religious and national fundamentalisms, to false prophets and fake tribes. In an over-legalised world, rules and norms discourage people from thinking independently and discovering their own relation to themselves, to others, to language and history." See Douzinas, "Human Rights," 199.

76 Best, *Fugitive's Properties*, 16.

77 Hartman, *Scenes of Subjection*, 119.

78 Hartman, *Scenes of Subjection*, 6. For another influential argument that accuses contract law of systemizing routine patterns of racial oppression, see Mills, *Racial Contract*.

79 Blackmon, *Slavery by Another Name*.

80 Alexander, *New Jim Crow*.

81 Hong, *Keywords*, 181.

82 Harris's landmark essay exemplifies such a style and method of reasoning. See Harris, "Whiteness as Property"; Lowe, *Immigrant Acts*, 24–25.

83 Weber, *Political Writings*, xvi.

84 Patterson, *Slavery and Social Death*.

85 Cacho, *Social Death*, 5.

86 Cacho, *Social Death*, 6, 9.

87 Cacho, *Social Death*, 23.

88 Cacho, *Social Death*, 13.

89 Cacho, *Social Death*, 8.

90 Cacho asserts the need for "refusing 'the lure of legibility.'" See Cacho, *Social Death*, 31–32. See also Dayan, *Law Is a White Dog*.

91 Weheliye, *Habeas Viscus*, 7, 11. For Weheliye's counter to Agamben's cynicism, see Weheliye, *Habeas Viscus*, 131–32.

92 Weheliye, *Habeas Viscus*, 76.

93 Weheliye, *Habeas Viscus*, 11, 13. Weheliye instead prefers "relationality" as a metric better geared to capture the incalculable, extrajuridical design of a justice that is clearly antinomian.

94 See Anker and Meyler, "Introduction."

Interlude: Anatomy of Paradox, or a Brief History of Aesthetic Theory

1 For Derrida's return to this text, see Derrida, *Psyche*.

2 Sears, "The Two-Way Text."

3 Plato, *Republic*, 64.

4 Plato, *Republic*, 269, 272.

5 Colie, *Paradoxica Epidemica*, 33. My gratitude to my colleague Jenny Mann for alerting me to this reception of Plato. Cognizance of that history helped to synthesize and spur many of this book's arguments.

6 Sidney, in *Norton Anthology*, 493.

7 Diderot, *Paradox*.

8 Wilde, *Intentions*, 2–3.

9 Wilde, *Intentions*, 10.

10 Greenblatt, *Renaissance Self-Fashioning*, 15, 31.

11 Butler, *Gender Trouble*, 175.

12 Wilde, *Intentions*, 10.

13 Kierkegaard, *Fear and Trembling*, 65, 89, 63, 99.

14 Kierkegaard, *Fear and Trembling*, 90.

15 Kierkegaard, *Fear and Trembling*, 81, 70. For a contemporary statement of this, see Žižek et al., *Monstrosity of Christ*.

16 Burke, *Philosophical Enquiry*, 57.

17 Jameson, *Postmodernism*, 44.

18 Relatedly does Kant's 1790 notion of art's "purposiveness without a purpose" stage such a quandary of how best to label art's mysterious influence.

19 Brooks, *Well Wrought Urn*, 3, 9.

20 Brooks, *Well Wrought Urn*, 7, 212–13.

21 Schiller, *Aesthetic Education*, 80, 74.

22 Schiller, *Aesthetic Education*, 63, 80. See Spillers, "Mama's Baby," 80.

23 As Jameson continues to explain realism, he insists on "the irrevocable antagonism between the twin (and entwined) forces in question: they are never reconciled, never fold back into one another in some ultimate reconciliation and identity; and the very force and pungency of the realist writing I here examine is predicated on that tension, which must remain an impossible one, under pain of losing itself altogether and dissipating if it is ever resolved in favor of one of the parties to the struggle." Jameson, *Antinomies*, 11.

24 Watt, *Rise of the Novel*, 130.

25 Slaughter, *Human Rights*, 45.

26 Ricoeur, *Freud and Philosophy*, 23, 27.

27 Lukács, *Theory of the Novel*, 41.

28 For an important overview of the "Quarrel between the Ancients and the Moderns" in the sixteenth and seventeenth centuries, see Calinescu, *Five Faces of Modernity*, 23–35.

29 Bakhtin, *Dialogic Imagination*, 35, 12.

30 Bakhtin, *Dialogic Imagination*, 7.

31 Bakhtin, *Dialogic Imagination*, 366.

32 Bakhtin, *Dialogic Imagination*, 7, 10.

33 Alexander Pope's 1733–34 "An Essay on Man" explains away "All discord, harmony, not understood." Thanks to Caroline Levine for helping with this point.

34 Ricoeur, *Freud and Philosophy*, 88.

35 Marcus and Best, "Surface Reading."

36 Jameson, *Political Unconscious*, 80.

37 Žižek, *Sublime Object*, 16.

38 de Man, "Resistance to Theory," 10.

39 de Man, "Resistance to Theory," 18.

40 de Man, "Resistance to Theory," 17.

41 Dean, "Art as Symptom," 22.

Chapter 3: Redeeming Rights, or the Ethics and Politics of Paradox

1 Moyn, *Last Utopia*.

2 Moyn, *Last Utopia*, 118.

3 Moyn, *Last Utopia*, 47, 85, 220.

4 Moyn, *Last Utopia*, 121.

5 Ross, *May '68*.

6 Moyn, *Last Utopia*, 106–7.

7 Moyn, *Last Utopia*, 121.

8 McCann and Szalay, "Do You Believe in Magic?," 436.

9 McCann and Szalay, "Do You Believe in Magic?," 440, 444. C. Wright Mills is typically credited for the notion of the "cultural apparatus."

10 McCann and Szalay, "Do You Believe in Magic?," 451–52. Such thinking is rife within radical democratic theory. For instance, Jason Frank, drawing on Rancière, exalts what he calls the vox populi, or the "inability of the people to speak in their own name" as "the ongoing condition of possibility" for democracy. Frank, *Constituent Moments*, 5–6.

11 Goodman, "Archives, Institutions, and Imaginaries."

12 See Nobel Prize, Amnesty International, https://www.nobelprize.org/prizes/peace/1977/amnesty/facts/.

13 For a recent example of such thinking, see Stanley, *How Fascism Works*.

14 Lefort, *Political Forms*, 299.

15 DeLillo, *White Noise*. The novel concludes by poking separate fun at the interrelated instinct to gaze upon apocalypse and disaster in expectation of redemption. In the aftermath of public fears of exposure from an "Airborne Toxic Event," the novel's conclusion nevertheless finds Gladney and his family dazzled by the sublime sunsets that result.

16 Scarry, *Body in Pain*.

17 Scarry, *Body in Pain*, 54, 27.

18 Scarry, *Body in Pain*, 14.

19 Scarry, *Body in Pain*, 29.

20 Balfour and Cadava, "And Justice for All?"

21 Eagleton, *Function of Criticism*, 99.

22 Žižek, *Did Somebody Say Totalitarianism?*, 101, 126.

23 Lefort, *Political Forms*, 246.

24 Lefort, *Political Forms*, 251.

25 Lefort, *Political Forms*, 256–57.

26 Lefort, *Political Forms*, 256.

27 Lefort, *Political Forms*, 260.

28 Lefort, *Political Forms*, 256–57.

29 Bakhtin, *Dialogic Imagination*, 67, 159.

30 Bakhtin, *Dialogic Imagination*, 285.

31 Bakhtin, *Dialogic Imagination*, 255–56.

32 Balibar, *We, the People*, 94.

33 Rousseau, *Social Contract*, 71. Reinhart Koselleck focuses at greater length on Hobbes and the "logical paradox" underlying his account of the social contract. See Koselleck, *Critique and Crisis*, 32.

34 Ricoeur, *History and Truth*, 253, 250.

35 Ricoeur, *History and Truth*, 261, 254.

36 Bosteels, "Introduction," 2, 4.

37 Bosteels, "Introduction," 11.

38 Bosteels, "Introduction," 7–8.

39 Bosteels, "Introduction," 9.

40 Honig, *Emergency Politics*, xv.

41 Honig, *Emergency Politics*, xvi–xvii.

42 Honig, *Emergency Politics*, xvi.

43 Honig, *Emergency Politics*, 3.

44 Comparable tensions inform Derrida's definition of the sign, which "represents the present in its absence" and therefore "is deferred presence." See Derrida, *Margins of Philosophy*, 61.

45 Derrida, *Writing and Difference*, 280.

46 Derrida, *Writing and Difference*, 289–90.

47 Derrida, *Writing and Difference*, 91.

48 Derrida, *Writing and Difference*, 83. For Derrida, this logic manifests in diverse tenets. Along with the conceit of an original unity or center, Derrida censures the privileging of speech over writing; belief in unmediated access to transcendental knowledge; and scientific positivism with its premise of objective truth.

49 Derrida, *Writing and Difference*, 91.

50 Notably, Derrida does not enlist the specific term "paradox" in "Violence and Metaphysics," although he does with frequency in his later writing.

51 Derrida, *Beast and the Sovereign*.

52 Derrida, *Rogues*, 39.

53 Derrida, "Force of Law," 929.

54 Derrida, "Force of Law," 931.

55 The original lecture was delivered in French at the University of Virginia. Derrida, *Negotiations*.

56 Derrida, "Declarations of Independence," 7.

57 Derrida, "Declarations of Independence," 8.

58 Derrida, "Declarations of Independence," 9–10.

59 Derrida, "Force of Law," 945.

60 Derrida, "Force of Law," 947.

61 Derrida, "Force of Law," 957–59.

62 Derrida, "Force of Law," 923.

63 Culler, *Theory of the Lyric*, 16.

64 Derrida, "Force of Law," 953–55.

65 Derrida, "Force of Law," 945–47.

66 Similar comments explain democracy in *Rogues*, as Derrida states: "To speak democratically of democracy, it would be necessary, through some circular

performativity and through the political violence of some enforcing rhetoric, some force of law, to impose a meaning on the word democratic and thus produce a consensus...." Derrida, *Rogues*, 73.

67 Although as one colleague pointed out, at least within Paul de Man's thought a paradox is not a very complicated figure.

68 Derrida, *Writing and Difference*, 108.

69 Anderson, "Cryptonormativism and Double Gestures."

70 Lacan, *Ethics of Psychoanalysis*, 259.

71 Lacan, *Ethics of Psychoanalysis*, 278.

72 Lacan, *Ethics of Psychoanalysis*, 279.

73 "Lacanian Works" (website), 1. http://www.lacanianworks.net/?p=236. Accessed Sept 15, 2017.

74 As Juliet Flower MacCannell puts it, "Lacan found the implications of Kant's maxims—the voice within—scandalously close to Sade's." MacCannell, "Facing Fascism," 73. See also Salecl, *Spoils of Freedom*.

75 Lacan, "Kant avec Sade," 56.

76 Lacan, "Kant avec Sade," 69.

77 MacCannell, "Facing Fascism," 72.

78 Lacan, "Kant avec Sade," 58.

79 Lacan, "Kant avec Sade," 75.

80 Lacan, *Ethics of Psychoanalysis*, 279.

81 Lacan, "Kant avec Sade," 59.

82 Lyotard, *The Inhuman*, 2.

83 Lyotard, *The Inhuman*, 4.

84 Lyotard, "The Other's Rights," 136.

85 Lyotard, "The Other's Rights," 136.

86 Lyotard, "The Other's Rights," 146.

87 Derrida, too, takes up the status of testimony, which he defines as "heterogeneous to producing proof or exhibiting a piece of evidence" to conclude that its legal incorporation "risks losing its value." See Derrida, *Sovereignties in Question*, 75, 68.

88 Lyotard, *The Inhuman*, 144–45.

89 Lyotard, "The Other's Rights," 145–46.

90 See Julia Kristeva, *Powers of Horror*.

91 Lyotard, "The Other's Rights," 143.

92 Pheng Cheah is another excellent candidate for a lengthier discussion here. See Cheah, *Inhuman Conditions*.

93 Butler, *Giving an Account*, 37, 39.

94 Butler, *Giving an Account*, 106. Butler attributes this recognition and structure of analysis to Adorno.

95 Keenan, *Fables of Responsibility*, 41.

96 Keenan, *Fables of Responsibility*, 138.

97 Keenan, *Fables of Responsibility*, 141.

98 Indeed, Keenan draws on Lefort only to double down on Lefort's earlier positions. See the assertion, "we need only add [to Lefort] that politics is here thought and experienced as a paradox, in the strictest sense, an ungrounded or aporetic predicament...." Keenan, *Fables of Responsibility*, 171.

99 Rancière, "Who Is the Subject?"

100 Notably absent from the essay is an extended confrontation with Marx, although Rancière explains that, in the immediate postwar era, "it was obviously impossible to revive the Marxist critique." Rancière, "Who Is the Subject?," 298. See also Rancière, *Dissensus*.

101 Rancière, "Who Is the Subject?," 301–2.

102 Rancière, Hatred of Democracy, 61.

103 Rancière, *Dissensus*, 33.

104 Rancière, *Politics of Aesthetics*, 13. See also Rancière, *Hatred of Democracy*, 58–59.

105 Rancière, *Dissensus*, 132, 140.

106 Rancière, *Dissensus*, 304.

107 Rancière, *Dissensus*, 139.

108 Rancière, *Dissensus*, 94.

Chapter 4: The Politics of Exclusion

1 For example, see Cheah, *Inhuman Conditions*; Slaughter, *Human Rights*.

2 Kennedy, "Critique of Rights," 181.

3 Matsuda, "Looking to the Bottom," 333. See also Williams, *Alchemy of Race and Rights*.

4 Matsuda, "Looking to the Bottom," 149, 161.

5 MacKinnon, *Feminism Unmodified*, 34, 39

6 The imprint of a thinker like Carole Gilligan is here vivid. See Gilligan, *In A Different Voice*.

7 Crenshaw, "Demarginalizing the Intersection of Race and Sex," 140.

8 Crenshaw, "Demarginalizing the Intersection of Race and Sex," 154.

9 Harris, "Race and Essentialism."

10 Matsuda, "Looking to the Bottom," 326.

11 Harris, "Race and Essentialism," 592, 608–9.

12 Crenshaw, "Demarginalizing the Intersection of Race and Sex," 153.

13 Crenshaw, "Demarginalizing the Intersection of Race and Sex," 153.

14 Crenshaw, "Demarginalizing the Intersection of Race and Sex," 44.

15 Crenshaw, "Demarginalizing the Intersection of Race and Sex," 5.

16 Crenshaw, "Demarginalizing the Intersection of Race and Sex," 37.

17 Notwithstanding that pervasiveness, of equal importance are outliers that do not short-circuit the translation of their theoretical insights into practical, viable stakes or strategies. One other example from the chronicles of feminism can *both* illustrate such reasoning's ongoing authority *and* its amenability to more outwardly normative interventions. As we have repeatedly seen, the structure of a paradox is to be contrary and thus exceptional to as well as frequently parasitic upon a doxa or dominant. "Family law exceptionalism" (FLE) within legal scholarship similarly leverages the critical potency of submerged exclusion in order to rethink certain of the assumptions that inducted family law as a field. Theorists like Janet Halley, Kerry Rittich, and Chantal Thomas have therefore questioned the conceit that the family is "special," autonomous, or otherwise "exceptional" relative to public or market-based domains, disputing that marginalization of the family. Further emphasizing its "invented" status, Halley and Rittich delineate the methodological goals of FLE according to what might appear familiar markers: as seeking to uncover (or, we could say, to give voice to) the interactions "ideology masks," in the process revealing contract and family law to be "mutually constitutive." Rather than "peripheral," the family, Halley and Rittich show, has been "central to the making of the modern global legal order" and especially to neoliberal governance. For Halley and Rittich, those recognitions demand a self-reckoning *within* family law as a field; hence, another itinerary of FLE is to expose family law scholarship's own "complicity with this backgrounding." But while such reasoning certainly shares many instincts with a thinker like Butler, its critiques of exclusion have not derailed a more normative outlook, among other things to propose a reconstruction of that academic field. Halley and Rittich, "Introduction," 755, 757.

18 Ju, "Women's Studies at Cornell."

19 Menand, *Marketplace of Ideas,* 85.

20 University of Chicago English Department faculty statement in response to Black Lives Matter protests, July 2020. Accessed July 8, 2020, https://english .uchicago.edu.

21 Guillory, "Sokal Affair," 485. See also Guillory, *Cultural Capital.*

22 Delgado, "Storytelling for Oppositionists."

23 Guinier et al., "Becoming Gentlemen," 5.

24 Dworkin, "Is Law a System of Rules."

25 Matsuda, "Looking to the Bottom," 324.

26 Edwards, "Introduction," vii.

27 Edwards, "Introduction," xiv.

28 Du Bois, *Souls of Black Folk.*

29 Gates, "Introduction," xxxii.

30 Gates, "Introduction," xxxii.

31 Stepto, *Behind the Veil,* 91.

32 Gates, "Introduction," xxxiv.

33 This Kierkegaardian sense of paradox importantly continues to inform schools of theology (such as radical orthodoxy and weak theology) influenced by theory. See Žižek et al., *Monstrosity of Christ*.

34 Kierkegaard, *Fear and Trembling*, 95, 97.

35 Butler, *Gender Trouble*, 55.

36 Butler, *Gender Trouble*, 182.

37 Butler, *Gender Trouble*, 182.

38 Butler, *Gender Trouble*, 7.

39 Butler, *Gender Trouble*, x.

40 Moi, *Revolution of the Ordinary*, 135.

41 Matsuda, "Looking to the Bottom," 335.

42 Gates, *Signifying Monkey*, 25.

43 Gates, *Signifying Monkey*, 35.

44 Spivak, "Subaltern Studies."

45 Kennedy, "Form and Substance."

46 When I asked Kennedy about what precipitated this shift, he explained, "Well, we were reading Derrida."

47 Gabel and Kennedy, "Roll Over Beethoven," 11, 6.

48 Gabel and Kennedy, "Roll Over Beethoven," 3.

49 Gates, *Signifying Monkey*, 27.

50 Gabel and Kennedy, "Roll Over Beethoven," 19.

51 Gabel and Kennedy, "Roll Over Beethoven," 8.

52 Gabel and Kennedy, "Roll Over Beethoven," 47.

53 Gabel and Kennedy, "Roll Over Beethoven," 12.

54 Gabel and Kennedy, "Roll Over Beethoven," 11–13.

55 Gabel and Kennedy, "Roll Over Beethoven," 186, 176.

56 Gabel and Kennedy, "Roll Over Beethoven," 14. Berry's music also inaugurated an unprecedented cult of the popular, indexing another common fear of the left intelligentsia: of losing touch with and thereby inadvertently excluding the very masses to whom one purports to give voice. Hence, one might read here a yearning to forge the Gramscian "organic intellectual." For such debates see also Matsuda; Bell, "Serving Two Masters."

57 McLeod, "Law, Critique, and the Undercommons," 253.

58 Butler, *Gender Trouble*, 177.

59 Butler, *Gender Trouble*, ix.

60 See Horwitz, *Transformation of American Law*.

61 Small, *Value of the Humanities*.

62 Young, "Idea of a Chrestomathic University."

63 Eagleton, "Slow Death of the University."

64 Deresiewicz, "Neo-liberal Arts."

65 Brown, *Undoing the Demos*, 196.

66 Sommer, *Work of Art in the World*, 98–99.

67 Kindley, "The Calling."

68 Young, "Idea of a Chrestomathic University."

69 For a discussion of whether postcritique represents a "humanist retrenchment" or "new scientism" or both, see Fleissner, "Romancing the Real."

70 For an overview of that dispute, see Ortolano, *Two Cultures Controversy*. See also Small, *Value of the Humanities*, 37.

71 Latour, *We Have Never Been Modern*.

72 As suggested, although Menand argues that antidisciplinarity is a bygone phenomenon, we will see that it continues to be alive and well. See Menand, *Marketplace of Ideas*.

73 Brooks, "Misunderstanding the Humanities."

74 Butler, "Ordinary, Incredulous," 30.

75 Rancière, *Emancipated Spectator*, 63.

76 See Allen, "Future of Democracy."

77 Spivak, *Death of a Discipline*, 26.

78 Brown argues: "to preserve the kind of education that nourishes democratic culture and enables democratic rule, we require the knowledge that only a liberal arts education can provide." Brown, *Undoing the Demos*, 200.

Chapter 5: The Pedagogy of Paradox

1   Brooks, "Introduction," 11.

2   Harris, "Whiteness as Property."

3   Sedgwick, *Touching Feeling*.

4   Anzaldúa, *Borderlands/La Frontera*, 99.

5   It is also a project of "breaking down the unitary aspect of each paradigm." Anzaldúa, *Borderlands/La Frontera*, 102.

6   Anzaldúa, *Borderlands/La Frontera*, 102.

7   Anzaldúa, *Borderlands/La Frontera*, 60.

8   For example, see Cheah and Robbins, *Cosmopolitics*.

9   Bhabha, *Location of Culture*, 13.

10 Bhabha, *Location of Culture*, 173, 28.

11 Bhabha, *Location of Culture*, 23–24.

12 Bhabha, *Location of Culture*, 23–24.

13 Bhabha, *Location of Culture*, 18.

14 Bhabha, *Location of Culture*, 185.

15 Spivak, "Righting Wrongs," 526.

16 Spivak, "Righting Wrongs," 532, 546.

17 Spivak, "Righting Wrongs," 558, 546.

18 Spivak, "Righting Wrongs," 524, 526; See also Spivak, *Critique of Postcolonial Reason*, 147.

19 See Sanders, *Complicities*; Attridge, *J. M Coetzee*.

20 See Brooks, "Misunderstanding the Humanities."

21 Eagleton, *Significance of Theory*, 33.

22 Stommel, "Digital Humanities."

23 hooks, *Teaching to Transgress*, 29, 31, 7.

24 hooks, *Teaching to Transgress*, 7–8.

25 hooks, *Teaching to Transgress*, 90.

26 hooks, *Teaching to Transgress*, 90–91.

27 Felman, "Education and Crisis," 19.

28 hooks, *Teaching to Transgress*, 67.

29 hooks, *Teaching to Transgress*, 68.

30 hooks, *Teaching to Transgress*, 79.

31 Dawes, "Why A Man Eats Another Man's Heart."

32 Dawes, "Why A Man Eats Another Man's Heart."

33 Gikandi, "Globalization and the Claims of Postcoloniality," 653.

34 Gikandi, "Globalization and the Claims of Postcoloniality," 630.

35 Gikandi, "Globalization and the Claims of Postcoloniality," 649.

36 This is a phrase Bhabha used repeatedly on a panel at the 2018 MLA meeting.

37 Bhabha, *Location of Culture*, 175.

38 Bhabha, *Location of Culture*, 35–36,

39 Bhabha, *Location of Culture*, 241.

40 Bhabha, *Location of Culture*, 175.

41 Leys, *Trauma*, 17.

42 Fassin and Rechtman, *Empire of Trauma*.

43 Of course, it also created the conditions for developments like today's opioid epidemic. See Quinones, *Dreamland*.

44 Gersen, "Socratic Method."

45 Scarry, *Body in Pain*.

46 Felman, "Education and Crisis," 18.

47 Langer, *Age of Atrocity*.

48 See Felman and Laub, *Testimony*, 6; Caruth, "Trauma and Experience," 8.

49 Caruth, "Trauma and Experience," 4.

50 Caruth, "Trauma and Experience," 10.

51 See Felman, *Juridical Unconscious*. We can recall a parallel insistence on the "necessary failures" of representation within Butler's theory of gender.

52 Kearney, *On Stories*, 5; Kearney, "Narrating Pain," 56.

53 Whitehead, *Trauma Fiction*, 3, 87.

54 Clift, *Committing the Future*, 182.

55 Clift, *Committing the Future*, 6.

56 Whitehead, *Trauma Fiction*, 140.

57 Scarry, *Body in Pain*, 30; Caruth, *Unclaimed Experience*, 5.

58 Craps, *Postcolonial Witnessing*, 2.

59 Felman and Laub, *Testimony*, 5; *Juridical Unconscious*, 8.

60 Felman, "A Ghost," 257.

61 Felman, "A Ghost," 155.

62 Felman, "A Ghost," 11.

63 Caruth, *Unclaimed Experience*.

64 Weheliye, *Habeas Viscus*; Snorton, *Black on Both Sides*.

65 Spillers, "Mama's Baby," 65.

66 Spillers, "Mama's Baby," 78.

67 Spillers, "Mama's Baby," 78.

68 Spillers, "Mama's Baby," 79–80.

69 Sharpe, *In the Wake*, 16.

70 Sharpe, *In the Wake*, 14.

71 Sharpe, *In the Wake*, 21, 17.

72 Sharpe, *In the Wake*, 22.

73 Leys, *Trauma*, 10–11.

74 La Capra, *Representing the Holocaust*.

75 Fassin and Rechtman, *Empire of Trauma*, 95.

76 See Fassin and Rechtman, *Empire of Trauma*; Craps, *Postcolonial Witnessing*.

77 *Unclaimed Experience*, 274.

78 Felman and Laub, *Testimony*, 197.

79 Felman and Laub, *Testimony*, 57.

80 Fogarasi, "On Second Front Doors."

81 See Craps, *Postcolonial Witnessing*, 2.

82 See Fassin and Rechtman, *Empire of Trauma*, 19.

83 For Toril Moi, this is broadly true of theory descended from post-Saussurean linguistics; such theory's preoccupation with the arbitrariness and gaps separating word from meaning foregrounds chronic epistemological uncertainty at the expense of attention to "action and responsibility." See Moi, *Revolution of the Ordinary*, 13, 135.

84 It is this parasitism of trauma on a repressive status quo that often renders witnessing performative. See Leys, *Trauma*.

85 Scott, "How the Right Weaponized Free Speech."

86 Brown, *In the Ruins of Neoliberalism*.

87 "Microaggression," Wikipedia; January 2021. https://en.wikipedia.org/wiki/Microaggression.

88 Gersen, "Socratic Method," 2340.

89 Lasch, *Culture of Narcissism*.

Interlude: A Different Kind of Theory

1   Felski, *Limits of Critique.*
2   Latour, "Has Critique Run out of Steam?"
3   See Lesjak, "Reading Dialectically."
4   For the "new incrementalism," see Love, "Small Change." See also Williams, "New Modesty."
5   For the phrase "the new academic downsizing," see Hensley, "Curatorial Reading."
6   Marcus and Best, "Surface Reading."

Chapter 6: What Holds Things Together

1   Woolf, "Room of One's Own," 72–73.
2   As discussed, Rosalie Colie refers to paradox as a "hall of mirrors." Colie, *Paradoxica Epidemica.*
3   This book's appeals are influenced by Bernard Williams's work on integrity, and especially his efforts to separate notions of truth from truthfulness. See Williams, *Truth and Truthfulness.*
4   See Connolly, *Why I Am Not a Secularist,* 26.
5   As I hope is also clear, this chapter's investment in noncontradiction and synthesis by no means proposes a reversion to the linear construction of analytic philosophy.
6   Povinelli, *Cunning of Recognition,* 3.
7   Puar, *Right To Maim,* 70–71.
8   Puar, *Right To Maim,* xviii.
9   Puar, *Right To Maim,* 75, 82.
10 Puar, *Right To Maim,* 81.
11 Puar, *Right To Maim,* 75–76.
12 On Horkheimer and Adoro, see Habermas, *Philosophical Discourse.*
13 Kurnick, "A Few Lies," 363.
14 Among other recent interventions, see Anderson, "Therapeutic Criticism," 322, 325; Williams, "New Modesty"; Sedgwick, *Touching Feeling.*
15 Davis, *Enabling Acts,* 15, 19.
16 Davis, *Enabling Acts,* 251.
17 Davis, *Enabling Acts,* 15.
18 Davis also emphasizes certain differences between disability and civil rights demonstrations.
19 LeBrecht and Newnham, *Crip Camp.*
20 Davis, *Enabling Acts,* 79.
21 Davis, *Enabling Acts,* 56.
22 Davis, *Enabling Acts,* 5.

23 Davis, *Enabling Acts*, 245–46.

24 Davis, *Enabling Acts*, 251.

25 Davis, *Enabling Acts*, 238–39.

26 Davis, *Enabling Acts*, 251.

27 Scott, *Only Paradoxes*, 168–69, 175.

28 Scott, *Only Paradoxes*, 175.

29 Scott, *Only Paradoxes*, 89.

30 Scott, *Only Paradoxes*, 171.

31 Scott, *Only Paradoxes*, 168.

32 Scott, *Only Paradoxes*, 168.

33 Muñoz, *Cruising Utopia*, 115, 292, 327.

34 Scott, *Only Paradoxes*, 174.

35 Scott, *Only Paradoxes*, 172.

36 Mansbridge, *Why We Lost the ERA*.

37 Mansbridge, *Why We Lost the ERA*, 47, 59.

38 Mansbridge, *Why We Lost the ERA*, 117.

39 For a discussion of these dynamics, see Levine, "From Nation to Network."

40 Woolf, "Room of One's Own," 89.

41 Rankine, *Citizen*. See text notes below.

42 Spillers, "Mama's Baby," 79–80.

43 Woolf, "Room of One's Own," 52, 83. Woolf similarly presents herself as having "thought how unpleasant it is to be locked out; and thought how it is worse perhaps to be locked in; and thinking of the safety and prosperity of the one sex and of the poverty and insecurity of the other and of the effect of tradition and of the lack of tradition upon the mind of a writer...." Woolf, "Room of One's Own," 24.

44 Woolf, "Room of One's Own," 67, 86, 94, 83.

45 Woolf, "Room of One's Own," 22–23.

46 Woolf, "Room of One's Own," 87.

47 Woolf, "Room of One's Own," 42.

48 Woolf, "Room of One's Own," 41.

49 The temptation to dismiss these distinctions as essentializations of the masculine versus feminine is certainly one indicator of the extent to which Woolf's vision eludes available conceptual schema.

50 Rankine, *Citizen*, 159.

51 Woolf, "Room of One's Own," 72.

52 Rankine, *Citizen*, 154, 151, 153.

53 For this sort of distinction, see Williams, *Truth and Truthfulness*.

Bibliography

Ackerman, Bruce. "The Storrs Lectures: Discovering the Constitution." *Yale Law Journal* 93 (1984): 1013–72.

Agamben, Giorgio. *Homo Sacer: Sovereign Power and Bare Life*. Translated by Daniel Heller-Roazen. Stanford, CA: Stanford University Press, 1995.

Agamben, Giorgio. *Remnants of Auschwitz: The Witness and the Archive*. Translated by Daniel Heller-Roazen. New York: Zone, 1999.

Alexander, Michelle. *The New Jim Crow: Mass Incarceration in the Age of Color Blindness*. New York: New Press, 2010.

Allen, Danielle. "The Future of Democracy." *Humanities* 37, no. 2 (Spring 2016).

Althusser, Louis. *Reading Capital: The Complete Edition*. Translated by Ben Brewster and David Fernbach. New York: Verso, 2015.

Anderson, Amanda. "Cryptonormativism and Double Gestures: The Politics of Post-Structuralism." *Cultural Critique* 21 (Spring 1992): 63–95.

Anderson, Amanda. "Therapeutic Criticism." *Novel* 50, no. 3 (2017): 321–28.

Anderson, Carole. *Eyes Off the Prize*. New York: Cambridge University Press, 2003.

Anker, Elizabeth, and Bernadette Meyler. Introduction to *New Directions in Law and Literature*. New York: Oxford University Press, 2017.

Anzaldúa, Gloria. *Borderlands/La Frontera*. 4th ed. San Francisco: Aunt Lute, 2012. First published 1987.

Appadurai, Arjun. *Modernity at Large: Cultural Dimensions of Globalization*. Minneapolis: University of Minnesota Press, 1996.

Arendt, Hannah. *The Origins of Totalitarianism*. New York: Harvest, 1968. First published 1951 by Harcourt, Brace.

Asad, Talal. *Genealogies of Religion: Discipline and Reasons of Power in Christianity and Islam*. Baltimore: Johns Hopkins University Press, 1993.

Attridge, Derek. *J. M Coetzee and the Ethics of Reading: Literature in the Event*. Chicago: University of Chicago Press, 2004.

Badiou, Alain. *Ethics: An Essay on the Understanding of Evil*. Translated by Peter Hallward. New York: Verso, 1993.

Badiou, Alain, Pierre Bourdieu, Judith Butler, et al. *What Is a People?* Translated by Jody Gladding. New York: Columbia University Press, 2016.

Baehr, Peter. Introduction to *The Protestant Ethic and the "Spirit" of Capitalism and Other Writings*, by Max Weber. New York: Penguin Classics, 2002. First published in English in 1930 by Scribner.

Balfour, Ian and Eduardo Cadava. Introduction: "And Justice for All? The Claims of Human Rights." *South Atlantic Quarterly* 103, nos. 2–3 (Spring/Summer 2004).

Balibar, Etienne. "Is a Philosophy of Human Civic Rights Possible?" *South Atlantic Quarterly* 103, nos. 2–3 (Spring/Summer 2004): 312–22.

Balibar, Etienne. *We, the People of Europe? Reflections on Transnational Citizenship*. Translated by James Swenson. Princeton, NJ: Princeton University Press, 2003.

Bakhtin, Mikhail. *The Dialogic Imagination: Four Essays*. Edited by Michael Holquist. Translated by Caryl Emerson and Michael Holquist. Austin: University of Texas Press, 1981. First published 1975.

Baucom, Ian. *Specters of the Atlantic: Finance Capital, Slavery, and the Philosophy of History*. Durham, NC: Duke University Press, 2005.

Bell, Derrick. "Serving Two Masters: Integration Ideals and Client Interests in School Desegregation Litigation." *Yale Law Journal* 85, no. 4 (March 1976): 470–516.

Benjamin, Walter. "Critique of Violence." In *Reflections: Essays, Aphorisms, Autobiographical Writings*, edited by Peter Demetz, 277–300. Translated by Edmund Jephcott. New York: Schocken, 1978.

Bentham, Jeremy. *Anarchical Fallacies: Being an Examination of the Declaration of Rights Issued During the French Revolution*. First published 1796.

Berman, Marshall. *All That Is Solid Melts into Air: The Experience of Modernity*. New York: Penguin, 1988. First published 1982 by Simon and Schuster.

Berman, Marshall. *Modernism in the Streets: A Life and Times in Essays*. Edited by David Marcus. New York: Verso, 2017.

Best, Stephen. *The Fugitive's Properties: Law and the Poetics of Possession*. Chicago: University of Chicago Press, 2004.

Best, Stephen. *None Like Us: Blackness, Belonging, and Aesthetic Life*. Durham, NC: Duke University Press, 2018.

Bhabha, Homi. *The Location of Culture*. New York: Routledge, 1994.

Blackmon, Douglas A. *Slavery by Another Name: The Re-Enslavement of Black Americans from the Civil War to World War II*. New York: Doubleday, 2008.

Bosteels, Bruno. "This People Which Is Not One." In *What Is a People?* by Alain Badiou, Pierre Bourdieu, Judith Butler, et al. New York: Columbia University Press, 2016.

Brooks, Cleanth. *The Well Wrought Urn: Studies in the Structures of Poetry*. New York: Harcourt, 1942.

Brooks, Peter. Introduction to *The Humanities and Public Life*. Edited by Peter Brooks with Hilary Jewett. New York: Fordham University Press, 2014.

Brooks, Peter. "Misunderstanding the Humanities." *Chronicle Review*. December 15, 2014.

Brooks, Peter. *Troubling Confessions: Speaking Guilt in Law and Literature*. Chicago: University of Chicago Press, 2000.

Brown, Wendy. *In the Ruins of Neoliberalism: The Rise of Antidemocratic Politics in the West*. New York: Columbia University Press, 2019.

Brown, Wendy. "'The Most We Can Hope For ...': Human Rights and the Politics of Fatalism." *South Atlantic Quarterly* 103, nos. 2–3 (Spring/Summer 2004): 451–64.

Brown, Wendy. "Suffering the Paradoxes of Rights." In *Left Legalism/Left Critique*, edited by Wendy Brown and Janet Halley, 420–34. Durham, NC: Duke University Press, 2002.

Brown, Wendy. *Undoing the Demos: Neoliberalism's Stealth Revolution*. New York: Zone, 2015.

Brown, Wendy, and Judith Butler. Preface to *Is Critique Secular?: Blasphemy, Injury, and Free Speech*. New York: Fordham University Press, 2013.

Brown, Wendy, and Janet Halley. *Left Legalism/Left Critique*. Durham, NC: Duke University Press, 2002.

Burke, Edmund. *A Philosophical Enquiry into the Origin of Our Ideas of the Sublime and Beautiful*. Oxford: Oxford World's Classics, 1990. First published 1757 by R. and J. Dodsley.

Butler, Judith. *Gender Trouble: Feminism and the Subversion of Identity*. New York: Routledge, 1990.

Butler, Judith. *Giving an Account of Oneself*. New York: Fordham University Press, 2005.

Butler, Judith. "Ordinary, Incredulous." In *The Humanities and Public Life*, edited by Peter Brooks with Hilary Jewett, 15–38. New York: Fordham University Press, 2014.

Butler, Judith. *The Psychic Life of Power: Theories in Subjection*. Stanford, CA: Stanford University Press, 1997.

Cacho, Lisa Marie. *Social Death: Racialized Rightlessness and the Criminalization of the Unprotected*. New York: NYU Press, 2012.

Calinescu, Matei. *Five Faces of Modernity: Modernism, Avant-Garde, Decadence, Kitsch, Postmodernism*. Durham, NC: Duke University Press, 1987. First published 1977 by Indiana University Press.

Caruth, Cathy. "Trauma and Experience: Introduction." *Trauma: Explorations in Memory*. Baltimore: Johns Hopkins University Press, 1995.

Caruth, Cathy. *Unclaimed Experience: Trauma, Narrative, and History*. Baltimore: Johns Hopkins University Press, 1996.

Chakrabarty, Dipesh. "Postcoloniality and the Artifice of History: Who Speaks for 'Indian' Pasts?" *Representations* 37 (Winter 1992): 1–26.

Chakrabarty, Dipesh. *Provincializing Europe: Postcolonial Thought and Historical Difference*. Princeton, NJ: Princeton University Press, 2000.

Cheah, Pheng. *Inhuman Conditions: On Cosmopolitanism and Human Rights*. Cambridge, MA: Harvard University Press, 2006.

Cheah, Pheng, and Bruce Robbins, *Cosmopolitics: Thinking Beyond the Nation*. Minneapolis: Minnesota University Press, 1998.

Clift, Sarah. *Committing the Future to Memory: History, Experience, Trauma*. New York: Fordham University Press, 2014.

Cohen, Joshua. "Minimalism About Human Rights: The Most We Can Hope For?" *Journal of Political Philosophy* 12, no. 2 (June 2004): 190–213.

Colie, Rosalie L. *Paradoxica Epidemica: The Renaissance Tradition of Paradox*. Hamden, CT: Archon, 1976.

Connolly, William E. *Why I Am Not a Secularist*. Minneapolis: University of Minnesota Press, 1999.

Cover, Robert. *Narrative, Violence, and the Law: The Essays of Robert Cover*. Edited by Martha Minow, Michael Ryan, and Austin Sarat. Ann Arbor: University of Michigan Press, 1995.

Cover, Robert. "Nomos and Narrative." *Harvard Law Review* 97, no. 4 (1983).

Craps, Stef. *Postcolonial Witnessing: Trauma Out of Bounds*. New York: Palgrave, 2013.

Crenshaw, Kimberlé. "Demarginalizing the Intersection of Race and Sex: A Black Feminist Critique of Antidiscrimination Doctrine, Feminist Theory and Antiracist Politics." *University of Chicago Legal Forum* 139 (1989): 139–67.

Culler, Jonathan. *Literary Theory: A Very Short Introduction*. New York: Oxford University Press, 1997.

Culler, Jonathan. *Theory of the Lyric*. Cambridge, MA: Harvard University Press, 2015.

Davis, Lennard J. *Enabling Acts: The Hidden Story of How the Americans With Disabilities Act Gave the Largest US Minority Its Rights*. Boston: Beacon, 2015.

Dawes, James. "'Why A Man Eats Another Man's Heart,'" *CNN*, May 16, 2013: http://www.cnn.com/2013/05/15/opinion/dawes-syria-video/.

Dayan, Colin. *The Law Is a White Dog: How Legal Rituals Make and Unmake Persons*. Princeton, NJ: Princeton University Press, 2011.

Dean, Tim. "Art as Symptom: Zizek and the Ethics of Psychoanalytic Criticism." *diacritics* 32, no. 2 (2002).

DeGooyer, Stephanie, Alastair Hunt, Lida Maxwell, and Samuel Moyn. *The Right to Have Rights*. Brooklyn, NY: Verso, 2018.

De Gouges, Olympe. *Le bonheur primitif de l'homme*. Paris, 1788.

Delgado, Richard. "Storytelling for Oppositionists: A Plea for Narrative." *Michigan Law Review* 87, no. 8 (August 1989): 2411–41.

DeLillo, Don. *White Noise*. New York: Viking, 1985.

de Man, Paul. "Literary History and Literary Modernity." *Daedalus* 99, no. 2 (Spring 1970): 384–404.de Man, Paul. "The Resistance to Theory." *Yale French Studies* 63 (1982): 3–20.

Deresiewicz, William. "The Neo-liberal Arts." *The Atlantic*, September 2015.

Derrida, Jacques. *The Beast and the Sovereign*. Translated by Geoffrey Bennington. Chicago: University of Chicago Press, 2009.

Derrida, Jacques. "Declarations of Independence." *New Political Science* 15 (Summer 1986): 7–16. Reprinted in *Negotiations: Interventions and Interviews, 1971–2001*. Edited by Elizabeth Rottenberg. Stanford, CA: Stanford University Press, 2002.

Derrida, Jacques. "Force of Law." Translated by Mary Quaintance. *Cardozo Law Review* 11 (1989–90): 920–1045.

Derrida, Jacques. *Margins of Philosophy, a Derrida Reader: Between the Blinds*. Translated by Alan Bass. Chicago: University of Chicago Press, 1985.

Derrida, Jacques. *Psyche: Inventions of the Other*. Stanford, CA: Stanford University Press, 1987.

Derrida, Jacques. *Rogues: Two Essays on Reason*. Translated by Pascale-Anne Brault and Michael Naas. Stanford, CA: Stanford University Press, 2005.

Derrida, Jacques. *Sovereignties in Question: The Poetics of Paul Celan*. New York: Fordham University Press, 2005.

Derrida, Jacques. *Writing and Difference*. Translated by Alan Bass. Chicago: University of Chicago Press, 1978.

Diderot, Denis. *The Paradox of the Actor (Paradoxe sur le comédien)*. Translated by Walter Herries Pollok. Createspace, 2015. First published 1830.

Douzinas, Costas. *The End of Human Rights*. Oxford: Hart, 2000.

Douzinas, Costas. "Human Rights, Humanism and Desire." *Angelaki* 6, no. 3 (December 2001): 183–206.

Douzinas, Costas. *Human Rights and Empire: The Political Philosophy of Cosmopolitanism*. New York: Oxford Cavendish, 2007.

Dworkin, Ronald. "Is Law a System of Rules." *Philosophy of Law* 52 (1977).

Edwards, Brent Hayes. Introduction to *The Souls of Black Folk*, by W. E. B. Du Bois. Oxford World's Classics edition. New York: Oxford University Press, 2007. First published 1903.

Eagleton, Terry. *The Function of Criticism*. New York: Verso, 2005. First published 1984.

Eagleton, Terry. *The Significance of Theory*. Cambridge, MA: Blackwell, 1990.

Eagleton, Terry. "The Slow Death of the University." *Chronicle Review*. April 6, 2015.

Esposito, Roberto. *Immunitas: The Protection and Negation of Life*. Malden, MA: Polity, 2011.

Fassin, Didier, and Richard Rechtman. *The Empire of Trauma: An Inquiry into the Condition of Victimhood*. Princeton, NJ: Princeton University Press, 2009.

Felman, Shoshana. "Education and Crisis, or the Vicissitudes of Teaching, "*American Imago* 48, no. 1 (1991).

Felman, Shoshana. *The Juridical Unconscious: Trials and. Traumas in the Twentieth Century*. Cambridge, MA: Harvard University Press, 2002.

Felman, Shoshana, and Dori Laub. *Testimony: Crises of Witnessing in Literature, Psychoanalysis, and History*. New York: Routledge, 1992.

Felski, Rita. *The Gender of Modernity*. Cambridge, MA: Harvard University Press, 1995.

Felski, Rita. *The Limits of Critique*. Chicago: University of Chicago Press, 2015.

Fischer, Sibylle. *Modernity Disavowed: Haiti and the Cultures of Slavery in the Age of Revolution*. Durham, NC: Duke University Press, 2004.

Fleissner, Jennifer. "Romancing the Real: Bruno Latour, Ian McEwan, and Postcritical Monism." In *Critique and Postcritique*, edited by Elizabeth Anker and Rita Felski, 99–126. Durham, NC: Duke University Press, 2016.

Fogarasi, Christina. "On Second Front Doors and Other 'Symptoms': Disentangling Sexual Assault and Trauma." Unpublished manuscript, last modified July 1, 2021.

Foucault, Michel. *Discipline and Punish: The Birth of the Prison.* Translated by Alan Sheridan. New York: Vintage, 1977.

Foucault, Michel. *The History of Sexuality: Volume I. An Introduction.* Translated by Robert Hurley. New York: Vintage Books, 1990. First published 1976.

Foucault, Michel. "Nietzsche, Genealogy, History." In *The Foucault Reader*, edited by Paul Rabinow, 76–100. New York: Pantheon, 1984.

Foucault, Michel. "What Is Enlightenment?." Translated by Catherine Porter. In *The Foucault Reader*, edited by Paul Rabinow, 32–50. New York: Pantheon, 1984.

Frank, Jason. *Constituent Moments: Enacting the People in Postrevolutionary America.* Durham, NC: Duke University Press, 2010.

Freud, Sigmund. *Civilization and Its Discontents.* Translated by James Strachey. New York: Norton, 2010. First Published 1930.

Frye, Northrup. *The Anatomy of Criticism.* Princeton, NJ: Princeton University Press, 2000. First published 1957.

Gates, Henry Louis. Introduction to *The Souls of Black Folk*, by W. E. B. Du Bois. Norton Critical Edition. New York: Norton, 1999. First published 1903.

Gates, Henry Louis. *The Signifying Monkey: A Theory of African American Literary Criticism.* New York: Oxford University Press, 2014. First published 1988.

Gersen, Jeannie Suk. "The Socratic Method in the Age of Trauma." *Harvard Law Review* 130, no. 9 (October 2017): 2320–47.

Gikandi, Simon. "Globalization and the Claims of Postcoloniality." *South Atlantic Quarterly* 100, no. 3 (Summer 2001).

Gilligan, Carole. *In A Different Voice: Psychological Theory and Women's Development.* Cambridge, MA: Harvard University Press, 1982.

Glendon, Mary Ann. *A World Made New: Eleanor Roosevelt and the Universal Declaration of Human Rights.* New York: Random House, 2002.

Golder, Ben. *Foucault and the Politics of Rights.* Stanford, CA: Stanford University Press, 2015.

Goodman, Brian. "Archives, Institutions, and Imaginaries: Human Rights and Literature." Paper presented at NYU symposium March 2–3, 2018.

Greenblatt, Stephen. *Renaissance Self-Fashioning: From More to Shakespeare.* Chicago: University of Chicago Press, 1980.

Guillory, John. *Cultural Capital: The Problem of Literary Canon Formation.* Chicago: University of Chicago Press, 1993.

Guillory, John. "The Sokal Affair and the History of Criticism." *Critical Inquiry* 28 (Winter 2002): 470–508.

Guinier, Lani, Michelle Fine, and Jane Balin. "Becoming Gentlemen: Women's Experiences at One Ivy League Law School." *University of Pennsylvania Law Review* 143, no. 1 (November 1994): 1–110.

Gumbrecht, Hans Ulrich. "Mythographer of Paradoxes." *Critical Inquiry* 42, no. 2 (Summer 2016).

Habermas, Jürgen. *The Philosophical Discourse of Modernity: Twelve Lectures (Studies in Contemporary German Thought).* Translated by Frederick G. Lawrence. Cambridge, MA: MIT Press, 1990.

Halley, Janet, and Kerry Rittich. "Introduction to Special Issue, Critical Directions in Comparative Family Law: Genealogies and Contemporary Studies of Family Law Exceptionalism." *American Journal of Comparative Law* 85 (2010): 753–75.

Hamacher, Werner. "The Rights to Have Rights (Four-and-a-Half Remarks)." *South Atlantic Quarterly* 103, no. 2/3 (Spring/Summer 2004): 343–56.

Harcourt, Bernard. *Critique and Praxis*. New York: Columbia University Press, 2020.

Harris, Angela P. "Race and Essentialism in Feminist Legal Theory." *Stanford Law Review* 42, no. 3 (February 1990): 581–616.

Harris, Cheryl. "Whiteness as Property." *Harvard Law Review* 106 (1993): 1709–91.

Hartman, Saidiya. *Scenes of Subjection: Terror, Slavery, and Self-Making in Nineteenth-Century America*. New York: Oxford University Press, 1997.

Hensley, Nathan K. "Curatorial Reading and Endless War." *Victorian Studies* 56, no. 1 (Autumn 2013): 59–83.

Hiley, Scott. "The Basic Contradiction of Capitalism." Website for Communist Party USA. October 11, 2016. Accessed May 8, 2021. https://www.cpusa.org/article/the-basic-contradiction-of-capitalism/

Hong, Grace Kyungwon. "Property." In *Keywords for American Cultural Studies*. 2nd ed. Edited by Bruce Burgett and Glen Hendler. New York: NYU Press, 2007.

Honig, Bonnie. *Emergency Politics: Paradox, Law, Democracy*. Princeton, NJ: Princeton University Press, 2011.

hooks, bell. *Teaching to Transgress: Education as the Practice of Freedom*. New York: Routledge, 1994.

Horkheimer, Max, and Theodor Adorno. *Dialectic of Enlightenment*. New York: Continuum 1947.

Horwitz, Morton J. *The Transformation of American Law, 1870–1960: The Crisis of Legal Orthodoxy*. New York: Oxford University Press, 1992.

Hunt, Lynn. *Inventing Human Rights: A History*. New York: Norton, 2007.

Ignatieff, Michael. *Human Rights as Politics and Idolatry*. Princeton, NJ: Princeton University Press, 2001.

Ignatieff, Michael. *The Lesser Evil: Political Ethics in the Age of Terror*. Princeton, NJ: Princeton University Press, 2004.

Jameson, Fredric. *The Antinomies of Realism*. New York: Verso, 2013.

Jameson, Fredric. *The Political Unconscious: Narrative as a Socially Symbolic Act*. Ithaca, NY: Cornell University Press, 1981.

Jameson, Fredric. *Postmodernism, or, the Cultural Logic of Late Capitalism*. Durham, NC: Duke University Press, 1991.

Johnson, Paul. *Intellectuals*. New York: Harper Collins, 1988.

Ju, Anne. "Women's Studies at Cornell Evolves." *Cornell Chronicle*, November 4, 2009.

Judt, Tony. *Postwar: A History of Europe since 1945*. New York: Penguin, 2005.

Keane, Webb. *Christian Moderns: Freedom and Fetish in the Mission Encounter*. Berkeley: University of California Press, 2007.

Kearney, Richard. "Narrating Pain: The Power of Catharsis." *Paragraph* 30, no. 1 (2007).

Kearney, Richard. *On Stories*. New York: Routledge, 2001.

Keenan, Thomas. *Fables of Responsibility: Aberrations and Predicaments in Ethics and Politics*. Stanford, CA: Stanford University Press, 1997.

Kennedy, David. *The Dark Sides of Virtue: Reassessing International Humanitarianism*. Princeton, NJ: Princeton University Press, 2004.

Kennedy, Duncan. "The Critique of Rights in Critical Legal Studies." In *Left Legalism/ Left Critique*, edited by Wendy Brown and Janet Halley, 178–228. Durham, NC: Duke University Press, 2002.

Kennedy, Duncan. "Form and Substance in Private Law Adjudication." *Harvard Law Review* 89 (1976): 1685–1778.

Kennedy, Duncan, and Peter Gabel. "Roll Over Beethoven." *Stanford Law Review* 36, no. 1 (January 1984): 1–55.

Kierkegaard, Soren. *Fear and Trembling*. Translated by Alastair Hannay. New York Penguin, 1985. First published 1843.

Kindley, Evan. "The Calling." *Dissent* (Winter 2015).

Kornbluh, Anna. *Realizing Capital: Financial and Psychic Economies in Victorian Form*. New York: Fordham University Press, 2014.

Koselleck, Reinhart. *Critique and Crisis: Enlightenment and the Pathogenesis of Modern Society*. Cambridge, MA: MIT Press, 1988. German edition 1959.

Koselleck, Reinhart. *Futures Past: On the Semantics of History Time*. Translated by Keith Tribe. New York: Columbia University Press, 2004.

Kristeva, Julia. *Powers of Horror: An Essay on Abjection*. New York: Columbia University Press, 1982.

Kuhn, Thomas. *The Structure of Scientific Revolutions*. Chicago: University of Chicago Press, 2012. First published 1962.

Kurnick, David. "A Few Lies: Queer Theory and our Method Melodramas." *ELH* 87, no. 2 (Summer 2020): 349–74.

Lacan, Jacques. "Kant avec Sade." Translated by James B. Swenson Jr. *October* 51 (Winter 1989), 55–75.

Lacan, Jacques. *Seminar VII: The Ethics of Psychoanalysis: 1959–60*. Translated by Dennis Porter. New York: Norton, 1992.

La Capra, Dominick. *Representing the Holocaust: History, Theory, Trauma*. Ithaca, NY: Cornell University Press, 1994.

Langer, Lawrence. *The Age of Atrocity: Death in Modern Literature*. Boston: Beacon, 1978.

Lasch, Christopher. *The Culture of Narcissism: American Life in An Age of Diminishing Expectations*. New York: Norton, 1979.

Latour, Bruno. "Has Critique Run out of Steam? From Matters of Fact to Matters of Concern." *Critical Inquiry* 30, no. 2 (Winter 2004): 225–48.

Latour, Bruno. *We Have Never Been Modern*. Translated by Catherine Porter. Cambridge, MA: Harvard University Press, 1993.

LeBrecht, James, and Nicole Newnham, dirs. *Crip Camp*. 2020; Good Gravy Films and Higher Ground Productions.

Lefort, Claude. *The Political Forms of Modern Society: Bureaucracy, Democracy, Totalitarianism*. Edited by John B. Thompson. Cambridge, MA: MIT Press, 1986.

Lesjak, Carolyn. "Reading Dialectically." *Criticism* (Spring 2013).

Levine, Caroline. "From Nation to Network." *Victorian Studies* 55, no. 4 (Summer 2013): 647–66.

Leys, Ruth. *Trauma: A Genealogy*. Chicago: University of Chicago Press, 2000.

Loughlin, Martin and Neil Walker, eds. *The Paradox of Constitutionalism: Constituent Power and Constitutional Form*. New York: Oxford University Press, 2007.

Love, Heather. "Small Change: Realism, Immanence, and the Politics of the Micro." *Modern Language Quarterly* 77, no. 3 (September 2016).

Lowe, Lisa. *Immigrant Acts: On Asian American Cultural Politics*. Durham, NC: Duke University Press, 1996.

Lukács, Georg. *The Theory of the Novel: A Historico-philosophical Essay on the Forms of Great Epic Literature*. Translated by Anna Bostock. Cambridge, MA: MIT Press, 1971.

Lyotard, Jean-François. *The Inhuman*. Stanford, CA: Stanford University Press, 1991.

Lyotard, Jean-François. "The Other's Rights." In *On Human Rights: The Oxford Amnesty Lectures 1993*, edited by Stephen Shute and Susan Hurley, 135–47. New York: Basic, 1993.

MacCannell, Juliet Flower. "Facing Fascism." In *Lacan, Politics, Aesthetics*, edited by Willy Apollon and Richard Feldstein, 65–100. Albany, NY: SUNY Press, 1996.

MacIntyre, Alisdair. *After Virtue: A Study of Moral Theory*. Notre Dame, IN: Notre Dame University Press, 1981.

MacKinnon, Catharine. *Feminism Unmodified: Discourses on Life and Law*. Cambridge, MA: Harvard University Press, 1987.

Mahmood, Saba. "Religious Reason and Secular Affect: An Incommensurable Divide?" *Critical Inquiry* 35 (Summer 2009).

Mansbridge, Jane J. *Why We Lost the ERA*. Chicago: University of Chicago Press, 1986.

Mao Tse-tung. "On Contradiction." 1937. Marxists Internet Archive website. Accessed May 8, 2021. https://www.marxists.org/reference/archive/mao/selected-works/volume-1/mswv1_17.htm.

Marcus, Sharon, and Stephen Best. "Surface Reading: An Introduction." *Representations* 108, no. 1 (Fall 2009): 1–21.

Marx, Karl. *Capital*. In *The Marx-Engels Reader*. 2nd ed. Edited by Robert C. Tucker. New York: Norton, 1978. First published 1867.

Marx, Karl. *The Economic and Philosophical Manuscripts of 1844*. Moscow: Progress Publishers, 1959. First published 1932.

Marx, Karl. "On *The Jewish Question*." In *The Marx-Engels Reader*. 2nd ed. Edited by Robert C. Tucker. New York: Norton, 1978. First published 1844.

Marx, Karl, and Friedrich Engels. "Manifesto of the Communist Party." In *Marx/Engels Selected Works, Vol. 1*. Moscow: Progress Publishers, 1969. First published 1848.

Matsuda, Mari J. "Looking to the Bottom: Critical Legal Studies and Reparations." *Harvard Civil Rights-Civil Liberties Law Review* 22 (1987): 323–99.

McCann, Sean and Michael Szalay. "Do You Believe in Magic? Literary Thinking after the New Left." *Yale Journal of Criticism* 18, no. 2 (2005): 435–68.

McCleod, Allegra. "Law, Critique, and the Undercommons." In *A Time for Critique*, edited by Didier Fassin and Bernard E. Harcourt, 252–70. New York: Columbia University Press, 2019.

Menand, Louis. *The Marketplace of Ideas: Reform and Resistance in the American University*. New York: Norton, 2010.

Mills, Charles W. *The Racial Contract*. Ithaca, NY: Cornell University Press, 1997.

Moi, Toril. *Revolution of the Ordinary: Literary Studies after Wittgenstein, Austin, and Cavell*. Chicago: University of Chicago Press, 2017.

Mouffe, Chantal. *The Democratic Paradox*. New York: Verso, 2000.

Moyn, Samuel. *The Last Utopia: Human Rights in History*. Cambridge, MA: Harvard University Press, 2010.

Muñoz, José Esteban. *Cruising Utopia: The Then and There of Queer Futurity*. New York: New York University Press, 2009.

Mutua, Makua. *Human Rights: A Political and Cultural Critique*. Philadelphia: Pennsylvania University Press, 2002.

Nietzsche, Friedrich. *On the Genealogy of Morals*. In *Basic Writings of Nietzsche*, translated by Walter Kaufmann, 437–600. New York: Random House, 2000. First published 1913.

Ortolano, Guy. *The Two Cultures Controversy: Science, Literature and Cultural Politics in Postwar Britain*. New York: Cambridge University Press, 2009.

Patterson, Orlando. *Slavery and Social Death: A Comparative Study*. Cambridge, MA: Harvard University Press, 1982.

Perugini, Nicola, and Neve Gordon. *The Human Right to Dominate*. New York: Oxford University Press, 2015.

Posner, Eric. *The Twilight of Human Rights Law*. New York: Oxford University Press, 2014.

Posner, Richard. *Law and Literature*. Cambridge, MA: Harvard University Press, 1988.

Povinelli, Elizabeth A. *The Cunning of Recognition: Indigenous Alterities and the Making of Australian Multiculturalism*. Durham, NC: Duke University Press, 2002.

Puar, Jasbir. *The Right to Maim: Debility, Capacity, Disability*. Durham, NC: Duke University Press, 2017.

Quinones, Sam. *Dreamland: The True Tale of America's Opiate Epidemic*. New York: Bloomsbury, 2015.

Rancière, Jacques. *Dissensus: On Politics and Aesthetics*. New York: Continuum, 2010.

Rancière, Jacques. *The Emancipated Spectator*. New York: Verso, 2009.

Rancière, Jacques. *Hatred of Democracy*. New York: Verso, 2006.

Rancière, Jacques. *The Politics of Aesthetics*. Edited and translated by Gabriel Rockhill. New York: Bloomsbury, 2013. First published 2004.

Rancière, Jacques. "Who Is the Subject of the Rights of Man?" *South Atlantic Quarterly* 103, no. 2/3 (Spring/Summer 2004): 297–310.

Rankine, Claudia. *Citizen: An American Lyric*. New York: Graywolf Press, 2014.

Ricoeur, Paul. *Freud and Philosophy: An Essay on Interpretation*. Translated by Denis Savage. New Haven, CT: Yale University Press, 1970.

Ricoeur, Paul. "The Political Paradox." In *History and Truth*. Edited by Charles A. Kelbly, 247–70. Evanston, IL: Northwestern University Press, 1965. First published 1955.

Rorty, Richard. *Contingency, Irony, and Solidarity*. New York: Cambridge University Press, 1989.

Ross, Kristin. *May '68 and Its Afterlives*. Chicago: University of Chicago Press, 2002.

Rousseau, Jean-Jacques. *The Social Contract and Other Later Political Writings*. Edited by Victor Gourevitch. New York: Cambridge University Press, 1997. First published 1762.

Russell, Bertrand. *The Philosophy of Logical Atomism*. 1918.

Said, Edward. *Orientalism*. New York: Random House, 1979.

Salecl, Renata. *The Spoils of Freedom: Psychoanalysis and Feminism after the Fall of Socialism*. New York: Routledge, 1994.

Sanders, Mark. *Complicities: The Intellectual and Apartheid*. Durham, NC: Duke University Press, 2002.

Scarry, Elaine. *The Body in Pain: The Making and Unmaking of the World*. New York: Oxford University Press, 1985.

Schiller, Friedrich. *Letters Upon the Aesthetic Education of Man*. Translated by Reginald Snell. Mineola, NY: Dover, 2004. First published 1795.

Schmitt, Carl. *The Concept of the Political*. Translated by George Schwab. New Brunswick, NJ: Rutgers University Press, 1976. First published 1932.

Schmitt, Carl. *Political Theology*. Translated by C. J. Miller. Albuquerque, NM: Antelope Hill Originals, 2020. First published 1922.

Scott, David. *Conscripts of Modernity: The Tragedy of Colonial Enlightenment*. Durham, NC: Duke University Press, 2004.

Scott, Joan. "How the Right Weaponized Free Speech." *Chronicle of Higher Education*. January 7, 2018.

Scott, Joan. *Only Paradoxes to Offer: French Feminists and the Rights of Man*. Cambridge, MA: Harvard University Press, 1996.

Searle, John. "Reality Principles: An Interview with John R. Searle." Edited by Steven Postrel and Edward Feser. *Reason* (February 2000). https://reason.com/2000/02/01/reality-principles-an-intervie/.

Sears, Diane E. "The Two-Way Text: Ponge's Metapoetic 'Fable.'" *L'Esprit Createur* 31, no. 2 (Summer 1991): 50–57.

Sedgwick, Eve Kosofsky. *Touching Feeling: Affect, Pedagogy, Performativity*. Durham, NC: Duke University Press, 2003.

Sharpe, Christina. *In the Wake: On Blackness and Being*. Durham, NC: Duke University Press, 2016.

Sidney, Sir Philip. "The Defence of Poesy." *Norton Anthology of English Literature*. 10th ed. Vol. 1. New York: Norton, 2018. First published 1595.

Slaughter, Joseph. *Human Rights, Inc.: The World Novel, Narrative Form, and International Law*. New York: Fordham University Press, 2007.

Small, Helen. *The Value of the Humanities*. New York: Oxford University Press, 2013.

Snorton, C. Riley. *Black on Both Sides: A Racial History of Trans Identity*. Minneapolis: Minnesota University Press, 2017.

Sommer, Doris. *The Work of Art in the World: Civic Agency and Public Humanities*. Durham, NC: Duke University Press, 2014.

Spillers, Hortense. "Mama's Baby, Papa's Maybe: An American Grammar Book." *Diacritics* 17, no. 2 (Summer 1987): 64–81.

Spivak, Gayatri Chakravorty. *Critique of Postcolonial Reason: A History of the Vanishing Present*. Cambridge, MA: Harvard University Press, 1999.

Spivak, Gayatri Chakravorty. *Death of a Discipline*. New York: Columbia University Press, 2005.

Spivak, Gayatri Chakravorty. "Subaltern Studies: Deconstructing Historiography." In *The Spivak Reader: Selected Works of Gayatri Spivak*, edited by Donna Landry and Gerald MacLean, 203–36. New York: Routledge, 1995.

Spivak, Gayatri Chakravorty. "Writing Wrongs." *South Atlantic Quarterly* 103, no. 2/3 (Spring/Summer 2004).

Stanley, Jason. *How Fascism Works: The Politics of Us and Them*. New York: Random House, 2018.

Stepto, Robert. *From Behind the Veil: A Study of Afro-American Narrative*. Champaign: University of Illinois Press, 1979.

Stommel, Jesse. "The Digital Humanities is About Breaking Stuff." *Hybrid Pedagogy*. September 2, 2013. Accessed July 16, 2020. https://hybridpedagogy.org/the-digital-humanities-is-about-breaking-stuff/.

Strauss, Leo. "Notes on Carl Schmitt." In *The Concept of the Political*, translated by George Schwab. New Brunswick, NJ: Rutgers University Press, 1976. First published 1932.

Taylor, Charles. *Sources of the Self: The Making of Modern Identity*. Cambridge, MA: Harvard University Press, 1989.

Waldron, Jeremy, ed. *Nonsense Upon Stilts: Bentham, Burke and Marx on the Rights of Man*. New York: Methuen, 1987.

Warner, Michael. "Uncritical Reading." In *Polemic: Critical or Uncritical*, edited by Jane Gallop, 13–38. New York: Routledge, 2004.

Watt, Ian. *The Rise of the Novel: Studies in Defoe, Richardson, and Fielding*. Berkeley: University of California Press, 1962.

Weber, Max. *Political Writings (Cambridge Texts in the History of Political Thought)*. Edited by Peter Lassman. Translated by Ronald Speirs. New York: Cambridge University Press, 1994.

Weber, Max. *The Protestant Ethic and the Spirit of Capitalism and Other Writings*. Translated by Peter Baehr and Gordon C. Wells. New York: Penguin, 2002. First published in English 1930 by Unwin Hyman.

Weheliye, Alexander. *Habeas Viscus: Racializing Assemblages, Biopolitics, and Black Feminist Theories of the Human*. Durham, NC: Duke University Press, 2014.

White, Hayden. *Metahistory: The Historical Imagination in 19th-Century Europe*. Baltimore: Johns Hopkins University Press, 1973.

Whitehead, Anne. *Trauma Fiction*. Edinburgh: Edinburgh University Press, 2004.

Wilde, Oscar. *Intentions*. New York: Brentano, 1905.

Wilde, Oscar. *The Picture of Dorian Gray*. New York: Penguin, 2009. First published 1891.

Williams, Bernard. *Truth and Truthfulness: An Essay in Genealogy*. Princeton, NJ: Princeton University Press, 2002.

Williams, Jeffrey. "The New Modesty in Literary Criticism." *Chronicle of Higher Education*, January 5, 2015.

Williams, Patricia. *The Alchemy of Race and Rights*. Cambridge, MA: Harvard University Press, 1991.

Woolf, Virginia. "A Room of One's Own." New York: Quality Paperback Book Club, 1992. First published 1929 by Hogarth Press.

Young, Robert J. C. "The Idea of a Chrestomathic University." *Torn Halves: Political Conflict in Literary and Cultural Theory*, 290–351. Manchester: Manchester University Press, 1996.

Žižek., Slavoj. *Did Somebody Say Totalitarianism? Five Interventions in the (Mis)Use of a Notion*. New York: Verso, 2011.

Žižek., Slavoj. *The Sublime Object of Ideology*. New York: Verso, 2001.

Žižek., Slavoj, and John Milbank. *The Monstrosity of Christ: Paradox or Dialectic?* Edited by Creston Davis. Cambridge, MA: MIT Press, 2009.

Index

INDEX

307, 334n43; gender in, 266–68, 292–93, 297–300, 334n43, 334n49; integrative criticism and, 28, 267–72, 291–92, 300–301, 307–8, 310; on integrity, 266–68, 298–301, 307; paradox and, 291–93, 298, 308, 310
Roosevelt, Eleanor, 88, 320n34
Rorty, Richard, 38, 50, 130–31
Ross, Kristin, 142–43
Rousseau, Jean-Jacques, 78, 155–57, 219
Russell, Bertrand, 13

sacramental, paradox as, 93, 175, 198
Sade, Marquis de, 168–70, 326n74
Said, Edward, 53, 56
Saussure, Ferdinand de, 201–5
Scarry, Elaine, 147–48, 241–42
Scenes of Subjection (Hartman), 105
Schiller, Friedrich, 129
Schlafly, Phyllis, 289–91
Schmitt, Carl: Agamben and, 98–101, 107; Arendt and, 96–97; on exception, 8, 73, 77, 93–94, 97, 107; Honig on, 157; on law, 93–97
Scott, David, 63–67, 180, 189
Scott, Joan, 64–65, 68, 180, 189, 256. *See also Only Paradoxes to Offer*
Searle, John, 19–20
secularism, 55–56, 95
Sedgwick, Eve, 262, 264, 278
self-help industry, paradox in, 258–60
Seminar VII (Lacan), 19, 44, 167–70
semiotics, 287; Derrida and, 158–61; in *Gender Trouble*, 201–5; hybridity and, 228. *See also* post-Saussurean linguistics; Saussure, Ferdinand de; sign
Sharpe, Christina, 247–48
Shoah (film), 245
Sidney, Philip, 117–18
sign, 158, 167, 202; Lyotard on, 171; Saussure on, 201
signature, 113, 160–61
The Signifying Monkey (Gates), 205–6
singularity, 8, 121–23, 230, 279
Slaughter, Joseph, 132
slavery, 83–84; in anti-legalism, 104–6; paradox and, 246–47
Slavery and Social Death (Patterson), 106
Small, Helen, 213, 215
social constructivism, 283

The Social Contract (Rousseau), 78, 155
Social Death (Sexton), 106–7
social justice: exclusion and, 182–83, 187; theory and, 16, 78, 196, 210, 269, 280
Sommer, Doris, 214, 219
The Souls of Black Folk (Du Bois), 195–200
Sources of the Self (Taylor), 53
South Africa, 145
sovereign, 8, 93–94, 96–97, 100
Soviet Union, 141, 143, 145, 150–51, 156
spectacle, 60–63, 68, 286
Specters of the Atlantic (Baucom), 83
speech: authoritarianism opposed by, 140–41, 146–53; Cold War and, 145–46, 152; CRT on, 188; in feminism, 187–88; free, 140–41, 145–47, 256; inarticulate, contentless, 145–48, 256, 324n10; Lefort on, 150–53, 158; performative, 160; racist, xenophobic, 257–58; rights and, 145–46, 149–53, 158, 177, 256; rights-as-utterances, 149–53, 177; "Roll Over Beethoven" on, 208; trauma theory and, 147–48, 172, 249–51, 254–58
speechlessness, 122–24, 223. *See also* inarticulate speech
Spillers, Hortense, 130–31, 246–48, 295
Spivak, Gayatri Chakravorty, 53, 126, 219; on exclusion, 181, 206, 230–31; on pedagogy, 127, 230–31
staging, of contradiction, 126
Stepto, Robert, 197
strategic essentialism, 206
Strauss, Leo, 94
structural oppression: *Citizen* on, 293–95; disability studies on, 274–77, 281–83
The Structure of Scientific Revolutions (Kuhn), 1
style: in aesthetics, 128, 130, 136; of Arendt, 90; in exclusion, politics of, 210–11; *Gender Trouble* on, 210; integrative criticism and, 264, 292, 306; in justice, Derrida on, 162–66; theory, critiques of, and, 262–64. *See also* rhetoric
subject: in ethics, 19, 44, 170–71, 229; in modernity, 43–45; of rights, 15. *See also* "Who Is the Subject of the Rights of Man?"
sublime, 122, 124–25, 243
Surkis, Judith, 192
suspicion, hermeneutics of, 38–39, 53, 132
symptomatic reading, 38–40, 53, 135–36, 251
Szalay, Michael, 144–45

Taylor, Charles, 44, 53

Teaching to Transgress (hooks), 231–32

testimony, 171, 326n87; legal, 251; in pedagogy, 225, 231–32, 236; in trauma theory, 232, 242–43, 250–55, 252, 254–55, 332n84

theology, 117, 183; Derrida and, 165; Du Bois and, 197–200; in exclusion, politics of, 197–200, 203, 206; in *Gender Trouble*, 203; Lyotard and, 172; political, 93–97; theory and, 8–9; trauma theory and, 245, 250

theory: aesthetics and, 8–9; agency of, 128, 271, 273, 311; *Citizen* and, 295, 305–10; Cold War and, 6–7, 144, 150; eclecticism of, 20; ethics of theory era, 261; exclusion, politics of, and, 182–83, 220; genetics of, 4–10, 25; integrative criticism and, 268–69, 305–11; integrity and, 301; linguistic turn and, 7, 112, 158, 160; meta-theoretical, paradox as, 135–36; modernity and, 39–40, 46–47; paradox in, 4–11, 25, 33, 111–13, 135–36, 197, 268–69; post-theoretical, postcritical alternatives to, 19, 262–64; praxis and, 19, 268–69, 273, 286, 305–11; rights and, 26, 76, 112–14, 139–44; rise, institutionalization of, 5–7, 26, 31, 112–13, 138–39, 141–42, 144; "A Room of One's Own" and, 301, 308; theology and, 8–9; valuation, economy of, in, 70–71

Theory of the Lyric (Culler), 163

Theory of the Novel (Lukács), 52, 268

therapeutic, paradox as, 27, 240–41, 259–60

torture, 147–48

totalitarianism: Agamben on, 99, 321n66; democracy and, 153–55; Derrida on, 159; Lacan on, 168–69; Lefort on, 138, 146, 152–54; paradox and, 138–40, 149, 152–56; rights and opposing, 145, 149–53; speech and opposing, 146–52, 146–53

Totality and Infinity (Levinas), 165

Trauma (Leys), 248

trauma theory: anti-legalism in, 244–45, 253–55; antinormativity in, 252–53; *Citizen* and, 293, 295–96; critiques of, 248, 252, 255; CRT and, 245–46; Du Bois and, 246–47; exceptionalism in, 249–50, 252, 255; exclusion in, 27, 184, 222–23, 240–46, 249, 252, 255, 258; formalism in, 242, 252–53; Holocaust and, 243, 249–50, 252, 254–55; legal system and, 251, 254–55;

pain in, 147–48, 240–42, 241; paradox in, 222–24, 240–54, 257, 260; pedagogy and, 27, 221–25, 232–36, 240–41, 245, 258; racist, xenophobic speech, and, 257–58; as redemptive, paradox in, 222, 243, 246–50; representation in, 241–44, 249–52; right-wing appropriation of, 256–57; speech and, 147–48, 172, 249–51, 254–58; testimony in, 232, 242–43, 250–55, 332n84; theology and, 245, 250; on voicelessness, 249–51, 254–55; Yale school, 148, 171, 222, 241–42, 245–46, 248

Truth, Sojourner, 189

UDHR (Universal Declaration of Human Rights), 88, 142, 146, 160

Undoing Gender (Butler), 181

Undoing the Demos (Brown), 84

United States (US): Communist Party, 34; Declaration of Independence, 160–61; property in, 105–6

Universal Declaration of Human Rights (UDHR), 88, 142, 146, 160

university, neoliberalization of, 213–14

University of Chicago, 191–92

unpredictability, 116, 125–26; of trauma, 249

unrepresentability, 122

unverifiability, 122, 253, 257, 295

US. *See* United States

utterances, rights as. *See* speech

valuation, economy of: in aesthetics, 128, 136–37, 179; critique, paradox, and, 45; in Derrida, 164; in humanities, defenses of, 217, 219–20; on modernity, 59; negative, 128, 137, 164, 211, 217, 219–20, 251; in rights, paradox and, 149; in theory, 70–71; in trauma theory, 251

"Violence and Metaphysics" (Derrida), 158–59, 165

voice: in canon wars, 191; CRT on, 188; to exclusion, giving, 184, 187–88, 191–94, 219, 221, 225, 236, 240–41, 255; feminism on, 187–88; in pedagogy, 193, 221; trauma theory on voicelessness, 249–51, 254–55

Waldron, Jeremy, 80

Warner, Michael, 45, 55

Watt, Ian, 129–30, 132

Weber, Max, 37, 40–41, 69, 106
We Have Never Been Modern (Latour), 46
Weheliye, Alexander, 101, 107–9, 323n93
The Well Wrought Urn (Brooks, C.), 114
What Is a People? (Badiou, Bourdieu, Butler, et al.), 156
"What Is Enlightenment?" (Foucault), 42, 51
"What Is Enlightenment?" (Kant), 42
White, Hayden, 65, 316n76, 318n117
Whitehead, Anne, 243–44
"Whiteness as Property" (Harris, C.), 106, 225
White Noise (DeLillo), 147, 324n15
"Who Is the Subject of the Rights of Man?" (Rancière), 176, 178–79, 327n100
Why We Lost the ERA (Mansbridge), 289–90

Wilde, Oscar, 1–2; Butler and, 119–20; on lying, 118–19, 123; on modernity, 3; Plato and, 118–20, 123
Williams, Patricia, 186, 188
Williams, Serena, 309
women's studies, 190
women's suffrage, 284–85
Woolf, Virginia. *See* "A Room of One's Own"
World War I (Great War), 39, 91
World War II, 88–89, 98, 320n38

Yale school, of trauma theory. *See* trauma theory
Young, Robert J. C., 213, 215

Žižek, Slavoj, 18, 36, 135–36, 150, 315n15
Zong massacre, 83